THE UPPER ROOM

Disciplines

2013

UPPER
ROOM BOOKS®
NASHVILLE

AN OUTLINE FOR SMALL-GROUP USE OF DISCIPLINES

Here is a simple plan for a one-hour, weekly group meeting based on reading *Disciplines*. One person may act as convener every week, or the role can rotate among group members. You may want to light a white Christ candle each week to signal the beginning of your time together.

OPENING

Convener: Let us come into the presence of God.
Others: Lord Jesus Christ, thank you for being with us. Let us hear your word to us as we speak to one another.

SCRIPTURE

Convener reads the scripture suggested for that day in *Disciplines*. After a one- or two-minute silence, convener asks: What did you hear God saying to you in this passage? What response does this call for? (Group members respond in turn or as led.)

REFLECTION

- What scripture passage(s) and meditation(s) from this week was (were) particularly meaningful for you? Why? (Group members respond in turn or as led.)
- What actions were you nudged to take in response to the week's meditations? (Group members respond in turn or as led.)
- Where were you challenged in your discipleship this week? How did you respond to the challenge? (Group members respond in turn or as led.)

PRAYING TOGETHER

Convener says: Based on today's discussion, what people and situations do you want us to pray for now and in the coming week? Convener or other volunteer then prays about the concerns named.

DEPARTING

Convener says: Let us go in peace to serve God and our neighbors in all that we do.

Adapted from *The Upper Room* daily devotional guide, January–February 2001. © 2000 The Upper Room. Used by permission.

THE UPPER ROOM DISCIPLINES 2013

© 2012 by Upper Room Books®. All rights reserved.

The Upper Room Web site: http://www.upperroom.org

Cover design: Left Coast Design, Portland, Oregon

Cover photo: Valerie K. Isenhower

Revised Common Lectionary copyright © 1992 Consultation on Common Texts. Used by permission.

Scripture quotations not otherwise identified are from the New Revised Standard Version Bible © 1989, Division of Christian Education of the National Council of the Churches of Christ in the United States of America. Used by permission. All rights reserved.

Scripture quotations marked ASV are from the American Standard Version of the Bible.

Scripture quotations designated AP are the author's paraphrase; AT, author's translation.

Scripture quotations marked CEB are from the Common English Bible. Copyright © 2010 Common English Bible. Used by permission.

Scripture quotations marked ESV are from The Holy Bible, English Standard Version® (ESV®), copyright © 2001 by Crossway, a publishing ministry of Good News Publishers. Used by permission. All rights reserved. Scripture quotations marked (GNT) are from the Good News Translation in Today's English Version—Second Edition Copyright © 1992 by American Bible Society. Used by Permission.

Scripture quotations designated KJV are taken from the King James Version of the Bible.

Scripture quotations designated as THE MESSAGE are from *The Message* by Eugene H. Peterson, copyright © 1993, 1994, 1995, 1996, 2000, 2001, 2002. Used by permission of NavPress Publishing Group. All rights reserved.

Scripture quotations designated NIV are from the HOLY BIBLE, NEW INTERNATIONAL VERSION, NIV®. Copyright © 1973, 1978, 1984 by International Bible Society. Used by permission of Zondervan. All rights reserved.

Scripture quotations designated REB are taken from the Revised English Bible, copyright © Oxford University Press and Cambridge University Press 1989. All rights reserved.

While writers of various books of the Bible may be disputed in certain circles, this volume uses the names of the biblically attributed authors.

ISBN: 978-0-8358-1086-9

Printed in the United States of America

CONTENTS

Darkness surrounded me. The batteries in my flashlight ran out when I was halfway between the shower house and my tent at Girl Scout camp. I panicked for a moment. It would be easy to veer off the path into the woods or trip on the rocky surface. I still had a long way to go. What was I going to do? I stood contemplating my situation.

Then a peace came over me. I knew this path. I had traveled it hundreds of times over the two summers I had worked at the camp. I took a few deep breaths, centered myself, and recalled the curves and bumps ahead. My eyes slowly became acclimated to the darkness. I could actually see a little bit. If I moved slowly and carefully I could make it to my destination.

I arrived safely at the tent and offered a prayer of thanksgiving. The words of Psalm 119:105 came to mind, "Your word is a lamp to my feet and a light to my path." At the time I did not realize the full connection between my experience and the words of the psalmist. My only thought was that I was guided down the path to my destination.

The dark night on the trail is a paradigm story for my daily walk. The experience taught me the importance of familiarity, moving slowly, and letting my eyes adjust to the light available. Now, I apply these components to my faith journey.

I walk the path of Bible study during my devotional time every morning. I read a psalm along with another text from the daily lectionary. Sometimes, I conduct a word search to see what the Greek or Hebrew word means. Or, I read a commentary to see what the author says about the text. However, most mornings I just read the text slowly and reflect on it in my journal. What is this text saying to me today? How can I apply it to my life? What words or phrases will I try to carry with me all day long?

When I read the text slowly, more of it stays with me during the day and the days to come. I see more because my eyes do not skip over words or situations. It also allows me the opportunity to ask questions like: What was the person feeling and am I feeling the same way? How did the Triune God relate to the person, and have I ever experienced that? Who are the people in this story, and which one do I relate to?

Every day I walk the pages of the text I become more familiar with it. I allow the Bible to be part of my memory just as the path was at the camp. A slow reading means I open more avenues for the story to touch my soul just like walking slowly allowed my feet to touch solid ground on the path. When I am faced with dark moments or even the times of choice, I can reach into my memory and find a passage that sheds light on my situation. The psalmist says God's word is a light for my path. However, my eyes adjust to that light only when I can recall God's words.

"Your word is a lamp to my feet and a light to my path." May the discipline of your daily reading of the Bible shine light on your spiritual path.

—Valerie K. Isenhower
Executive Director, Water in the Desert Ministries
Albuquerque, New Mexico

Editor's Note

New in this edition: Each week will open with a Scripture Overview and Questions and Thoughts for Reflection—for both group and personal use. The overview explores the ties among the several scripture passages for each week. Then, four questions or thoughts for reflection help stir understanding.

Light in Darkness

JANUARY 1–6, 2013 • TOM APPEL

SCRIPTURE OVERVIEW: The coming of God into the world is often understood as the coming of a brilliant light. That light carries the power to transform Israel so that Israel is restored and those outside Israel are drawn to the light. Matthew 2 draws on imagery of the king and his enthronement, rather than the appearance of light. Ironically, the Matthew passage concerns the birth of an infant king whose power and longevity are seriously threatened by another king who acts only to protect himself. The story of the infant Jesus, already king, poses the question of where authentic power lies and what constitutes genuine kingship.

QUESTIONS AND THOUGHTS FOR REFLECTION

• Read Isaiah 60:1-6. What does Isaiah's imagery about light teach us about our role in God's kingdom?

• Read Psalm 72:1-14. This psalm alludes to the qualities of the one truly just leader that Christians affirm Jesus to be. How can we demonstrate justice in our everyday dealings?

• Read Ephesians 3:1-12. What mysteries of God have been revealed to you; how do you share them with others? How can you maintain your enthusiasm and passion for the gospel and share it effectively?

• Read Matthew 2:1-12. The wise men left their familiar lives behind in search of God. In what ways do you ensure your awareness of God's voice for direction in your life?

Community organizer and writer, living in Nashville, Tennessee

Agood parable for a New Year with new resolutions. I'm struck by the fact that the sheep seem just as surprised as the goats by the way they have acquired their inheritance. Surely this equality of incredulity provides an important clue to understanding the way of both sheep and goats. The surprise of the sheep seems to rule out any idea that we can somehow discipline ourselves and strive our way into sheepishness; that we can wake up each morning and say, "Oh, you beautiful sheep, you are so good at blessing people! Now get out there and clothe naked Jesus, help stranger Jesus, and give food and drink to hungry and thirsty Jesus." Neither do the goats (or so it would seem from their equally surprised response in this passage) go through life thinking, *I am going to turn my nose up at dirty homeless Jesus, and I am certainly not going to visit murderer Jesus at the penitentiary.*

If neither the sheep nor the goats went about intending to serve *or* neglect Jesus respectively, how can we choose to live as one or the other? I don't imagine that my neighbors wake up desiring to snub those on the outskirts of society, and I know that I don't have this sinister goal—yet I get a lump in my throat when I read this passage because I know that I am often rather goatish. What can we do? Surely we all want to line up with the sheep! Yet, it seems that despite our good resolve, the end result remains surprising.

What if the only way to see the lost and broken as Jesus did comes in getting to know Jesus so well that we can't help but see the subtle and not-so-subtle glimpses of the divine even in the dirtiest of street people and those most broken?

> *Lord, apart from you I cannot see the world in love. Thank you for this precious gift; please open my eyes each day so that I become an instrument of your mercy and grace. Amen.*

Even though it comes at the beginning of a new year, the month of January can feel a little dreary. The holidays are past; spring still feels miles away; and it can be quite cold and gray in many places. In the gray days of life like these, we must learn to rejoice in God's light. We remember that Isaiah's words come at a horrible time in Israel's history—the Babylonian captivity. When the Lord instructs Israel to "Arise, shine" and later in the passage promises the nation prosperity, I wonder how well the Israelites received this news. The people have always had a strong connection to the land; in fact, their journey to and eventual capture of the Promised Land has shaped much of their historical identity. Psalm 137, written about this time period in history, illustrates the emotion of the Israelites with images of weeping by the rivers of Babylon and being unable to sing the Lord's songs in a foreign land. We can easily imagine the Israelites being able to relate to the first half of Isaiah 60:2. "See, darkness covers the earth and thick darkness is over the peoples," (NIV). But the rest of the words may have felt like salt water to a parched mouth—the promise of luxury in the face of poverty.

Yet, the promises of God are realized, though perhaps not in a timetable that suits the people of Israel. This passage calls us to trust God. A command accompanies God's promises in this passage: arise and shine. In the midst of darkness and seemingly impossible odds, God's word calls us to trust in attitude and action. Many times I have been unhappy with the timing of God's help—of the fulfillment of promises in my life. In the face of darkness and depression I believe God commands us to arise and shine; then the Lord will meet us in that place to sustain and strengthen us.

What is the darkness over your life right now? Pray for strength to hold on to God's promises and to arise and shine in the midst of it all.

THURSDAY, JANUARY 3 ~ *Read Isaiah 60:1-6*

The prophecy in verse 3 that promises nations and kings will be drawn to Israel's light is as intriguing as the Lord's command to arise and shine in the midst of a dark and dreary exile. God demonstrates in the scripture again and again a preference to reveal divine power and glory through broken people. The Holy One intends that the people of God shine in a way that attracts those who do not yet know God. God partners with us to reveal the wonder of grace to the world. Yet, in practice, the drawing-others-by-reflecting-God's-light thing can throw us off track. Often Christians either will try really hard to be shiny and end up projecting their own little light instead of shining God's marvelous light or will be so intimidated by the concept of shining God's light that they try to hide the glory that is meant to shine through.

When I worked as a youth pastor, I had the privilege of watching God's love transform young people. When they understood the love of God demonstrated through the work of Jesus, it made an amazing difference. However, these youth had a hard time shining God's light into their families or groups of friends. They would often either think they had to be perfect now, or they would keep the "churchy" part of them hidden—both options leading them to feel like failures and frauds. I advised that the only responsibility of a reflecting object, if it wants to reflect well, is to stay in the light. Israel isn't given instruction for how to be their shiny best or how to attract the most nations and kings. Instead the passage reads, "the LORD rises upon you" (NIV)—that's the reason people come to your light. May we learn to keep our focus on God's light and remain in it so that our shining becomes a natural and wonderful aspect of being a child of God.

Thank you, Lord, for the privilege of shining with your light in a dark and hurting world. Amen.

Most of us desire a strong sense of justice in our leaders. Most politicians these days work hard to portray the competition with the opponent as a battle between right and wrong. Often the challenger runs for office to challenge an injustice. We, like the psalmist, pray for a leader who will be just, righteous, and a defender of the weak. If we perceive a leader as being unfair or manipulative of the system, there is little grace for him or her.

Why do Christians and non-Christians alike value justice so highly? Perhaps because right and wrong are most clearly demonstrated by injustice. We can debate moral issues, but when people are treated unfairly or taken advantage of, the behavior is not deemed acceptable. This psalm is an earnest prayer of support for one who longs to rule with justice; whose priority is the well-being of the people. This desire stands in stark contrast to another king we consider during this season of Epiphany—King Herod. A puppet king of an occupying Roman Empire, Herod demonstrates the horrific lengths to which he will go to protect his own interests. Those lengths include not only dishonesty and conniving but mass murder as he flails about in a desperate attempt to keep the promised Messiah from usurping his power.

Although King Solomon (the name associated with this psalm) does not live up to all the desires expressed in this prayer, the psalmist paints a wise picture of the archetypal just leader. But would the world accept a leader who delivered the needy and the afflicted, took pity on the weak, and rescued them from violence because "precious is their blood in his sight"? In this season of Epiphany we celebrate that the Prince of Peace has fulfilled the psalmist's prayer: "May he judge your people with righteousness, and your poor with justice."

Thank you, Lord, for your justice and mercy. Amen.

SATURDAY, JANUARY 5 ~ *Read Ephesians 3:1-12*

I really enjoy a good spy movie, as well as crime fiction books that involve some mystery—some journey of discovery for the protagonist. Paul, in this letter to the believers in Ephesus, speaks about a mystery that has been revealed to him by God for the purpose of sharing it. God's grace offered through the sacrifice of Jesus is for everyone. Perhaps this doesn't sound like such a mystery to us today, but imagine how controversial and groundbreaking Paul's message of salvation by grace through faith for *all* people would have been in his time.

At this time people associated the gods with a particular place. People had regionalistic pride in their gods, perhaps like people today have in our modern sports franchises. The idea of a God who is near and who offers relationship with all people would have been quite a head-scratcher. If someone were to write a mystery story about God's relationship with people, the detective protagonist would find clues throughout the Hebrew Scriptures and would be working on an insatiable hunch that this God had a plan to save the world. The big reveal of course is Jesus, who turns the expectations that many Jewish people had about the Messiah upside down while simultaneously fulfilling messianic prophecy in their history. What a wonderful paradox and great mystery story! The writer of John's Gospel writes about Jesus this way: "the light shines in the darkness, but the darkness has not understood it" (John 1:5, NIV). Let us consider afresh today the great and wonderful mystery of salvation by grace through faith in Jesus Christ. And in the places where understanding does not come, where the mystery of life is too difficult or painful to fathom, let us look to the light of Christ and trust that God will guide us in the way we should go.

Lord, help me today to share the good news about Jesus, in words and in action. Amen.

EPIPHANY

In many Christian traditions, Epiphany is an important cele-bration, a time to commemorate the coming of the Magi. This story draws our attention because of its monumental assertion that Jesus came into the world for the sake of *all* people, Jews and Gentiles alike. The Magi, though distinctly foreign visitors, celebrate the birth of Christ with a seeming awareness that this child is significant to them and to their people.

We know why the Magi made this trip: they saw "his star in the east and have come to worship him" (NIV). But consider the preparation that trip required. As men of status they had the means to make such an ambitious journey and offer costly gifts. Their reputations warranted an audience with the king. They were seekers who searched the sky for something greater than themselves. These wise ones, in a time when travel was not easy, risked their health and safety, their fortune, and their reputations to follow a light that they believed to be significant.

And though the Magi did seek Herod's help in locating the newborn king, their concern centers more on a warning dream than on the wrath of King Herod when he finds out they haven't reported back to him. What sort of people act in such incredible ways that fly in the face of culture's norm, all because of a star? It seems they highly valued seeking the truth. They valued find-ing this particular child enough to undertake the journey, though they didn't know exactly where to find him.

We cannot know all the mysteries of our God; but let us, like the Magi, be willing to chase after the deep truths about God's nature, which might require a difficult journey in order to be found.

Lord, help us to seek and value truth. Give us strength not to shy away from this endeavor in the face of persecution. Amen.

Your Servants Are Listening

JANUARY 7–13, 2013 • STEVEN H. SHUSSETT

SCRIPTURE OVERVIEW: Baptism for most Christian communities is the sacrament by which new converts are received into communing fellowship, the sign and seal of their incorporation into Christ. The New Testament texts connect the presence of the Spirit with baptism. The Gospel text claims that the very divine presence that came upon Jesus that day in the Jordan comes upon Jesus' followers. The Spirit is a powerful reality that cannot be domesticated or bought and sold like a commodity on the market. Baptism is also an acknowledgment of one's belonging to God. The voice from heaven at Jesus' baptism declares him to be God's own Son. He is the servant, the agent of God's reign, a sovereignty so eloquently praised in Psalm 29. His followers in baptism are also commissioned to be subjects of God's rule and empowered agents of reconciliation.

QUESTIONS AND THOUGHTS FOR REFLECTION

* Read Isaiah 43:1-7. How does it feel to be loved by God as much as Isaiah describes? How do you feel led to respond to this vast love?

* Read Psalm 29. In what ways have you heard God's voice in your life? Mindful of the creative and destructive power portrayed in the psalm, how has God invited you to build up and to break down?

* Read Luke 3:15-17, 21-22. Throughout your life, who has been a John the Baptist for you, pointing toward Jesus?

* Read Acts 8:14-17. As you review your life, decade by decade, what have been the "high water marks" of your faith journey?

Minister of Word and Sacrament, called as the Teaching (Executive) Presbyter of Lehigh Presbytery in eastern Pennsylvania

MONDAY, JANUARY 7 ~ *Read Acts 8:14-17*

Upon learning that I was raised a Jew, Christians often want to know how I came to follow Jesus. "When were you baptized?" is quickly asked; but as Acts demonstrates, it isn't an easy question to answer.

I'm blessed to know the moment when God went from a fuzzy "Somebody out there" to the One revealed in Jesus Christ. I can tell stories of my baptism by water and the gift of having my gracious, if perplexed, family attend. But when asked the simple-sounding question, "When were you baptized?" I find myself taking a deep breath and long pause before stammering my response.

Was I baptized in the Spirit when friends asked me to attend church with them and I went, even though nothing in my life hinted at accepting such an invitation? What of the many college classes I took on Christianity, participating and engaging professors more than I did in other courses? Or when all I listened to was contemporary Christian music as it put into understandable words the faith that I couldn't understand?

The people of Samaria accepted the word of God as their cornerstone, living faithful lives that others could see. Peter and John come onstage and the Spirit enters the scene in a way that no one then or now can witness or prove, that wind that "blows where it chooses, and you hear the sound of it, but you do not know where it comes from or where it goes" (John 3:8).

If asked, "When were you baptized?" what would the Samaritans say? And when someone asks you that same question, will you point to your infancy or a day marked in red on your calendar? Or will you too pause and stammer, trying to sum up a lifetime of accepting the word of God?

O God, may I know your presence with me, confess my absence from you, and celebrate the faith-full life that is mine by grace. Amen.

TUESDAY, JANUARY 8 ~ *Read Psalm 29:1-9*

We associate God's voice, God's hovering over the waters, with creation, as in Genesis 1. But here God hovers; God speaks; God breaks, shakes, and strips the forests bare. This does not sound like creation in process but destruction. But is that from God's infinite perspective or our own limited view?

Mount St. Helens erupted in Washington state in 1980. If we listened with the ears of the psalmist, we would agree that God's voice was indeed powerful that day. Flames of fire flashed forth; the wilderness shook; the mountain skipped and bucked. Not only did the trees break, they whirled. And what was once as life-filled a place as any on earth was now as dead as the moon.

Or so it seemed. Over time, however, it became obvious that new seeds had taken root, and animals never before seen on that mountain were making their homes there. Now the mountain teems with new colors, new sounds, new life. Upon entering that temple, all say "Glory!"

Life in this world holds many crosses, both large and small. Death rarely charges up to us to swing one mighty blow. Rather, it comes through the thousand cuts of an unkind word here, an innocent if biting oversight, a dream stillborn before its first breath. At that moment we feel as if we are stripped bare, shaken, broken. But even as the scars remain—our trust or confidence tossed to and fro—the God of glory hovers over us, not thundering but whispering, calling into life the new seeds of possibility within us. It may take days or weeks or months or years, but over time we become a new creation. And as we are able to receive and embrace this promise, then from deep within the temple of the Holy Spirit that is our body, we too will cry out, "Glory!"

God of power and might, may we hear your voice of love and grace over the clamor of our fears and anxiety. Amen.

WEDNESDAY, JANUARY 9 ~ *Read Psalm 29*

It has been my long-standing practice to introduce the passing of the peace with a relevant scriptural passage. The psalmist's coda, "May the LORD give strength to his people! May the LORD bless his people with peace!" followed by "The peace of Christ be with you," sets a powerful context for worship, promising the peace that passes understanding.

If we are honest, God's peace often lies beyond our understanding. This psalm is a hymn of praise to the One whose energy bursts like ten thousand suns. We look at our lives and the world around us; we see trees break, nations shake, and mountains leap. In honesty, we cannot deny these events. In faith, we trust that we are not alone in them.

Real peace is not the lack of turmoil or anxiety but a deep rootedness in the God who sits enthroned over any flood. The anchor that holds us in faith is not secured in the slipping sands of "It will be okay" or "It can't get any worse." Rather, as the fourteenth-century mystic Julian of Norwich reminds us, Jesus did not say there would not be storm or fatigue or discomfort, but he did promise we would not be overcome.

I have heard it said that the amount of water in the world remains constant, recycled through humidity and ice, salt and fresh. To remember Jesus' baptism is to claim our own, because the waters of the Jordan are the waters of our baptism as well. God, who sits enthroned forever, became one with us through the Son, and in the waters of baptism we become one with him.

The storms will come. But God through Jesus Christ is with us in the midst of it, blessing the people with peace.

Lord, you reign over all, and in the midst of life you whisper in love too deep for words, "Peace, be still." May we have ears of the heart to hear. Amen.

We can approach scripture in many ways. For some it gives an account of God's covenant through Israel and Jesus Christ. For others it serves as a collection of nonfiction, fiction, and poetry, while for still others it is history. But how often do we read the Bible as an expression of God's love for us? Can we read it and hear it as a love letter from God?

Military veterans from World War II are nearing the end of long lives. It is not unusual for a child or parent to discover their letters written during the war years to friends or loved ones. These letters might reflect the tedious nature of day-in, day-out life, punctuated by the hard realities of combat. Some share the honest fear felt in the midst of dire circumstances; others minimize such things out of concern for the reader. But taking the time to write, that in itself says so much. The writer wants the reader to know *I am thinking of you; you are in my heart; we are connected by love and affection.*

This reading from Isaiah reminds us that God is our Parent, our Loved One, who created and formed us, who went so far as to name us and to claim us. And although we often face our own trials and tribulations, whether war or sickness or any number of other things, God is with us, God will protect us. As Christians, we believe and affirm that God has already given God's only Son for us. All because we are precious in God's sight, honored and loved.

> *Hear God's promise to you. Read this passage aloud, saying your own name after each instance of the word "you." Substitute your name for the printed name where necessary.*

Jesus' ministry begins with his baptism and ends with his ascension, from living with us in a particular time and place to being worshiped as the One who reigns over all time and space. Isaiah speaks to this grand vision when God says, "Peace, peace, to the far and the near" (57:19), or as Jesus ascends, commanding the disciples to "be my witnesses in Jerusalem, in all Judea and Samaria, and to the ends of the earth" (Acts 1:8).

Each time we celebrate the Lord's Supper, we live out this promise of God's summons in word and in deed. I find few moments more profound than the invitation to the Table, "Friends, this is the joyful feast of the people of God. Men and women and children will come from north and south and east and west—'everyone who is called by my name'—to sit at table in the kingdom of God."

And even more than this cloud of witnesses surrounds us The prophet reminds us not once, not twice, but six times that God is active among us, no matter from what direction we come.

At a conference some years ago, our worship leader spoke the words as noted in the paragraph above before we celebrated Communion. No, she more than spoke them; Laura danced them. Slowly, gracefully, arms broadly and gently extended, she pirouetted the invitation to come from wherever we were, whoever we were, to share in the feast that Jesus had prepared. In that moment, grace moving through the grace of another, we were reminded that what God desires will not be denied. All people, every people, are invited to come together, share together, because God made us, named us, and claimed us.

Stretching your arms, take a deep breath and pray to the God who is as wide as the oceans, and as close as your heart.

After a poor introduction to church-shopping, I walked into a second church a little wary, uncertain of my reception as a new visitor and as a non-Christian. My answer came in minutes as a group of older women surrounded me, smiling and full of questions. By the time the service began they knew my height, weight, favorite color, and food allergies! For someone who felt like an outsider, that welcome became a life lesson.

The people who braved the wilderness to see John did not get there by accident. Such a trip would take planning and commitment, and these do not come without some anticipation: "the people were filled with expectation." They had something in mind, some sense of who John was and what he would say.

But the people find themselves surprised. John does not cleanse so as to set apart folks by greater purity—as a ritual bath might suggest. Rather, being baptized as Jesus was baptized set aside the illusion of being "pure" for the truth of being human. It is for our humanity—the good and the ill of it—that Jesus will die. By accepting the baptism by John, Jesus rejects the simplicity of wheat versus chaff, in order to be with the world full of people who are both wheat *and* chaff. For someone who came to church believing one had to be "good" to be a Christian, this was good news indeed.

When those women surrounded me, and subsequently that congregation and ultimately the church, it was not as chaff or tares at risk of burning. Despite my expectations, they did not lovingly intend to make me "right" but simply to have me grow alongside them.

Lord, help me first to see not the differences between myself and others; but as I trust your Spirit is in me, to trust that the same Spirit resides in them. Amen.

Elsewhere in the Bible, writers compare God's voice to a peal of thunder. For many, thunder causes unease; and when we are confronted by the living God—in confession or calling—that unease seems appropriate.

But God's presence manifests in ways other than thunder. In Luke's Gospel, a voice that speaks of love accompanies Jesus' baptism—no loud boom here, only the tickle of dove's wings. I was baptized in my midtwenties in a church more familiar with infant baptism. Though of average height, I felt the need to bend low at the waist, to keep my head over the font. I didn't want to make a mess!

I didn't consider how I looked until I heard the peals—of laughter, not thunder! Somehow I sensed that the members were laughing with me, not at me. Laughing in joy with an adult who is now going where too often only infants dare to tread. Laughing in joy with the stranger who had found a home.

At the Jordan River, with so many baptized, among waves of confession and forgiveness, it was new life like a cup running over. And then, to top it off, God's Son joins this new family, wading into the swirling waters of dying and rising, peril and promise. In our holy washing, is it laughter that we hear? Laughter not from having been caught in sin but rather from having been freed from it!

I frequently look back on that day, remembering how I could have been laughed at, judged, or considered a stranger. Instead, I experienced a love that carried me through those infant steps of faith and allowed me to hear God's call in my life. And with ears of the heart to hear it, I suspect I might have heard God laughing all along.

Lord, may my first reaction to life's unexpected events be joy in your presence. Amen.

Catching the Vision

JANUARY 14–20, 2013 • AMORY PECK

SCRIPTURE OVERVIEW: The Old Testament texts contain references to "dawn," "burning torch" (Isa. 62:1), and "light" (Ps. 36:9), which are familiar symbols for the Epiphany season; and the miracle of changing the water to wine at Cana is a traditional text for this part of the Christian calendar. The common theme is the overwhelming generosity of God. The psalmist sings of it in terms of God's "steadfast love," which comes in times of opposition and threat. The voice of Isaiah 62 can hardly contain itself. Jerusalem's vindication is at hand. In the story at Cana in John 2, Jesus answers the emergency of a depleted wine supply with provisions that both quantitatively and qualitatively go beyond what the original host could supply. First Corinthians 12 reminds us of the abundant gifts of the Spirit, leading first to a confession of Jesus as Lord and then to a variety of services for the common good of the church.

QUESTIONS AND THOUGHTS FOR REFLECTION

- Read Psalm 36:5-10. Picture the surroundings where you live. Where and when are you most likely to find comfort in the shadow of God's wings?

- Read Isaiah 62:1-5. When have you felt the most desolate? How did you move into a sense of delight?

- Read John 2:1-11. Jesus performs his first miracle and then his disciples believe in him. Can you recall a specific situation when you saw and *then* believed?

- Read 1 Corinthians 12:1-11. There are numerous ways of being in service. How does your church or faith community help people identify their spiritual gifts?

Retired teacher/trainer, living lakeside in the Pacific Northwest

The Cascade Mountains extend from Southern British Columbia, through Washington and Oregon, to Northern California. The tectonic forces that shaped the Cascades also tightly folded the layers of 55 million-year-old sandstone, shale, and coal to create the Chuckanut Mountains. During the last Ice Age, glacial ice more than 5,500 feet deep covered the Chuckanuts. As the glacier advanced and retreated over the rocks, Lake Whatcom was created. Nearly twelve miles long and a mile wide at its broadest point, Lake Whatcom has thirty miles of shoreline and holds about 250 billion gallons of water.

Kokanee salmon, cutthroat trout, and smallmouth bass inhabit Lake Whatcom. Ringing the lake, Pacific tree frogs and Northwestern garter snakes share the area with great blue herons, the bald eagle, and downy woodpeckers. Mountain beavers, striped skunks, red fox, as well as deer and coyotes roam the area. Western hemlock and Douglas fir cover the hills. Salmon berries and red elderberries can be found.

Those are the facts of the area where I live. Every season gives me joy, every mood and look of the surroundings speaks to me. But the psalmist reminds us that the reality of it all is so much more than a beautiful world. The psalm assures us that God's love is as high as those mountains, as deep as the sea. God's steadfast love enfolds me, enfolds all of us, including the eagles, foxes, and trout.

My retired life is filled with family, friends, good books, and volunteer work. I also live with congestive heart failure. When I let my thoughts linger on that piece of who I am, I feel diminished. That's when I look to the world around me. The strength of those depths and heights is the very reach of God. I rest, with a grateful heart, in the assurance of steadfast love.

Creator God, creatures great and small are blessed to live in the protective shadow of your wings. Amen.

A "Back to Church Sunday" YouTube clip featured a number of people explaining why they were not part of a faith community. Their heartfelt reasons included "I've got to get my life together first," and "It would make me nervous to go," and "I don't believe everything they believe." The saddest comment for me to hear was "If they knew me, they wouldn't want me."

The ad countered each worry with reassurance. A faith community *is* the place to get your life together; you'll feel right at home; and you don't have to believe everything—you can still belong. Most reassuring was "It's okay not to be okay. Really."

These words from Isaiah describe the people of the time: people crushed by daily worries who understood themselves as forsaken and desolate. This description still rings true. On a global level, so many are, indeed, forsaken and desolate. Their images come vividly to our minds. On a personal level, most of us have times of feeling that wretched.

Yet, we and the Israelites hear these words from the prophet and joyfully affirm the action of One who vindicates us and with whom we have relationship. In this relationship, we no longer have the names of Forsaken and Desolate. The Lord renames us; we become My Delight Is in Her, and Married—names that convey a life of relationship.

The YouTube clip described church as a place of new beginnings, a place that welcomes imperfect people and declares us all of infinite worth. We discover our true value in the names given us by the One who loves us into relationship. For, as the prophet Isaiah says, "the LORD delights" in us.

O Lord, may we believe that you claim and rename us; may we be a delight to you. Amen.

WEDNESDAY, JANUARY 16 ~ *Read Isaiah 62:5*

We read about the One who vindicates us, calls us into relationship, and offers us a new name of hope. And in this season of Epiphany, we note the images of light: the vindication that "shines" like the dawn and salvation like "a burning torch." Perhaps that very light draws us and others out of forsakenness and desolation. Verse 5 lifts up the fact that we enter a committed relationship with God, just as a bride and groom commit to each other—each rejoicing over the other. In the past few years I've seen the faces of my nephew and nephew-in-law as they watched their brides come toward them—spellbound in delight.

Dakota, the two-year-old son of church members, is a wonderfully free spirit, unbelievably quick on his feet. On a recent Sunday, he came forward with the other children for children's time but flitted away before the story's conclusion. When he heard the other children being dismissed for Sunday school, he came flying down the aisle to catch up with his friends. In some way that most of us didn't see, he reentered the sanctuary, only to fly back down the aisle later to sit expectantly on the chancel steps. Dakota's attentive parents were aware of his whereabouts at all times. Only the rest of us thought that he seemed a sprite—of the moment and a delight to our congregation.

This passage from Isaiah tells me that the Lord delights in me, in all of us. The Lord views us with the same unabashed joy as we view little Dakota.

The Lord rejoices over us, just as bridegrooms rejoice in their brides. I am filled with awe at the wonder of that.

Dear God, whenever my spirit starts to slip, help me remember this astonishing message: you delight in me. Amen.

Several years ago our newly assigned supervisor asked each local church in his care to complete an assessment instrument. The self-assessment form asked that members evaluate how effectively our congregation engaged the mission field surrounding our church, how we incorporated new disciples into the life of our church, and how we supported the ongoing spiritual development of our church family.

At my local church, a small group of members met to talk through the questions. We began talking fairly superficially; but as we gained focus and talked together more prayerfully, our responses became more insightful and honest. We were especially startled to realize how much more we could be doing in our church to equip ourselves as disciples of Jesus Christ. We confessed our lack of focus and pledged, as leaders in the congregation, to begin changing that reality. We vowed to help one another learn how to talk about our beliefs and to encourage one another in spiritual growth. The assessment form became a wake-up call.

In today's reading Paul asks for another type of assessment as he writes to the early Christians in Corinth, informing them of their new life as believers. They, like us today, needed to set aside life as it had been, in order to put on their new lives as disciples of Jesus Christ. Clear in their new commitment and trusting in Jesus, they could live out their lives using the spiritual gifts given to them.

Those early Christians learned. We, in my home church, learned. Paul asserts that our ability to affirm Jesus as Lord is itself a gift of the Spirit. So we remember and affirm the source of our faith and begin anew.

Dear God, may our self-assessment always come in the light of your reign. Amen.

Paul then discusses the variety of gifts among us—we who confess that Jesus is Lord. These gifts, services, and activities come from the same Spirit, the same Lord, the same God. Why are we so different from one another as Christians? Our differences exist because our gifts and diversity are based on God's character. All are necessary to support the common good.

During the 1980s I had several opportunities to attend workshops conducted by Marlene Wilson, the founder of the Volunteer Connection, Boulder County, Colorado. Her book, *How to Mobilize Church Volunteers* (Augsburg Publishing House, 1983) became, and remains, despite its early publication date, one of my most valuable resource books.

All these years later I vividly recall one particular exercise. Ms. Wilson asked each of us to think of our favorite volunteer task in the church. Then she asked us to think of our least favorite. She called on one person, asking, "What's your favorite? What's your least favorite?" Hearing the responses, she would then ask who had that least favorite as their favorite? In that large group, every time someone mentioned a task they didn't enjoy, another mentioned their delight in that particular job.

Ms. Wilson noted that a major difficulty in congregations is that busy leaders are often reluctant to recruit others to do the jobs they themselves find distasteful. That, of course, leads to disgruntled leaders and underused laypeople.

God, in divine wisdom, kindness, and good humor, has scattered out a wide variety of gifts. Thank God for those good souls who, from their deep passion, teach our Sunday school classes, sing in our choirs, chair our committees, organize our prayer chains, and tackle the mystery of church kitchens. Gifts, talents, and skills from God—all for the common good.

Inventive God, you sprinkled out a marvelous variety of gifts. Thank-you for the spiritual gifts I've received. Amen.

There was a wedding in Mercer Island, Washington. Friends and family had been invited. The bride was having an at-home wedding and had hired her niece as the caterer. This occasion would debut the niece's new catering business. I was there early to help out, and I heard the young woman worrying aloud: "I haven't prepared nearly enough. There won't be food for everyone." Well, there was. Everyone ate well, and the fledgling business owner felt relief and pride.

There was a wedding in Cana of Galilee. Friends and family had been invited. Preparations had been made for food and wine for the guests. But well before the celebration's end, the wine was running out. Mary, the mother of Jesus, knew that would mar the joy of the celebration. She turned to her son for a solution. After a bit of family fuss between mother and son, Mary turned to those serving the guests and said, "Do whatever he tells you." I delight in this vision of Jesus as he takes time to participate in the joy of the day and chooses to begin his ministry of miracles in such a spirit of overflowing, abundant hospitality.

As I read more deeply, though, I realize that more than just a wedding reception is at hand. Despite the best intentions of the host family, the reception is about to disintegrate into chaos. What has been is no longer enough. Instead, something new— some new intervention is needed. The old will be redeemed by the new. At this moment in time, everything is about to change. Jesus, surrounded by his disciples and his mother, will usher in a time of new life, a life of abundance and salvation.

What an honor to be present at this moment—the wedding banquet goes so much beyond expectations.

Jesus, you've invited us to a wedding banquet. Help us to imagine the inclusive, expansive, life-giving gathering that awaits us. Amen.

It was a marvelous sight and a mighty sound as the eleven grandchildren came drumming their way around the corner of the house and onto the family reunion stage. Earlier in the day their Aunt Elizabeth had gathered them for a drum-making session. Elizabeth had spent weeks searching out used buckets and plastic flowerpots for the base of the drums, heavy balloons for the drum heads, and lots of colored tape and stickers. She had brought ordinary items, and from those she and the children created extraordinary drums. Their enthusiastic drumming was a highlight of the evening's entertainment.

Let us switch to another setting. The guests at the wedding in Cana are disappointed; the wine has run out. Perhaps they grumble about the stinginess of the host family. Jesus takes the six stone jars at hand and has the servants fill them with water. From these simple items Jesus creates fine wine. Gallons and gallons of wine. One hundred eighty gallons of the finest wine. Hospitality overflowing.

I can think of many instances within my church's administrative council meetings where people bemoan a lack of resources. We could welcome newcomers more effectively if only the church could afford to hire a Web master. We could spread our net wider if only the church had the money for extensive publicity. We could feed more homeless people if only the kitchen were larger. We could, we could—if only.

Jesus' water-into-wine example warms and encourages me, just as the used buckets-into-drums experience impressed me. What a lesson to learn: all I need, all *we* need to delight others is at hand, waiting to be created from the ordinary.

Provider God, too often we feel lost in life's challenges. Help us remember that we have all we need, right at hand. Blessings overflowing. Amen.

Deep Listening to God's Word

JANUARY 21–27, 2013 • YOUNGSOOK CHARLENE KANG

SCRIPTURE OVERVIEW: It is appropriate that the people of God be reminded time and again that they live by the divine word, ancient but ever new. Nehemiah 8 records the story of the people of the reconstituted community of Israel gathered as one to listen to Ezra read the Torah. That same delight in the Torah makes it the object of praise in Psalm 19. It renews the soul, instructs the ignorant, brings joy to the heart and enlightenment to the eye. But it functions also to expose secret and proud sins so that God's servants can live in total dependence on divine mercy. The Gospel text reminds us that the word of God can also bring rejection and rage as well as delight (Luke 4). The epistle lesson from First Corinthians does not focus immediately on the word of God, but it depicts for us a community constituted by the word, a community grappling with the very diversity Jesus explained from the Isaiah text.

QUESTIONS AND THOUGHTS FOR REFLECTION

- Read Nehemiah 8:1-3, 5-6, 8-10. In what ways do you rejoice when hearing the word of God?
- Read Psalm 19. The psalmist praises the Lord as "my rock and my redeemer." What name for God expresses your experience of the divine?
- Read 1 Corinthians 12:12-31a. Paul points out that we have differing gifts. What gifts do you possess, and how do you use them for the body of Christ?
- Read Luke 4:14-21. Jesus calls us to a specific mission. How are you involved in bringing the good news of Jesus Christ to your neighbors?

District superintendent of The United Methodist Church, Denver, Colorado

The walls of Jerusalem stand restored, but the Israelites still face many challenges. The land to which they return after seventy years of captivity is not a tension-free utopia—despite their high hopes. They feel uncertain about the future of their community.

One challenge requires that the people determine what is essential or indispensable and what can be set aside. They realize that they have indeed lost what was most essential to them—their spiritual heritage. They now see the need to restore the foundation of their faith.

So the people ask the scribe Ezra to bring the book of the law of Moses. They stand when he opens the book. Men and women listen to the word of God attentively as Ezra reads from early morning to midday. Ezra reads, and the Levites interpret among those who gather; the occasion becomes a time of spiritual reawakening. The power of the written word and the acknowledgment of the gap between the law's expectations and their daily lives and practice bring the people to tears. God's word convicts. Though the people weep, Nehemiah declares this day to be a holy day, one set apart by God. Such a day is one of celebration with eating, drinking, and fellowship, "for the joy of the LORD is [y]our strength."

Now the people finally "get it"; they understand the reading that has been given them. They go off to feast, "eating and drinking and including the poor in a great celebration" (THE MESSAGE, Neh. 8:12). God's word convicts *and* restores. Truly, the joy of the Lord comes in the joy of returning to God's word.

O God, convict and restore us. May we celebrate the joy of knowing you as the source of our strength and salvation. Amen.

Recently a friend and I climbed to the top of a hill behind a retreat center in Cody, Wyoming. We saw numerous piles of stones, or cairns, as we ascended—often one at each turn of the narrow path. Some piles were high; others were low. Some stones were quite big; others were small. Perhaps people stacked the stones to mark the path. But I imagined that people left them as symbols of their prayers; marking each turning as a sacred place, placing stones as they prayed a special prayer. Some may have prayed for loved ones. Some may have indicated a desire to leave their past behind and move forward. Others may have wanted to build a little tower of aspirations and dreams.

These stones do not speak a word. But to me they speak volumes about the hearts of those who pray and build cairns. Not only do the heavens and the firmament tell of and proclaim God's work, but these small stones pour forth speech. They declare knowledge of people's hopes and dreams.

As my friend and I hiked up the hill, I stopped at some cairns and joined my prayers with those who had gone before me. I placed a few small stones as a token of my prayer. Oh, yes, I realized that this gesture on my part and others was how these cairns grew higher and higher. As I placed the stones, I uttered a prayer of hope. I joined all of creation, which day to day and night to night prays and praises the Creator. Finally, I picked up a stone and prayed the psalmist's words: "The signposts of GOD are clear and point out the right road. The life-maps of GOD are right, showing the way to joy. The directions of GOD are plain and easy on the eyes" (THE MESSAGE). Truly, our ultimate direction in life comes from the word of God.

O God, as we follow your leading, may we leave cairns of prayer and praise that bear witness to you. Amen.

Each year the Vietnamese Children's Choir from a local church sings at a church-district annual celebration. Not only Vietnamese but Ghanaian, Pakistani, Korean, Japanese, Tongan, Hispanic, African American, and Anglo congregations come together to celebrate our ministries. Different languages, cultures, and traditions meet as we share in worship and lift up our common ministry goals and visions in Christ. For me, this annual gathering is indeed a culmination of the church as a diverse but unified body of Christ.

Yet, some of these immigrant congregations hear from within and without the church this message: "Go home. You don't belong here." Paul emphasizes a different approach to belonging. For him, all are necessary and precious parts of one body. Diversity is a gift of God, and no gift is more essential than another. "The eye cannot say to the hand, 'I have no need of you.'" With our Spirit-infused gifts, we bring specific capabilities to the body: hearing, sense of smell, the gift of sight. Each person's particular gift enhances the body. We need one another.

Paul invites the members at Corinth, and us, to embrace the gifts that each brings. Our barriers of language, elitism, education, race, culture give way in communion and relationship in the body. We find ourselves enriched by one another's love and wisdom.

A pastor relates that a dear friend told him that he was a better person for knowing him. Would that that were true for us as individuals and as a church. We may disagree with one another; but in our diversity, which is a gift of the Spirit, we come together and are stronger for the gift.

Gracious God, may we come to value our differences as strength rather than weakness. Amen.

The text Jesus chooses to read recapitulates his concern for the excluded and the outcast. It is as if he were saying, "I am anointed to bring the good news to the marginalized." As I read this passage, I am reminded of Bishop Aldo Etchegoyen of Argentina who took seriously his role as a Christian and a bishop and put this passage in practice.

In 1976 Argentina came under military dictatorship. Some thirty thousand people disappeared over a six-year period of time; about two hundred women were among the prisoners in Buenos Aires. Three Protestant women requested that Bishop Etchegoyen bring Communion to them in prison. Although it was considered dangerous to relate to any political prisoners, Bishop Etcheogyen was not afraid of providing this service to them. He wanted to share the love of Christ who sets the prisoners free. Each time he attempted it, however, the bishop was not allowed to pursue his offering. The bishop decided to keep in the freezer a loaf of bread that he would use at the time he would be allowed to serve Communion. Argentina returned to civilian democratic rule in 1983 after a seven-year military dictatorship. When he was finally permitted to serve Communion to these women, Bishop Etchegoyen used the bread that he had kept in the freezer. He recalled that the bread was hardened but could not be broken by dictatorship but only by the power of Jesus Christ. A few days later, the women were released from prison.

Bishop Etchegoyen's faithful obedience to the gospel of Jesus Christ helped bring God's liberating presence to those in captivity. God calls and anoints us to bring good news to the poor, to proclaim release to the captives, and recovery of sight to the blind, to let the oppressed go free.

O God, may we continue Christ's ministry of healing, reconciliation, and transformation. Amen.

FRIDAY, JANUARY 25 ~ *Read Psalm 19:7-14*

A Two-Year Academy for Spiritual Formation made quite an impact on my spiritual practice. If *radical* means "getting to the root" of how God works in our lives, I can state that my Academy experience has been a radical one. I've been led to reach the roots of my faith through deep listening to God's word. I realized that God's word does indeed guide my life. "Otherwise how will we find our way?" (THE MESSAGE).

I tend to make matters complex. I often equate *profound* with *complex*, while regarding *simple* as *simplistic*. But through the Academy experience I discovered that God's way is challenging *and* profound—but simple. Looking back, each of the eight sessions helped me move from the pursuit of intelligence and complexity to the pursuit of God's "simple" way. The psalmist says, "The decrees of the LORD are sure, making wise the simple." Now I, as the simple, want to be made wise!

Notice the many words the psalmist employs to describe God's word: *law*, *decrees*, *precepts*, *commandments*, and *ordinances*. As the psalmist proclaims, "The revelation of God is whole and pulls our lives together" (THE MESSAGE). Just as the sun's heat encompasses the earth, so too does God's instruction encompass and enrich the world. As we learn to depend on God's word, we find ourselves in harmony with all creation. Attentiveness to God's voice revealed through the word and the world helps us stay in touch with the roots of our faith.

As we listen to God's voice, we find ourselves rooted, forgiven, and restored.

"Let the words of my mouth and the meditation of my heart be acceptable to you, O LORD, my rock and my redeemer." Amen.

In October 2011, I went to Haiti as part of a work team that would help with a recovery construction project at two Methodist schools that were damaged by the devastating 2010 earthquake. In addition to our common physical labor activities, team members were assigned different responsibilities: team leader, physical labor crew chief, team nurse, music leader, photographer, videographer, blog coordinator, journalist, and leader for children's activities. I was so glad that my assignment was to lead children's activities. I acknowledged my shortcomings in the physical labor area; I was not much help in construction work. Our work team effort required all the different gifts from our various members.

Paul asks a self-evident question: "Do all possess gifts of healing? Do all speak in tongues? Do all interpret?" No, Paul makes it clear that our diversity is a gift from God and part of God's larger plan as we live out God's mission as the body of Christ. No gift is more valued than another; all people need one another. That dependence fosters a care for the other. When one suffers, all suffer; when one rejoices, all rejoice.

God's design through our various gifts models our understanding of our lives together as a church: every part is unique and dependent on every other part. My mission team to Haiti served well because of the diverse and unique gifts the members brought to the team. Our team was "the body of Christ and individually members of it."

O Christ, we pray that we may serve you and the church with our diverse gifts. Amen.

Jesus, in a place of worship, stands and reads from the scroll of the prophet Isaiah. It is noteworthy that he chose this particular passage to read as one of his first acts of public ministry. He has returned to Galilee after facing the devil's testing. He comes now to set forth his plan of action. In Luke's Gospel, God's reality is a world in which the poor and marginalized matter, the freedom of captives matters.

As Jesus reads the message of recovery of sight to the blind and setting the oppressed free, he tells his listeners to open their eyes and let drop their shackles in order to witness the shape of his ministry. Through this reading, Jesus gives people a glimpse of what it will be like to follow him as their teacher and Lord.

The proclamation of the year of the Lord's favor may refer to the Jubilee year (every fifty years) when the ground lay fallow and slaves were released. Jesus ties the coming of the kingdom to the year of Jubilee and the transforming power of God. "The word of God is living and active," said the writer of the Hebrews (4:12). Jesus' reading of the Isaiah passage helps the hearers and readers understand that his ministry will serve to fulfill his anointing by the Spirit. When he finishes, Jesus states, "You've just heard Scripture make history. It came true just now in this place" (THE MESSAGE).

The Gospel of Luke invites us to see the world through the lens of these verses and to see what it means to follow Jesus. The reign of God is at hand. What if we as people of faith choose these values to guide us? How does our vision of the kingdom change if we understand this passage as Jesus' vision for our community of faith?

God, may we know and understand Christ's way on earth and follow him as our teacher and Lord. Amen.

Fulfilling Our True Selves

JANUARY 28–FEBRUARY 3, 2013 • AUDREY MISKELLEY

SCRIPTURE OVERVIEW: This week's lessons affirm the reality and illustrate the remarkable results of being known, claimed, and called by God. God "knew" Jeremiah even before he was "formed ... in the womb" (Jer. 1:5). Paul's teaching to the Corinthians about love is grounded in the affirmation that "I have been fully known" (1 Cor. 13:12). In language reminiscent of Jeremiah, the psalmist professes that it was God "who took me from my mother's womb" (71:6). The fulfillment of the scripture that Jesus announces in Luke 4:21 involves the claim of God on his life: "The Spirit of the Lord is upon me" (4:18). To be known, claimed, and called by God means to be equipped "to accomplish abundantly far more than all we can ask or imagine" (Eph. 3:20). The lessons offer an opportunity for us to consider God's claim on us. The good news is that a share of God's Spirit is ours as well, to equip and empower us in every circumstance to live and love in accordance with God's righteous purposes for us and the world.

QUESTIONS AND THOUGHTS FOR REFLECTION

- Read Jeremiah 1:4-10. How does an awareness of God's knowledge of you—even before the womb—affect your beliefs and living?

- Read Psalm 71:1-6. Where do you give voice to your personal lament? Where do you find sustenance and healing?

- Read 1 Corinthians 13. Where do you fail to fulfill the scriptural message of love in your relationships?

- Read Luke 4:21-30. When have you allowed assumptions to blind you to the truth of a person's being? What did you learn from that experience?

Canon Evangelist, Diocese of Lexington, Kentucky

God's call to the young man Jeremiah follows the prophetic pattern in scripture: God calls; prophet responds negatively to the call; God empowers. Many of us have had just such responses to the call of God on our lives. God's call brings fear as often as delight. God involves Jeremiah in a lifelong commitment to which Jeremiah expresses doubt of ability, but God promises to deliver and sustain.

Even before Jeremiah's birth, God has consecrated him to this task. Many of us have a difficult time grasping thoughts of time "before" the womb. I have no grasp of me before me. Yet God reminds us that we have a "before" and that place is God's. And, we remain God's in our "nows" and our "afters" too!

Imagine being called. Close your eyes and try to close your mind as well, turning off distracting thoughts about this coming week as much as you can.

The voice began singing to you when you were still safely in your mother's womb, singing to you the song of your life, telling you stories about a loved and devoted child, gifted by God and then sent out to fulfill the wonders of God's kingdom among the beloved of God's children. The story of our lives rests deeply inside each of us; it is the song that God sings to us. We can hear the familiar tune if we will only pause our minds and our lives long enough to hear its simple melody. Perhaps in his youthfulness, Jeremiah could hear the refrain.

I pray, gracious God, that I may hear your song and sing your words of my life. Amen.

I cannot hear or read this scripture passage without fond memories of the summer of 2010 when I officiated over fourteen weddings. It was a busy summer season, to say the least. It was also the summer that I had the opportunity to listen carefully to this passage in its entirety, without judgment.

We often allow Paul's lovely poetic language to lull us into sweet and blissful thoughts about the nature of love. But Paul writes to the Corinthians to address a group of quarrelsome church people who are squabbling over the spiritual gifts. He writes in practical words to explain that—whatever the gifts and religiosity among them—without a loving relationship, those aspects do not matter.

This passage from First Corinthians is the most often read scripture at marriage ceremonies, but I wonder if any of us hear the message it contains. I struggled as I developed homilies around the words of this biblical text that every couple wanted read. As a fallen human being, my own cynicism eagerly inserted itself into the reading and distorted the truth that lay at the heart of my relationship with God and with my neighbor.

Paul reminds us of life's truth: we are to live in love and charity with our God first and foremost. This achievement bears witness to the second great commandment: that we love our neighbor as ourselves.

In acknowledgment that we are fully known by God, let love be our mantra, leading us from moment to moment and from person to person. Let love be at the heart of our environments, our thoughts. When moments of anger or stress arrive, as they surely will, may we close your eyes and release the tension by reciting the following:

Rejoice! I will rejoice in the truth of God's love for me and extend the truth of that love to you.

The author of this psalm raises a personal lament. But the psalmist moves from petition, to complaint, to expression of trust, and then to praise. A lifelong commitment to God and to divine care issues in the psalmist's trust in God's righteousness. We too voice our petitions and complaints to God in trust, perhaps having "leaned" upon God from our birth. I look to God in trust for my safety. That relationship, formed before I was aware of it, lives in me and courses through me and shines out of me.

For many churches Wednesday is a blessed day of healing and respite, a day to respond to the petitions and needs of God's weary and battered children—a sacred space for healing and renewal. Wednesday in the company of the faithful provides a midweek boost to sustain us through to Sunday, our day of sabbath. But finding a midweek time and place to rest our worn-out human lives does not require the four walls of a church building.

I find considerable rest within the language of the psalmist who offers to us a reality checked with the cries of human emotion: pain, sorrow, joy, fear, and even anger. During my seminary years I came to enjoy and appreciate the real-life human drama that unfolds throughout the Psalms and began to rely on these ancient voices to give comfort to my own small life discomforts.

From time's beginning, our God has invited us into divine presence and provided a space where we can open our hearts and minds and offer up to God all the realities of our lives, wherever they may fall on life's continuum. The psalmist reminds us that we are God's refugees in this world where we live but do not belong, where we minister as good stewards but do not own, where our heart is captivated but cannot be held captive.

Pray to God on this day for the will to rest in the comfort of God's divine tent city.

As we begin to wind down this week of work, study, play, or rest, our minds may wander ahead to the weekend. We live so much of our lives waiting for the weekend to arrive and for the "fun to begin" that we easily get caught up in not being where we actually find ourselves. Our day-to-day anxiety keeps us from fully living our lives where we actually find ourselves and instead knits into our daily routines the desire to be somewhere else.

For Jeremiah, God's assertion of presence and deliverance creates a prophet. Despite his fears and anxiety about his youth and his inability to speak, God's support empowers him to fulfill the call. The reminder that our Lord accompanies us through our life circumstances becomes essential to *hearing* God's words for us and *fulfilling* God's call.

When the theme song of anxiety creeps into our minds, it brings with it the fear of failure, the fear of success, the fear of change, the fear of letting go, and all the many fears that tend to stop us mere human beings in our tracks. A visual image that I use when I feel tense or anxious is that of walking hand in hand with Jesus; the two of us are always walking away and up a slight incline, and I am always a little girl.

Knowing that my Lord holds me safely gives me comfort and support. With God as companion and deliverer, I find my courage to live where I am—even when where I am is not much fun. It is my God who calls me to follow, and it is through this day and with this divine companion that my path leads.

On this day I will write upon my heart the generous love of God and find courage to live out God's call on my life.

Hearing. Listening. Being where we are. Answering the call. How many of us can honestly say that we hear? Oh, we hear all the noise of the world around us: the news, the music, the voices of family and friends, perhaps even the voices in our own heads. But to whom do we listen?

Those in the synagogue listen with amazement to Jesus as he reads from the scroll of Isaiah. They know this young man: "Is not this Joseph's son?" Yet their very assumptions interfere with their ability to hear God's call: "Today this scripture has been fulfilled in your hearing." But wait a minute—"is not this Joseph's son?" We know this guy, and we know what he has to offer.

All of us have preconceived ideas and assumptions about our world; through these preconceptions we can close ourselves off from God's miracles of salvation, grace, and love. Our expectations limit the way we allow God to work in our lives. Truly the Word has been fulfilled in our hearing, and we are deaf to understanding.

This story from the Gospel of Luke challenges us to let go of preconceived notions—and to be amazed at the gracious workings of God. It is time again to close our eyes and to quiet our noisy heads, to meditate on God's call to us, to hear God's love song, and to know that each of our lives has been born out of the seeds of God's love. Those seeds have a purpose and a life that connects us integrally to our God and to one another. "Today this scripture has been fulfilled in your hearing."

On this day I will listen for God and hear the words of my Savior Jesus speak the blessing of my life.

Jesus lives out his true self, and the hometown crowd grows uneasy. Jesus identifies the conflict that begins even as his ministry begins using a traditional phrase: "No prophet is accepted in the prophet's hometown." God never promises that following the call of our lives will be an easy path, only that we will always be graced with God's ever-abiding presence.

Perhaps in today's feel-good environment of "me first" living, Jesus' example of sacrifice, hardship, and faithfulness seems silly and wholly unnecessary. After all, we see ample evidence of success around us. Jesus stands in front of that hometown crowd of the faithful, but they cannot see or hear the words of the God he proclaims because their world values a different idea of success—and Jesus was not it. Rather than proudly stand as the "hometown boy does good" example, Jesus' life and ministry will portray such a diversion from the commonly held belief of the day that he will be eliminated.

Jesus was different. He caused fear and anxiety by calling for both change and a return. Being different creates an environment of hostility that many of us are unable or unwilling to tolerate for long periods of time, if at all.

Do we ignore our call for fear of being different? Does our need for acceptance within the human family exert more influence than God's voice? Jesus' acceptance of his call leads to conflict and hostility, teaching and healing. His words fill the members of the synagogue with a rage that moves them to violence. But with God's ever-abiding presence, he passes through the crowd and goes on his way.

Our lives are God's whether we acknowledge the connection or not. May we live out our true selves.

"The truth is . . . " Ah, here the *reality* of our lives meets the *ideas* of our lives; now seems to be a good time to consider which is which and upon what path we will walk.

The hometown boy who, up to now, seems to bring pride to the home folks begins to "meddle." Jesus, like Elijah and Elisha before him, comes to minister to those in need, not just the faithful of Israel. Matter of fact, in the stories he relates, God's favor resides with those outside the fold. The repeated refrain of "none of them" (either widows or lepers of Israel) strikes home to his listeners, and they become irate.

I have always been rather blunt. I prefer to live my life that way, and I prefer for others to be as straightforward with me as possible. I don't want to be attacked, but I do want your truth. Jesus offers the truth: the words are true; the stories are true; and the truth hurts. Jesus confronts us all with the truth of our lives. What are we doing with that truth?

I hear the truth with an anger and resentment turned against the God who loves me and has such hope for me. After my initial shock at being reminded of my limited faith and perceptions, I begin to search for the redeeming power of Jesus. I open up the space needed to grieve my own failings, which in turn allows space for healing and renewal.

Let us pray in this Epiphany season for the courage to embrace the truth of God, for the faith to follow the call of God, for the love to do the work that God has given us to do. As we close our eyes in this prayer, we hear the heartbeat of our mother's womb where God sings to us the song of our life. Amen.

The Mountaintop

FEBRUARY 4–10, 2013 • TOM ARTHUR

SCRIPTURE OVERVIEW: The texts for Transfiguration Sunday insist that glory *is* the right word for God as well as those touched by God's presence. The psalmist praises the exaltation of God above all people. The Exodus text depicts God's glory and its consequences for human beings. Moses, by virtue of speaking with God, undergoes a change so dramatic that the people of Israel cannot even look on his face. In the passage from Second Corinthians, Paul draws on this story of Moses to make the radical point that in the Christ-event, God enables all to participate in the glory of God. All can see the glory of God (3:18) and, indeed, as Paul states in a verse that follows our lection, all believers have "knowledge of the glory of God" in Jesus' face (4:6). As Peter learns, God's glory can be neither reduced nor controlled.

QUESTIONS AND THOUGHTS FOR REFLECTION

- Read Exodus 34:29-35. What mountaintop experiences have you had with God? How did they change you? Did others notice? Why or why not?

- Read Psalm 99. Where are you tempted to keep faith personal and ignore the injustices around you? What injustice is God calling you to address?

- Read 2 Corinthians 3:12-4:2. What improvements are you seeing in your life? In what areas do you still struggle?

- Read Luke 9:28-43. When are you tempted to surround yourself with a protective bubble and ignore the needs for healing around you?

Second pastor of Sycamore Creek Church, Lansing, Michigan

We all long for mountaintop experiences, even the most reserved and stoic of us. Deep down we want to experience such a closeness to God that the inner transformation spills out into the world through the shine on our faces. When we're down in the valley, we wonder when we'll next meet God in such a powerful way.

I enjoy backpacking. One of my favorite memories is sitting on the top of Clingman's Dome in The Great Smoky Mountains National Park. It was my first backpacking trip. I found it exhilarating to be higher than anything else, but I had hated every moment of climbing up that mountain. Three days of hiking over twenty miles with five stream crossings, signs warning us of bear activity, and seriously painful feet were some of the costs. While most of us value mountaintop experiences, we sometimes forget how much work it takes to get there.

In today's reading, Moses has a mountaintop experience and encounters God in a powerful way. I wonder what it cost Moses to climb that mountain. While it took a heavy physical toll to get up there, I think the bigger cost was probably what Moses brought back down the mountain: the spiritual work of the covenant.

When God makes a covenant with us, our life changes; when our life changes, something must die for something new to be born. What did Moses have to leave on the top of that mountain to come down a transformed man? What old life, habits, customs; old ways of thinking, being, and doing did he have to leave behind to fulfill that covenant? That's the real work of having a mountaintop experience—the spiritual work of dying to self in order to covenant with God.

God of the mountaintop, give us strength to do the work that we must do in order to meet you there. Amen.

Let's face it; when you have a mountaintop experience and then come back down to earth where everyone else lives, you may seem a little odd—even scary. After a mountaintop experience you don't fit in quite the same way you did.

I enjoy backpacking and climbing mountains, but when I get back to civilization, I don't have a shine that everyone can see. Rather, I've got a stink that everyone can smell! I'm no longer very civilized until I hit the shower.

Moses had a similar experience. When he came down from the mountaintop, having done the hard spiritual work of covenanting with God, he seemed a bit scary to those around him. They could see that he was a changed man.

When we see someone else changed by an experience with God, we may fear whether God will ask us to make some changes. Will we have to be odd too? Will the change be so obvious that other people can actually see it? Will we be unable to keep our faith a private thing between us and God?

Moses answers these questions for the Israelites by reading to them the commandment of the covenant. The answer is yes. If you want to know and love and serve God, then you will be a little odd. You'll have to follow the commands of the covenant, and those commands will most likely make you stick out from the culture around you.

So what do we usually do when we encounter those who have submitted their life to God so fully? We suggest that they put a veil on, for heaven's sake! Keep that shine to yourself!

Perhaps we need to encourage that shine!

God who transforms, give us courage to be a little odd for you. Give us an openness to learn from those who don't quite fit in because they've covenanted with you. Amen.

A mountaintop experience can never be just about me and God. While transformation may begin with a personal encounter with God, it can never stay there. Today's psalm reminds us that the God of transcendence on the mountaintop is a God of justice in the valley.

Too often we separate personal holiness and salvation from social holiness and communal transformation. We experience God on the mountaintop, and it changes our lives. We may think that the whole point of the encounter is for personal transformation. But it's not. Moses brings down from the mountain with him the covenant and its commandments, and he shares them with the community. Ultimately that covenant is a covenant made with a Mighty King of justice and equity.

Like Moses, John Wesley sought both personal and social holiness. He called individuals to personal repentance of sins and reception of God's grace, and he called Methodists to reach out to the poor in friendship and generosity. He expected Methodists to visit the poor and the sick and to live simply so that they could give most of their money away. Wesley understood that the mountaintop experience of the forgiveness of sin ultimately puts within the heart a desire to transform society through the right use of all one's resources: time, talent, treasure, and testimony.

While the Mighty King is a God of mercy and forgiveness, this psalm offers a glimpse of what can happen when justice and equity aren't part of our personal transformation. The earth quakes! The people tremble! God is an "avenger of . . . wrong-doings." Justice entails judgment. Don't keep that mountaintop experience to yourself. Share God's covenant with others and work to bring an end to oppression and injustice.

Mighty King, change our hearts to love justice. Use us to establish equity and to execute justice and righteousness. Amen.

While mountaintop experiences are powerful, transformation in our lives often occurs in more mundane ways. Paul describes this kind of transformation as taking place "from one degree of glory to another." Incremental change is the kind of change that happens in the valley—change that we sometimes barely notice.

Like most men in our sexualized culture, I have struggled much of my life with lust. I find it hard not to look at a woman and objectify her based on her body. I've often prayed for a mountaintop experience where God would instantaneously and finally take this temptation and sin away. God has yet to do so in any grand kind of way. But one night I experienced a small degree of transformation.

I was in seminary and out on the town celebrating a friend's birthday with several other seminarians. At one point we bumped into a beer rep from a local brewery who was trying to sell us beer. He had brought along with him a "beer girl." I didn't realize that there were actually girls just like in the beer commercials. She dressed to catch the eye; but instead of lusting, I found myself thinking, *She must be really uncomfortable walking around in that skimpy outfit and those high heel shoes.* I had somehow managed to think of her not as an object to view but as a human worthy of empathy.

I've contemplated that night several times. *Why did I have that different kind of response?* The only answer I can come up with is that slowly but surely God has been transforming my mind, eyes, and heart as I've spent time with God in prayer, Bible study, worship, fasting, small groups, and other spiritual disciplines day in and day out. That's transformation—not on the mountaintop but one degree at a time.

Holy God, change us so imperceptibly that there's no way we can think it is anything but your Spirit at work in us. Amen.

Staying on the mountaintop can endanger your health. While backpacking in the Grand Tetons, my wife and I were climbing over a pass when an afternoon storm set in. The wind picked up. Rain pounded down. Thunder boomed. Lightning cracked. We set a new personal record for getting up and over that pass. While I feared getting caught in the worst of the storm, I also felt a little frustrated that after two days of hiking we couldn't hang out at the top of the mountain. That's a lot of hard work just to go up and over without taking time to pause and enjoy a scene I may never have again.

Peter wants to stay on the mountaintop. He recognizes the beauty, mystery, and sacredness of this time. Jesus is talking with Moses and Elijah! Suddenly he and the other two disciples find themselves in a cloud, an "afternoon storm." But this is no ordinary storm—the voice of God speaks from the cloud. When God finishes speaking, the cloud dissipates, and Peter, James, and John find that they are alone with Jesus. Peter would like to enshrine the experience, but Jesus knows that you can't hold on to that beauty, mystery, and sacred moment. To do so would be to lose it all. It has come and gone, and now it is time to go back down the mountain and carry on with life.

How much time do you spend trying to hold on to powerful moments of the past? How does your attempt to grasp hold of the mountaintop experience and memorialize it indicate your fear that you won't meet God again? Unlike Peter and his companions, Jesus seems unfazed by the moment that has come and gone. His strong faith trusts that God will continue to be present.

Gracious God, give us faith to let go of our experiences of you in the past so that we might fully know you in the present. Amen.

Why do I have to go back to work on Monday? I'm always a little despondent about the whole transition from worship on Sunday to work on Monday. I have to deal with all the petty things that my vocation entails. I run up the mountain in worship on Sunday and then find myself in the valley on Monday morning.

Jesus has just experienced a singularly unique event with Moses, Elijah, and God on the mountain. Then we read, "On the next day, when they had come down from the mountain, a great crowd met him." Isn't that just perfect? From the peace and comfort of Sunday to the craziness of rush-hour traffic on Monday. Why can't those crowds of people get their needs met somewhere else?

It's hard not to hear a little exasperation in Jesus' response to his disciples' inability to meet the needs of the crowd. He says, "You faithless and perverse generation, how much longer must I be with you and bear with you?" Didn't I call you to take care of that so I didn't have to deal with it? Don't you know that you're in the wrong department for that issue? Didn't I answer that same question for you last week? And yet amidst exasperation with the crush of needs around him, Jesus heals a boy of his unclean spirit.

That's the kind of mountaintop experience I want to have: the kind where I come back down into the valley, and while the needs still drive me a little crazy, I've got renewed strength and determination to bring healing to those around me.

God of the weekday crowd, give me patience with the needs that sometimes feel like they are going to crush me. Use me to bring healing to my friends, family, community, and world. Amen.

Today is Transfiguration Sunday, the last Sunday of Epiphany. Next Sunday begins the season of Lent. The church turns a corner on this day. It turns a corner from the infant Jesus toward the crucified Jesus. Lent begins to prepare us for the hard work of Holy Week, and Transfiguration Sunday helps us turn the corner from a baby in a manger to a prophet who is not heard in his own hometown.

Like getting up to the mountaintop, Lent will be a lot of work. We will have to take a hard look at ourselves and discern with the help of others what sin still remains. We will, by God's grace, have to repent and seek a new life in Jesus Christ.

The hard work of Lent is sure to be valley work. If we are to experience transformation in the season of Lent, it will most likely come in degrees rather than in mountaintop experiences. We will slowly be changed by the means of grace we practice on Monday through Friday.

Lent will challenge us not to keep our holiness to ourselves, but to seek justice for those around us. Sin is not just personal. It is corporate too. The God who speaks in a mountaintop cloud will not allow us to ignore the least, last, and lost.

Like Peter in the transfiguration, we find it tempting to want to dwell continually with the celebration of Jesus as an infant in a manger, to stay with that tender moment. That is a much more pleasant scene than the one we will eventually see in Holy Week. But staying in the Epiphany season can endanger our spiritual health. Jesus was born not only so that we could coo at an infant but also so that our sinfulness could be made visible by his life, forgiven by his death, and redeemed by his resurrection.

God who comes as an infant, help us turn the corner from the mountaintop of the manger to the valley of the cross. Amen.

The Word Is Very Near You

FEBRUARY 11–17, 2013 • SUSAN A. BLAIN

SCRIPTURE OVERVIEW: What does it mean to call on God? Israel exists because it cries to God out of its bondage, and God delivers. The psalmist is convinced of the personal and profound manner in which he has offended God and shattered their relationship. In casting himself on God's grace, the psalmist acknowledges God's role as the unique savior of faithful people; and the result of God's intervention is a changed and redirected life. The story of Jesus' temptation offers a strong rejoinder to those who would claim that loving God and calling on God result in rescue in any and all circumstances. God's care is not a commodity to be gained by human beings through wheedling; it is, instead, a promise that no one ventures outside the realm of God's care. To call on God is not to ask for power to be dispensed but to acknowledge human finitude and divine providence.

QUESTIONS AND THOUGHTS FOR REFLECTION

- Read Deuteronomy 26:1-11. The common memory of the faith community retains its story across the generations. What stories does your faith community tell?

- Read Psalm 91. The psalmist places utter trust in the Holy One, describing a desert place full of danger. From what danger do you need protection? What rescue do you seek?

- Read Romans 10:8b-13. "The word is very near to you, on your lips and in your heart." How can you access with confidence that word so near? What keeps you aware of the divine presence?

- Read Luke 4:1-13. Where do you find the wisdom to know what is of God and what is of the Tempter?

Minister for Worship and Spiritual Formation in the United Church of Christ

Transfiguration ecstasy seldom lasts long. We get glimpses of glory only, as the disciples discover when they try to persuade Jesus to stay apart with them on the mountaintop. Isn't it enough to have this vision, this clarity, this moment of meeting God?

But Jesus is already ahead of them, hurrying back down into the world of suffering, complexity, sin. He knows, and they must discover, that the holy does not linger in such isolation. A struggling people calls, and Jesus will respond. Following the call to Jerusalem, where his life will end and new life begin, will take all Jesus' prayerful courage.

The season of Lent invites us to follow Jesus on this journey to Jerusalem, deeper into the midst of the struggles of the world. If we have eyes to see and ears to hear and hands willing to work, we may discover some unexpected place where God is calling us to the work of transformation. Isaiah decries false righteousness while calling the people to justice and true righteousness. Only through repentance may false righteousness give way to a change of life. Isaiah points the way—the cries of those yoked by injustice, hunger, illness. Can engaging their need become our point of meeting God?

Despite the people's fear of God's abandonment, verses 9-12 encourage possibility of restoration: "*If* you remove the yoke . . . *if* you offer your food to the hungry," *then* your light shall rise" (emphasis added). God intends salvation, not condemnation. If we can find prayerful courage, Isaiah tells us that meeting God will offer its own kind of ecstasy: our own parched places may become a watered garden, and we will find the glory of God in strength, confidence, and creativity to repair the breach and restore the streets.

Holy One, give us prayerful courage to seek you, and in finding you, give us joy to join your work of transformation. Amen.

If Isaiah pushes us out into a broken world to find the holy, the psalmist pulls us deep inside our own broken hearts. Before we face the world, we must face ourselves—more prayerful courage needed. Honest and brave self-examination is the theme for Psalm 51. The psalmist provides a language for the feelings—disappointment, remorse, paralysis, contrition—and we fill in the gaps: "I know my transgressions; and my sin is ever before me." Within the tender framework of Psalm 51, we can examine our lives and let our hearts be broken open so that we may be made whole.

The unbroken heart wants protection; it builds walls and takes no risks. The broken heart wants mercy for the risks it has taken and the mistakes it has made. The unbroken heart calls its limited knowledge the truth; the broken heart asks for wisdom to know truth. The unbroken heart keeps secrets; the broken heart wants its secrets revealed, accepted, forgiven. The heart broken open is the image the psalmist weaves throughout Psalm 51: grace can do its healing work only on the broken heart.

Sorrow for sin is lodged in the broken heart, but so is desire for wholeness and healing. "Create in me a clean heart, O God . . . restore me [to] joy . . . sustain in me a willing spirit."

The clean heart, the joyful heart, the whole heart is ready for service. The heart which has known God's mercy can confidently tell of that grace and draw on that power for the world.

Tender God of mercy and love, take our broken hearts and mend them. Make us strong in the broken places and send us into your world in courage and joy to join you in the work of reconciliation. In Jesus' name we pray. Amen.

Ash Wednesday

In Ash Wednesday's Gospel text, Jesus tells us how to pray—modestly and humbly. And where to pray—in a secret place. Pray, fast, give alms without any fanfare, noticed only by God.

What might be the content of our modest, secret prayer this Lent? Perhaps the traditional prayer for the placing of ashes on the forehead offers a hint: "Remember you are dust, and to dust you shall return" (Gen. 3:19). A theme of relationship between Creator and created surfaces here and sets the tone for Lent. "The Lord God formed the human from the topsoil of the fertile land and blew life's breath into his nostrils. The human came to life" (Gen. 2:7, CEB).

This stuff of creation, earth, raw material, is given life by the Holy One. Simple dust holds the breath of God. The human being is one with all created things who depend on God's love constantly breathing through them—God breathes us into being and sustains us in life. We are limited, yes, but empowered by God; mortal, yes, but precious, returning to the earth God loves. Trust may grow out of that understanding and even a desire to use every precious, created particle of our lives to praise the God of creation.

Lent invites us to follow Jesus, who breathed most fully that divine breath and knew with all of us the limits and pain of mortal life. Jesus lived our life fully, trusting God with his life, his death, and his resurrection.

Repeat the words of the traditional Ash Wednesday prayer a few times slowly; give careful attention to your breathing:

Remember you are dust,
(*pause, breathe in; wait, breathe out*)
and to dust you shall return.

Let God breathe in and through you, and know the wonder and trust of Jesus.

THURSDAY, FEBRUARY 14 ～ *Read Psalm 91:1-2, 9-16*

God calls us out on a journey each Lent, away from what we know and take for granted, away from our comfortable havens. God calls us to follow Jesus into a desert of unknown challenges. No wonder the lectionary provides such a comforting psalm to encourage us on the way! If we choose God and love God, Psalm 91 promises that we will find in God's faithfulness our dwelling place: our shelter for safety, refuge in fear, fortress of strength. A moveable dwelling, of course, for we are called not to stand still but to venture forth.

Perhaps the psalm's most challenging suggestion is that we dwell in God's shadow, in God's shade. Shade: outside, open to the elements—but still there is welcome refreshment there and rest. Together with Jesus, the "Human One" (CEB) who has no place to lay his head, we make our way under the starry skies, over the shifting sands into a future that risks hope.

These days, our troubled world is full of "desert places" where people struggle for shelter. And what of those who find themselves in the "desert places" of our troubled world: in refuge camps, fire-trap slums, and forlorn foreclosures? How do they hear these images of God's faithfulness in Psalm 91? Do those of us who try to dwell in the shelter of the Most High, and abide, vulnerably and trustfully, in the shadow of the Almighty, have something to offer those who suffer without worldly shelter these days? Can we, God's fellow travelers, create a space of justice; of refuge, shelter, and fortress for those in need?

O God, our shelter and our shade, let us know your presence so thoroughly and intimately that we may set forth into the challenge of Lent trusting in your refreshment and your protection. In Jesus' name. Amen.

Past and present come together in this beautiful passage. The people of Israel are instructed to give thanks for their safe deliverance from slavery by telling their story and offering the "first fruits"—the earliest and best of their harvest—to their faithful God. More than by memory, the Israelites tell the story by heart. The story of past ancestors living as aliens in a foreign place suddenly becomes the story of the present community: "the ancestors" become "us"; their past struggle becomes "our" struggle; the injustices, the pain, the hard labor of strangers in Egypt all are felt afresh. In this moment, the ancient anguish is felt again in the community, and the need for God is known. God's saving action is not a past glory but a present reality in the lives of this people! The past bears fruit in the present, and they invite all to give thanks with them, even the aliens and strangers living in their midst.

Can we, this Lent, enter our stories of faith once again to immerse ourselves in them so as to tell them "by heart"? Can we fall into step beside the disciples and try to understand what Jesus is about? Can we celebrate at his table and struggle to stay awake in the Garden? Can we sense the challenge of owning up to knowing him or the defeat of denying him in our world and our work? Can we choose, with the women, to stay with him even at the cross and the tomb? Can "their" story become "our" story, so that we can tell it by heart, knowing the anguish and the triumph as our own in our own life circumstances? Can we let our past story bear fruit in our present and transform our lives right now?

O God of past and present, you invite us to be part of a people who know you afresh in each generation. Help us take our place in your story and bear witness with our lives to your life in us. In Jesus' name. Amen.

"The word is near you, on your lips and in your heart." So Paul assures the young community at Rome: Rome, a crossroads for the world and fertile ground for planting the gospel of Jesus. Cultures come together here in unexpected ways; everything old becomes new again. The new insight into ancient truth to which Paul bears witness—that the Holy may be encountered and known in Christ Jesus—is available to all, not only the Jews, followers of the law; but also to Gentiles, strangers, aliens, newcomers to faith. One may come to know Jesus in all sorts of ways: through the law; through the stories; through community; through heart-felt experience, like Paul's own. Faith in Christ is possible for all.

But it is not enough simply for us to know "by heart"; we need to speak what we know! Paul bids us believe in our hearts and confess with our lips the truth about God and Jesus. He insists on that powerful pairing of heart and voice, of hidden and public, of knowledge received and knowledge proclaimed, so that knowledge may shape our lives and our world.

The word is very near us, in our hearts and on our lips. Paul's Rome and our world have much in common: a global crossroads, experienced today in ways unimagined by Paul; strangers and friends sharing a fragile, complex environment— today in cyberspace as well as face-to-face reality. So many ways to open our hearts to Jesus, so many ways to proclaim what we come to know about Christ, so many ways to shape our world out of that knowledge, welcomed in our hearts and proclaimed by our voices.

O Holy Wisdom, within us and around us, give us eyes to see and ears to hear and voices to proclaim what we know in our hearts: that Jesus is your Word and your life! Amen.

SUNDAY, FEBRUARY 17 ~ *Read Luke 4:1-13*

FIRST SUNDAY IN LENT

The Holy Spirit leads Jesus from the moment of baptism ecstasy at the Jordan into the desert experience of solitude, hunger, and temptation. Jesus, the "Beloved," is alone now; no food to refresh, no friends to encourage—only a famished human being encountering temptation at his weakest point. The Tempter is a vivid presence here in the desert. Where is God?

God is as near as Jesus' own hunger, a fast that empties him of all distractions from his encounter with God. Jesus knows, in his hunger, what food he needs to nourish him; and it will not come from the seeds of manipulation that the Tempter tries to sow. What hunger will nourish us this Lent?

God is as near as the scriptures that Jesus knows by heart; he has brought with him into the desert the faith tradition that has formed him. Knowing, loving, serving *God* is power, and it is not in the gift of the Tempter. Where will we look for empowerment this Lent?

God is as near as the wisdom Jesus makes room for through his desert prayer; God is power, presence, source of life to be sought after in prayer, in ministry, in risk, in study—not a magician whose worth will be proved with the cheap trick the Tempter demands. Where will we seek wisdom this Lent?

The Spirit that led Jesus into the desert now leads him back into the world, where, nourished and empowered, he takes up his ministry of transformation. Day by day, Jesus will teach, heal, challenge, and reveal the presence and power of God in our midst.

Desert-dwelling God, you challenge us to seek you where you are to be found: in our hungers, in our aloneness, in our hearts. Meet us and strengthen us to recognize and resist the Tempter in our lives that would keep us from knowing you. In Jesus' name. Amen.

Refuge and Hope

FEBRUARY 18–24, 2013 • CRAIG MITCHELL

SCRIPTURE OVERVIEW: The contradiction between appearance and reality runs through several of the readings. Hearing God's assurance of protection, Abram reminds God that he and Sarai are childless. Hearing God's promise once again, Abram believes; but he believes in the face of all the evidence. Paul often struggles to articulate the difference between what can be seen with the eyes and the reality that can be seen only by faith. In Philippians, he employs the powerful language of citizenship to explain that Christians live as citizens of another realm; believers live out of an allegiance that cannot be witnessed with ordinary vision. "Herod wants to kill you," Jesus is warned. Yet Jesus' death will not prove an end to the threat he poses to either Roman or religious authority. If Psalm 27 does not so clearly distinguish between appearance and reality, it is because the psalmist knows on whose side reality lies. He anticipates a time when things will appear the way they actually are—in God's very presence.

QUESTIONS AND THOUGHTS FOR REFLECTION

- Read Genesis 15:1-12, 17-18. What legacy do you hope to leave?

- Read Luke 13:31-35. When have you experienced the tenderness of God as mother?

- Read Psalm 27. How and where do you experience God's shelter?

- Read Philippians 3:17–4:1. "Our citizenship is in heaven." How does this concept shape your living?

Faculty member, Uniting College for Leadership and Theology; Adelaide, South Australia

My father, aged eighty-two, passed away following unsuccessful heart surgery. Hearing the testimonies at his funeral from family, friends, and coworkers, I felt amazement, gratitude, and a sense of pride. Several weeks later, my twin daughters turned twenty-one, and I was struck by the question "What will be my legacy?" What strengths and values of my dad are alive in me? How good a father have I been? How will I be remembered?

Not all of us have children or grandchildren. Yet most persons hope to leave the world a better place because of their living in it—to love and be loved, to do good and show respect, to act justly and fairly, to care well for the earth in our small patch of the planet.

In an ancient land of many gods, a land marked by territorial wars between small kingdoms, the member of a small group receives an unlikely call and a bold promise from the one God who claims sovereignty and allegiance. In Genesis 12, Abram accepts God's call to gather up his people and journey to a new place. Later, in Genesis 15, after politely rejecting gifts from King Melchizedek, Abram is gifted by Yahweh, told that he and Sarai will bear children and prosper.

This small group had few of the assets that might ensure security in today's world. Yet God promises that they will grow and have their own dwelling place. In truth, the coming increase of this tribe looks far from pretty. Yahweh's declaration invites faith; it does not ensure a trouble-free future. Abram's trust in God's promise is deemed righteousness: he is worthy of God's blessing. In a sense, Abram's legacy begins with his choosing to be predisposed toward the promise and blessings of Yahweh.

God of hope, I look to the heavens. May I see the stars of your blessing in my life and in our world. Amen.

Today we revisit the story of Abram and Sarai. Allow yourself to reread the text with fresh eyes to see what arises.

Like a strong river current, the theme of covenant runs deep in the Hebrew Scriptures. In these early narratives of their history, the people of Israel recall the astonishing drama of Yahweh's choosing them to be a light to the nations. Their radical claim, testified to by generation after generation, is to have encountered the one true God. What's more, this God binds the divine self to them in covenant love. God meets Abram's despair for the future with a promise of divine companionship.

On the occasion of my wife's and my thirtieth wedding anniversary this year, I felt privileged yet again to have married a remarkable woman. I was also grateful and humbled that she had chosen me! She also has managed to live through the ups and downs of what that decision has meant for both of us.

Yahweh's covenant relationship with the people of Abram and Sarai is mutual but not equal. God chooses to be revealed; God chooses to speak; God chooses to bless; God chooses to forgive. In each instance, Abram and Sarai are invited to hear, to accept, to trust, to follow, and ultimately to love this Creator-Deliverer God.

As people of the new covenant in Christ, how do we see the church's future—through eyes of despair or eyes of hope? The fulfillment of God's promise involved the Hebrews traveling to a new place, intermarrying with foreign tribes, engaging in conflicts both within and beyond themselves, and yet bearing witness to the existence of the one God, Yahweh. How might this story of revelation, promise, and trust speak to us as Christ's "tribe" today?

Covenant God, may we as your church know that we are deeply loved, strongly claimed, and boldly sent by you into new territory to be your witnesses today. Amen.

WEDNESDAY, FEBRUARY 20 ~ *Read Psalm 27:1-6*

The Lord is my light and my salvation. Whom shall I fear?" Light and fear. Two opposites? Light is bright and white. If you were to assign a color to fear, what would it be? A chaplain friend speaks of the journey from anxiety to depression as going through darkening shades of blue.

We know from neuroscience that stress, anxiety, and fear can be related. In midlife I am learning to uncover and name my deeper fears. My compulsive desire for perfection at work, along with the anxiety and stress it produces, are fueled by my fear of failure. As a parent, my anxieties for the safety and success of my children arise in part from my fear that I cannot make everything in their life just right.

Yet, if I'm honest, those seem like rather middle-class fears. Turn on the TV news anytime. People in the Middle East, parts of Africa and Mexico fear for more than their popularity or status. Like the psalmist, their very lives are at risk from violence. This psalm does not simply promise a feeling of peace in response to inner turmoil but a much deeper confidence in God in the face of genuine threat.

Take some time to contemplate your own experience of fear, anxiety, or stress. Write the three words on a piece of paper. Reflect on what causes these emotions. What connections do you see between these emotions and their causes? Then close your eyes and imagine yourself in a place of shelter, a place where God is present. Imagine yourself being bathed in light, the light of God's saving love. Say to yourself, "The LORD is my light and my salvation; whom shall I fear?" Sit in the light and give thanks.

> *God of light, shine into the fearful or anxious places in my life with the assurance of your saving love and persistent presence. Amen.*

At age twenty I left home for my first job, a move that took me hundreds of miles from my family. That was just over thirty years ago. As I have grown, married, and had children who are now full-grown, the homecomings have changed. Yet in a real way, the home hasn't. Although my parents have aged, the family home has always offered safety, comfort, and acceptance. A month ago I helped my mother move out of the house that she sold after my father's death. Coming to terms with this strange loss of place became possible only when I began to pray that the new homeowners, a young family, would make a home that was as richly blessed as ours had been.

Psalm 27 offers not a *prescription* but a *description* of how we might seek refuge in God when times are tough.

Seek God's place. When the psalm writer feels embattled and alone, he flees to the temple to find sanctuary with God. At times when life batters and bruises you, go to a place—real or in your imagination—where you have found safety and comfort.

Seek God's face. In times of difficulty, God may seem hidden or absent from us. In this safe haven, be still and seek to know that God is truly present.

Seek God's favor. For Israelite people, the holiness of Yahweh meant that one could never truly see God's face. The psalm is rather a prayer for God's favor, to experience blessing rather than suffering.

Seek God's way. "Teach me your way, O LORD." The writer has confidence that God can show him a way to live free of persecution or at least faithfully in its presence.

See God's goodness. We can learn to trust that if we wait patiently, we will see God's goodness, all in good time.

God of grace, as I seek your face this day, may I be assured of your close presence in all I do. Amen.

WWJD. *What would Jerry do?* In a new job with new responsibilities, I felt unsure what to do or say in complex situations. I instinctively found myself asking a close colleague in my previous workplace what he would do. His words and attitudes gave me enough direction that I could swim and not sink.

WWPD. *What would Paul do?* The apostle Paul invites people to consider his example and seek to imitate it in their lives. That's pretty arrogant, isn't it—like a holier-than-thou Christian who seems to have standards that the rest of us are supposed to aspire to?

Except in this case, Paul opposes such people. Some Jewish Christians were teaching that new Christians, presumably Gentiles, had to be circumcised and obey Jewish ritual laws about food. The apostle rails against them, saying that he has as much right as anyone to claim how zealous he has been. Then, in a memorable few sentences (verses 7-11), Paul states that he has thrown all of this behind him. He counts his attainments as rubbish. All he wants is to "gain Christ and be found in him," and to receive the righteousness that comes from Christ.

WWJD. *What would Jesus do?* We're not meant to try to be as good as Paul but to imitate him in not relying on our own goodness. Instead, like him, we are to die and rise in Christ. Paul says that his opponents, in piling extra requirements onto what it means to be Christian, actually worship the body, not God. But those who are in Christ, already citizens of heaven, will find their bodies transformed as part of Christ's body.

God of heaven and earth, may I see my life as clothed in Christ's goodness. Free me of my efforts to justify myself before you and others. Amen.

A new leader emerges from the masses with a clear message and a prophetic voice. First she is a curiosity; then she gathers a small following. Later, as her popularity grows, she is feted by business leaders, politicians, religious officials. Then slowly the tide begins to turn. Questioned about her past. Criticized for lack of experience. The old guard gathers its forces. Public opinion is divided. Trial by media ensues. The hopeful is denounced and disgraced. A promising career buried.

Such is life in the capital, where authority is centered and public opinion paramount. As the political and religious center of Israel, Jerusalem holds both real and symbolic power. Jewish King, Roman governor, and high priest all wield authority; the Temple holds a central place of religious celebration and faithful pilgrimage.

As the seat of the Hebrew faith, the Temple is a common target of the Old Testament prophets. False teaching, foreign cultic practices, abuse of privilege and power, hypocrisy, and self-interest were a recurring litany of indulgence and unfaithfulness. Jesus' message to priest and king alike resonates with prophetic spirit, God's consummate appeal to change their ways.

Just as Zechariah and Uriah were put to death in Jerusalem (2 Chronicles 24 and Jeremiah 26), Jesus foretells his own death as a prophet, confirming again his status as God's messenger even as he condemns himself to their fate.

Perhaps conflicts with principalities and powers will inevitably ensue when people proclaim God's prophetic word against idolatry, abuse, and the denial of life. Jesus' persistence in the face of threat seems foolish, reckless. Yet his very determination to bring freedom and healing speaks the word of a God whose love will not be denied.

God of justice and freedom, continue to speak your word of life in the corridors of power in our land. Amen.

SECOND SUNDAY IN LENT

A carpenter's rough-hewn arms and shoulders, shaped by apprenticeship at the workbench . . .

A healer's tender touch, gently daubing eyelids so a blind man sees . . .

A tradesman's hearty laugh, jesting on the job with down-to-earth fishing folk . . .

A scribe's eye for detail, citing chapter and verse in scholarly query . . .

A father's joy, beckoning children with warmth and welcome . . .

A teacher's wisdom, opening truths with story and sign . . .

A prophet's holy rage, firing wrath upon corruption and greed . . .

A priest's presence, mediating grace to others in prayer and promise . . .

A servant's compassion, offered humbly to friend and stranger . . .

A mother's love, brooding over a city of wayward, disobedient children . . .

"Who do you say that I am?" asks the Christ. As the Gospels take us to Jerusalem, the glimpses of divine intent become clearer. When offered an early exit, Jesus responds with bold resolution. Yet the intimate portrait of these few verses reveals the vulnerable heart of a mothering God who broods with love over Creation, who aches for those who would respond not with gratitude but with denial and betrayal.

In the humanity of God, Emmanuel, we see the fullness of being truly human. Jesus' vulnerability reveals a God who is strong in brokenness, truthful in despair, and grace-filled even to death.

Mothering God, teach us the strength of vulnerable love. Amen.

God's Sustaining Mercy

FEBRUARY 25–MARCH 3, 2013 • PAMELA C. HAWKINS

SCRIPTURE OVERVIEW: The need for introspection and repentance looms large during this season of the church year, yet there is also room for joy. The joy that issues from the Isaiah text is generated by the prophet's realization that God's mercy is close at hand and available to any who will draw on it. Psalm 63 expresses a strong confidence in God, praising God for past out-pourings of mercy. The longing for sustenance is transformed into a "rich feast," which satisfies the innermost being of the psalmist. Paul views the lives of his fellow Christians in Corinth against the background of ancient Israel's experiences of exodus and wilderness wanderings. The Corinthian believers are exhorted to learn from the example of these Israelites, lest they too be judged by God. Paul balances the warning with a promise: God's grace is active, even in times of greatest pressure to forsake God's calling. The Luke reading stresses the urgent need for repentance.

QUESTIONS AND THOUGHTS FOR REFLECTION

- Read Isaiah 55:1-9. When, in the past year, have you been aware of God's activity in plans that you made and lived out?

- Read Psalm 63:1-8. Recall a place in your home where you have experienced closeness to God. Describe the feeling you have when you are in this place, aware of God's presence.

- Read 1 Corinthians 10:1-13. Using other words, rewrite this verse: "God is faithful."

- Read Luke 13:1-9. Imagine that Jesus is sitting with you in a quiet place. He asks, "What would you like to change?" What is your response?

United Methodist pastor serving at Belmont United Methodist Church, Nashville, Tennessee; author of three books published by the Upper Room

He was young, tired, hot, and skeptical. Since early morning, he had been selling papers at the intersection in an upscale business area. Homeless for months, he still felt awkward on the streets, unsure how to approach cars waiting for the light to change, whether to make eye contact or not, or where to find a restroom if he needed one.

When the young woman drove up to the corner and rolled down the car window to buy a paper from him, he wondered if he had heard her right. "What?" he asked.

"When you are done, come to our office and get some lunch and water. We're right down the street," she replied.

"What does it cost?"

"Nothing."

"What do I have to do? Listen to a talk or something?" he asked, having been warned by the street veterans.

"No, nothing. Just come get some lunch and water. We have plenty," she said again. "I hope to see you."

Nothing makes sense here. How can anyone get food without money in this neighborhood? This is a trick, some undercover plot to get another homeless person off the street. Or it might be a humiliating joke at the expense of an inexperienced young man. Water for nothing here? Food at no cost?

"All of you who are thirsty, come to the water! Whoever has no money, come, buy food and eat!" (CEB). Different words from a different time and place, but in this Lenten season both invitations, that of Isaiah and of the woman in the car, remind us of God's life-giving, covenant-shaped feast. A feast set by love when those who are faithful share what we know to be true: that God's love is everlasting and is for everyone.

God of hope, you are bread for our hunger and water for our thirst. You sustain us by your Spirit that we might become bread for the world. May we listen, change, and love. Amen.

Where else but in God do we receive the true freedom not to have to know, achieve, or strategize a plan? In a time when business plans, traffic plans, payment plans, political plans, and personal plans overlap and guide our minutes, hours, and days; where but in God are we given the full relief and assurance that God's plans for us and ways for us are more mysterious, intentional, and generous than anything we can conceive or project on our own?

We are conditioned and rewarded in human terms to do all we can to plan and control our lives. We are measured by our ability to outscheme and overachieve, and we are exhausted by the pace we set for ourselves and for one another.

But this passage from Isaiah calls us to turn around, to look back toward God who, with compassion and forgiveness, waits to restore in us a different plan for living, a plan we need not and cannot fully know. Our lives were not our ideas in the first place, nor are they ours to plot and plan on our own, as hard as we try to do so. God delights in leading, inspiring, nourishing, and filling us with wonder, gifts, and presence.

In this season of Lent, we are given, not by our design but by God's, enough time and space to seek what is holy, restorative, and fruitful for ourselves, our neighbors, and all of creation. We are invited to trust God's ways, especially those that point us higher and beyond ourselves.

Creating God, fill us with your generous mercy and grace that we may seek you all the more, having been nourished to our roots and sustained to the core of our souls. In the name and spirit of Jesus. Amen.

When parched, our body knows its deepest need: water. Every cell thirsts, every muscle craves what is needed for restoration. Our memory begins to work, reminding us of what we yearn for—wet, refreshing water that can, in a moment, bring us back to life. We are created with this inner knowledge, this internal gauge by which we sense when we need sustenance beyond ourselves. We are also created with this inner capacity to recall what has before refreshed our tired spirits and bodies. God has made it so.

In these verses of Psalm 63, the psalmist speaks to this universal human need and memory. When in the desert, parched and worn, his whole being longs for what is needed in his soul. He yearns for what is needed for life. Like a longing for water when his body is dried out, he longs for God when his soul languishes in a spiritual desert-time.

Is this not true for us all? When seasons of life drain all that we have reserved, when we have traipsed across difficult landscapes or felt the heat of intense discernment, do we not sense deep within that we must find a source of restoration and life? And do we not, in those same inner contours, begin to recall sources of hope, even if in the faintest distance of our memory?

Just as we are created to long for water to keep us alive, we are created to long for God. Our need for God and God's capacity to sustain us in every season through which we pass are imprinted in every cell of our being. Better than life itself, God's love for us and in us is unwavering and unforgettable in the deepest places of our spirits.

O God who will not let us go, you are light in the darkness and shade in the heat of the day. Our whole being thirsts for you. Our longing hearts ache for you because you are our ever-present source of life. Amen.

THURSDAY, FEBRUARY 28 ~ *Read Psalm 63:5-8*

King David was known to be a strong man. A leader in battle and politics, he was revered by some and feared by others. He was a man whose image would be nothing less than focused, determined, and driven. From the story of his youth when he slew Goliath with a simple slingshot to the story of his kingship as he waged fierce battles against enemies of his people, this man of God's choosing is well-known and remembered for his boldness and authority.

Yet in these verses from Psalm 63, a psalm often attributed to David, we gain insight into the willingness of this same man to be vulnerable before God. In the dark of night, alone in his bed, David does not fear turning to God. He does not fear clinging to God and acknowledging his dependence on the one who chose him to lead God's people.

Here we receive a powerful image for this season of Lent. If a leader as strong and confident as David publicly acknowledges that on his bed in the middle of the night he too ponders and meditates on his need for God's help and protection, how much more can we allow ourselves to do the same?

If a powerful king clings to God with every fiber of his being, if he can confess his love and need for God, and tell us so, can we not do the same? Whether we are presidents, CEOs, grandmothers, pastors, teachers, soldiers, mothers, doctors, students, or carpenters, we are all dependent on God. And God longs for us to ponder and meditate on the never-ending love that is ours to receive and share—love that will protect and help us in every time and season of life.

God of day and night, you are our help in every trouble and our light in every time of joy. Amen.

God's Sustaining Mercy

Anguish had a face this day. I knew the word but had not been in its presence until the morning of the accident. As I held my friend in my arms, both of us still stunned by her husband's sudden death, all we could do was cling to each other. No words of comfort would come; only unfettered, embodied anguish.

After what seemed like an unreal forever, my friend whispered words I could not hear. I pulled away so that we could look at each other, and asked what she had said. "I want to scream at God," she told me. "I want to scream at God. How can God let this happen?" Quietly grieving in deep sobs, she dropped her face back onto my shoulder.

"Then scream. Tell God. Scream at God what you feel. You can do that," I said to my friend. "There is nothing you want to say that God does not want to hear."

Weeks later, after beginning to put her family's life back together, we sat in her kitchen. She told me that until that day, she never knew it was acceptable to be openly angry with God. She was taught that a faithful person can handle anything without being tempted to question or rail against God. Yet, in that morning of inexpressible pain, the temptation to throw the anger and despair exploding in her soul toward God had been real. She had not known that other faithful people felt the same. Yet encouraged to trust God with her deepest self, she began to pray her anger and despair. What she discovered was not distance from God but closeness that will not let her go.

Our reading reminds us all that God has been, is, and will be faithful through every situation and temptation that we experience. God is with us whatever we face or endure. God will "supply a way out" (CEB).

God of infinite grace, wherever we go and whatever we endure, you are with us. We give you thanks. Amen.

We find it tempting to point out someone whose faults are worse than our own. "She started it!" has a familiar ring. Workplace and courtroom arguments form like building-block towers, one person's wrongdoing balanced on top of another's. Whose guilt is worse? Who started it?

As Jesus listens to those gathered with him, they are busy pointing fingers at some Galileans killed by Pilate for sacrificing in the wrong way at the wrong time. Clearly, "those" Galileans were in the wrong, and Jesus would have to agree. And not only agree, but Jesus surely would also commend the storytellers for being in the right.

So with fingers still pointed in the air and satisfied nods, the ones around Jesus wait for his "yes." Yes, the ones who died were in the wrong and more at fault than others. But Jesus does not see it that way, and he must startle them out of their smug certainty when he says no. "No, I tell you, but unless you change your hearts and lives, you will die just as they did" (CEB).

What? This is not what the people around Jesus expect to hear. Surely they misunderstand him. But before they can rebuild their case, Jesus builds his own by changing roles and becoming the storyteller, this time about the tower of Siloam. His point is the same. The ones killed when the tower fell were not guiltier than everyone else. They did not need to change more than everyone else.

No, according to Jesus, everyone must change—no one is exempt; no one is better; no one is finished with the kind of change desired by God. And the change desired by God is a change of heart and life, a change made visible and real through Jesus who started it for us all.

Potter God, may we trust our lives to your hands. Make us new, reshape us in gospel ways that we might follow Jesus ever more closely. Amen.

THIRD SUNDAY IN LENT

What good will another year do? The landowner's frustration leaps from the page of our reading as he looks at the barren fig tree. Enough is enough for him; he tells his gardener to cut the tree down. For three years this landowner has taken time to walk over to this puny tree, to check on it, look at it, judge it, and let it live in the care of someone else. But the landowner sees nothing worth rescuing this time. No fruit in three years' time. Nothing has changed in the landowner's view, and nothing is likely to change.

But the gardener senses, or maybe imagines, that the tree is worth giving air, space, and water to. This tree holds a promise that the gardener can still see, maybe because the gardener has spent time near the tree, touching its bark, watching birds rest on its branches and children dance around it. In the eyes of the gardener, this tree has a future, so much so that he will get on his hands and knees to care for it and nourish it through another season.

Change holds promise in eyes that will see what is not yet but can be. In our story, the gardener sees what can still be and willingly commits himself to bring that change to pass. So it is with God for us. Through the eyes of God we each hold promise for becoming what we are created to be—people rooted and grounded in God's love. May we use this Lenten season to tend patiently to the possibilities of change that will be life-giving for God's creation.

Timeless God, we thank you for being slow to anger and abounding in steadfast love. Guide us into patience, vision, and hope that we may bloom where we are planted. Amen.

A Forgiving Spirit

MARCH 4–10, 2013 • DAN MOSELEY

SCRIPTURE OVERVIEW: A common theme of these passages is that of joy over the restorative love of God. Joshua 5:9-12 describes the first celebration of Passover in the Land of Promise. God's promise has been realized; the goal of the Israelites' lengthy journey is beneath their feet. The psalmist, aware of the devastating nature of human sin, celebrates the reality that confessed sin is a means of reconnecting with God. Paul acknowledges certain consequences of Jesus' death: (1) the cross opens up a new way of knowing, (2) to see with the eyes of the cross is to see a new world, (3) God's reconciling love is clearly revealed, and (4) Christ's followers are commissioned to be engaged in the ministry of reconciliation. The familiar parable of the prodigal son is concerned with matters of recognition and nonrecognition. The younger son comes to his senses about his own situation, and his repentance is recognized by the father.

QUESTIONS AND THOUGHTS FOR REFLECTION

- Read Joshua 5:9-12. What change of heart is required for "wilderness" people to become productive of a new order?

- Read Psalm 32. How can we slow our pace of struggle for doing right to celebrate God's gift of righteousness?

- Read 2 Corinthians 5:16-21. How can we be free to partner with God in the creating of a reconciled world?

- Read Luke 5:1-3, 11*b*-32. How can we create space to reconnect with those from whom we have been alienated?

A writer and speaker who helps people deal with loss and change; author of *Lose, Love, Live: The Spiritual Gifts of Loss and Change* (Upper Room Books, 2011); ordained pastor of the Disciples of Christ, living in Indianapolis, Indiana

Parables break open to reveal treasures. The diverse gifts appeal to different tastes and interests. Consequently parables are always old and ever new because the one who hears is ever changing and always in a different place.

One of the treasures of this parable resides in its revelation of disappointment and loss. The father in charge of the family has a plan. But the son who asks for his inheritance early (thus implying that his father has already died to him) throws a monkey wrench in that plan. His son has a different idea about how life will turn out—an idea that deeply disappoints the father.

The father's disappointment calls to mind our own experiences. Our dreams and plans, while good, often don't work out. Change seems to be stalking the edges of our life's designs. Our hard work to secure a desirable future often results in disappointment and grief. With change being the one constant that we can count on in life, loss becomes the consistent reality.

This reality can burden our moving forward into the future. The son's decision undoubtedly saddens the father; he may struggle to stay on an even keel. His son's leaving brings shattered dreams and a broken heart.

We too experience such loss and grief in our lives. We face disappointment when life doesn't turn out the way we think it should. Moving beyond the pain of the losses of the past requires that we open ourselves to the forgiving spirit of God's love. If we cannot grieve the losses and accept the freeing forgiveness for the future, the weight of that ungrieved loss will break us. What loss do you need to name and grieve?

Give heed to my pain, O God, and give me courage to face my disappointment. Amen.

The Hebrew people have experienced it all. They had freedom but famine drove them into hunger. Their hunger drove them into Egyptian slavery. In their suffering they cried out for liberation. God sent Moses to lead them to freedom. They discovered that freedom isn't easy. Their interminable wandering and fear freed them from their dependency on slave masters and opened them to trust in the God who accompanied their ancestors Abraham and Sarah.

Now the Hebrews are moving into the land that has been opened to them. They cross the Jordan freed from their identity as slaves yet uncertain of their identity as Israelites. They create new symbols to represent the journey. They reclaim practices to remind them of their identity.

The people discover that they are being called to a new beginning, a new self-understanding. They can no longer count on manna; planting, harvesting, and securing their own food falls to them. The work of deconstructing their identity as slaves was over. In this new land they now could construct a new people. They had work to do.

We too move through wilderness places where we lose our sense of identity and security. Like our Hebrew ancestors, we too experiment and learn from our experience. We too receive forgiveness from God, who has been with us in our wandering.

But then the time comes to embrace our freedom and contribute to the building of a new self. God works to help us forgive the past so it doesn't control our future, but we have a responsibility to contribute to the emerging of the new self. What work are you now doing to create your grace-filled, forgiven self?

Accompany us, good God, as we wander, and embrace our new creative energy as we become your new creation. Amen.

In the midst of conflict between family members, the changes that offend and alienate and the losses of innocence and identity that result from those changes, certain longings and actions follow. The son who left home, insulted his father, and spoiled the family plans for the future, comes to his senses. He discovers that his longing for an independent and individualistic future is not as powerful as his longing for home and relationships with those who love and sustain him. In the absence of home, he discovers a hope for home.

Out of his loss and emptiness, he goes to his father and confesses his mistake. He names the losses that he and his family suffered. In humility he realizes that he cannot return to his former family status. He is not worthy.

But in confessing, an interesting thing occurs. The son discovers that the onerous burden that he and his family experienced has lifted. His father has been holding in his heart a pool of grace for his son. The family will never be the same. The experiences of the past will always shape the future. His father welcomes him back as a son, but no one will be the same. Grace and forgiveness do not restore life as it was. They simply reconnect the wounded and scarred, offering a chance to build anew.

In God's future, shalom is a reality. God's agenda of freeing people from the power of the past to control their future encourages a rebuilding out of the scattered stones of separation and alienation. The psalmist sings of the burden that is lifted when the heart confesses and affirms God's deliverance. How have you contributed to God's agenda in creating a heart of grace that reformation might take place?

Grant us the courage to confess, O God, and open ourselves to reconnection. Amen.

It seems the reuniting of a family would be cause for unbridled celebration rather than hurt and separation. But betrayal and abandonment cut deep. The brother who remained at home feels wounded. He not only suffered the loss of his brother who deserted him, but he was left to share his father's pain. When someone we love gets hurt, the cut goes even deeper.

So, when the happy reunion occurs, the older brother doesn't join in. He could have performed his duty and joined the festivities, but anger was deep. He not only remained the responsible one while his brother wasted his inheritance, but he must now share the remainder since his brother is a son again. He grieves not only the past but the loss of the future he had anticipated.

Does it seem fair to ask the older brother to forgive his younger brother? If the brother honors the father's desire for family unity, then he has no choice. But don't ask him to like it. Overcoming deep and shaming pain is an arduous process. Forgiveness isn't simply declaring that it's over. Grieving the loss of the world you knew and the world you hoped for takes time. Being freed for a new tomorrow requires a forgiving spirit that must grow toward that liberated future. It takes patience; it takes small steps. It takes prayerful conversation with the offending party and your own soul.

Also keep in mind the heart of the father. While the younger son has new opportunity and suffers no permanent separation, the older son has benefited from the father's steadfast presence and affection. While it may appear that the gifts of grace are only for those who do grievous offense, there is constant and faithful presence for those who never know the pain of separation. Hold on to God's constant grace.

Hold us, patient Redeemer, in your constant state of grace. Amen.

Parables invite imagination. We don't know what happened to the prodigal's family members as they worked life out together after the party. If their life resembled ours, we can envision trial and error, effort and failure, miscues and mistakes, tears and struggles. When life confronts us with situations that are without precedence, we must make up what happens next. We don't always know the best thing to do. We don't know the outcome of actions until we try them.

Living this way can be scary because we *will* make mistakes—unintentional and simply the result of life lived by experimentation and discovery. We will make choices that work out well and some that will create more pain and confusion. Recreating life after the scattering and breaking of alienation requires patient testing of direction and action.

Paul shares with us insights as to how God creates a healing space for experiments gone awry—a way to keep us from becoming the mistakes that we make. He talks of a God who does see us from a human point of view. God in Christ is in the business of innovation—of making a new creation. God so desires that we join in that creative process that the Divine self is given to overcome our mistakes and our separation.

This forgiveness releases the innovative energy that we humans can share and thus break down the walls that separate us from God and each other. We too can take the initiative, not seeing others as humans do, locking each other into our mistakes. We try to view others as God does, as humans who make mistakes. This frees us all to join God's journey of new creation. Can you develop the divine eyesight and join in that journey?

Holy Initiator, be patient with us as we make our way to your will. Amen.

God loves creation. Divine life creates the world and declares it good. All creatures are gifts of the Holy One. God enjoys being in right relationship with the created order and gives us partners with whom to discover a full and faithful way of life. The goal is the reign of God on earth as it is in heaven.

Therefore, God does not hold our sins against us but acts to reconcile us with one another and with the divine will. God wants to break down the walls of pain and injustice that divide us from the created good. Those who claim Christ as Lord become partners in the creation of a new world that reflects the divine desire for justice and mercy.

That new world will be different from the previous one. Our experiences, our mistakes, our discoveries, our achievements and failures will all be taken into the divine heart through "the one who knew no sin" and will give shape and form to the new world that is being created. Because God returns to us and does not hold our mistakes against us, we can live boldly, trying and failing, picking ourselves and each other up and trying again. The future world of a reconciled people keeps calling us forward into new action.

When we allow the mistakes, the hurt and pain of past offenses to capture us and create prison bars to keep us away from a new and reconciled future, we deny God the insights of our experience. We are kept from offering ourselves, broken and incomplete, for the service of God's design. Therefore, receiving divine forgiveness is the devotional imperative of those who seek to follow Christ. How free are you to join God in an innovative future of grace and justice?

Beloved of all, take our hands and walk with us into your divine future. Amen.

FOURTH SUNDAY IN LENT

This is the day to take a breath. This is a day of celebration. The father, whose overwhelming delight with the return of the lost, initiates a party. He suspends the compulsion that often captures those who are responsible for providing the resources for sustaining life. Get the best food and the party hats, and let us take time out to rejoice.

When the alienated ones finally reunite, when the hard work of forgiveness is underway, when interrupted conversations begin again, even haltingly—it is time to party. Acknowledgment that something new is happening brings with it a time to taste the first fruits of God's reign. Happiness overflows amid shouts of joy.

All too often we fail to join this party. We can be so caught up in holding people accountable for their mistakes that we can't experience the joy of forgiveness and the freedom to discover a new way. The burden of ungrieved loss and disappointment weighs us down, and we are lost in the prison of the past, unable to move forward into that new world of abundant life designed by God's forgiving spirit.

Open your heart to God who longs for you to join the journey toward a new creation. Allow your burdens to be lifted so that, at least from time to time, maybe each Lord's day, you might set aside your struggle to be right and allow God to give righteousness as a gift to you. Then you can celebrate with the father, with the wayward child, and the steady child who stayed home. Won't you join the party?

Thanks, Giver of new life, for putting a new song in our hearts. Amen.

Looking Back, Going Forward

MARCH 11–17, 2013 • K. CHERIE JONES

SCRIPTURE OVERVIEW: The Isaiah text portrays the redemptive activity of God that is about to be introduced into Israel's life. All paradigms lie shattered before the enormity of God's grace! The joy of Psalm 126 is occasioned by the memory of God's act of redemption in the past and also by the anticipation that a similar intervention is imminent. Paul's autobiographical sketch directed to the Philippians confesses the change that has come into his life as a result of "knowing Christ Jesus my Lord." The story of Mary's anointing of Jesus' feet must be read in the context of Jesus' looming passion. Jesus sets Mary's actions in their proper perspective by linking them to his own death, even as he deflects Judas's counterfeit compassion.

QUESTIONS AND THOUGHTS FOR REFLECTION

- Read Isaiah 43:16-21. How do you respond to this God who insists on doing new things for the sake of the people?

- Read Psalm 126. Pray this psalm three times: (1) pray all the verbs in the past tense in thanksgiving; (2) pray all the verbs in the future tense as a prayer for help; (3) pray verses 1-3 in the past tense, verses 5-6 in the future tense. Which was hardest to pray?

- Read Philippians 3:4b-14. What props or credentials do you need to let go of?

- Read John 12:1-8. What motivations does your discipleship reflect?

Retired United Methodist pastor; member of the California-Pacific Annual Conference

Memory of God's works takes different roles in our faith. Sometimes we recall the past to remind ourselves that God remains with us. I sat with a friend who was suffering greatly from the complications of a rare form of cancer. We talked about hope in the midst of a bleak outlook. She recalled times when she experienced God's provision and faithfulness. It did not change her circumstances, but it encouraged her and renewed her awareness of God's presence and faithfulness.

In this reading, memory plays another role. The people are *not* to recall the past so that they will be ready for God's new work. The opening verses evoke the memory of the Exodus, specifically when God brought the people safely through the sea and into the wilderness—a place of struggle as well as a place of revelation. There they dealt with scarce resources and murmured against God. Now God promises to do a new thing by making a way in the wilderness where rivers will run and praise will resound.

Forgoing that Exodus memory is not a critique of the memory; rather, the focus shifts to awaiting the new thing that God will do for the people. As in every generation, our task is to remember the past but even more to ready ourselves for what God seeks to do *now*.

This readiness does not come easily—especially to those who "remember the former things." The church has wrestled with many issues, such as slavery, style of worship, war, role of women. It has taken much prayer, conversation, and discernment. It can take a long time, if ever. Still God promises to do new things and calls us to follow on that new way.

O God, you continue to do new things for your creation. Help us to see and respond to your action. Amen.

Twenty years ago, my spiritual director taught me to pray the psalms. The psalms teach us to pray and bring the truth of our lives to God, including the emotions and habits we would prefer to ignore. Praying the psalms gives us words when we cannot find them on our own. The psalms also teach us about the One to whom we pray and who expects us to need to pray these words at different times in our lives.

Today's psalm is one of the Songs of Ascent the pilgrims prayed as they traveled to Jerusalem for the high holy days. In the Christian tradition, we pray this psalm during Advent and Lent and often at Thanksgiving.

The Bible translation you use when you pray this psalm will shape your prayer. The challenge comes in determining the verb tense of the psalm. Some translate all the verses in the past tense, making the psalm a prayer of thanksgiving. Others translate all the verses in the future tense, making the psalm a prayer for help. Still others split the difference by translating verses 1-3 in the past tense and verses 4-6 in the future tense; this results in remembering God's past acts of salvation and requesting help from God now.

Perhaps this very ambiguity or flexibility among the translations is God's gift as it encourages us to pray this psalm in different ways, depending on the situation. During Advent and Lent, it is a psalm of praise as we ponder anew the humble birth, violent death, and resurrection of Jesus. Other times, it is more appropriately a prayer of praise and a plea for help.

As we continue our approach to Holy Week, perhaps praying this psalm will give voice to the cries of our hearts.

O God, thank you for the gift of the psalms. I take comfort in praying the words that your people have found so helpful. Amen.

In this dinner at the home of the family Jesus loved, we witness discipleship in several forms. First we see Mary anointing Jesus' feet with an expensive perfume, then wiping it away with her hair. Here we see part of the dynamic of discipleship: Jesus loves and cares for her, and Mary responds with an act of devotion. She has listened to and learned from Jesus, has seen him raise her brother from the dead and has put some of the pieces of discipleship together. She intuitively knows how to respond extravagantly to Jesus—even before he washes his disciples' feet and commands them to love others. Mary chooses the right action for the right reasons and models faithful discipleship.

We see another example of discipleship in Judas's response. Perturbed by Mary's actions, he offers a critique that seems rational when he asks, "Why was this perfume not sold . . . and the money given to the poor?" The question of how to respond to God's persistent commandments to care for the poor is appropriate, one that every generation of faithful people wrestles with. But the Fourth Evangelist essentially asserts that Judas's motivation for asking the question involves greed rather than compassion for the poor. Judas knows scripture and talks piously but does not follow through on his words; thus, he models unfaithful discipleship.

This story calls us to check our motivations as well as our actions to be sure that we are taking the right actions for the right reasons. It also gives us permission to offer extravagant gifts of devotion to Jesus, even a donation to the poor.

> *Lord Jesus, you know the contours of my heart. I may know the right answers, but I don't always do the right things for the right reasons. Continue to teach me how to be your disciple. Amen.*

THURSDAY, MARCH 14 ~ *Read Philippians 3:4b-14*

I serve on a committee of clergy and laity that meets several times a year to certify candidates for ordained ministry in our denomination. There are criteria for the candidates: seminary education, psychological assessments, recommendations from church leaders, etc. During the meetings, we pray, listen carefully to the candidates and to God, and discern if we confirm a call to ministry and if the candidates seem ready to move on in the process. We expect them to meet the criteria and show fluency in theology, leadership skills, and pastoral care. We also want them to be mature Christian disciples who trust in God wholeheartedly.

In this reading, Paul lists the ways in which he met the criteria for being a faithful Jew: by birth, zeal, and keeping the law. He knows that while these credentials are good, even God-given, knowing Jesus puts him in a right relationship with God. So he gives up putting his trust in his credentials and instead puts his total trust in Jesus. This does not mean that Paul stopped using the skills of debate or knowledge of the Law that he had honed as a Pharisee or stopped being energetic in living out his faith. When Paul chose to rely first on Jesus, he placed his credentials in the right place, the right order. They then became tools with which he could serve God in remarkable ways.

Whether clergy or lay, we easily slip into relying on our credentials—how long we have attended church or how many mission projects we have gone on—as a way to be right with God. Paul reminds us that we are to trust in Jesus, not in our credentials—no matter how good they are.

Lord Jesus, it is so easy to rely on accomplishments and credentials rather than on you. Please help me to keep all this in the right order. Amen.

In this short, autobiographical snippet, Paul recaps his little life and places it within the big story of God's activity. He recounts his credentials and religious heritage, then mentions his need for reevaluation of all in light of "knowing Christ." He goes on to state his present intention. Paul's "knowing Christ" has reoriented his entire perspective on life, creating new priorities for his life's direction and how he chooses to expend his energy and for Whom he will "press on toward the goal."

Rachel Beckwith had a goal that reoriented her perspective. At church she learned about the desperate need for clean water in other countries. Shocked that children her age did not drink clean water, Rachel decided to raise $300 for water wells in Africa. She canceled her ninth birthday party and urged her family and friends to contribute $9 each to the project. She set up a Web page to make it easier to contribute. It disappointed her to raise only $220 by her birthday, but she decided to keep trying.

Six weeks later, a traffic accident involving the Beckwiths left Rachel critically injured. Friends began to contribute to the fund to signal their support. The giving far exceeded her goal of $300. On July 23, 2011, three days after the accident, Rachel was taken off life support and died. But Rachel's dream lived on. As the media picked up the news about her dream of clean water, the contributions poured in. The account was closed on September 30, 2011, with total contributions of over $1.2 million that would help over 63,000 people.

By God's grace, Rachel's death was not the end of the story. What are your dreams for reaching out to others with Christ's love? How are you helping others press on toward their goals?

Holy God, thank you for giving me dreams of how to share your love with others. Give me the courage to see these dreams through. Amen.

On September 11, 2001, my friend Michael Hingson and his guide dog, Roselle, went to work in his office on the 78th floor of the North Tower of the World Trade Center. What started off as a normal day turned into an extraordinary day when the hijacked American Airlines Flight 11 jet was flown into their building. Not knowing what was going on, Michael and Roselle walked down 1,463 steps and exited the North Tower.

Minutes later, the South Tower collapsed some one hundred yards from them. As the pair turned to flee from the debris, Michael, who had prayed throughout the morning, cried out to God, "Why did you get us out of the building only to let another fall on us?" In the chaos, he heard God's voice inside his heart, *Don't worry about the things you cannot control. Focus on running with Roselle and the rest will take care of itself.* In what was now an urban wilderness, God's words comforted and calmed his heart.

Michael and Roselle ran, dodging debris and then being enveloped by the toxic three-hundred-foot dust cloud. In the utter chaos of those moments, Michael felt God's presence and experienced the "peace of God, which surpasses all understanding" (Phil. 4.7). The deep peace allowed him to totally focus on running with Roselle, who was now temporarily blind from the dust. Michael, who learned echolocation at the age of four, and Roselle simultaneously heard an opening into a subway station and ducked out of the wilderness into a refuge.

It was a few years before Michael talked about his mystical experience publicly, but now he alludes to God's guidance in the wilderness whenever he tells his story. God made a way for Michael on that terrible day. How has God made a way for you in the wilderness?

Thank you, faithful God, for meeting and guiding me in the wild places. Amen.

FIFTH SUNDAY IN LENT

Fifteen years ago, on the Fifth Sunday of Lent, our organization underwent upheaval. I served on the staff of the General Board of Discipleship of The United Methodist Church. That morning our coworker, Donna, went missing. It soon became clear that she had been murdered. Eight days later, on Monday of Holy Week, a beloved retired staff person named Bobby died of natural causes. On Wednesday, a coworker named Verlia died, also of natural causes.

The deaths of three trusted colleagues and friends rocked the organization. The first response of the staff was to meet daily in worship. We affirmed God's faithfulness and lamented our loss. We prayed for Donna, her family, and those searching for her. During Holy Week, we added the families of Bobby and Verlia to our prayers. We looked for ways to support their families, especially their children. The staff somberly tried to concentrate on work, and conversations were muted. Walking into the building felt like walking into a tomb.

The words of the psalmist resonated: "Restore our fortunes, O LORD." Corporately we had experienced God's faithfulness many times in the past but we desperately needed God's help and faithfulness again—help with our grief and with how to continue in ministry.

Easter brought a new depth of hope in the Resurrection. God met us as we gathered weekly in worship and felt the prayers of so many people outside the organization. Slowly and surely, God gave us the help we needed, and we experienced divine faithfulness anew. I remember the day when, walking through the halls, I heard laughter once more. I knew we had turned a corner and offered a prayer of gratitude to the Faithful One.

Eternal God, thank you for your faithfulness in times of need. Be with those who need your help today. Amen.

The Stone the Builders Rejected

MARCH 18–24, 2013 • JEFF TAYLOR

SCRIPTURE OVERVIEW: Palm/Passion Sunday is a time of celebration over the coming of the King, but it is also a time of foreboding because the celebrants know that the King is soon to die. This King is a king like no other, yet he goes almost unrecognized by those over whom he rules. Isaiah 50:4-9 portrays a servant of God who is aware of deep trouble yet faces it with bold confidence. The confidence emerges from a sense that the servant is doing the will of God, but this does not diminish the hostility or render the servant less vulnerable to it. The servant's single purpose is to affirm the rule of God. Psalm 118 celebrates the reality that the rejected building stone "has become the chief cornerstone" (v. 22). The epistle lection sings of Christ's humiliation and exaltation. Luke narrates Jesus' entry into Jerusalem: Jesus enters as king and his greeters extend to him a royal welcome.

QUESTIONS AND THOUGHTS FOR REFLECTION

- Read Psalm 118:1-2, 19-29. How do you describe God's goodness and steadfast love in the world and in your own life? Reflect on ways that creation tells the story of God's goodness and steadfast love.

- Read Luke 19:28-40. Imagine yourself as the owner of the colt that is requisitioned by Jesus' disciples. What are you willing to give up because "the Lord needs it"? What role can you see yourself playing in the first Palm Sunday processional? Are you a participant or a bystander? What are you shouting?

President, United Methodist Foundation of West Virginia, Inc.; member, Johnson Memorial United Methodist Church, Huntington, West Virginia

MONDAY, MARCH 18 ~ *Read Psalm 118:1-2*

What does it mean to say that God is good? In our every-day speech we proclaim the goodness of everything from food to movies. We wear our *good* shoes with our *good* clothes. When my dog does what he's expected to do during our morning walk, he's a "good boy." We relax with a good book, fight for a good cause, and shop for a good buy, which is not to be confused with our common farewell: good-bye.

One of the most common adjectives in English, *good* is often the first word in the morning and the penultimate word at night. Good is not bad, but it's not that great either. In the world of modifiers, *good* seems middle-of-the-road—perhaps even boring.

So what does it mean that God is good?

This psalm, intended for use in worship, gives the community the opportunity to proclaim in unison God's goodness. In ancient times and today, no matter what we bring with us to worship—our pain, our failures, our sin, our disagreements—we can declare one thing in full accord: God is good!

The worshiping community, in proclaiming God's goodness, highlights the covenantal relationship between God and God's people. God not only created the universe and reigns over all, but God is good! The Holy One faithfully fulfills the covenant, without regard to and even in spite of our human failure to be obedient. And that's a good thing.

The only conceivable response to such one-sided benevolence is thanks and praise.

Dear God, we give you thanks and praise for your goodness. As we reflect on our own lives in the light of your goodness, we can see more clearly the ways we have failed to live up to your desires. Forgive us, and strengthen us to fulfill your purposes. Amen.

This psalm describes God's love as steadfast. Like goodness, God's steadfast love indicates God's faithfulness to the covenantal relationship with the people despite the community's failure to live up to it. To be steadfast is to be unchangeable and unaffected by external forces. We attribute steadfast love to God alone. External forces do not affect God.

Although we experience desert times in our lives when it seems that God is absent, from the perspective of looking back, we can see where divine love sustained us and brought us through and beyond the desert place. Two years ago I spent most of a week with Mom and other family members in hospital waiting rooms and intensive care units as Dad's sudden hemorrhagic stroke took his life. That devastating time came as a shock. I sat with Mom as she watched the love of her life slip from consciousness. I sensed she feared the future, and that frightened me.

In that entire experience, I had the powerful sense of God's steadfast love and comforting presence: in the care of the nurses and treating professionals at the hospitals, in the visits from friends and neighbors, in the cards, in the prayer shawls knit by church members. I felt God's presence in the e-mails and calls from caring friends who didn't know what to say but let us know they were thinking of us. I sensed God's presence as my pastor and my mentor stayed all night with Dad and with me in the hospital after Dad was taken off life support. I felt it through my colleagues who picked up my workload so that I could be where I needed to be.

In the darkest moment of my life, evidence of God's steadfast love shone abundantly. That experience gives me hope and reassurance for the future as well.

Dear God, in our darkest times and deepest pain, we know you are with us and your steadfast love endures forever. Amen.

When Christians read verse 23, we usually think of Jesus Christ as the stone rejected by the builders who becomes the cornerstone. We tend to think of the builders as the religious leaders of the day who failed to recognize the obvious signs of Jesus' identity. The cornerstone represents God's triumph in Jesus Christ. Our perspective tends to be as the cornerstone, not the rejected stone; the victor, not the victim; the resurrected, not the dead.

But I wonder if the psalmist could still pen this verse today. If so, who are the builders? Who are the stones rejected by the builders—or by us?

Every day, I make choices that reject Jesus' messiahship in favor of my own self-interest. I do what I want to do instead of what I know God requires. I react to situations out of anger and self-preservation instead of responding out of love. I work and plan to conserve my own nest egg instead of leaving a legacy of compassion and generosity. These choices reject Jesus' call to radical discipleship.

Even more troublesome than my and your personal failures and rejections are the ways we complacently and complicitly condone the communal rejection of Jesus. Our churches, our communities, our governments build walls, both literal and figurative, to protect us and to reject others. We hoard and waste scarce resources while others live in poverty and starvation. We create systems that ensure cheap food and clothing for ourselves and ignore the working conditions of those who labor to provide them. We build up our own "temples" for joyful worship while the marginalized remain on the outside.

What would it look like today if the rejected stone became the cornerstone?

Dear God, may our rejoicing and gladness move us to compassion for those who have been rejected by society. Amen.

Today's reading marks the climax of the travel narrative, Luke's account of Jesus' journey to Jerusalem. Jesus and his disciples have reached the Mount of Olives. It will play a prominent role in the Passion narrative, but now it is the place of preparation for the entry into Jerusalem. Jesus sends two disciples as advance agents to commandeer a colt—not just any colt, but a certain colt, tied in the village, that has never been ridden.

The disciples do as Jesus instructs. As they untie the colt, the owners stop them just as Jesus warned they might. "The Lord needs it" is the disciples' only explanation; and with that, the colt's owners become unlikely heroes in God's saving action through Jesus Christ.

I cannot imagine being as compliant as the colt's owners. If I caught two strangers helping themselves to my automobile, the police would have been notified by the time I got the explanation that "the Lord needs it." I would have missed the chance to participate with God in fulfilling God's purposes.

How often have I failed to act on an opportunity to cooperate with God's divine grace? It may come in the form of a need lifted up in church to clean the yard at the parsonage. It may come in the form of an announcement in the community to bring gently used coats for the needy. It may come in the form of a look or a sign from a person on the street. I can hear "the Lord needs it," but I drown it out with a cacophony of excuses disguised as busyness, inconvenience, or caution.

The colt's owners took a chance. Did they get their colt back? We don't know, but that didn't seem to matter to them. It was enough for them to know that the Lord needed it. They obeyed, no questions asked.

Dear God, help us see and hear your needs clearly so that we can seize opportunities to cooperate with your grace to fulfill your purposes in the world. Amen.

FRIDAY, MARCH 22 ~ *Read Luke 19:28-40*

The high point of this week begins with crowds hailing the long-awaited Messiah and then descends to Temple cleansing, arguments, denial, arrest, betrayal, trials, judgment, and crucifixion.

I have often wondered how many details of the entry into Jerusalem were worked out in advance. Did the owners of the colt know in advance that their animal would be requisitioned? Were the people watching and waiting for Jesus to emerge on the colt? Had they planned to spread their cloaks and shout their praises? Or was the first Palm Sunday processional a grass-roots movement that gathered momentum?

Luke's account has no palm branches in the triumphal entry, but certain clues indicate that the writer perceives the entry into Jerusalem as an intentional act of asserting Jesus' messiahship. Zechariah foretold the Mount of Olives as the place where the Lord would become king over all the earth (14:4-9). The colt directly refers to Zechariah's prophecy that the king would ride in on a colt (9:9). The actions of the crowd in spreading their cloaks in front of the processional allude to similar actions for royalty elsewhere in the scriptures. The shouts of praise are a direct quotation from the Psalms, except the "one who comes" is replaced with the "king who comes."

Yet some witnesses present did not participate. From the perspective of looking backward from this side of Easter, however, we can see the triumph. What would it have been like on that day? I often wonder what I would have been shouting. Would I have joined in the praises for the king who comes in the name of the Lord? Or would my voice have joined those of religious leaders shouting that Jesus demand his disciples to stop?

Dear God, with the benefit of hindsight we recognize you. Give us grace to recognize your presence in our midst daily. Amen.

Jesus tells the Pharisees that even if the disciples stop shouting, the stones will cry out. God does not depend on us to tell the story. The natural wonders of creation tell the story of God's continuing presence in and with creation.

In many ways, stones do tell the story of God's saving acts. David defeated Goliath with a stone. Jacob marked divine interactions with stones. Stones intended for capital punishment help us learn something about self-righteousness and judgmentalism. Jesus refers to Peter as the rock upon which the church will be built. The rejected stone becomes the chief cornerstone.

The story of God's goodness and steadfast love as demonstrated through the life and ministry of Jesus Christ has proven to be too great to silence. Later in this week, which starts with a triumphal entry, it may seem that the movement has been silenced. Jesus' closest disciples will be nowhere to be found. The shouts will be something other than praises to the king. And in the depths of darkness and despair, God's enduring, steadfast love will be evidenced by a single stone, a stone that is rolled away from the tomb.

Jesus was right, of course. The stone told the story when it appeared that it might not get told. And news of the stone spread across millennia and around the world that Jesus Christ is Lord.

> Blessed is the king
>> who comes in the name of the LORD!
> Peace in heaven,
>> and glory in the highest heaven!

Dear God, we give thanks for the wonders of your creation, which tell the story even when our voices are silenced by fear. Amen.

PALM/PASSION SUNDAY

A tension exists in the way this Gospel depicts Jesus' entry into Jerusalem. Luke portrays Jesus as uncharacteristically assertive in claiming his kingship and authority by riding a colt. The disciples' acts of spreading their cloaks on the road before him further evidence the claim. However, riding on a colt displays humility that does not meet some expectations of a royal or triumphal entry.

Another element of tension exists in the fact that just as Jesus and his disciples enter Jerusalem, Herod Antipas enters from the other side with an entourage of warriors. They arrive to remind those attending the Passover celebration that they are under Roman authority and to discourage any confrontations. Jesus rides on an animal that symbolizes humility; Herod likely rides on a mighty steed, a symbol of war. The tension mounts and eventually erupts into conflict.

We may feel tempted to judge the Pharisees for not getting it—for missing the signs of who Jesus was. But what would a triumphal entry look like today? Would it include a military armada? Would we follow a leader who didn't live up to our regal, powerful, and affluent expectations?

The tension continues today. We celebrate the triumphal entry, when the Prince of Peace heralded a new day; but in reality we are not at peace. We are yet at war; the language of war is embroiled in our political, social, and economic discussions.

Has peace triumphed?

Dear God, on this Palm Sunday, we want to celebrate a festive processional, yet at the same time we know that before this week ends, the triumph turns tragic. Give us the grace to join with you in the triumph of peace and justice. Amen.

Strange, Wonderful Week

MARCH 25–31, 2013 • WILL WILLIMON

SCRIPTURE OVERVIEW: [*This Scripture Overview and questions accompany the lections listed for Easter Sunday.*] The common themes of death's reality, the powerful intrusion of the delivering God, and the manifold responses to resurrection run prominently through the texts. The psalmist rejoices at an occasion of divine deliverance, remembering death as a threat from which God has provided rescue. In the Gospel lection, Mary acknowledges the devastation of death and begins to come to grips with her grief and consternation. All four texts announce God's deliverance from death, the divine "power play" that brings life not only for "the one ordained by God as judge of the living and the dead" (Acts 10:42) but also for God's people (1 Cor. 15). Jesus' resurrection makes possible a radical style of new life.

QUESTIONS AND THOUGHTS FOR REFLECTION

- Read Acts 10:34-43. What situations have helped you understand that "God shows no partiality"?

- Read Psalm 118:1-2, 14-24. What events have you celebrated with your faith community when you acknowledged God's steadfast love?

- Read 1 Corinthians 15:19-26. The arms of the risen Christ receive all persons. What in your life bears witness to the work of the Spirit in you?

- Read John 20:1-18. Mary cannot initially "see" the fact of an empty tomb as witness to resurrection—but only as a stolen body. When have you been unable to see the resurrection work of God?

Retired United Methodist bishop, professor at Duke Divinity School, and author of *Why Jesus?*

It's an odd way to begin a week, even for the Gospel of John. Jesus is in Bethany being entertained by his good friends Mary and Martha. The Gospel writer casually remarks that Lazarus, whom Jesus has just raised from the dead, sits there at table with them.

Whom he has just *raised from the dead*? Imagine the oddness of being seated at that table!

"You know our rabbi, Jesus, and next to him is our brother, Lazarus, who died last week but now, thanks to Jesus, is back among the living. Make yourself comfortable in the seat between them."

"What sort of week have you had?" you ask politely.

Your dinner companion replies, "Well, I was sick unto death, then I was entombed for three days. Now Jesus has raised me from the dead, and I'm here at my sisters' dinner party. How was your week?"

Where are we? Welcome to the wonderfully strange world of the Gospel of John and to the holiest week of our year. God is on the move. Jesus sits at table with us and whenever Jesus shows up, hold on to your hat: corpses rise from the dead; we face the shock that God is more than we imagined; the predictable, dull world is rendered strange; and even a dinner table can be a dangerous place.

It's Holy Week. Be prepared to be shocked by Jesus; made uncomfortable, confused, raised from the dead, and the familiar world made odd. Our salvation draws near, too close for comfort. Something odd is about to happen, God with us.

Come, Lord Jesus. This week shock, surprise, wake us up, startle us with your strange glory. Amen.

W e wish to see Jesus," say these Greeks to Philip. And so say we. That's one reason we went to church last Sunday and are reading this meditation on Tuesday. We want better to see Jesus.

Jesus responds by predicting the hour of his glory. Yes, that's what we really want to see, and that's what we most expect out of God—*glory*.

"Show us your glory!" Moses asked God. Down through the ages, that has been our demand: Lord, let us see your undeniable, irrefutable glory. And yet, down through the ages, God—who by definition is glorious—has just never been quite glorious enough for us. Wouldn't it be easier to believe and to serve if God met our glorious expectation more tangibly and visibly?

"We want to see you," we demand of Jesus. Then Jesus shows who he is. He speaks to us of death, loss of life, humble service, obedient following, and judgment. And Jesus calls this his hour of glory?

It's hard to understand this sort of talk as glorious. We want a god who is all-powerful, all-sufficient, high and lifted up.

This week we get the God who defeated our expectations for godliness by being high and lifted up—on a cross.

If we would see Jesus, we must be willing to have our definitions of glory, God, and good rearranged. Jesus continues on his way this week to show us the heart of God as God is, rather than as we would have God to be.

Behold the one who came to us in complete love, the one betrayed, rejected, and by us crucified. And yet Christians are taught to call this week and this God on a cross as glorious a God as we ever hope to see.

Open our eyes, Lord Jesus, to see your peculiar glory. Amen.

No sooner have the disciples settled in at the table than Jesus drops his bombshell: "One of you will betray me." And all of them have the effrontery to ask indignantly, "Lord, who would do such a horrible deed?"

The Gospel writer says that Satan enters Judas, leading him to betrayal, even as he receives the bread from Jesus' hand. But I recall that all the disciples are at table and all flee into the darkness when the soldiers come to arrest Jesus. *All.*

Presumably Satan doesn't need to trouble the hearts of the other disciples to incite them to desertion; among them and us, unfaithfulness to Jesus comes naturally. The shocking, horrible truth is this: If we are looking for Jesus' betrayers, look first among his best friends whom he lovingly gathers at this table.

"Were you there when they crucified my Lord?" we sing. Each of us knows the answer. We meet no sin among Jesus' enemies that we disciples do not first encounter in our own hearts.

And yet (here is the good news), with whom does Jesus choose to spend his last meal, whose feet does he wash, to whom does he offer himself and this meal? With his betrayers—that is, *all of us.*

Jesus is on his way to glory, but he will not be glorified alone, insisting on one last meal, one final night of conviviality with his most beloved friends who also happen to be his most sinful betrayers.

You'd have to be a disciple of Jesus to know why we call this glorious good news.

We give thanks, Lord Jesus, that you died for sinners, some of whom are your close friends—but sinners all. Amen.

MAUNDY THURSDAY

As the Gospel writer begins his account of Maundy Thursday, he says that Jesus, "having loved his own . . . loved them to the end." Until this night and its aftermath, we knew neither the full breadth and depth of God's love for us nor how painfully, deadly difficult it would be for God to love people like us.

This night Jesus dramatically redefines both God and us. Jesus himself kneels and acts as servant, washing the feet of his disciples. Even his disciples protest; they do not understand. We do not understand.

We thought that God was loving but somewhat distant from us: God, transcendent, high and holy, vaguely benevolent.

Tonight God signals the divine determination to come too close for comfort, God getting personal—no matter the pain and the cost. Any God less determined to love us, even unto death, wouldn't do us much good. We are a bloody, death-dealing lot who tend to treat our enemies and our saviors the same way.

In daring, in love to make people like us "his own," God in Christ foreordained that the journey from God to humanity that began in a manger at Bethlehem would end at Golgotha on a cross.

What a comfort to know that the same God who says, "I love you" is willing to love us all the way "to the end."

Your body broken for us, your blood shed for us, Lord Jesus. In the end we, though unworthy, depend so greatly on your costly love! Amen.

GOOD FRIDAY

After Jesus had spoken these words, he went out with his disciples." Jesus, the great preacher, has ended his sermons. Not words but costly deeds will consume the rest of the Gospel's dramatic narrative.

Now it's time for Jesus' disciples to speak up and to speak out. Peter, premier disciple, stands outside the high priest's chamber in the cold darkness, his fear rendering him mute. A serving maid accosts him, "You are not also one of this man's disciples, are you?"

Peter replies with denial, "I am not."

Earlier Jesus had called Peter "the Rock," had praised him for his faithful confession, and had said he would build his church upon him. But tonight, in the early hours of this fateful Friday, Peter denies his discipleship. When put to the test and given his chance to speak to the world about Jesus, Peter fails.

Here in the darkness we are witnessing the birth of the church—a group of half-understanding, often cowardly people trying but not always succeeding to follow Jesus as he leads us down a path few of us really want to go.

And yet this day, this night, alone the Lamb of God walks the path for us. The good news is he will not be deterred in his hard path up Calvary. His bold love for us is unlimited by our failures to love him courageously.

That's why we call this horrible day of crucifixion good.

Jesus, give us the grace to speak up to the world about the gift you gave us this day. Amen.

HOLY SATURDAY

"And the Word became flesh and lived among us" (John 1:14). Jesus, Emmanuel, God-With-Us, came near with openhanded love—and thereby brought out the worst in us.

Jesus, living among us, proved to be God too close for comfort. "This whipped, suffering, crucified Jew cannot be our Messiah," we said. "The God we worship is lofty, holy, lifted up, at some remove from us."

Now Jesus' limp body has been taken down, lamented by the women, and prepared for burial. Nicodemus, who earlier feared being caught in the light of day with Jesus (John 3:1-21), now loves him openly, providing a regal store of spices to dress the body. The condemned criminal whom Pilate mocked as "King" will receive, at the hands of Joseph of Arimathea (patron saint of morticians) and Nicodemus, a royal burial.

Outside of town.

The One who spent his ministry in solidarity with ordinary people, living the life we lived, who made his move into the heart of the Holy City; he who taught and healed, fed and blessed us, was tortured to death rather than received with joy by us. Crucified outside the city, he is now buried outside of town, sealed shut in a tomb.

Can we now get back to normal? Have we reestablished a convenient and safe distance between God and ourselves? Is this quiet sabbath the last we shall hear from this disruptively close Word made flesh?

Who knows? As always, the next move is up to God.

Lord Jesus, having done our worst, we are once again dependent upon you to do your best. Surprise us, Lord! Amen.

EASTER SUNDAY

The first thing that impresses the two disciples on the first Easter is absence. They run out to the tomb, peer in; it is, alas, . . . empty. They assume, quite rationally, that in one final indignity, someone has stolen Jesus' dead body. So they sigh deeply, give up, and go back home.

Mary, in her grief at the loss, lingers. Someone appears. Mary, who assumes that the person is the gardener, says, "They have taken the Lord out of the tomb, and we do not know where they have laid him." The gardener calls her by name, and Mary responds in startled recognition.

Our story with God does not end at the cross on Friday, as we expected. The risen Christ shows up, transforming our painful sense of absence by his presence. In steadfast love God refuses to leave us. Christ shows up and appears to the very ones (his own disciples) who betrayed and disappointed him. We don't have to go looking for Jesus; he's looking for us. We don't have to search and find him; as he did with Mary, he finds us. Who is a Christian? A Christian is someone to whom Christ has shown up.

What is your great hope in life, in death, in life beyond death? The same persistent Savior who shows up to Mary will, in your living and in your dying, keep showing up to you—often when you least expect him.

I know another who has spent a lifetime evading God's claim upon his life. I warned him to be careful, to keep looking over his shoulder—because after Easter, just when his guard is down, Christ shows up.

Happy Easter! Christ has not only risen, risen indeed; Christ has shown up.

Lord Jesus, it would have been enough victory if this day you had simply defeated death. Beyond that, you showed up. Amen.

Encouragement

APRIL 1–7, 2013 • HOLLY G. MILLER

SCRIPTURE OVERVIEW: The texts help us grasp what it means to be "witnesses" of the Resurrection. Acts 5 depicts the apostles in Jerusalem announcing both the resurrection of Jesus to those who shared in his death and his exaltation as Savior. The apostles witness by means of verbal proclamation, through which the Holy Spirit functions as divine authorization. Revelation 1:4-8 continues the theme by declaring Jesus as "the faithful witness, the firstborn of the dead, and the ruler of the kings of the earth" (1:5). Identification with Jesus produces a body of people that intercedes before God on behalf of the world and stands before the world on behalf of God. John 20 records the transformation of Thomas, for whom analysis and debate give way to confession: "My Lord and my God!" (20:28). The psalm's call to praise becomes a summons to live one's life in the context of God's powerful rule.

QUESTIONS AND THOUGHTS FOR REFLECTION

- Read Acts 5:27-32. When have you been rebuked for sharing your faith?
- Read Psalm 150. Recall a worship service that included unfamiliar music and rituals. What parts could you relate to, and what parts seemed uncomfortable or even alien?
- Read Revelation 1:4-8. How do you bring imagination and emotion to the reading of this text?
- Read John 20:19-31. When have you doubted the truth of an experience of the holy?

Author or coauthor of fourteen books; communication consultant to several foundations; living in Anderson, Indiana

Depending on the situation, we might view persons who practice civil disobedience as activists, heroes, and martyrs. Or, if we don't agree with their cause, we might dismiss them as dissidents, troublemakers, and rebels. Paul urges us to "be subject to the governing authorities" and warns that "whoever resists authority resists what God has appointed" (Rom. 13:1-2). His rationale is that God has chosen society's leaders; therefore, they are worthy of our obedience. But what happens when a leader's word seems at odds with God's word? Which takes priority?

The apostles clearly defy local authorities when they continue to preach and perform miracles after the high priest has ordered them to stop. Does their defiance make them heroes or rebels? martyrs or dissidents? "We must obey God rather than any human authority," explains Peter, who has no misgivings about standing firm against the governing council. The apostles bear witness to God's work in history through Jesus Christ to those who bear some responsibility for his death. They courageously stand before the council stating that Jesus was raised by the God of Israel; God has exalted him as an act of mercy toward Israel and will offer repentance and forgiveness to Israel.

The apostles' unshakable faith and Spirit-filled lives affirm their understanding of accountability to a higher power. God has commissioned them to carry on the work of Jesus Christ, and nothing will deter them from that assignment.

History is replete with persons who risked their lives for the faith. Like the apostles, they adhered to their principles even if civil disobedience meant incarceration or death. We tell and retell their stories to encourage a new generation of activists, heroes, and martyrs.

Lord, may we never confuse human laws with your law. May we respect the former but worship the latter. Amen.

A seventieth birthday always offers a good reason to celebrate, but what made Father Henry Kuykendall's party extra special was the guest list. For the first time in anyone's memory, the two ethnic groups that make up Nativity Catholic Church's membership came together to sing, dance, share a meal, and even do some congenial "table-hopping," according to Father Henry, the parish priest and honored septuagenarian.

The small church in Evansville, Indiana, had been bilingual since Father Henry invited the neighborhood's growing Hispanic population to make Nativity their parish home. Partly because of the language barrier and partly because of worship traditions, the Sunday services that evolved were equal but separate. Mass at 9 AM was conducted in English and included liturgies and music preferred by the older Anglo members. The tempo picked up at noon when Mass was celebrated in Spanish, with liturgies and music familiar to the younger Latino members.

The birthday party marked a coming together of the two communities. At its heart was a shared love for the parish priest and a shared belief in Jesus Christ.

Psalm 150 opens with an invitation to praise. *All* the earth and its creatures—in the sanctuary, in the firmament—are to use all means at their disposal to praise God's surpassing greatness. As our society becomes increasingly pluralistic, we can't allow petty differences to distract us from shared core beliefs. Whether we praise God with majestic hymns or lively choruses; whether we employ harp, lyre, flute, tambourine, or drums in our rituals, we join all voices lifted in praise to our Lord.

A Dio el Padre celestial, whenever we feel at odds with fellow believers, help us to focus on what draws us together, and then join in praise to you. Amen.

When Thomas Ken wrote the familiar words of the doxology for students at Winchester College, he warned the young scholars to use the verse only as part of private devotions in their dormitory rooms. Why all the secrecy? The year was 1674, a time when church leaders in England insisted that any hymn's lyrics come directly from scripture, preferably the Psalms. To create an original hymn suggested that the author had the audacity to amend the Bible, which was dangerously close to blasphemy.

Ken, an Anglican priest and prolific poet, audaciously wrote many hymns in his lifetime, but none is more revered than the closing lines of his long poem, "Awake, My Soul, and with the Sun." In his defense, he based the stanza loosely on Psalm 150, but church leaders in the seventeenth century had little tolerance for poetic license. Restricting the lines to private use by prep school students seemed the safer plan.

How ironic that such secrecy shrouded the hymn now known as the Doxology. Today even the most casual churchgoer can recite its lyrics from memory. It spans religions and denominations within religions. Embraced by Christians and Jews, it conveys a command that offends no one's beliefs: "Let everything that breathes praise the Lord." That message, simple and direct, serves as a unifying call for all believers, whether they gather in holy cathedrals, stately synagogues, storefront chapels, big box churches, revival tents, or underground cells. Regardless of our differences in ritual, governance, or scriptural interpretation, we are in harmony with the call to praise the one and only God who reigns over heaven and earth.

Praise God, from whom all blessings flow; praise him, all creatures here below; praise him above, ye heavenly host; praise Father, Son, and Holy Ghost. Amen.

Involvement in frontline ministry is exhausting, especially for those assigned to small congregations in out-of-the-way locations. Like members of the early church, these pastors may feel isolated from the religious and secular communities that surround them. They need encouragement, but peers may be in short supply. They want to get back in touch with "him who loves us and freed us from our sins by his blood." Too little time and too many responsibilities get in the way.

A few years ago, a group of Benedictine nuns at a monastery near Indianapolis felt such empathy for their ordained Protestant sisters that they designed a program that blended prayer, rest, exercise, learning, and friendship. They invited female clergy from across the country to spend several days as their guests on the Our Lady of Grace campus. Denominational differences disappeared as hosts and guests explored common beliefs and experienced different ways of expressing those beliefs. For the first time, the nuns celebrated Communion administered by a female; for the first time, the guests learned the power of silence in a worship service.

John's "apocalypse" appeals to imagination and emotion. It proclaims the sovereignty of Christ, "the faithful witness," who releases us from sin. In verse 1, the author reaches out and unifies the scattered churches in Asia with the gentle greeting, "Grace to you and peace from him." The Benedictine nuns reach out and unify a fragmented clergy with a program for wholeness. Both actions strengthened the church at large and fostered a much-needed bond of fellowship . . . and sisterhood. Both John's writing and the time apart at the Benedictine monastery call forth imagination and emotion from those who are freed from sin and united.

Blessed are those who build bridges and remove barriers in the name of the Lord.

We live in an "-er" world. Think about it. We dream of being rich-*er*, thinn-*er*, young-*er*, smart-*er*, happi-*er*, and healthi-*er*. We want to live long-*er* and achieve success fast-*er*. We welcome as heroes those persons who claim the ability to show us the way to a bett-*er* life. We buy their books; we attend their seminars; we visit their Web sites; and we await their miracles. When no miracles materialize, we lose interest and move on in search of the next hero who has products to sell and promises to offer.

As Jesus' ministry unfolded, his fame grew and his reputation preceded him wherever he traveled. "This is the Great One," whispered townspeople privy to his amazing deeds. "Here is the miracle worker who turned water into wine. This is the man who restored the sight of two blind men with a mere touch of his hand and called Lazarus from the dead!" By the time Jesus entered Jerusalem he was accorded a hero's welcome: "Clear a path for his entourage," the crowd shouted. "Cushion the road with your coats; distribute palm branches, and greet him with cheers and songs of praise. He's coming! Let the miracles begin."

The celebration—although short-lived—was well deserved. The Great One was among them, just as he is among us today. "'I am the Alpha and the Omega,' says the Lord God, who is and who was and who is to come, the Almighty." By comparison, all humans fall short. Jesus Christ, "the faithful witness," who releases us from sin and is exalted by God stands as the one hero worthy of our unending adoration and reverence. For that reason we continue to greet him with songs of praise and an understanding that even in this "-er" world, a full-*er*, rich-*er*, bett-*er* life is available to anyone who becomes a follow-*er* of the true source of wisdom and joy.

Lord, strengthen our power of discernment so we will recognize and embrace your son as the giver of eternal life. Amen.

For years my "bucket list" included enrolling in the Master Gardener Program supported by Purdue University in my home state of Indiana. Not until I paid my registration fee, bought the necessary tools, and attended my first meeting did I learn the depth of the curriculum.

This serious business involved much more than trading tips on where to plant perennials or how to eradicate beetles. To earn my "badge" as a Master Gardener, I would have to study the contents of a thick three-ring binder, agree to apply my new knowledge not just to my own backyard but also to a public green space, and abide by the group's mission statement. The wording of the latter surprised me. The statement didn't ask me to help others grow plants; instead, it asked me to "help others grow." The omission of the word *plants* implied more complex expectations.

I have often heard sermons that use gardening as a metaphor for propagating our faith. Evangelists plant the seeds of faith in persons who are unchurched; the local congregation nurtures those seeds; and society reaps the harvest when Christians mature to the point that they pass along the faith to others. This tradition is rooted in scripture. "As the Father has sent me, so I send you," explains Jesus to his disciples. He then invites them to "receive the Holy Spirit." This act—giving and receiving the Holy Spirit—empowers them to serve as God's representatives on earth. What an enormous responsibility!

As followers of Christ we study God's word and apply it in our everyday lives. But our responsibility doesn't stop there. When we receive the Holy Spirit, we assume an obligation to pass our faith on to others. We accept as our mission the charge "to help others grow."

Gracious God, may we continue to grow as Christians as we study your word and share our faith with others. Amen.

Is it possible to be a Christian by faith and a journalist by profession? As one who has taught media-writing to students at a Christian university for more than two decades, I've wrestled with that question. The words *Christian* and *journalist* seem at odds with each other. An oxymoron, perhaps. As educators, we train future journalists to be skeptical and to take little at face value. In the classroom we stress the importance of asking probing questions; we teach students to insist on corroboration from several sources before accepting information as the truth. We require them to study the work of diligent reporters whose skepticism has brought sins and misdeeds to light and who have earned prestigious prizes for the effort. And yet in our Christian education classes our message differs vastly. We instruct students to have faith, to trust, and to believe . . . even when tangible proof is unavailable.

Perhaps Thomas would have made a better journalist than a disciple. He insists on seeing and touching the evidence before he will concede that, yes, Jesus has risen and walks among them. He secures the proof he requires, along with a gentle lesson from the master teacher. That lesson seems especially valid for us more than two thousand years later: "Blessed are those who have not seen and yet have come to believe." Jesus doesn't call us to be naïve or gullible. He doesn't ask us to accept blindly the words and deeds of an imperfect being. Instead, he assures us that we can believe unequivocally in him and in the One who sent him, that we might "come to believe that Jesus is the Messiah, the Son of God."

Lord, help us to recognize the difference between that which is holy and that which is human. May we never doubt the Holy, that by believing in him we too will have eternal life. Amen.

Full Disclosure

APRIL 8–14, 2013 • JOHN F. C. DORNHEIM

SCRIPTURE OVERVIEW: Moments of disclosure can free us to go on with life. Such a disclosure came to the disciples after a long night of unsuccessful fishing. They hear a voice directing them to let down the nets on the right side. As they do so and find an enormous catch of fish, they wonder who has such insight about the waters. The beloved disciple voices the revelation, "It is the Lord!" Just so, the light that flashed on the Damascus road and the voice of identification constituted such a moment of disclosure for Paul. In reflection, the psalmist sings about such a moment for himself. These texts relate revelations of the divine mystery. The scene in Revelation puts it most clearly. The scroll that not only explains the final events of human history but sets them in motion is to be opened, but who is worthy to do it? "The Lion of the tribe of Judah, the Root of David."

QUESTIONS AND THOUGHTS FOR REFLECTION

- Read Acts 9:1-20. God's grace changed Paul's course of life. When has God transformed your attitudes or rerouted your direction?

- Read Psalm 30. When have you experienced God's comforting presence in your grief or despair?

- Read Revelation 5:11-14. We are created for God's glory. When and how do you make time for daily praise of God?

- Read John 21:1-19. Our love for Jesus motivates us to serve God. The more we listen to God, the clearer our mission becomes. Be silent, and ask Jesus to speak to you.

Ordained in the Evangelical Lutheran Church in America, currently serving as Protestant Campus Pastor on the C. W. Post campus of Long Island University

The day stretches out, full of promise like so many others before it. Nothing will deter Saul from his task. He is, after all, a professional, a professional persecutor, a man on a mission—no one is safe. Or so he thinks. However, he underestimates the God he serves.

Often religious fanatics, extremists, start out with the best intentions, but then they begin to believe that they can do better, that they know better. Sometimes they set out to build a better mousetrap.

Saul is in for a rude awakening. He has spent a great deal of time developing his vision of the work that God intends that he do. Saul is not the first to put his imprimatur on God's work; but in that post-Resurrection era, he may have been the most ruthless. Taking his cue from the Pharisees, he sought to be a Pharisee *par excellence*. Wrapped in the cloak of the law rather than being warmed by the gospel, he acknowledges the work to be done. The death of Jesus has not squelched the movement, and he finds himself determined to erase from the face of the earth all of Jesus' adherents who sought to keep the message alive. After all, God has called him to do this; it has become his all-consuming vision.

In order to correct that vision, God takes the drastic step of dimming Saul's sight, even to the point of blinding him for three days. That might not seem like a long time considering the number of years that Saul has persecuted Christians. At the right moment, God sends Ananias to Saul to help guide him to the Light. The eyes of Saul have been shut, but now those eyes will see God's purposes more clearly.

Think about a time in your life when your understanding of God's plan proved wrong. Whom did God send to assist you?

"Why is this happening to me? I've been good. Why would God let this happen?" On more than one occasion, as a hospital chaplain, I have heard these questions in conversation with a patient. "God," I would say, "does not always cure people of their ills, but God always heals."

Psalm 30 is a twofold psalm. On one hand, it is a psalm of lament. The poet has suffered terribly, even to the point of death, and believes that God has inexplicably allowed it to happen. After having been established like a rugged mountain, the psalmist feels that the foundation has crumbled. We don't know what happened to the poet except to say it was so bad that he (perhaps) not only succumbed but suffered the further indignation of being assigned to the Pit. Sheol. Hell. What could be worse than that for someone who fully believed that a life of greatness lay ahead? Yet, from the depths, the poet calls upon God for healing, and it is granted.

Hence the other hand. This is also a psalm of thanksgiving. God has heard the plea of the poet, has raises the poet from the Pit, and reestablished him. God removes the sackcloth; the poet wipes off the ashes and breaks into song and dance! "Weeping may linger for the night [down in the Pit], but joy comes with the morning [healing]." The experience of pure joy comes after the enduring of great sadness or despair. We bear in mind our total dependence upon God, as well as God's eternal presence. The poet writes as though he is on a roller coaster yet fully believes that in all of the twists and turns, the ups and downs, God has always been with him.

Remember a time when you (or a loved one) were on that same roller coaster. Did you feel abandoned, or was God next to you in the car? When you experienced God's healing presence, could you turn to joyous dancing?

W hen I was in college, work had begun on the new hymnal for my denomination. All the liturgy came from scripture, and congregations sang, "Worthy is Christ, the Lamb who was slain" to many tunes. Taken from these verses in Revelation, the liturgy seemed to burst forth in all its fullness.

I think that is John the Revelator's intention. He writes to a church that is undergoing tremendous persecution from the civil authorities. Many people find it a time of despair. In this book, John always refers to the crucified Christ as "the Lamb" and, in these short verses, he seeks to connect the Lamb to the One who sits upon the throne. These hymns of praise are normally directed to that one on the throne, God, the first person of the Trinity. But John now assigns this one to Jesus, the Lamb. It is as if he tells the persecuted, "Look, here is the Lamb that has been slain yet now reigns triumphantly in heaven. All is not lost. The persecution that you now endure will not last." His words remind us of those of the psalmist: "Weeping may linger for the night, but joy comes with the morning."

Most of us will not experience the travail that those of the early church endured. Yet, sometimes, it seems that we do. In those times, we need only look to the death, resurrection, and ascension of Jesus. As he overcame death and the grave, so shall we rise above those things that seek to defeat us.

But that is easier said than done. We see throughout this week's lessons the reality of persecution, despair, and eventual triumph. As the preacher once said, there is nothing new under the sun.

When you experience a difficult circumstance, how do you respond? How do you move past the despair and emerge triumphant?

---

*It might help to read the entire chapter to understand the context of these verses.

Trying to forget their woes, the disciples go night fishing. Perhaps they cannot concentrate even there on the sea. They work all night and catch nothing. Only when Jesus appears (although they do not recognize him) do they haul in 153 fish. Then, like Saul, their eyes are opened.

If you happen to be one of those people who take the scripture literally, what do you make of verse 14? Earlier in verse 11, the Gospel writer seems quite specific about the number of fish that the disciples haul in—153. I can't recall any speculation as to the accuracy of this number. Most folks wonder *Why 153** rather than wondering *Are you sure that it wasn't 152*?

But here, in verse 14, the Gospel writer mentions that this is the third appearance of the risen Christ to the disciples. Oh, really? I can understand a miscounting of the fish; that's a lot of fingers. But the third appearance? If you are keeping score, there are four appearances: to Mary, to the disciples *sans* Thomas, to the disciples *cum* Thomas, and now here on the beach.

How could John have been so accurate in verse 11 and not so here? Well, I think it is the old biblical numbers game. The frequency is less important than the risen Christ's appearances. Each appearance has its own gifts: of peace, of Spirit, of fish. All a bounty.

> *How do you recognize the appearance of the Lord? In whom do you see the appearance of the Lord? When have you exclaimed, "It is the Lord!"?*

---

*Some commentators suggest that 153 was the acknowledged number of nations in the world at that time.

If I had to pick one verse of scripture with which I resonate most closely, it would be this one. I wish it had been the text of the sermon preached at my ordination. I graduated from seminary quite confident of one thing: I would return home to Long Island and serve the church there where I would spend the rest of my life. I didn't. After my ordination, I went to south central Pennsylvania, then to Baltimore, before returning to Long Island some sixteen years later. I have heard it said that if you want to make God laugh, share your plans with God. This week's lessons highlight one big learning: *our* plans are not always God's.

The disciples all seemed eager to respond to Jesus' "follow me." Do they take time to mull it over? No. Do they really know what they are getting into? No. Do they even know where Jesus is going? No. Truly he puts some belts around their waists and off they go. Yet only at this point in the Gospel does Jesus utter these words.

I am often somewhat amused when I see a toddler at the end of a leash in a shopping mall. I am also upset, but that's not the point here. Sometimes, it appears as though the child is leading the parent to places that he or she had no intention of going. In these situations, the leashed is leading. In our passage, Jesus does the leading; the leashed are along for the ride. For the most part, the disciples seem fairly cool with that. There wasn't much digging in of their heels.

When has God led you in a direction that you did not intend to go? How trusting were you? Did you follow willingly?

On that dark night of Jesus' arrest, people ask Peter three times if he knows or associates with Jesus. Three times, Peter says no, and each time his heart must break a little more.

Jesus, always knowing what we need, gives Peter the same number of chances to heal the situation. But Peter, as usual, seems slow on the uptake. Jesus' questions sound redundant, and they are ones to which Jesus should already know the answers. Three times Jesus asks if Peter loves him. Three times Peter, exasperated, affirms what Jesus already knows. Three times Jesus requests a task* of him.

"Feed my lambs." The ones most vulnerable, Peter, come first. Whatever else you do, put my lambs first on your to-do list. The children, the marginalized, the downtrodden, the outcast need special protection.

"Tend my sheep." These sheep are maturing lambs who are learning to steady their legs and move about on their own. Their curiosity and eagerness to get out into the fold and find what is there marks them as ones who have begun to grow in the faith. With the right guidance, they will continue to go in the proper direction.

"Feed my sheep." These are the rams and the ewes who have matured; but to ensure their survival, their productivity, they will still need guidance, a watchful eye or two. Left to their own devices, they may wander off track.

All sheep need a shepherd. Sheep tend to keep their heads down, walking and nibbling at the grass with little concern as to direction. A faithful Shepherd makes sure that they do not nibble themselves away.

If you too love Jesus, how are you feeding his lambs? How are you tending and feeding his sheep?

---

*Interpretation of the author

Dan Berrigan, Jesuit priest, writer, and activist, has made many prophetic utterances. The one I recall is this: "If you are going to follow Jesus, you'd better look good on wood." I wonder if any of the disciples thought this would happen to them. Yet when Jesus invites them to follow him, they accept.

We often respond rather impetuously to the significant decisions that we are called to make. When it comes to the insignificant ones, we spend a lot of time hemming and hawing, weighing the pluses and minuses, committing then changing our minds and then recommitting. We give following Jesus—an invitation that comes to each of us—scarcely a thought. Of course, we want to follow Jesus. Who wouldn't?

Peter received several invitations. Shortly before his arrest, Jesus had that conversation with Peter, and Peter responded like he always did. But Jesus said, "You will, just not yet. Even after Peter denies him thrice, Jesus, on the beach that morning, extends the invitation one more time. Peter will follow, being led to places that he will not wish to go, to events yet unforeseen; but he will follow to the end. Even upside down, Peter will, indeed, look good on wood.

God seems a persistent old cuss—constantly sending invitations to which we RSVP, even though we never fully understand what we are getting into. We forget; we lose the directions; we get distracted. But throughout our lives, the invitation comes, awaiting a full response. Like Peter on that morning on the beach, we finally commit. We finally begin to follow fully.

The lambs hear the voice of the shepherd, and they respond. The lambs hear the voice of the Lamb upon the throne, and they respond. All in God's good time.

How often have you have been invited to follow? What led you to respond?

Goodness and Mercy

APRIL 15–21, 2013 • CHERYL SOMERS-INGERSOL

SCRIPTURE OVERVIEW: All four passages voice the providential care of a loving God, whose concern reaches out to needy folk. The widows in the Acts account are saintly but are also vulnerable in the broader society and subject to manipulation by ruthless scoundrels. Peter becomes an instrument of divine mercy for their leader, Dorcas. In the vision in Revelation, the great, diverse host of people "have come out of the great ordeal," but they now experience deliverance, shelter, and a way to the "springs of the water of life" (7:17). Both Psalm 23 and John 10 relate God's providential care. To be a part of the shepherd's flock means to be watched carefully so that no foe can snatch the sheep from the hands of the divine caretaker.

QUESTIONS AND THOUGHTS FOR REFLECTION

- Read Psalm 23. How does the Good Shepherd lead and guide you and provide for your needs?
- Read Acts 9:36-43. How has the presence and power of Christ dispelled the "shadow of death" in your life?
- Read John 10:22-30. How do other commitments or distractions interfere with your ability to see Jesus clearly or to hear his voice?
- Read Revelation 7:9-17. How does this vision of the new heaven and new earth encourage and empower you in your Christian life?

Spiritual Director, currently serving a United Methodist Church in the Kansas City area; leader of annual mission trips to Guatemala

When I was a child, Psalm 23 became a security blanket for me. I whispered the words in bed when I heard strange noises in the night. I repeated them as I walked home from school, taking a shortcut through the woods. I clung to them at age thirteen when the Navy chaplain came to our home to bring word that my father's plane had disappeared into the ocean.

"Yea, though I walk through the valley of the shadow of death, I will fear no evil: for thou art with me, thy rod and thy staff they comfort me" (KJV).

As a pastor, my first funeral was for a nine-year-old boy who died of leukemia. Instinctively I turned to Psalm 23 as the text for the homily. I've included it in every funeral since, often inviting the congregation to join in praying the words with me.

But Psalm 23 is not just about comfort in dark times. It is not just about the shadow of death. Ultimately it's about life and living—which is why I always require youth in the confirmation program to memorize it. Psalm 23 involves living life in the constant awareness of God's leading, presence, and provision. It invites our trusting God in green pastures and through dark valleys. Finally, we let God's promises of goodness and mercy dwell in us until we become confident that nothing can separate us from those promises and from God.

"Surely goodness and mercy shall follow me all the days of my life: and I will dwell in the house of the LORD for ever" (KJV). When and how has Psalm 23 been a security blanket for you? How has it reminded you of God's leading, presence, and provision? How has God's goodness and mercy "chased" after you (THE MESSAGE), bringing you safely home to God?

Shepherd us, O God, in green pastures and dark valleys, every day of our lives, always leading us home to you. Amen.

Commentators identify Psalm 23 as a prayer of trust. The psalmist recounts in vivid detail God's provision for his every need ("The LORD is my shepherd, I shall not want"). Yet how simple and basic are these provisions—green pastures, still waters, right paths, rod, staff, table, cup, oil. Yet note their power: they refresh, restore, comfort, bless, sustain. In a world of smart phones, iPads, HDTVs, and other manufactured "needs," do the psalmist's metaphors still relate? How can these simple, basic provisions be everything we need?

The power of the psalm's images is twofold. First the images evoke what Rabbi Abraham Heschel once noted was most missing in the twentieth century—our sense of "creatureliness." Despite our technological sophistication, we have the same basic needs for food, water, rest, and protection as all our fellow creatures. Second, as the images move from creation to table to temple, they remind us of deeper, more soulful needs. In the midst of our work in creation, we need rest and restoration, hospitality at table, and an assurance of God's goodness and mercy. We need to know there is a place for us in creation, at the table, in the temple. "He makes me lie down in green pastures; he leads me beside still waters. . . . You prepare a table before me in the presence of my enemies. . . . I shall dwell in the house of the LORD my whole life long."

How are you finding rest, restoration, and re-creation in the midst of creation? How have you experienced God's hospitality at the table? How have your deep, soulful needs been met in creation, at the table, in God's house?

Creator, Provider, Redeemer, you refresh, restore, comfort, bless, and sustain us. As your creatures, we ask that you help us to remember that you provide everything we need. Amen.

Nothing undermines our trust in God more than the reality of death. When we walk through the"valley of the shadow of death," we wonder if death does have the last word. This passage reflects the community's distress because one of their own, Tabitha, a disciple whose "life overflowed with good works and compassionate acts on behalf of those in need" (CEB), has become ill and died. The disciples send for Peter. When he arrives, the sounds and rituals of death fill the house: "They washed her body, . . . laid her in an upstairs room." Then they take Peter to the room and "all the widows stood beside him, crying as they showed the tunics and other clothing Dorcas made when she was alive"(CEB).

Into this death-shadowed reality, Peter, after sending everyone out of the room, kneels and prays. And through the name of the One who shares the same life-and-death-giving power as the Creator, Tabitha is restored to life. When the community sees Tabitha alive once more, it both restores and multiplies their trust. "The news spread throughout Joppa, and many put their faith in the Lord" (CEB).

Several things strike me about this story: first, Peter sends everyone out of the room. Jesus did this too in a similar situation (Mark 5:40). It seems as if the name, presence, and power of Jesus are incompatible with the overwhelming signs of death. Second, death cannot triumph over a life as overflowing with love and compassion as Tabitha's. This story, like the psalm, reassures us that even in the "valley of the shadow of death," God is with us. Death does not have the last word.

God of life and death, restore and multiply our trust in your power and love to triumph over all things, even death. Amen.

This Gospel reading takes us back to winter, to Hanukkah, the festival of Dedication. Jesus walks around the Temple during a time when his contemporaries are especially mindful not only of the liberation and restoration of the Temple under the Maccabees but also of kings and kingship. Perhaps that mindfulness prompts the question, "How long will you keep us in suspense? If you are the Messiah, tell us plainly."

Jesus replies that he has told them, and they did not believe. Therefore, he will not testify on his own behalf: "The works that I do in my Father's name testify to me."

Indeed Jesus has told them in figurative language, using a series of "I am" statements: water, wine, bread, light, shepherd, sheep, gate. The images reveal or conceal depending on the hearer's heart disposition. "I have told you, and you do not believe," Jesus said. We know *credo*, the Latin word for "believe," but its deeper meaning is "I give my heart to." Clearly Jesus' questioners have no predisposition to believe—to give their heart, to hear his voice, to follow him.

These verses prompt reflection in at least two ways. First, what is the disposition of your heart? Are you predisposed to belief in Jesus: to give your heart to him, to hear his voice, to follow him? Or do other commitments or loves interfere with your belief, your ability to see clearly who Jesus is? Second, Jesus says his works (healing, feeding, comforting, freeing) testify to his identity. How do our works testify to our identity as his followers? Do others "know we are Christians by our love"? In a world of information overload and cheap, meaningless words and promises, perhaps the saying often attributed to Saint Francis could be our motto: "Preach the Gospel at all times; when necessary, use words."

Lord Jesus, may we give our heart to you and embody our belief in our lives by following your way. Amen.

The themes of trust, belief, life, death, provision, protection, sheep, and shepherd continue. "My sheep hear my voice. I know them, and they follow me. I give them eternal life, and they will never perish. No one will snatch them out of my hand."

Oh, how we yearn to hear our name called, to know and be known, to trust that nothing can separate us from God! Pastors sometimes joke about the "Cheers" church, "where everybody knows your name and they're always glad you came." Our yearning for such a place resides deep in our souls and in our culture. We long for a safe place where we can be known completely—yet accepted, welcomed, and loved.

Jesus does know us—the good and the bad, the gracious and the petty, the lovely and the ugly, the hopes and the fears, the achievements and the failures—the whole truth of our being. He knows us completely and still promises us a relationship with him (and thereby with the Father) that is imperishable. Jesus assures us that when we believe (give our hearts to him), we will recognize his voice so we can follow. And as we believe and hear and follow, we enter into life in his name.

What is that safe place where you can know and be known, hear your name called, and relax in the arms of God? You may find it in a small group, in worship, on a retreat, in nature, during a time of prayer. As that old hymn goes: "Softly and tenderly Jesus is calling, calling for you and for me; see, on the portals he's waiting and watching, watching for you and for me. Come home, come home; you who are weary, come home; earnestly, tenderly, Jesus is calling, calling, O sinner, come home!" (*The United Methodist Hymnal*, #348)

Loving Shepherd, may we hear your voice and follow you home. Amen.

W e come full circle with this reading from the book of Revelation. In Psalm 23, the Lord is our shepherd who leads us
and supplies our every need. In the reading from John, Jesus is
our shepherd and the relationship between the shepherd and
the sheep is so close that we know each other's voice. We rest
safely in his hands. Now here in the Revelation to John, the
shepherd who knows us, who calls our names, who leads and
protects us, is also the Lamb. "The Lamb at the center of the
throne will be their shepherd."

Of course, the Lamb is Christ—"the Lamb of God who takes
away the sin of the world!" (John 1:29). Yet in light of the Resurrection, where Christ is made new and death is overturned,
the place of the lamb is also overturned, flipped. The sacrificial
lamb, usually viewed as vulnerable and helpless, is no longer.
The powerless victim has become the Victor. And the proper
response to such a paradox, such a wonder is this: "They fell on
their faces before the throne and worshiped God!"

When I read through Revelation, I am always struck by how
much of our hymnody, especially contemporary praise music,
comes from this book. Yet as uplifting and positive as the images
at first appear, a heaviness exists, a "shadow of death," still present. The white-robed, worshiping "sheep" have come through an
ordeal; "they have washed their robes and made them white in
the blood of the Lamb."

Again, like Psalm 23 and John 10, the writer's experience
of thoughtful and deep faith engenders a radical trust in God
amid all the uncertainty, challenges, and deathly realities of life.

*O Lamb who is also our Shepherd, guide us to the springs of
the water of life, where you will wipe away every tear from
our eyes. Amen.*

SUNDAY, APRIL 21 ～ *Read Revelation 7:9-17*

This text embodies not only a radical trust but also a radical hope. A great multitude, from every tribe and nation, gathers around the throne of God, robed in white with palm branches in their hands. When they cry out in a loud voice, the first word in their song is *salvation*—or "save us" or "hosanna." The scene reminds us of Palm Sunday, but the historical resonances go even deeper. People also used palm branches during the festival of Tabernacles when all of Israel was encouraged to journey to Jerusalem, where pilgrims put up makeshift huts (tabernacles) in remembrance of Israel's time in the wilderness when they had no home. This festival was celebrated at various times but became especially associated with the rededication of the Temple or the festival of Dedication (the setting of the Gospel lesson).

Now this scene in Revelation gathers up all these hopes and memories. Here, all nations and all people have come together before the Lamb and before the throne for a new dedication. Here they are reminded of their salvation, their new home, the new heaven and earth. Here they receive the promise that "they will hunger no more, and thirst no more; the sun will not strike them, nor any scorching heat." Instead, the Lamb at the center of the throne will be their shepherd. And this shepherd, like the Shepherd of Psalm 23, will guide them to the springs of the waters of life where God will wipe away every tear.

The longing for home, for provision, for protection, for salvation runs deep in our souls. So too do the promises and hope of our faith. In light of these promises and hope, may God grant us courage and wisdom in the living of our faith.

Save us and lead us, O God, from death into life. Amen.

All Things New

APRIL 22–28, 2013 • DERREK BELASE

SCRIPTURE OVERVIEW: The New Testament witnesses affirm the radically new era ushered in with the advent, death, and resurrection of Jesus Christ. It is a time of excitement and expectation. In the Gospel of John, perplexed disciples are instructed by Jesus before his departure; they are given "a new commandment." Peter learns about the new strategy in a dream. The contention between the old and the new sometimes reaches a fever pitch. The epistle lesson promises a time when the conflicts between old and new will have completely faded (Rev. 21:1-6). In the light of Easter and the anticipation of a new heaven and a new earth, Psalm 148 becomes a marvelous expression of praise to God. Voices from heaven and from earth; voices of angels, animals, and humans; voices of women and men, young and old join in a splendid harmony to the One who makes all things new (Rev. 21:5).

QUESTIONS AND THOUGHTS FOR REFLECTION

- Read Acts 11:1-18. When have you included someone whom others shunned? How did the "included" person react? How did others react?

- Read Psalm 148. The psalmist summons all creatures to praise. How might you join other creatures in offering a new act of praise to the Creator?

- Read Revelation 21:1-6. What images of the new Jerusalem do you have? What sources inform those images?

- Read John 13:31-35. How might you love others the way Christ loves you?

Pastor, Highland Park United Methodist Church, Stillwater, Oklahoma

MONDAY, APRIL 22 ~ *Read Psalm 148:7-14*

People in the United States will celebrate Earth Day today. Since 1970, it has been observed to inspire appreciation for and awareness of our natural environment. In today's reading from the Psalter, humans (verses 11-12) as well as nonhumans (verses 7-10) are called upon to praise God.

But how exactly do sea monsters or mountains or fruit trees praise God? Just like humans, they praise their Maker by living out God's intent for them in their creation. Trees do not praise God simply by offering humans shade in the summer. Trees praise God by producing beautiful leaves in the summer, which then turn red, yellow, and even brown as fall turns to winter before producing new leaves again in the spring. Trees remind us that the God we praise is a God who creates and recreates, time and time again.

A few years ago, I was riding on a public boat/taxi that took me and a group of seminarians to a remote village in the jungles of the Amazon rainforest. The rainstorm that cooled us during the evening boat ride and the pink dolphins that greeted us by jumping in and out of the water the next morning were praising God by doing what they had been created to do.

We praise God not by using others, whether humans or nonhumans, to our own advantage but by allowing them to exist for their created, intended, and unique purpose. Do we treat trees, mountains, and sea creatures as objects to use or as subjects that remind us of the creative artistry of God? You can celebrate Earth Day wherever you are this day by simply appreciating the many ways all of God's creatures praise God.

Creator God, along with all your other created beings, we praise you this day. Amen.

Though it has been almost a month since we celebrated the resurrection of Christ, you may still be able to hear the sounds of that glorious morning. Maybe you can still see your sanctuary so beautifully decorated with Easter lilies. Your olfactory senses may even be able to muster up the smell of the morning as you traveled to a sunrise service.

Most of us have put out of our minds the sights and sounds of Holy Week; we certainly do not want to remember the images of Good Friday. However, when I read the first few verses of Psalm 148, my mind wanders back to that fateful day when the whole earth testified that an important event was taking place.

Luke reminds us that "darkness came over the whole land" (Luke 23:44), lasting from noon to three in the afternoon, and that the "sun's light failed" (Luke 23:45). The curtain in the Temple was torn in two (Luke 23:45); and at the foot of the cross, an official of the Roman government declared, "Truly this man was God's son" (Mark 15:39). It is as if every single thing in the entire universe gave witness to the gruesome nature of the events on a hill outside Jerusalem.

This psalm opens with a series of commands about who is to praise the Lord. The list begins with a variety of celestial beings including angels, the sun, the moon, a host of heavenly beings, and stars just to name a few. How do these praise the Lord? The drama of Holy Week bears witness as to how each testifies to God's work in the world.

The praise expressed by these celestial beings signifies more than spiritual commotion; all created beings direct their praise toward the one who created the heavens and the earth. Like them, what else can we do but testify and praise?

God, may the sun, moon and stars remind us to praise you. Amen.

Table fellowship is an important element in the life of any community. Beyond gathering around the Lord's Table on the first Sunday of each month, our church hosts a monthly fellowship luncheon and a yearly neighborhood ice cream social. Gathering around a meal can bind us together.

Acts 11 gives us a brief glimpse into the importance of table fellowship in the life of the early Christian community. Because of the various food and dietary restrictions, Jews and Gentiles rarely dined together. One day Peter, the faithful Jew, has a vision in which a voice declares that all food is clean. Shortly thereafter, he accompanies three Gentile men to Caesarea and enters the house of Cornelius. Acts 10 narrates both sides of the story, in which Cornelius has a similar vision.

Why does this matter? Cornelius, as an uncircumcised Gentile, ate nonkosher food; Jews considered Gentiles unclean. Yet, Peter proclaims to the household a message he received from God, "Do not call anything impure that God has made clean" (NIV).

Oftentimes in life, we vacillate between clean and unclean. We feel sure about who is "in" and who is "out." We clearly know, maybe even better than God, who deserves to be a part of our ministry or a member of our church. We spend so much time and energy drawing lines to keep others out that we cannot hear God saying to us, "Do not call anything impure that [I have] made clean."

Like Peter, we have opportunities to sit down and fellowship with others—believers and nonbelievers. Over the table, we might just find that we have more in common than what separates us. Jesus taught us to love and cherish our neighbors as much as we do ourselves. Peter exemplifies this when he sat down to eat with Cornelius.

O God, you alone are the one who declares what is clean and unclean. Amen.

Who was I that I could hinder God?" Peter asks during the culmination of his speech in Jerusalem. It seems like an obvious question. Who among us has the right or authority to hinder the work of God?

Peter makes this statement in regard to his religious experience. Often, we, like the circumcised believers in Jerusalem, quickly dismiss someone's experience if it does not line up with ours. And if another's experience falls outside our interpretation of scripture, then we surely cannot understand it.

While I believe that scripture is chief among the ways God chooses to reveal God's self to us, it is certainly not the only way. In United Methodist circles, we often talk about the Wesleyan Quadrilateral, a theological method that places tradition, reason, and experience alongside scripture as ways to interpret the word of God in our world today.

We lose the richness of God's activity when we limit our understanding of it to scripture alone. In fact, we cannot really understand the Acts of the Apostles until we can come to grips with experience. This is a book full of experiences!

Most of us interpret the scriptures based on our experiences. We spend time in Bible studies, but often we sense God at work in life around us. The ordinary experiences of life provide the most fertile ground for seeing the words of scripture sprouting to life before us.

Peter's experience leaves no doubt in the minds of his hearers that God's Spirit has worked in an amazing way in the Gentile population. The Spirit is free and frees, working always for the good of those for whom Christ died. What might the Spirit have in mind for us? Rather than doubt or question the validity of others' experiences, we might first ask, "Who am I that I could hinder God?"

Lord, may we never hinder your Spirit. Amen.

Tears are our first language." When my friend and colleague, Tish Malloy, spoke those words, they immediately transported me to the small room where my daughter was born. I can remember holding Madison in my arms just after her birth and kissing away her tears—her first expression to us, her parents.

A tear is simply a small droplet of salty discharge emanating from our eyes, right? While that is scientifically correct, we all know that some tears come from a deeper source. "It's cancer," the doctor says. "Your son has been killed in a car wreck," the police officer states during the official notification. "It's so good to see you," says your spouse after a particularly bad day at work. Tears shed in situations like these come from the heart.

The writer of Revelation tells us of a time when death, mourning, crying, and pain will be no more. All "first things" have passed. God in Jesus Christ makes all things new: "a new heaven and a new earth"—the entire cosmos recreated. And perhaps most stunningly, God will live among mortals. In the new Jerusalem, God will wipe the tears from our eyes. Sometimes good news seems hard to find in Revelation; but this is good news, and we long for these future tearless days. But what about present tearful days?

Every day, we encounter people who are shedding tears. Maybe we cannot see visible tears, but we know these people are hurting. We have the opportunity to wipe those tears from their eyes by offering a shoulder on which to cry, writing an encouraging note, or being a listening presence.

As long as we are on this side of the new Jerusalem, tears remain an ever-present reality. Who will wipe them away? You will do it for me, and I will do it for you.

Dear God, when we see a tear on the face of another, give us the courage to wipe it away and offer a word of hope. Amen.

My grandmother and I sat in the dining room eating pizza while my dad, on the other side of the wall, was slipping away from this life to the next as cancer devoured the remainder of his once healthy, vibrant body. "No parent should have to bury their child," she said, with tears streaming down her face.

In less than a week, my grandmother was doing exactly that. Though my dad was forty years old, in her eyes he was still the little boy she had reared into a fine husband, father, and business owner. I did not fully understand her statement until I had a child myself, and now I understand it more than I want to.

When my dad died, we mourned together; but as we stood at his grave, calm seemed to prevail. A calm that had not been present for the eleven weeks of pain, agony, and suffering brought on by pancreatic cancer. The pastor pronounced these words, "I am making all things new. . . . Write this down, for these words are trustworthy and true."

Therein lay the hope. My father had moved beyond the pain of cancer. We could move past our grief. Even in death, God reigned victorious. While my grandmother and I stood at his grave side, my father was drinking from the spring of the water of life. He now resided in a place where death, mourning, crying, and pain were no longer. He had been made new.

My experience is not unique. It is repeated day after day in hospitals, funeral homes, and cemeteries. Parents lose a child. A child loses a parent. Mourners wonder if life can go on. We hear the good news that the Alpha and Omega is in charge. As the old saying goes, "We may not know what the future holds, but we know who holds the future." That is enough for me.

We thank you, loving God, that mourning and grief are temporary, but that your love for us is forever. Amen.

Today's reading takes us back to a pre-Crucifixion moment when Jesus shows the depth of his love for the disciples by washing their dirty feet and offering them a new commandment: they are to love one another. Really? Are we to assume that loving others is a new commandment?

As far back as the levitical code (Lev. 19:18), scripture commanded faithful Jews to refrain from grudges and to love their neighbor. So how is Jesus offering a *new* commandment? Why does Jesus use this very personal and crucial moment to reiterate a centuries-old commandment? Loving others had always been the minimum requirement. Now we discover that Jesus expects his disciples to love others *as he loved them*. He takes this loving to a new level. Jesus offers us his entire life and calls us to offer ourselves in a similar manner.

On either side of these four verses, denial and betrayal rear their ugly heads. Though he has just supped with those who have been closest to him during his entire ministry, Jesus predicts that Judas will betray him and Peter will deny knowing him. Yet, Jesus still loves them.

In that context, this love lesson becomes more evident. If Jesus can love these close friends after they turn their backs on him, can we not love when people hurt us? If Jesus willingly shared this last meal with two friends who will soon disappoint him in a callous way, can we not love those who disappoint us?

I find that when others love me, I can love them back quite easily. I have more trouble loving when love is a one-way relationship. Jesus knew this concept would present a problem for us, so in another important message, he reminds us that even sinners love those who love them (Luke 6:32-33). The bottom line is this: we are to love regardless of the circumstances.

Lord, help us love others as you have loved us. Amen.

Reflections on Home

APRIL 29–MAY 5, 2013 • DOREEN M. MCFARLANE

SCRIPTURE OVERVIEW: The heart of the gospel is that God loved the world, and the Easter proclamation is that Jesus Christ died and rose for the sins of the world. The texts warn us against the persistent temptation to make our God too small. In Acts, Paul takes the gospel to Macedonia, which fulfills Jesus' commission to the disciples "that repentance and forgiveness of sins . . . be proclaimed in his name to all nations." Psalm 67 also reminds us of the wideness of God's mercy. Revelation states that the immediacy of God's presence will be recognized by "the kings of the earth." In John 5 the unsolicited and undeserved healing expresses the "unprovoked grace" that flows from God's limitless love for the world and all its people.

QUESTIONS AND THOUGHTS FOR REFLECTION

- Read Psalm 67. Do you often think of yourself or your nation as particularly blessed? What about other nations? Do you pray for nations and people other than your own?

- Read John 14:23-29. How would your behavior differ if you took seriously the thought of God living and making a home in you?

- Read Acts 16:9-15. How do you exhibit your faithfulness to God? When has God "opened [your] heart to listen eagerly"?

- Read Revelation 21:10, 22–22:5. What aspects of the world you live in would you like to see changed? How might the light of God's love in you begin in some small way to bring about these changes?

Pastor, university and seminary professor, most recently serving the church as a "critical presence" in China; now living in Canada

Psalms are the texts for music sung in the ancient Temple in Jerusalem, music that has been lost in antiquity. Still, the words echo into our very souls to this day. We continue to be amazed at how often psalms address our modern issues. Psalm 67 sets a good example with its back-and-forth motion. This psalm leads us out from our inward focus, into the world, and then back. We can sing or pray this psalm. We might recite it alone or in worship. Psalm 67 is a "home and away" psalm. It begins with a "text within a text," the familiar words of Numbers 6:24-26 that declare God's blessing on Israel.

Then the psalm shifts away from Israel to other nations. Israel is chosen, but to be chosen always entails a task. God has made a home in Israel and blessed it so that, in turn, Israel may show to the world the wonders of what God can do. The psalm envisions all nations as happy and being judged fairly by God who cares for all creation. The concluding verses joyfully direct us back home, as the people thank God for a good harvest. They ask God to continue to bless them so they may bring the whole world to know this wonderful God.

In our times, we easily think of everything that is going wrong and forget the bounty of our lives. In our time, many people wonder about their purpose in life. It is good to realize that when we live out our faith to the best of our ability, we are fulfilling our purpose.

Great God, all creation is yours and everything in it. May all of the world find not only peace but also joy in living. May I do my part in living in your ways. Amen.

Ivalue traveling and have spent a good deal of my life in doing so. I enjoy the excitement and the change of seeing new places and meeting new people. Still, I am always amazed and surprised by how incredibly good it feels every time I return home. Isn't it interesting that, though we may visit other people's homes, no matter how big and beautiful these places may be, it's only our own home, however humble, that gives us that warm feeling inside? No matter how long we're gone, that feeling of returning home never seems to fail us.

In today's passage, Judas (not Iscariot) asks Jesus why he's not revealing his true identity to the world. We might expect that Jesus would respond by saying something like, "I am not telling them who I am because. . . ." But Jesus doesn't answer Judas directly. Rather, he chooses to talk about the meaning of his love and self-revelation, as well as "home." He says to Judas, "Those who love me will keep my word, and my Father will love them, and we will come to them and make our home with them." Home is so much more than a building; it's where we're understood and where our mistakes are forgiven, all because love is there.

We seldom try to share our hopes and dreams with people who will never understand us or be at home with us. All we can do is wish them well and go on. But when love happens, understanding surely follows; that's how we know we are home with others. Knowing that God is in us can direct us to understanding. Then, in turn, the love that we have from God can begin to teach us to make a home for others.

O Holy One, come. Make your home in me! Help me experience you as my true home, no matter where I live and act in the world. Amen.

I've always admired widows and widowers because they seem to have found the strength to go on over the years without their loved one. How do they do it? I think this passage offers a clue. The time has come too soon when Jesus will leave the disciples and go on to his death. Still, he promises that upon his leaving, "the Advocate" will come. They cannot receive this gift until he is gone from them.

We use many translations for this word *Advocate*: Holy Spirit, Helper, someone who is on our side, or God in action in community. Having that Advocate with us means we will never again need to feel completely alone. God will always be present in some way with us.

Jesus also promises the disciples something more—a peace that nothing else in the world can give! This peace gives us the strength to go on through any adversity. Jesus admonishes the disciples not to be afraid even though he is going to have to go away. While he is yet with them, his words prepare them for his coming suffering and death.

There are events in human life that nothing can really prepare us for, such as the loss of a loved one. Yet, in these most trying of times, Jesus promises two gifts in full measure, the same gifts that he gave the disciples: the presence of the Holy Spirit and the peace of Christ. The Spirit's presence means we are no longer alone. God walks with us. The peace of Christ offers us strength and the courage to go on.

O Holy Spirit, Advocate, during good times and bad, help us to know you are truly with us. And, along with your presence, lead us to know we also have your peace that passes all understanding. Amen.

Ionce met a man people called a dreamer. He always had new ideas and moved to try them out. Most of them didn't amount to anything substantial. But one day, while he was still quite young, he got the idea that he would raise money and build a school of the arts in the middle of the glorious mountain range not far from his home. Ten years later, that school existed as a summer school. Twenty years went by, and it had become a full campus, offering every aspect of the arts. People traveled from the area but also from long distances to enjoy the art and music. Now, after over fifty years, that school remains a year-round international center for the arts.

In the night, Paul receives a vision of need in Macedonia. He decides this vision actually comes from God, so without hesitation he acts on it. Paul sets sail to that place. As it turns out, his work in Macedonia contributed greatly to the building up of the early church and to the spread of Christianity.

Do we often have meaningless dreams? Of course we do. Still, at times our dreams or daydreams deeply move us. Do we act on them and hurry forward to make a change in the world, or are we more likely to push them aside as unrealistic?

We can be like the dreamer I mentioned. He let go of many of his dreams due to their impracticality. But one dream commanded his action. Even though others doubted, his compelling call took fear away and moved him forward with energy and courage. When we're willing to move out of our comfortable space to work for good, our dreams can lead to miracles.

O Great One, when we sense that our dreams are your dreams, give us the courage to act on them. Amen.

FRIDAY, MAY 3 ~ *Read Acts 16:13-15*

Paul and his followers spent a good deal of time away from home. They felt called to teach everyone willing to listen about Jesus Christ. Still, they must have often longed to be back at their own tables and in their own beds.

At one point in Paul's travels, he and those with him meet a woman named Lydia. She listens with her whole heart to Paul's teachings and extends a sincere invitation to come and stay at her home. They accept. Lydia, a successful businesswoman, evidences humility because she suggests that they come to her home *only* if they judge her faithful to the Lord.

Lydia, while good at business, seems to long for something more: to come closer to God and to be found faithful. The Lord opens "her heart to listen eagerly," and Paul baptizes her and her household. Lydia then invites Paul and his companions to her home; she extends an invitation into her life. At her home, they can talk, pray, and share the love of God. Some scholars have suggested that Lydia's home may have become one of the first "house churches" of the budding new faith, Christianity. She may have become a leader in the early church.

In our day, we carefully choose whom we invite into our homes and lives. Yet if we listen with eager hearts, we may be ready to receive those from whom we know we can learn good things and with whom we can share life's meaning. Let's be thankful for people who come into our lives and enhance them rather than taking the opportunity for granted. Good friends are God's gift. In turn, we can try to be this kind of gift for others.

O Christ, grant me humility and discernment to welcome you into my life and my home gladly. With deep thanks for the friends you have sent me, I ask that I may also be a good friend to others. Amen.

I once had a professor who was known to say on occasion, "Dear students, that was not what I meant to say. Please push the delete button." It was a joke—computer-age humor. Sometimes in life we wish we could push a button and make our mistakes and hurtful words go away. We can't do that, of course. When things aren't going well, sometimes it's good to relax and allow ourselves to think about something beautiful. Have you ever had a dream so good that you hated to wake up?

Here, in Revelation, the author writes about a magnificent dream. The new Jerusalem vision brings to mind images of peace and God's glory. Yes, our world is filled with suffering; we live in a troubled world. But we can approach our worldly tasks with new eyes once our mind's eye has had a chance to stop a while, reset, and focus for a time on the ideal.

Such is Revelation's dream of the perfect home, the world the way God would have it. The new Jerusalem offers ultimate security: the city has no gates, and night never comes. The nations and their leaders dwell in peace. The crystal waters flow, and fruit abounds.

Earlier this week we read about Paul's vision and his acting on it. How might we act on a vision like the one portrayed in these verses? How can we bring security and light to others' lives? How might we relate to others out of a sense of bounty rather than scarcity? What will heal our relationships?

The new Jerusalem dream cannot focus on our denial of reality. But such a vision gives respite, a chance to push the delete button for a while and, after rest and renewal, find the strength to go on.

O God, may we never lose sight of the dream of beauty that is still possible here on earth. We know that whatever happens, you always hold this world in your loving embrace. Amen.

Sam had worked a bit late. He got off the bus at the end of the line near where he lived and walked home in the dark. It was his birthday, but it seemed no one had remembered. He was feeling kind of sad inside and wanted to get out of the chilly night air. He fumbled with the key and unlocked the door. That's when the lights suddenly came on. "Surprise!" Smiling friends filled his kitchen. They'd come to give him a party. His sister, to whom he'd given a house key, had let them in. Sam's feelings turned to joy!

Did you ever open the door to your house at night and enter the room into complete darkness? When you turn on the lights, even though you may have been alone, I would guess that you felt your heart warmed by the light and, even more, by the familiar sights of home. If darkness had frightened you in any way on the outside, you now felt you were safe.

For millions in this world, even home is not a truly safe place. Today's passage assures us that the "world to come" in some future time will be a home that needs no light from sun or moon because God will be its light—our light and our home. Light as we know it is surely but total darkness in comparison to the light of seeing God. Even in our current state of veiled vision, we can serve as conduits for God's light, enabling others to walk more safely in the world until, together, we see God face to face.

O Light of the World, whenever darkness comes, help us release our fear and open our hearts to the truth that you are our light. Now and always, shine in our hearts. Amen.

Worshiping Together

MAY 6–12, 2013 • NICOLA VIDAMOUR

SCRIPTURE OVERVIEW: The continuation of the church when Jesus is no longer present is an acute issue. This fearful, waiting community, which is anxious and bewildered, has no power of its own. And yet, oddly, power is given that causes this fragile little community to have energy, courage, imagination, and resources completely disproportionate to its size. How can one speak about this changed situation that can only be attributed to the inscrutable generosity of God? The psalm for the week breaks out beyond reasoned explanation into wonder, awe, amazement, and gratitude. God's new rule is beyond our logic. We only see its effect in a transformed community. That community is uncertain what has happened but is sure enough to affirm its identity and embrace its proper work.

QUESTIONS AND THOUGHTS FOR REFLECTION

- Read Acts 16:16-34. Which hymns or songs would you sing if you were in prison? How does your faith liberate you?

- Read Psalm 97. What signs of the glory of God and the joy of the Lord do you see in your local area?

- Read John 17:20-26. What prevents you from experiencing the oneness that Jesus talks about in this passage?

- Read Luke 24:44-53. In what ways do you pass on to others the blessings that you have received from God? What or whom do you want to bless God for today?

- Read Revelation 22:12-14, 16-17, 20-21. How is God's grace transforming your faith community from a community of sinners into a communion of saints?

Methodist minister in London, England; editor of *Mesto Vstrechi*, the Russian edition of *The Upper Room*

The Methodist Church in Britain has recently produced a new hymnal called *Singing the Faith*. Charles Wesley, one of the two brothers who started the Methodist movement, was a prolific hymn writer; and Methodists have been well-known from their earliest days for the way in which they sing the faith.

Paul and Silas also sang their faith—even in the middle of the night while locked in prison after receiving a severe flogging. Despite their pain and suffering they still burst into song, offering praise and prayer to God.

It is believed that John Newton, the former slave trader, set the words of his famous hymn "Amazing Grace" to a tune he heard the slaves singing in the galley of a ship. African spirituals give powerful witness to the way in which black Christians have sung their faith in the midst of oppression and injustice.

Paul and Silas are imprisoned because they released a young slave girl from the spirit that possessed her, thus depriving her owners of the money she provided for them. This girl described her emancipators as "slaves of the Most High God." Paul and Silas are indeed bound and held captivate by God as well as by their prison chains; but their singing makes it overwhelmingly clear that their faith gives them a deep sense of freedom.

We sometimes talk about singing that "raises the roof" because of its volume and enthusiasm. When Paul and Silas sing "there was an earthquake so violent that the foundations of the prison were shaken; and immediately all the doors were opened and everyone's chains were unfastened." Paul and Silas—and all those who heard them singing their faith—are literally set free. Singing the faith is liberating!

God of freedom, help us to sing our faith until the walls of oppression come tumbling down. Amen.

The Psalms remind us that it is not only people who sing praise to God. In Psalm 97 the earth rejoices and "the heavens proclaim his righteousness." Psalm 148 expands this idea to show how the whole of creation gives glory to God. The very first verse of Psalm 97 announces the reason for this: "The LORD is king!"

Several years ago, Prime Minister Vladimir Putin visited the Russian city of Pskov, where I used to live. Before his visit, the city workers laid new turf and planted colorful plants in all the flower beds. After his visit, the city council workers removed all the beautiful plants and greenery, leaving the streets as grey and bare as they had been before!

I now live in one of the most deprived areas of London, England. There is a park just across the street from my home—but most of the local landscape is full of buildings and buses. One of our retired ministers commented at a recent lay preachers' meeting that most of the images we use in worship to portray the beauty of creation and the glory of God are quite rural. "We need to find images that enable people to see the beauty and glory of God here in the inner-city," he said.

Psalm 97 talks about the coast lands and the mountains. I find it easy to worship God when I stand by the ocean or lift up my eyes to the hills. However, Psalm 97 also talks about Zion, the holy city of Jerusalem. God's light dawns in the city as well as the country. The city itself is glad, and joy comes to her upright inhabitants. I am learning to worship God in the bustle and noise of the city.

Sing to the Lord, you cities of the world. Praise God, tower-blocks and corner shops, crowded trains and busy streets. Amen.

WEDNESDAY, MAY 8 ~ *Read John 17:20-26*

The pronouns we choose to use in worship are significant. Here in Britain, *The Methodist Worship Book* offers a choice for the assurance of forgiveness and the final blessing. The minister can either say *"your* sins are forgiven" or *"our* sins are forgiven"—and can pronounce the blessing of God on *you* or on *us.* Preachers also vary as to whether they include themselves in the instructions they give in their sermons. Some pastors speak about what *you* must do when they address their congregations. Others talk about what *we* must do.

This Gospel passage has a strong "them and us" feel to it. "There's you and me," says Jesus to his father, "and then there's them. And I want them to be like us!" This is part of Jesus' prayer for his disciples just before his arrest. He is about to be separated from them and prays that they might be one. However, Judas has already broken away from the "us" (John 13:30) and later that night Peter will deny three times that he is one of "them" (John 18:17, 25-27).

One faith community may comprise many "them and us" groupings. It sometimes seems that we will never achieve the oneness for which Christ prayed. Our divisions offer a poor witness to God's all-embracing love.

In this passage Jesus expresses his desire to share with us the unifying love that he and his Father enjoy. He no longer wants there to be a "them and us" but a single community where we can all pray together as Jesus taught us: "Our Father in heaven. . . . Give us this day our daily bread. . . . And do not bring us to the time of trial, but rescue us from the evil one" (Matt. 6:9, 11, 13).

Father, may we all be one so that the world may know your name, live in your love, and see your glory. Amen.

THURSDAY, MAY 9 ~ *Read Luke 24:44-53*

ASCENSION DAY

I once stayed in a home that had a sign hanging by the door: "All our guests bring us joy—some when they arrive and others when they leave!" Jesus ascends into heaven "while he was blessing them." Jesus brought his disciples great blessing while he was with them—and he is still blessing them as he leaves. How many of us will depart this earth with words of blessing on our lips? We strive to bring blessing to others in our daily lives, but will we still be doing so at the end of our life? What will our final words be?

None of us knows exactly when our time on earth will come to an end, so we need to live each day as if it were our last. We need to say to people today those words of blessing and encouragement that we want them to hear before we die.

Abraham was blessed to be a blessing (Gen. 12:2), and the disciples respond to the blessing they receive from their ascending Lord by being "continually in the temple blessing God." Having been blessed by God, they spend all their time blessing God. The second volume of Luke's Gospel—the Acts of the Apostles—reveals how the followers of Jesus do indeed bring blessing to others as they continue the mission and ministry that Christ had begun.

Now it is our turn to take up the baton and pass on to others the blessings that we have received. Many people in the world feel that they have been dismissed as worthless and insignificant. What we say to persons today can enable them to rise up with wings like eagles (Isa. 40:31) and lift up their heart with words of praise to God.

Uplifting God, may all our words today be words of blessing and love. Amen.

FRIDAY, MAY 10 ~ *Read Revelation 22:12-14*

I once saw a cartoon featuring a pair of disgruntled zebras who were waiting to board Noah's ark and had just been told that boarding would take place alphabetically! Most of us would probably prefer to be at the front of a line, rather than at the back—but Revelation 22:13 suggests that Christ is in both places: "I am the Alpha and the Omega, the first and the last, the beginning and the end."

However, this verse is not actually about *where* Christ is so much as *who* Christ is. This is one of the "I am" sayings of the Bible—the most well-known of which appear in John's Gospel (6:35; 8:12; 10:9; 10:11; 11:25; 14:6; 15:1) and in Moses' encounter with God at the burning bush (Exodus 3).

Christ is not just present at the starting line and at the finish. Christ actually is the source and the consummation of our life.

This revelation of who Christ is also helps us to understand who we are—and what the purpose of our life is. It doesn't actually matter very much where we feel we are in the line for heaven. What matters is the knowledge that it is God who brought us to birth and God in whom our life will find its completion.

God is eternal—not simply the beginning and the end. God has no beginning and no end. God is. God requires only the present tense because what God has been, God always will be. Nevertheless, at times God acts in history in particular ways—and this final chapter of the Bible combines a proclamation of the unchanging being of God with a repeated announcement that "I am coming soon."

Eternal God, my life is nothing without you. You are my beginning and my end. Amen.

My earliest memories of going to church include the words "Come, for all is now ready" being said as an invitation to receive Holy Communion. These words come from the parable of the dinner party in Luke's Gospel (14:17) but are also echoed in today's reading from Revelation: "The Spirit and the bride say, 'Come.' And let everyone who hears say, 'Come.' And let everyone who is thirsty come. Let anyone who wishes take the water of life as a gift."

Having established that Christ is not only the source and the seed of David but also the dawn of a new day, the writer says that all is indeed ready for the feast of eternal life to begin. The invitation to "come" is issued by Christ himself, by the Spirit, by the bride (the church), and by everyone who hears. Having such an inclusive list of inviters is likely to make the guest list more inclusive too.

Sometimes the question "who is doing the inviting?" has to be asked when positions in the church and membership of conferences and committees are being decided. This is because the inviter has more power than he or she might be aware of and may consciously or subconsciously exclude certain people. The invitation in Revelation can be issued by anyone who has heard it—and everyone is welcome to respond.

Another important aspect of this invitation is that the water of life is offered "as a gift"; the only requirement made of the guests is thirst. There is something incredibly simple and open about the invitation that Isaiah voices: "Ho, everyone who thirsts, come to the waters" (55:1). How does this compare with the invitations that your faith community issues?

Lord, thank you for inviting us to your table. Show us whom we are excluding from ours. Amen.

Do you consider yourself to be a saint? I like the way the apostle Paul addresses his letters to the saints in the various communities to which he writes. The final verse of the last book in the Bible also refers to "the saints."

Nowadays, we tend to think of "the saints" as those people who have been canonized and given the title "Saint" with a capital *S*. However, the New Testament makes it clear that "the saints" are ordinary Christian people—all those who strive to be holy and to follow the way of Christ.

One Saturday evening—the night before I was due to be preaching in a church where I had never been before—one of my colleagues gave me the following advice: "Offer them heaven." What he meant by those words was this: "Don't tell them that they are sinners and that they are going to hell. Tell them that, through God's grace, the doors of heaven are open to them."

Saints are also sinners—but they are sinners who have allowed the grace of God to transform their lives. The first book of the Bible explains how we became sinners. The last book of the Bible assures us that we are saints.

The grace of God turns sinners into saints. So if you are looking for a simple sentence with which to pray for those with whom you will worship this Sunday, then turn to the concluding words of Revelation: "The grace of the Lord Jesus be with all the saints. Amen."

How has God's grace turned you from a sinner into a saint? How is God's grace transforming your faith community from a community of sinners into a communion of saints?

"The grace of the Lord Jesus be with all the saints. Amen."

Come, Holy Spirit

MAY 13–19, 2013 • MARY LOU REDDING

SCRIPTURE OVERVIEW: The very nature of the Spirit defies our attempts to explain or control. In the account of the Day of Pentecost in Acts 2, the Holy Spirit gives new life to a dispirited band of disciples. The church is born. Birth imagery is present too in Romans 8 where "all who are led by the Spirit of God are children of God." In John, the Spirit or Advocate's presence will continue to make life possible for the disciples in the absence of Jesus' physical presence. In Psalm 104 the Spirit of God is responsible for the origin and sustenance of all creation. The life-giving power and presence of the Spirit is a gift—unsolicited, unexpected, undeserved. But life in the Spirit is life as God intends, to know a peace that the world cannot give.

QUESTIONS AND THOUGHTS FOR REFLECTION

• Read Acts 2:1-21. Where have I experienced the power of the Holy Spirit, and where do I want to experience it more?

• Read Psalm 104:24-34, 35*b*. What evidence do I see of God's continued loving involvement with Creation? How am I called to be part of that?

• Read Romans 8:14-17. By what means does the Holy Spirit lead me?

• Read John 14:8-17, 25-27. How is "Spirit of truth" an accurate name for the work of the Holy Spirit in my life?

Former Editorial Director of T*he Upper Room* magazine, has written numerous small-group studies, including *The Lord's Prayer: Jesus Teaches Us to Pray*; lives and writes in Brentwood, Tennessee, with her spoiled and aging miniature poodle, Annabelle, at her side

"Come, Holy Spirit. Fill the hearts of your faithful. . . . "

For over a decade, I have met weekly with several other women in a discipleship group. Each Thursday we begin by praying the "Prayer to the Holy Spirit"* that I quote from above. After all these years, bidding the Spirit to come into my heart feels quite natural. But apparently praying in this way is not common.

Several years ago when leading a workshop on discovering spiritual gifts, I opened with a prayer addressed to the Holy Spirit—appropriate, I thought, given our subject. When the workshop ended, one of the participants made a point of coming to say to me, "I have never heard anyone pray to the Holy Spirit before."

If we looked back over our recent worship experiences, the Holy Spirit is likely to be the person of the Trinity least addressed. Other than at Pentecost, we seldom talk about the Spirit or address the Spirit except in hymns.

Discussing the Holy Spirit makes many of us feel uncomfortable. It raises questions to which we have no answers and opens doors we'd as soon leave shut. Today's reading includes the account of people speaking in tongues. Discussion of this passage usually ends up devoting significant time to that phenomenon, diverting attention from the role of the Spirit's less spectacular but far more pervasive role in our daily life.

Going back to the prayer familiar to me: What would happen if we prayed from the heart each day, "Come, Holy Spirit"? This week as we approach Pentecost, we'll be considering what it means to invite the Holy Spirit into our lives.

Holy Spirit, help me to open my heart and my life to you. Amen.

---

*Adapted from The Walk to Emmaus, used by permission of Upper Room Books.

"Come, Holy Spirit. Fill the hearts of your faithful and kindle in them the fire of your love. Send forth your spirit and they shall be created . . . ."

A fierce wind and flames resting on people who speak all kinds of languages they've never learned. What a show! Though a fire can be welcoming on a cold night, people tend—wisely—to draw back from flames. An out-of-control fire means destruction. But as the story of Moses and the burning bush shows us, the fire that God sends does not consume; it draws attention to God and God's power. We must ask this question: Do we want to open ourselves to what could happen?

We would not want to go overboard. Our educated, restrained, excessively moderate spirituality is quite enough. Perhaps we even fear being consumed, overwhelmed, or having our uniqueness wiped out.

A story from the Desert Fathers tells of Abba Lot who went to see Abba Joseph, saying, "I fast a little, I pray and meditate, I live in peace and as far as I can, I purify my thoughts. What else can I do?" Abba Joseph stood, extended his hands toward heaven, and his fingers shone like ten flames of fire. He replied, "If you will, you can become all flame." (*The Desert Fathers: Sayings of the Early Christian Monks*, Benedicta Ward, trans. [London, England: Penguin Books, 2003], 131).

Rather than consuming us or obliterating our uniqueness, opening ourselves to the Holy Spirit releases us to live more freely. As Paul wrote to the Corinthians, "Where the Spirit of the Lord is, there is freedom" (2 Cor. 3:17). Peter's transformation from one who would not acknowledge relationship with Jesus to that of a bold preacher to thousands shows us that as we open ourselves to the Holy Spirit, we become more fully who we are meant to be.

Come, Holy Spirit, and make me all flame. Amen.

"Come, Holy Spirit. Fill the hearts of your faithful and kindle in them the fire of your love. Send forth your spirit and they shall be created, and you shall renew the face of the earth."

Lost in thought, I gradually became aware of two young voices coming from the back seat of the car. "Will not." "Will too!" "Nuh-uh." "Uh-huh." Then, "Mommy, there will so be animals in heaven, won't there?"

I asked for a recap of the discussion. "Ashley says there won't be animals in heaven, but heaven is going to be full of all the things we love; so there have to be animals or it won't be heaven, right?" For those like me and my daughter, relationships with animals make life fuller—and so they will be part of God's healed cosmos.

Is this weird theology? Not alongside today's psalm. (See also Isaiah 11:6-9.) The Bible makes it clear here and in many other places that the life God breathed into humans also shapes and sustains the rest of creation.

God created the vast seas. Ships (fragile and temporary human creations) are borne upon waves that God created; "Leviathan," the huge, mythic beast that often symbolizes chaos, the uncontrollable forces of the universe, "plays" beneath those same waves. God, master even of chaos, continues in loving relationship with the animals and the earth: All creatures wait for God to give them food; God gives them breath and makes the ground "brand-new again" (CEB).

God is not equivalent to nature and nature is not God, but for those who have eyes to see, as Elizabeth Barrett Browning said, "every common bush [is] aflame" with life from God. Why do we view the power displayed at Pentecost as such a surprise?

Holy Spirit, show me how to live in loving relationship with all creation. Amen.

"Send forth your spirit and they shall be created, and you shall renew the face of the earth."

This amazing passage from Ezekiel reads like a scene synopsis from an Indiana Jones movie. It pictures dramatically the power of God's *ruach*—the Hebrew word translated as both "wind" and "spirit" (as is the equivalent Greek word in the New Testament). The prophet's startling and unforgettable vision shows the breath of God reviving not someone who has recently died, as when Jesus raised Jairus's daughter or the widow's son or even Lazarus, but God giving flesh and breath to bodies that have been long dead.

The scene from Ezekiel brings to mind the Genesis account of Creation when God breathed life into inanimate clay to create humans. Here we see an act different in degree, not kind. Here, as with the psalmist's words yesterday, we are reminded that all life—every speck of any life, anywhere—originates with God.

I heard a story that helps me remember how basic this truth is and how easily we forget it. As the story goes, seeing humans' imperfection, a man challenges God to a person-building contest. God agrees, and they set out the conditions of the contest. They are about to begin. But as the challenger bends down to scoop up some earth, God stops him, saying, "No, no, no—you have to provide your own dirt."

Pentecost is a reminder that during those days or weeks or months when we feel as lifeless and used up as those bleached bones in Ezekiel's valley, our God who gives life to every living thing is able and willing to breathe us to life again.

Come, Holy Spirit, to those places where I feel no more than dry bones, and breathe your life into me. Amen.

*"You shall renew the face of the earth. O God, who by the light of
the Holy Spirit did instruct the hearts of the faithful . . ."*

According to today's readings, the Spirit of God works *in* all
believers and will work *through* all kinds of believers. Peter
does not describe an exclusive club where an elite few know
the inside truth and others are shut out; he describes a fellowship where God speaks and acts through the weak, the old, the
young, even women.

The church that this Spirit inhabits is open to all kinds of
people—Cornelius, who has been seeking God on his own; the
Ethiopian eunuch who would not have been allowed into the
synagogue because he was incomplete, damaged, unworthy to
draw close to God; slaves and slaveholders together. This church
is open to all who call "on the name of the Lord," and whoever
"believes" in Jesus Christ will do the kinds of works that Jesus
does. The church, empowered by the Spirit, is utterly democratic.

The theory makes a fine speech, but the reality is not as
pleasant, of course. We know that in spite of Peter's words on
Pentecost, Acts later tells of the church arguing over who could
be admitted and what rules of Jewish law Gentile converts
would have to keep. After all, we cannot allow too much of that
sort of thing, welcoming everyone and talking about God working through anyone.

If we want to be the church that Peter envisioned and on
which Jesus poured out power, we might have to make some
changes. Who's absent from your fellowship? What is Christ
saying about what your fellowship could be, and what is your
part in it?

*Come, Holy Spirit. Empower me to be like Jesus, an agent of
healing and a life-filled illustration of the love of God. Amen.*

O God, . . . grant that by the same Holy Spirit we may be truly wise and ever enjoy your consolations. Through Christ our Lord. Amen.

If you love me, you will keep my commandments." This is where the rubber meets the road. And where the rub lies—except for the promise that follows: "I will ask the Father, and he will send another Companion, who will be with you forever" (CEB). Jesus knows that the disciples cannot go it alone, just as we cannot.

But this Companion, the Spirit of truth, can be received only by those who know Christ. Jesus tells the disciples that the world can neither see nor recognize this Spirit. Those in the world cannot begin to understand. As Paul told the Corinthians, "People who are unspiritual don't accept the things from God's Spirit. They . . . can only be comprehended in a spiritual way" (1 Cor. 2:14, CEB). This may explain much of the confusion people experience in trying to understand the Spirit.

Jesus also stipulates two more important functions of the Companion-to-come: the Spirit will remind them of what Jesus has said to them and, beyond that, will teach them new things. Jesus knows that they will forget his teachings, and he realizes that in the future they will face situations and challenges he has taught them about. Jesus is human, limited by time and space, but the Spirit is not.

The Holy Spirit is God with us in unlimited ways. When we go "off the grid," when we face situations that the Bible does not address, the Spirit becomes our source of wisdom. When we are asked to explain our faith in Christ, the Spirit will give us words in that moment. As far into the future as we can see, and beyond, the Spirit will be our companion—"forever."

Come, Holy Spirit, and help me to live what I believe. Amen.

PENTECOST

"O God, . . . grant that by the same Holy Spirit we may be truly wise and ever enjoy your consolations. Through Christ our Lord. Amen."

This passage from Romans acknowledges the unsettling fact that much of what we "know" about the spiritual life is subjective. And that includes what we know about the person and reality of the Holy Spirit. The early church did not have a clear understanding of the Spirit. Even the Ephesians when asked if they'd received the Holy Spirit, responded, "We've not even heard that there is a Holy Spirit" (Acts 19:3, CEB).

Perhaps because of believers' lack of knowledge, Paul later writes the epistles that give us the bulk of the Bible's direct teaching about the Spirit. Today's passage introduces the slippery concept of being "led by the Spirit." This idea opens one of those doors we don't want opened: People may do, and have done, all sorts of crazy things because of feeling "led."

What are people referring to? Something in the head? the heart? both? How can we know whether such "leadings" actually come from God? For me these questions go to the heart of our uneasiness: The Holy Spirit is beyond our understanding and cannot be domesticated. We're usually uncomfortable with what we cannot tame. And yet the Spirit is how we come to know that we are connected to God, when the "Spirit agrees with our spirit, that we are God's children" (CEB).

No one can identify the inner working of the Spirit for or within another person. No one can prove the reality of the Spirit's work except by pointing to changed people. Learning to recognize the voice of the Spirit for ourselves, within ourselves, is a personal experience—one that changes the rest of our life.

Come, Holy Spirit. Lead me to open my life to you. Amen.

God's Wisdom, Hope, and Promise

MAY 20–26, 2013 • LAURENCE HULL STOOKEY

SCRIPTURE OVERVIEW: The lessons for Trinity Sunday offer an additional opportunity to consider the work of the Holy Spirit. Romans 5 refers to God, Jesus Christ, and the Holy Spirit. Through their mutual work, the believer experiences peace. In particular, it is through the Holy Spirit that the love of God "has been poured into our hearts" (Rom. 5:5). The lesson from John is another passage in Jesus' "farewell discourse" that mentions the Spirit's role as teacher. Proverbs 8 opens the way to consider the feminine dimension of the Godhead. Psalm 8 suggests that the God-given "glory" of humanity is not incompatible with suffering. This conclusion is reinforced by Romans 5:1-5. To "boast in our hope of sharing the glory of God" (Rom. 5:2) means to "boast in our sufferings" (v. 3). As the Romans lesson from last week suggested of the relationship between the believer and Christ: "We suffer with him so that we may also be glorified with him" (8:17).

QUESTIONS AND THOUGHTS FOR REFLECTION

- Read Proverbs 8:1-4, 22-31. What role does Lady Wisdom play in your social order? To whom do you listen at the crossroads?

- Read Psalm 8. How does the awe of creation help you in times of distress?

- Read Romans 5:1-5. When, in your life, has suffering produced endurance?

- Read John 16:12-15. What might Jesus have to tell you that you are not ready to hear?

Professor of Preaching and Worship, Wesley Theological Seminary, retired; Pastor, Asbury United Methodist Church, Allen, Maryland

A casual reading of the opening lines of Proverbs 8 can seem to imply that what is known as "The Poem to Lady Wisdom" suggests the honoring of two deities: God the Lord and a female consort. But before jumping to that conclusion, ponder the fact that the Hebrew language has no neuter. Every noun must be designated as either "he" or "she"; there is no "it" available.

Further, poetic texts are not intended to be the basis of literalistic rationalism. Instead they are meant to stretch our imagination and send us off prepared for new insights, for deeper understanding. Wisdom is indeed a crucial attribute of the one God. But Lady Wisdom is neither a goddess nor a consort; let alone is she a temptress. But she graciously offers her priceless gifts to all who will listen in the public square, at the crossroads, at the gates and entrance portals of the town.

Who among us does not need and seek a greater depth of knowledge in order that we may more fully serve God? Perhaps we despair at achieving this. Despair may be justified if we try to manufacture wisdom ourselves. Today's reading reveals that what we seek has been characteristic of God since before creation and is available to us because it is in accord with the interior desire of the One whom we serve.

In the history of Christian thought and piety, divine wisdom as found in the book of Proverbs becomes the foundation upon which have been built our understanding of the Word of God (*logos*) and indeed of the Trinity itself. This we shall explore more fully as we pray our way through the week ahead.

Gracious God, to all who truly seek you, grant the holy wisdom that has forever been at the center of your redemptive love for your world. Amen.

Wisdom herself first describes her situation. Wisdom was created by God before all else. Before that there were no waters, no springs from which to drink, no seas to be kept within their assigned boundaries. Once creatures, mountains, and soil were formed, all was changed. Chaos was restrained by Wisdom who could say: "I was daily God's delight, rejoicing before him always, rejoicing in his inhabited world, delighting in the human race."

How often we come close to giving up on the whole human race and all else with it. Can you imagine in your mind's eyes and ears God dancing with delight over what has come out of chaos? Can you imagine a God who in sheer exuberance shouts for joy in the presence of what the old eucharistic liturgy called "angels, and archangels, and all the company of heaven" whose holy name we laud and magnify?

If you cannot imagine at least some of this, perhaps your view of God needs a drastic overhaul! Certainly there are times when weeping is in order and delighting in humanity seems an exercise in futility or even dishonesty. But the writer of the book of Proverbs knew all that. And in spite of it, God loved, and still loves, the whole creation. That which God loves are we not to seek to love also? And there is the agonizing work of seeking reconciliation where before there was only painful separation.

Because God in Christ crucified has loved us so sacrificially, what then shall we cry but this:

> *More love to thee, O Christ, more love to thee!*
> *Hear thou the prayer I make, on bended knee;*
> *this is my earnest plea, more love, O Christ, to thee;*
> *more love to thee, more love to thee.*

—Elizabeth P. Prentiss (1869)

Doesn't it seem silly to advise that if you are distressed or wallowing in negativity, that you, with the psalmist consider the heavens, God's handiwork? What good does it do to look at the stars? Isn't that simply to engage in a form of denial or avoidance?

I once served on a team of theologians visiting a mission station near the war-ravaged border between Zimbabwe and Mozambique. Around ten o'clock that evening we finished our agenda and walked out into the brisk night air. The skimpy use of electricity and lack of light pollution overhead revealed a view of creation I had never before imagined. I wept at the incredible majesty of the Milky Way.

But the problem of human animosity and greed still existed in this war-torn area and throughout the world. How could the starry sky lessen the agony on this tiny planet? What are we human beings that God is mindful of us and cares for us?

Yet there is hope for the human creature. We, designed by God, are seen by the psalmist to be but a bit below the Creator, crowned with glory and honor. Beneath our feet God has put all sheep and oxen and also the beasts of the field, the birds of the air, the fish of the sea, and whatever passes along the paths of the sea.

Imagine that! What responsibility this places upon us, lest we disappoint our Maker and ruin the divine image (the *imago dei*) that our hope-filled God has put within us.

How can we live up to the stewardship implied in this psalm? Only the grace that brought us into this world can guide and correct us on our journey through it. Yet God is faithful and will see us through.

For your cosmos created to give us an assurance of your enduring love, O Lord, we bless your holy name. Amen.

THURSDAY, MAY 23 ～ *Read Psalm 8*

We closed yesterday's meditation with these words: "Yet God is faithful and will see us through." But do we often live as if God has given us a blank check that we may use to spoil the gift of creation? If everything is put under our feet by our Maker, don't we have the authority to do whatever seems useful for our human welfare?

Surely both Lady Wisdom and the author of Psalm 8 would be shocked to hear such an interpretation (or misinterpretation) of their work. God's oversight of us holds in check any selfish desire on our part to waste, to spoil, to ruin the gift of love and life given to us by the Almighty. The proper understanding of our human role in caring for the cosmos in verses 1 and 9 of the psalm must take into account their identical assertion: "O LORD, our Sovereign, how majestic is your name in all the earth!"

Our God-given human "authority" is always hemmed in on all sides by the fact that God's will trumps our authority, as Jesus acknowledged in Gethsemane. When we do not choose to observe this truth, God can and will veto our arrogant assumption of infallible wisdom; and we will be humiliated by our own baseless pride. "The mouths of babes and infants" will contain more authority than all the proud "avengers" and foes of the present age; the latter will be silenced.

Take away from us, O Lord, all desires that are not in accord with your will. Let not the ways we deem to be wise overcome the virtues of restraint and humility, that you may be glorified and honored by all; through Jesus Christ, whose glory is set above the heavens. Amen.

FRIDAY, MAY 24 ~ *Read Romans 5:1-5*

Strange to say, let's start our complex reading at 5:5 and work our way back to the beginning at 5:1. "Because God's love has been poured into our hearts through the Holy Spirit that has been given to us," hope does not disappoint us. We read in 5:2 that "we boast in our hope of sharing the glory of God."

Yesterday the psalmist spoke to us about our human status: "a little lower than God, and crowned . . . with glory and honor" (8:5). If the believer has peace, hope, and love, it is God's doing. Full of confidence and trust in God, believers may indeed boast about these gifts of God. The apostle now writes of those attributes related to suffering:

> suffering produces endurance,
> endurance produces character;
> and character produces hope;
> and hope does not disappoint us.

And there we are, back at hope.

All this rests on Paul's undergirding article of faith that "we are justified by faith" and "have peace with God through our Lord Jesus Christ."

We have hopes for our own lives and for the lives of those whom we most deeply love. But God has a deep and abiding hope for the welfare of *all* created things. God has a dream for us in order that the world and all within it may find peace in God.

Holy Redeemer, if we in our rebellion or confusion have led astray others of your children, forgive us and be to them a guardian, guide, and stay. Amen.

Paul's relationship to the Christian church at Rome is somewhat murky. Many scholars think that while he may have known some of the Roman Christians, by and large he did not; they were brothers and sisters in the faith, yet not deeply personal friends. If this is in fact true, the apostle goes out of his way to extend warm greetings to these virtual strangers. In five brief verses he uses the inclusive "we" six times, "us" twice, and "our" four times: a dozen times within five verses.

But is it not a tribute to serious Christian faith that strangers can extend hospitality to one another as a matter of course, not as a matter of exceptional treatment? Paul intends that all of this hospitality engender hope within the little Christian community, frazzled by martyrdoms and rumors of still more martyrdoms. Nor is it just any kind of hope. It is the eschatological hope that the Caesars will be defeated and that Christ will triumph.

The children of God's people will survive so that future generations will thrive to sing the praises of God in the courts of the Most High. And angels again will do God's bidding where previously lions had roared in the Coliseum.

If older Christians, worn out from the battle, stay on the sidelines, younger women and men will faithfully run the course. The weary exhausted ones cannot hear everything Jesus might like to say to them just now. But when the time is right, Jesus will send the Spirit of truth who will guide the Christians into all truth. They will not be abandoned because of their momentary suffering.

Before the end comes, Lady Wisdom will again tread the streets and speak the truth at the city gates. Hope, once tired out, will gain its second wind; and the promises of Christ to his followers will be fulfilled.

Blessed be the name of the Lord. Amen.

We do not always receive God's words to us readily. Jesus knows that many of his followers will be "at sea" without some augmented seriousness, some assurance from Jesus before he, in bodily form, departs from this earth. So Jesus says to them, "I still have many things to say to you, but you cannot bear them now. When the Spirit of truth comes, he will guide you into all the truth."

Many to this day still do not understand the fullness of that promise. Have you ever heard a devout Christian say something like this: "I wish Jesus had not been taken from us. It would have been better if all Christian people could have escaped that loss." But Jesus' ascension was not a loss to us; it was a gain. The Lord, even in his ascending, received new power. Once he inhabited only a few hundred square miles; but now that he is risen, he is available to all people on the earth at all hours of the day and night. In his resurrection he became accessible in new and wonderful ways. The risen and ascended One is no longer hemmed in by the confines of time and space that encumber us in our daily lives.

Spiritual matters for us are far less confusing than they were during the forty-day span from Easter Day to Ascension Day. To wish you could turn back the clock denies the power of the Holy Spirit who can be with us in both our joys and our sorrows, in the times of trial and in the times of victory over sin. So, rejoice and be glad, for the Spirit gives to us far more than the ascension of the Lord could possibly remove from us.

Even more, the Spirit makes present to us and active among us promises that Jesus made during his ministry that we have largely forgotten. What we and our ancestors in the faith do not recall, the Spirit brings to a remembrance.

Holy Spirit, come among us, minister to us now and always. Amen.

Voices of Worship

MAY 27–JUNE 2, 2013 • SUSAN YOUNG HUCKABY

SCRIPTURE OVERVIEW: Who has power? Elijah has no power. He is but a "troubler of Israel." Yet Elijah's prayers summon the power of God. Paul has no power. The churches in Galatia have learned that Paul neglected to teach them to observe the law of Moses. He can only insist that there is one and only one gospel, no matter who preaches it. The centurion of Luke 7 does have power. The centurion himself knows his power, but he also knows its limitations. He is not worthy to have Jesus, the powerless one, enter his home. For this acknowledgment of where real power lies, Jesus demonstrates once again the power of God. The question of who has power finds its most direct answer in Psalm 96: "For great is the LORD, and greatly to be praised."

QUESTIONS AND THOUGHTS FOR REFLECTION

• Read 1 Kings 18:20-39. List the voices that attempt to pull you off-center and out of the range of God's voice. What can you do to set aside these voices and hear God's voice loudly and clearly?

• Read Psalm 96. Glance through the psalm and locate at least five different, active ways to worship.

• Read Galatians 1:1-12. On a scale of 1 to 10, where do you fall on the "people-pleasing" scale"? How strongly do you identify with Paul's statement that we cannot please people and serve the Lord?

• Read Luke 7:1-10. Recall a time when God's word, combined with music, gave you hope and comfort.

Director of Worship and Adult Discipleship at Trinity Church in Spring Hill, Tennessee; a campus of Brentwood United Methodist Church in Nashville, Tennessee

Worshiping God involves ears—the ears of our mind and heart! Voices saturate our world, each screaming to be heard above the other, vying for our attention. Hearing and following the voice of God is no easy task.

The Israelites, God's chosen people, have succumbed to multiple voices from false gods, and evidently they have accepted these gods into their lives. Elijah, Israel's sole remaining prophet, asks the people how long they will waver between two opinions. I imagine many among the crowd found Elijah's words confusing. *What's so wrong with what we're doing?* they may have thought. "We believe in the Lord *and* we follow Baal and Asherah. No harm done." When Elijah suggests a showdown between the Lord and the other gods, the people readily agree, saying Elijah's challenge is good.

How did the Israelites get to this place—a place of heeding two, maybe more, voices? I imagine it was a slow fade. The hearts of God's chosen people did not lose their ardor overnight, a thought that strikes me cold. We don't have to look far to realize we too are on a slippery slope. Our culture's voices profane God's name here, pander easy credit there, tease too much drink here, infiltrate prime-time television with soft porn there, promote adulation of sports figures here. . . . As Christians, we need not completely deny our faith in God in order for these gods, other voices, to speak into our lives. We were created, however, to worship *only* God (Exod. 20:3). Worshiping the Lord and heeding only God's voice may be a struggle, but we do not face the battle alone. We have God's promise of presence and strength in times of trial and temptation as we trust and obey the Lord.

O God, break through the cacophonous voices around us so that we may hear your loving, trustworthy voice and worship only you. Amen.

Elijah, the sole remaining prophet of Israel, never wavers in the face of 450 false prophets. His confidence in the Lord and the authority with which he speaks exemplify his dedication to God. Would we have been so bold?

Elijah is not perfect. The tone of his voice, along with his taunts and sarcasm during this Mount Carmel challenge, seem strange coming from a man of God; yet, they reveal the human side of this prophet and, perhaps, even a humorous side of God. When attempts to engage the other gods fail, Elijah's mocking ceases. He immediately calls the people to worship the Lord God.

Elijah understands worship. He leads the people in worship, first naming God for who God is and recalling God's mighty acts by naming Abraham, Isaac, and Jacob. Do our prayers focus too often on what we want God to do *now* or in our *future*? Remembering what God has done in the past can provide the faith-building rope God offers to pull us out of our current struggles. We can also encourage family and friends to recollect God's past blessings, guidance, and protection, allowing the Holy Spirit to bring hope for a seemingly despair-filled future.

The worship of Elijah and the Israelites engages their whole beings. "Bless the LORD, O my soul: and all that is within me, *bless* his holy name" (Ps. 103:1, KJV) comes to mind with this scene in First Kings. As with all good Israelites, Elijah understands the imperative to bless the Lord with all that he is. His encounter with these backsliding Israelites illustrates participatory worship. We witness praise, remembrance, prostrate prayer, drama, visuals, proclamation, submission, and confession. May our worship of the Lord God Almighty be so rich.

O Lord, you are God. There is no other. With all that is within us, we bless you for who you are and what you have done for us. Amen.

Pens, pencils, offering envelopes, chewing gum, photographs from Mom's wallet, the pictures in the middle of the Bible—it took all these plus the stern looks from my Dad to keep me quiet during worship services when I was a child. Our little church did not have children's church. Once the hymns were sung and the preaching began, I faced forty minutes of *enforced* self-control. My friend's father kept a switch up his coat sleeve and would show it to him from time to time to keep my friend's wiggly self under control!

Psalm 96 paints a different picture. The voice of worship is our own, and there is no hint of passivity. Dynamic words such as *sing, praise, proclaim, declare, ascribe,* and *rejoice* testify unequivocally that worshiping God requires full engagement. Robert Webber, in his book *Worship Is a Verb* encourages us to participate actively in worshiping God. Worship allows no room for spectators. Why is participatory worship important? Our praise can become rote, offered without thought or heart. Engaging body, mind, and soul helps keep our focus on the Lord.

The psalmist gives us ample reasons to worship. His words motivate us to rev-up our vocal cords and activate our bodies for worship: God is our salvation; the Lord is great and worthy of praise; the Lord made the heavens; the Lord is holy; God will judge the world in righteousness and the peoples in faithfulness. Other commands insist that even the seas, fields, and forests praise God. All these stir within us a great desire to worship the Lord, the Creator of heaven and earth, and the Creator of each one of us. How can we help but praise the Lord?

Creator God, you are great and greatly to be praised. May our voice of worship be heard by you and as a witness to you among the nations. In Jesus' name. Amen.

Worship Is a Verb, by Robert E. Webber (Hendrickson Publishers, Peabody, MA: 1996).

Offerings appear in over seven hundred places in the Bible (NIV). The passages reveal that giving an offering to the Lord serves as an important part of worship. Verse 8 declares we bring an offering and come into God's courts. Following this, the psalmist voices, "Worship the LORD in the beauty of holiness" (KJV). Offerings and worship go hand-in-hand.

Our offerings certainly take on a different look than offerings in Old Testament times. On this side of the cross and Jesus' sacrifice for our sins, we no longer bring grain offerings or offer animal sacrifices. Mark 12:33 (NIV) reads, "'To love [God] with all your heart, and with all your understanding and with all your strength, and to love your neighbor as yourself is more important than all burnt offerings and sacrifices." In other words, God does not need our money or gifts. God desires, instead, that we love God and have hearts full of love for others. I confess that I rarely think of the weekly offering time as worship. Often, I am more interested in the offertory music than I am in thanking God for my blessings or making things right with my neighbor.

Church people often joke about collecting an offering every time they get together, subtly hinting about budget needs. Pastors may stress the importance of giving so that programs can continue in the church. Neither of these is wrong. It comes down to a matter of emphasis. Do we keep the love of God and neighbor at the heart of our offerings? As we remember who God is, what God has done for us, and what God asks of us, we cannot contain our thanks! Some African worship services illustrate this beautifully. Praise music plays, and individuals bring their offerings forward, rejoicing—even dancing—as they give back to God a portion of what God has given them.

Lord, we gladly worship you with our offerings. May they be pleasing and acceptable to you. Amen.

Paul expresses astonishment at how easily the Galatians desert the gospel. They have accepted the teachings of people who alter the gospel, and he exhorts them to remain true to the original good news. Paul condemns those who pervert God's word, no matter how appealing they may be (even if it is a heavenly angel). "If I were still pleasing people, I would not be a servant of Christ." Paul minces no words in telling the Galatians and us that pleasing people and serving the Lord are incompatible; we cannot seek the approval of human beings *and* the approval of God. Specifically, we must guard against listening to provocative voices that lure us to accept a diluted gospel in our desire to please people.

My husband says I'm a people-pleaser and often tells me that I should be less concerned with what people think. Many of us find that difficult to do, for we are taught from toddlerhood to make others happy. We may wrap our self-worth up in gaining others' approval. As we worship God in our daily living, we should guard against loving and serving for human approval and seek to live for God's approval.

The irony of choosing God is that we "win" on both counts. Living our lives for God's approval results in loving and serving others and will likely bring the approval of those very people.

In verses 11-12, Paul reminds the Galatians that the gospel he teaches is not of his own making but was revealed to him solely from Jesus Christ. In other words, nothing less will do. May it be so in our own lives.

Gracious God, we long to please you because you are our maker, and you love us. Close our ears and mouths to anything less than your truth as you open our ears and hearts to your word. Amen.

We find two essential aspects of faith in Christ in today's scripture. One emphasizes the importance of personal faith, a solid faith in the Lord who gives us courage and strength. Can you identify with the centurion's desperation for his sick servant? Perhaps you have been in a similar situation.

When my husband suddenly became seriously ill several years ago, I cried out to the Lord for help. From my God-given faith nurtured in me since I was young and strengthened in me by the Holy Spirit, I knew the Lord was with us during that trying time.

Another aspect of faith comes to the fore when the centurion demonstrates the importance of supporting a faith community. Just as the centurion sent Jewish elders to plead with Jesus for the healing of his beloved servant, I called on church leaders and friends to entreat the Lord for my husband's restoration. The faith of the body of Christ is a powerful gift from God, a blessing and encouragement to us in difficult times.

We don't often think of Jesus as being amazed, yet something about the centurion's faith amazes him. Is it the centurion's boldness in sending liaisons to plead his case? Could it have been his humility, the unworthiness he felt to be in Jesus' presence? Perhaps the fact that the Gentile centurion believes in who Jesus is and trusts Jesus to act accordingly brings Jesus' amazement to the fore. I think it was a combination of all the above. The Lord feels pleased and honored, even marvelously amazed, when we approach him in faith. Today's voice of worship is the voice of our unwavering faith in Christ.

Lord Jesus, thank you for the gift of faith within each of us and the faith of our community around us. We pray for even greater faith that you will be honored in our words and actions. Amen.

The Roman centurion knows the power of words spoken with authority. His rank reveals this on two levels. It leads him to submit to the authority spoken from his own commanding officer, and his rank empowers him to issue commands to military personnel whose status fell below his. Today's passage shows the centurion's submission to Jesus as well as his recognition of the authority and power of Jesus' words.

Some people perceive submission as weakness. I am strong-willed, determined in personality. I often find it hard to take directions, to admit that I am incapable, or to say as the centurion states, "I am not worthy." Cultural influences don't help in this matter, with commercial voices touting, "I am worth it"; "I want it all, and I want it now"; and "have it your way." It has become commonplace to ridicule our government leaders. We seem to have lost the meaning of respect.

Here, however, we read about Jesus, the one who alone is worthy. The Israelites understood their place before God. Several Hebrew words for worship addressed submission to God. One such word, *shachah*, was the most widely used word for worship. It means "to bow down, prostrate oneself," or "to give homage." The focuses on a sense of humility with the creature bowing before the Creator, the unrighteous paying homage to the worthy God.

How do we worship in this way, submitting to authority or bowing down, when the concepts of humility and unworthiness are foreign to us? The centurion's humility warranted Jesus' praise; we in faith submit our lives to God. We worship God for who God is and all God has done for us. We have confidence in God's promises for our future.

Worthy is the Lamb that was slain to receive power, and riches, and wisdom, and strength, and honor, and glory, and blessing. (Rev. 5:12, KJV)

God's Provision

JUNE 3–9, 2013 • RUTH ANN TIPPIN

SCRIPTURE OVERVIEW: God intercedes powerfully for God's people. The reading from 1 Kings 17 continues the story of God's protection of Elijah from the wrath of Ahab, but God's protection here extends beyond his prophetic messenger to a non-Israelite widow. Psalm 146 reminds us that God alone may be trusted, for God is the one who cares for the outsider and the powerless, those rejected by human society and neglected by the "normal" standards of the world. In the Gospel lesson, Jesus encounters a woman whose position closely parallels that of the widow of Zarephath. For her also God intercedes, this time in the person of Jesus, whose own power restores the life of her son. Galatians 1:11-24 reminds us that God's intercessions do not always supply the pleasant fulfillments of our needs; sometimes they lead us where we would be happier not to go.

QUESTIONS AND THOUGHTS FOR REFLECTION

- Read 1 Kings 17:8-24. In what daily tasks might God surprise you this week?

- Read Psalm 146. Find a quiet place, and sing this psalm from your heart, making it your own. Don't worry about the melody. Let God form that in you. Consider writing your own psalm song!

- Read Galatians 1:11-24. How intentional are you about giving God time and space to re-create you, away from your life's work? How do you seek the revelation of God's enduring light?

- Read Luke 7:11-17. What do you most fear? What do you need to trust God for the most?

Raised in the Quaker tradition, now a recorded minister called into pastoral ministry among Friends; serving a congregation of Friends in West Branch, Iowa

Precarious—life is sometimes so precarious. At times, we, like this widow, have little left in the cupboard of our lives. We swing the doors wide open, searching the highest shelves, the furthest corners, and find only the smallest portion available. What do we do? The widow of Zarephath chooses to use what little she has to feed herself and her son. But she will not prepare it to sustain life; she will make the meal in preparation for death.

The widow goes to gather sticks, just as she does every day. This is the first item needed to make the meal: sticks. She leaves her home and son and heads to the city gates, probably a path she has traveled many times. But this time, she finds more than sticks. She finds a man asking for life and responds to his request with words to this effect: "How can I give you life, when I am preparing to die?"

Elijah's simple words offer her a new option. "Don't be afraid. Go home and prepare your meal but serve me first—before yourself and your son. In doing this, you will not die. Instead, you will live."

The widow could have stayed home. She could have given in to despair and waited for death. Instead, she performs the common, ordinary task of her every day. She follows her daily practice of gathering sticks—from this she receives life.

What do we do when life becomes precarious? Do we have a well-worn path of daily practice to follow? Do we leave everything behind and go in search of sticks? If so, surprised by God, are we willing to serve God first, even in our place of despair? Do we see our survival in seeking and serving God? "Do not be afraid . . . my provision for you will not fail" (AP).

Lord of Life, you have prepared a table before me. Lead me to feast with you there. Amen.

Elijah comes to Zarephath out of need for his own survival. God sends a survivor to a woman who is barely surviving herself. How strange of God to choose this way of bringing life from death. Not only given food and drink, Elijah finds shelter with a widow and her son. His life depends on her need for sustenance. Because she needs him, Elijah will find what he needs.

Fearing for his own life, Elijah had escaped to the Wadi Cherith, where ravens fed him each day. The intermittent stream of the wadi had dried up and, relying on God's direction, Elijah leaves there for the city of Zarephath.

Imagine how Elijah must have felt, leaving that isolated valley for a bustling town along the Mediterranean. Rather than ravens for company, Elijah will now be surrounded by humankind. He is literally coming out of hiding.

Elijah promises the widow that if she gives over what little she has, she will receive all she needs. If she serves Elijah, then she will see what God can do. Until the rains come again, they will never lack for grain and oil.

Imagine how the widow must have felt! Who is Elijah to tell her these things? But what does she have to lose? Her life is lost already. What she does not know is that Elijah has already seen what God can do. Day and night, down by the wadi, he has known God's faithfulness and found God trustworthy. Now she will discover the same truth about God.

Do we have the courage to step out, certain of God's trustworthiness, and ask of others the promises that God has made? Does our experience of and witness to God's commitment to life make us willing helpers to God's promises? Are we willing to come out of hiding?

Faithful God, draw us into the world with your power and grace. Amen.

How long has Elijah lived in the widow's home in Zarephath with her son? Apparently, not long enough for her to trust him. "You have come to me to bring my sin to remembrance, and to cause the death of my son!" Indicting herself, she blames Elijah for her son's death.

Elijah cries out to God, charging God with the death, but he does so with a question. "O LORD . . . , have you brought calamity even upon the widow with whom I am staying, by killing her son?" Elijah includes himself in the question.

When tragedy comes, we try to explain it; finding no reason, we assign blame. We often look to ourselves first, even as we accuse others. The widow feels overwhelmed with her own shortcomings, remembering every mistake, failure, and sin in her life. Elijah is upset that God would bring catastrophe anywhere near him. Regardless of our relationship to death, we want and need to find ways to make sense of it. We need clarity in the midst of confusion. We need truth.

The boy revives and returns to his mother. How does this happen? The Lord listens to Elijah. He hears Elijah's faith as well as his fear. God hears his call and answers his question. God hears the widow's cry and answers her accusation. The child does not die because of her sin. God does not choose to bring calamity on this household by killing the boy. Tragically, the child became severely ill and died. Miraculously, God brought the child back to life.

For the woman of Zarephath, life is truth. All that Elijah has said about God is true. Grain and oil sustained life, but her child, standing in front of her, is life. Jesus stands now, fully alive, ready to prove God true. Are we ready to ask God for life, even in the face of death?

God of truth, open us to speak with you in faith, even in the face of fear. Amen.

Is this your psalm? Is this a song you could sing, describing God's work in your life? I can imagine Elijah singing it. He has learned that humankind, especially those with great power, cannot be trusted. God is the one to trust for help and hope. God, who has created all things, will send birds to feed him, provide shelter in hidden valleys, and sustain him with water from flooded streams.

Do you hear the widow of Zarephath? She can sing praise to God as long as she has life. Indeed, because she has life! Her life is a gift—given and sustained by God. The God of Jacob has seen her, provided food, and upheld her son.

Another widow has yet to sing. She lives in Nain and will soon sing this same psalm. Her son, freed from the bonds of death, will be raised to live again. She will not die with him; instead, she will see her life extend through his into the next generation.

Is this your psalm? Can you begin and end a story in your life with praise to God? Can you sing out, through times of desolation, sorrow, fear? Do you hear God singing to you the sound and song of God's presence, even in the midst of those times? Do you remember times where justice was granted, release was given, and eyes were opened?

Just as God provided for Elijah, the widows, and their sons, so God provides for you. It may not be obvious. God may come as a flock of ravens or as an old fellow asking for a drink of water—but God provides. If you wonder about the truth of that statement, just start singing.

Lord of all, you have given my life the song of your presence. Help me form the words to sing it. Amen.

Known and unknown. Revealed and hidden. Recognized and unrecognized. Paul has felt and understood each of these experiences. What a remarkable work of God, to take someone so prominent, move him to near obscurity, and then return him to significance. How does this happen? Through revelation, the revelation of Christ Jesus.

Paul the persecutor became Paul the proclaimer as God called him to ministry by revealing the Son, Christ Jesus to him. Once a public figure, Paul leaves it all behind, moving into Arabia and Syria. He does venture back into Jerusalem to see Peter but for only fifteen days. People in Cilicia and Syria know him, but he remains unknown by sight to the churches in Judea. A once prominent and recognized member of the Jewish faith, Paul is now unrecognizable.

What a mercy! What a grace! This man who has been known throughout the region for his zealous persecution of those who follow Christ now refers to himself as one "proclaiming the faith he once tried to destroy."

God chooses to reveal Paul as a new person with a new personhood established in God's love, mercy, and grace. God chooses this person to reveal God, to glorify God, to proclaim who God can be in each person. Paul receives freedom—not only the freedom of soul and spirit but the freedom to be seen as Christ-in-Paul, not as Paul alone.

The work of revelation comes in being hidden away with God. From that "hidden" place, our ministry gains significance. This revelation becomes relationship, and an inner light endures.

Do we believe that God would choose to reveal God's self in us? Do we yearn to be hidden away in God? Do we believe that God's truth can be made real in us and through us?

God of light, reveal your truth to me that I may reveal it to others. Amen.

Jesus is compassionate, fearless, and powerful. Because of these traits, a young man will live; a widow's future will be secured; and God will be glorified.

Two groups of people approach the city gates of Nain; each will bear witness to God's favor. One group follows life; the other follows death. Jesus' disciples and a large crowd have traveled with him to Nain. Mourners have followed a funeral bier carrying the body of a widow's son through the same city, and these two groups meet at the city gates.

Jesus connects himself with the lives of the townspeople by acknowledging the widow, encouraging her not to cry. He could have easily ignored her, letting the funeral procession pass by. Not only does he speak to her in compassion, but he steps up fearlessly to the funeral bier that holds the body of her dead son. Now Jesus is connected to death and considered unclean for having touched the bier.

With the death of her son, and having no husband, this woman has lost her future. She has no one to care for and no one to care for her. She is bereft. Jesus knows this and determines to redeem her life, as well as that of her son. "Young man, I say to you, rise!" Jesus speaks the son into life, giving him back to his mother.

The followers of life and the followers of death join together in praise and in worship, as the power and glory of God overcomes them. "God has looked favorably on his people!"

This is the Jesus we follow—the compassionate, fearless, powerful Son of God who sees what we may not want to see, who takes risks that we may not want to take, and who speaks power where we may be afraid to speak. This is the Christ we follow. We follow life.

God of courage, teach us to be compassionate, fearless, and powerful as we seek to follow you. Amen.

SUNDAY, JUNE 9 ~ *Read 1 Kings 17:17-24; Luke 7:11-17*

Two widows. Two sons. Two deaths. None of the characters is made known to us by name—only by their place in their family. Hungering for life, the first widow struggles to save her son from death. He will eventually become ill and die. The second widow loses her son to death, as well. We are not given the reason—only the result.

Two cities. Zarephath, near the coast of the Mediterranean Sea, is known for its smelters and forges. Nain, whose name is translated as "pleasant," lies near Mount Tabor.

Two prophets. The first, a prophet of Tishbe in Gilead, who has counseled kings. The second, a man called a prophet, from Galilee, who will one day be known as the King of kings.

Two lives restored. Elijah calls out to God for the life of the boy and is not afraid to touch death in order that life might come. And, indeed, life came. Jesus took hold of death, literally stopping it in its tracks, and called out, as God in Christ, for life. And life came.

Two men serving one God. One God caring for two widows, two sons, two cities, two prophets. One God proving to be faithful, powerful, trustworthy, loving, and gracious. One God proving to be ultimately all that is needed.

Our lives are full of stories. Some we tell and retell. Some resemble those we hear others tell. Some stories are uniquely ours. As we retell our God-stories, we remember that God is always present, always listening, always answering, even when we, like Elijah or Jesus, first approach the city gates. Perhaps you are stepping through them just now.

God of hope, bless me with the sense of your faithful presence as I trust you with my life and the lives of those I touch. Amen.

Temptation

JUNE 10–16, 2013 • THE ROCK RECOVERY MINISTRY

SCRIPTURE OVERVIEW: In the story of Naboth's vineyard, Ahab and Jezebel act with unbelievable treachery against an innocent man. Only when Elijah confronts Ahab does the king acknowledge his sin against God. Psalm 5 powerfully recalls that only God may truly be called king and that the true king will not finally tolerate the wickedness of humankind. Both these passages remind us that the relationship between an individual and others reveals something powerful about the individual's relationship with God. The Gospel and epistle readings support the belief that an individual's relationship with God reveals something powerful about that individual's relationships with human beings. Paul attempts to deal with the boundaries some have attempted to reinforce between Jews and Gentiles. Luke's version of the woman who anoints Jesus with oil presents us with a Pharisee who does not understand that relationship to God involves social relationships as well. Jesus insists that the love of God requires loving generosity among human beings.

QUESTIONS AND THOUGHTS FOR REFLECTION

- Read 1 Kings 21:1-21a. What consequences have you faced because of giving in to temptation?

- Read Psalm 5:1-8. How does morning prayer help you develop a hedge of protection?

- Read Galatians 2:15-21. Paul points out that he had to die to the law and be reborn to Christ's law. Where in your life would this same principle apply?

- Read Luke 7:36–8:3. In what area of your life do you need to delve deeper and look below the surface?

A ministry of the Rock Church, San Diego, California; offering outreach and residential support for those struggling with addiction

Because we are members of a San Diego community of alcoholics and addicts, temptation touches our lives on a daily basis as we travel the road of recovery. We feel blessed to share with you a small slice of our serenity as God so graciously continues to bless us.

But why do we seldom feel satisfied with what God unselfishly blesses us with? As a society we have been conditioned to believe that more is always better, yet we can never obtain enough. Drugs and alcohol, money, food, clothes, sex, hi-tech gadgets; the list of our wants is infinite and our temptation to get them is almost overpowering. The temptation of greed can consume the soul as we selfishly succumb to its fatal grip. Greed strips us of our spiritual supply, and we trade in our moral standards for mere moments of make-believe bliss.

Jezebel's selfish decision to fulfill her husband's desires blinds her spiritual sight. She experiences no moral dilemma when deciding the death of another. It is a small price to pay for a piece of land. The voice of greed sounds louder than the voice of the Spirit. Her temptation results in a drastic choice.

Our culture bombards us daily with ads that encourage us to buy the next best thing. We watch media figures portray their popularity gained through sexuality, distracting us with endless supplies of eye candy that tempt us to look their direction. In an overstimulated society, who is surprised at what occurs behind closed doors? It becomes especially hard when temptation lures well-respected figures.

When temptation makes its stealth attack, how will you be spiritually prepared to strike back? Will you choose the armor of the Lord or the sackcloth of sin?

Heavenly Father, continue to feed us your spiritual word so that we never succumb to earthly temptation. Amen.

King Ahab gives no thought to Naboth's death and proceeds to secure the vineyard as his own. He disavows the consequences of his actions as he plunges into the bottomless abyss of his temptation to acquire more. Shortly after, Ahab's plans of personal gain become a deadly future of disaster. God sends the prophet Elijah to confront the king. Ahab has sold himself out to evil, yet he cannot bring himself to acknowledge the deed. Rather, he comments to the prophet: "Have you found me, O my enemy?"

Every day around the world people fail to recognize the alluring shades of evil. Distracted by the attractive sparkles of sin, we fail to see the evil of our actions as we pursue our desires. Our community of alcoholics and addicts constantly witnesses those who sell themselves to evil, falling into the dark depths of a spiritual death. They yearn for the comfort promised by sin, not realizing the length of its pleasure holds no comparison to what is sustained through the sacrifice given to us by our Savior. While the seduction of evil appears to be satisfying, it strips the soul of inner strength. Yet, the light of the Lord is everlasting, with an endless supply of love and serenity.

Through spiritual Lasik surgery, we receive new sight. We begin to see light in what was once dark and through continual seeking we can no longer be bought by the illusion of sin. Self-seeking still affects those who soak in temptation, making them unable to bask in the sunlight of the Spirit. Perspective on what's best in God's eyes can be seen only by following with faith the divine path. We prepare to follow with eyes wide open.

Father God, prepare us to see your path and not be diverted by the temptations that we see through our earthly eyes. Amen.

How often have we felt alone, crying out in despair, longing for the attention of anyone anywhere? Finding no immediate solution to the intolerable pain, we then at our weakest moment turn to anything. Anything to fill that vicious void of emotions that screams out quick solutions to satisfy the voices of not being ok with ourselves just as we are. Having exhausted all synthetic substitutes we, like the psalmist, sigh for God.

We begin to place our predicaments and pain in God's hands and witness divine patience that waits for the precise moment when the opportunity to place God at our center outweighs the best solution the world could ever supply. Slowly, as we increase our conversations with God, we discover that what used to tempt our minds easily has melted into calm mornings mesmerized by the simple beauty about us.

But how do we get to those mornings? This psalm expresses various times when the psalmist easily gives up and gives in to immediate gratification, a crafty gift composed by temptation. The psalmist wants to be heard, acknowledged, and paid attention to. How many of us relate to that desire?

But who has responded with the same patience displayed by the distraught psalmist? Many will and do impatiently reply yes to temptation by meeting discreetly with that coworker for a drink after work or replying to that e-mail from a singles' Web site while glancing down at an occupied ring finger. We all silently scream, "Pay attention to me!" But who is to say God is not paying attention to all of us? God asks for a small fee of faith paid through patience. The price procures a future of infinite fortune of an emotionally satisfying life.

God, may my mornings begin with a request for spiritual direction. Amen.

We wage the war of wickedness every day, forgetting that the most powerful weapon of choice is at our disposal: God, whose ways always predict the outcome as victory no matter how vicious the battle appears to be. When we think of wicked things, most of us visualize anything from senseless killings to harmful behaviors of deceit. They encompass the opposite of what God's loving hand created us for. Instead of lending to others, we become leeches. Instead of sharing from our overflow, we become hoarders. We rationalize our lies and seemingly forget how to treat one another with love and compassion, the commandment God has given us. Sounds like such a simple request from God. But in reality, it challenges even the most faithful.

In this psalm, the psalmist expresses a desire to find God's guidance toward the path of righteousness before his enemies conquer him. He knows that God does not delight in wickedness. He affirms his belief that God will protect him in the midst of murderers and deceivers.

We, like the psalmist, find ourselves tempted to step off the path that God places in plain view for all to follow. Why do we find it so enticing to divert from what we know to be the right way? Perhaps we may not sense God's immediate presence; maybe while sin stole our attention, our hedge of protection was slowly being pruned. The ways of the wicked are always at work, and often we are unaware.

So how will you follow God's "straight" way to enter God's house? Where will you seek God's guidance to be prepared? Preparation involves participation. Do you sharpen your sword on the rock of the Lord, or do you sit on the sidelines while sin saturates your soul? Through God's abundant and steadfast love, you too will enter God's house.

How will I prepare today against the ways of the wicked?

From our birth, we humans resemble little sponges that soak up all that surrounds us. As we grow we gain knowledge of life's rights and wrongs, the laws of the land. But whose laws in God's land shape our moral principles?

Our lives seem to be governed by laws set forth by society through centuries of experiences with issues that have been pushed to the limit. When considering issues like war, gay marriage, drug legalization, capital punishment, or premarital sex we may ask whose limit is being pushed: God's or mortals'? As God asks us to behave in one way, our world may demand that we conform to another, leaving us in a state of chaos with regard to compliance. Our moral compass goes off course when our minds tell us one thing and our hearts scream another. But is Paul attempting to set "believing" above "doing"? Paul does draw a distinction between "works of the law" and "faith in Jesus Christ." Do we react like Peter, who after an initial acceptance of Gentiles within the church fellowship, chose to withdraw from that group? Or do we, like Paul, acknowledge that living by the law nullifies God's grace to the point that "Christ died for nothing"?

We may be upstanding citizens in the eyes of society, but what use will that be when we leave our earthly boundaries? Entrance to the kingdom of God comes by faith in Christ. Obedience to earthly laws does not make us right with God. In fact, that obedience may lead to an outcome opposite the one we desire to attain: a home with God. Our old ways may be comfortable but how will they serve us in the world to come? Preparing for an eternal home begins with our obedient response to God in Christ today.

God, help me obey you regardless of what society may deem as right. Amen.

Many of us have experienced God's forgiveness for our many sins brought through temptation. But then we meet the Simons of the world, and the old phrase "don't judge a book by its cover" comes to life again. On a daily basis we draw conclusions about or speculate on what the surface of an event or person reveals. Sometimes we react out of convenience. Sometimes we do it because we fear taking a closer look. Perhaps we might see something of ourselves that we have tried to hide. Simon demonstrates what so many of us fall victim to. We fail to see others and situations with the loving eyes of God. Instead we assume and presume another person's character that comes out of sin and ignorance in the form of judgment.

The parable of the two debtors sheds light on how an ostracized soul who is forgiven his many sins has all the more love for the Lord. On the opposite side we see one whose love is much less apparent as a reflection of being forgiven for less. How easily we could misinterpret these verses as our needing to commit *many* sins in order to achieve a greater love and appreciation of God. But as we read deeper into the story, the lesson becomes plain. Just because society deems persons as sinners on a multitude of levels, that does not discount their standing with God. God welcomes all into the divine embrace no matter the size of the request for forgiveness.

Whether we consider ourselves to be open-minded or still tend to jump to instant conclusions, awareness of our attitudes and actions toward others lets us take a giant step in closing the gap that judgment continues to widen. Consciously making an effort toward acceptance of all will open our ears to Jesus' words: "Your faith has saved you; go in peace."

God, help me to pause today to see past my first perceptions of others and their situations. Amen.

Imagine Jesus going on tour. Here he, the disciples, and an entourage of others head out to the cities and villages. Many of those who follow along have been healed and witnessed miracles. What a spectacular sight that would have been! We read of the wonderful things he did, but to see Jesus in action would be more than mere words could describe.

Yet, if we think about it, do we not see Jesus' miracles performed to this day? In our recovery community we witness the miracle every day. We get a front row seat to the show. Alcoholics and addicts find themselves relieved of an obsession that no human power can have taken away. Those of us like Mary Magdalene receive forgiveness through our repentance and acquiring faith. We see the glory of God not just in our community but throughout societies of the world where only a mustard seed of faith is needed to initiate the growth of a spiritual sprout.

The power of what faith can achieve remains the same. Picture Jesus, his twelve disciples, and his entourage traveling in modern times. The kingdom of God remains the main attraction of the tour, with Jesus as the spokesperson. With such strong evidence supporting the work of God through Jesus, why do so many express skepticism? Perhaps the voices of earthly desires drown out those of the spiritual world. Yet, as a community we can continue to demonstrate the flow of God's power in and through us.

Faith knows no boundaries and moves beyond the limits of a select few. Opening our hearts and minds to the love of God can bring about much good in the world. Slowly connecting to the light of the Lord illumines the colors of every situation and every creature in the glow of forgiveness.

Where do you witness God's forgiveness at work?

God's Presence in Adversity

JUNE 17–23, 2013 • VAL WHITE

SCRIPTURE OVERVIEW: Acknowledging and serving God powerfully threaten the way the world generally does its business. Precisely because he has done the Lord's bidding in killing all the prophets of Baal, Elijah must flee from Jezebel's wrath. Utterly discouraged by the limitations of his own resources, Elijah proposes that he be allowed to die. God's response comes not in the form of words of encouragement but in the form of nurture, God's own presence, and finally in the form of yet another summons to work. The psalmist portrays the human need of God's presence and the human cry in the face of God's apparent absence. The words of Galatians call for liberation from anthropological boundaries of race, class, and gender. The Gospel lection poses a threat to the status quo. For the man possessed of demons, the arrival of Jesus Christ means freedom and the opportunity to serve.

QUESTIONS AND THOUGHTS FOR REFLECTION

- Read 1 Kings 19:1-15*a*. When has God come to you and asked, "What are you doing here?" How do you experience God's "voice" in your life?
- Read Psalm 42. How do you replenish your soul when you cannot be part of the faith community for a period of time?
- Read Galatians 3:23-29. Whom do you see as "other" in your world today?
- Read Luke 8:26-39. When have you experienced healing in your life? Did you go about proclaiming "how much Jesus had done" for you?

Minister of Discipleship and Evangelism, St. Luke's United Methodist Church, Danville, Virginia

I entered the ministry as a second career, having worked for years in the business field. I was zealous for the Lord and eager to get started, being assured by many that my business experience would prove to be a boon to my ministry. Consequently, I set out to save souls and the world as well. I knew I would succeed and thereby be worthy of God's calling on my life. How rapidly I learned otherwise, becoming greatly discouraged in the process! Ministry quickly became the hardest thing I had ever done in my life. In the midst of adversity, I turned to the scriptures for encouragement and rediscovered today's story of Elijah the prophet.

Today's scripture picks up after Elijah's stunning triumph over the 450 prophets of Baal and the 400 prophets of Asherah at Mt. Carmel. Yet instead of encountering a confident minister of God, we find the prophet running away to the desert in fear for his very life. Elijah gives the appearance of someone in the midst of a vocational burnout, going so far as to appear suicidal when he sits down under a broom tree to die. Elijah speaks to God with words to the effect, "I have had enough, Lord." Despite all the miracles Elijah has seen God perform, his attitude seems to be one of self-pity and resignation.

Have you ever had a similar experience, finding yourself in the midst of adversity and sorely tempted to just "throw in the towel" or abandon the cause? Do you wonder if God really cares? Does God hear your voice?

Sooner or later as we travel along life's journey, we will encounter some adversity that threatens to strip us of all that we believe. How we respond gives testimony to our faith.

Lord, give me strength in the face of whatever adversity I may encounter, and refill me with the hope of your promises. Amen.

We return to the story of Elijah, asking ourselves "What comes next?" For all Elijah's self-pity and frustration with God, God has provided for him. What a complete picture of the fickleness of humanity Elijah presents here! We might suppose that having been revived not once, but twice by God's messengers, Elijah might have stopped, built an altar, and praised and worshiped God! Instead Elijah gets up and travels quite a distance. This act seems hopeful and redemptive until we find that at journey's end he hides in a cave. Even God appears to wonder what is going on and asks this question, "What are you doing here, Elijah?"

Elijah's answer starts off well. He has been zealous for the Lord and served the Lord as he thought God desired. But then he bemoans that he is the only righteous believer left. At this point God tells Elijah that God is going to appear to him, "to pass by." A great rock-shattering wind occurs, followed by an earthquake and then a fire. Yet Elijah hears nothing of God's voice in any of this. Finally a great silence descends upon Elijah and in it Elijah encounters the divine voice. God again asks, "What are you doing here, Elijah?" and then sends Elijah forth with a mission.

God's question to Elijah is relevant for us today. What are we doing wherever we find ourselves? Do we trust God to be with us in the midst of adversity? Or do we trust only in our own capabilities? Time and time again I have seen God work miracles in my life, only to falter when the next adverse situation occurs. When God's question comes to you, how will you respond?

Lord, remind me of your great faithfulness no matter what situation I find myself in. Strengthen me in my weakness. Amen.

Ihave to confess that the opening words of this psalm, "As the deer pants for streams of water," have always annoyed me. Deer overpopulate the areas where I have ministered, wreaking havoc with landscapes, gardens, and field crops alike. Fewer deer in the environment would be a blessing to people who are trying either to feed their families or eke out a living. Yet, as is so often the case with us humans, I've been focusing on the wrong aspect of God's word! It's not the deer that should capture my attention but the human soul mentioned in the last part of this opening verse: a soul that "thirsts for God, the living God."

I'd venture to say that all of us have experienced "dry times" in our spiritual journeys, times when we feel that God has gone elsewhere and left no forwarding address. Our soul feels arid, as does the psalmist's. In my early twenties, a wise Christian teacher of mine made this statement, "When you feel like God has left you, look at where you are. Perhaps it's not God who has moved." The psalmist remembers with a heartfelt longing what it was like to be in the multitude of believers going to "the house of God." Without the ability to praise and worship God, the psalmist's life feels as barren as a desert.

For early Christians this psalm symbolized baptism: thirsty souls came to the baptismal font to drink the living water. In baptism they acknowledged, as do we, dependence upon God, God as the source of our being. So despite our despair and complaint, we bear witness with the psalmist to the bedrock of our faith: "Hope in God."

Lord God, remind me that you never leave me; that when I feel your absence in my life, perhaps I need to check where I am. Help me to find my way back to you. Amen.

Do you feel comfortable complaining to God? Or are you more like me, having been raised to believe that complaining or railing at God was not permissible because it showed a lack of faith in God? If you answer yes to either of these questions, you are in good company!

Few of us feel comfortable in lifting up our complaints and unhappiness to God. We believe somehow that God is too holy for us to approach in this manner. Yet, fully half of the Psalms are psalms of lament. How often do we access the psalms of lament for our personal devotion time, much less hear them read aloud in a worship service?

Psalm 42 is a psalm of lament. The psalmist has been unable to go to "the house of God" and worship the Lord. He is beside himself with grief having nothing but "tears for food each day and night." He complains, remembers, asks for vindication, and then raises his complaint again. His tremendous grief causes him to assail God with both his anger and doubt: "Why have you forgotten me?"

The psalmist has moved from spiritual thirst unquenched to the deluge of waves of trouble. Yet there is good news! The psalmist in all his agony remembers God's faithfulness in the past. This knowledge becomes a glimmer of hope, for at the close of this psalm the speaker stands ready to praise and worship the Lord once again.

In the midst of life's adversity, we can cry out to God with all our anger and bitterness. God is ready and able to hear our cries. The psalms of lament can give expression to our anguish and guide us back to God. The God of our lives is one of steadfast love, whose song is forever with us.

Lord God, may I remember your faithful promises to be with me always—even through the anger and bitterness of life. Remind me that you are "big enough" to hear my cries. Amen.

So far this week we have spoken about adversities that seem to be external in origin: Elijah flees from Jezebel, the psalmist experiences physical separation from God's presence. Today we encounter adversity that is more internal in nature, that of demonic possession.

Luke's first-century adherents lived in a culture that believed beings like demons, spirits, and angels exerted power over human beings. Today, we most likely interpret this story from the vantage point of mental illness. Those who routinely cope with issues like depression, bipolar disorder, and other mental health issues know well the great despair that can make them feel like they are possessed by a relentless force. Yet the adversity they struggle with is just as serious, just as real, as if we labeled it "demonic possession."

The sad ending to the human part of this story is that the community to which the demoniac belongs wants nothing to do with the healed man. Instead of rejoicing in his healing and restoration, people are suspicious and fearful. Their daily existence has changed; they want nothing to do with the person who brought this change about, bluntly telling Jesus to leave.

The joyous ending to this story from a faith perspective is the acknowledgment that God overcomes evil, in whatever form it manifests itself. The demoniac credits his healing to Jesus; Jesus credits the man's healing to God. When we receive healing from adversity in our lives, are we ready and able to give God all praise and glory?

Lord, help me to turn to you when I sense the presence of evil in my life. Let me not be so fearful that I resist your healing mercy. Amen.

The Gentile converts to Christianity face challenges to their faith in the church in Galatia. To better understand this situation we need to understand Paul's purpose in writing this letter to the Galatians.

We think of the apostle Paul as a preacher, but perhaps we would more aptly describe Paul as an evangelist—the Billy Graham of his day. We would refer to him as a church planter, and his primary target audience were Gentiles. In the region of Galatia, Paul had founded churches in Iconium, Lystra, and Derbe. He had preached the gospel of Christ's life, death, and resurrection and the sending of God's Holy Spirit upon all believers. He preached that Jesus was the Christ and therefore the fulfillment of God's law. Believers were justified—made right with God—through faith in Jesus, not through the keeping of Jewish law.

News reaches Paul that an extreme group of believers in the Galatian church called "Judaizers" are teaching the new believers that they must first keep the Jewish laws, before being welcomed as new Christians; and one of their demands is circumcision for all males. Paul is first dismayed and then angry that the Galatians are "so quickly deserting the one who called you by the grace of Christ and are turning to a different gospel" (Gal. 1: 6, NIV).

Here in today's few verses Paul sums up the law: "The law was put in charge to lead us to Christ that we may be justified by faith. Now that faith has come, we are no longer under the supervision of the law" (NIV). Jesus is the culmination of all God's covenants with humanity. Christ's centrality displaces all other loyalties.

God of grace, remind me that faith in Jesus is all that I need to be in relationship with you today, tomorrow, and always. Amen.

When faced with adversity we often want to name it. Then we can grasp hold of it and make some sort of sense out of what we are dealing with. In regard to relations among humans, labels such as "white," "black," "hispanic," "homeless," "addicted," or "lazy" often creep into our vocabulary; anything to distinguish between us and "them." Those who make us uncomfortable become "the Other." Once we have created "the Other," we then create a pecking order of characteristics that makes one group better than the other.

So it seems is the situation within the Galatian church. A group known as the "Judaizers"—strong-willed Jews who have become Christian believers—are trying to tell the new converts that they cannot consider themselves "offspring of Abraham" simply by believing in Jesus. These believers have labeled those who do not follow their teaching as "Other," using names such as "Greek" or "female" or "slave" to denote differences.

In these verses Paul makes it clear that *all* who are baptized into Christ are "clothed in Christ." Faith in Christ through belief and baptism as the entry into a new life in Christ makes a person a Christian. "There is neither Jew nor Greek, slave nor free, male nor female, for you are all one in Christ Jesus" (NIV). There is no "Other" in God's kingdom, only "All."

How quickly we forget this insight in our daily interactions. We continue to live in a world where we assign names and labels to different groups of people, where we routinely make distinctions between "us" and "them." Until we can completely appropriate the fullness of intent found in these words of scripture, God's kingdom on earth will remain but a dream.

Lord, help me to grow beyond my comfort zone in my relationships with others. May I be an instrument for equality among all your children. Amen.

Standing Firm

JUNE 24–30, 2013 • K. J. WUEST

SCRIPTURE OVERVIEW: The passing of a great leader of God's people gives rise to a crisis of sorts, for only the work of the Spirit of God can supply a newly empowered person around whom the people may rally. God does not abandon the people, and we see the fruit of the Spirit's work in the authorization of Elisha to fill the void left by Elijah's passing. Psalm 77 is a cry of distress from one in trouble, but the bulk of the verses have to do with the psalmist's meditation on the goodness of God, especially on God's saving deeds in the past. Galatians 5 is an important statement on the work of the Spirit. Freedom in Christ involves obligations to Christ and to others. The memory of Elijah is raised in the Gospel lection. However, unlike Elijah, Jesus rebukes his followers and invites further resistance by a series of statements concerning the nature of discipleship.

QUESTIONS AND THOUGHTS FOR REFLECTION

- Read 2 Kings 2:1-2, 6-14. When have you displayed great courage and conviction in order to stand your ground?

- Read Psalm 77:1-2, 11-20. When has someone close to you suffered a great tragedy, illness, or disappointment that you never knew about? How did you feel?

- Read Galatians 5:1, 13-25. Do you find Paul's words, "If you are led by the Spirit, you are not subject to the law" freeing or frightening?

- Read Luke 9:51-62. How are we today like the messengers sent ahead to make things ready for Jesus? What helps you persevere?

Writer, certified labyrinth facilitator, creative prayer and journaling retreat leader; member of Kent Lutheran Church, Seattle, Washington

It is not a sign of weakness to admit we are struggling, afraid, or in need of comfort, encouragement, and support. Unfortunately, many times we choose not to trust family and friends with the stark realities of life, and we do this believing we are saving them pain and worry. However, by choosing to shut people out, we actually cause pain, worry, anger, and mistrust. We also make it more difficult for God to share the love, support, comfort, and assurance that God so desperately wants to share with us. Crying out to the one we trust to hear us, we anticipate that our prayer for help will produce relief and release from our dark moments.

The concern then becomes, What do we do when relief does not come? The psalmist faces the issue of unanswered prayer. He cries out to God in the day and the night. His soul receives no comfort.

How do we stand firm in our faith, believing that God is with us, reaching out to comfort, console, and sustain us? Sometimes it helps to stop and reflect on times in the past when we felt this way. In our remembering other stressful or difficult times we have the benefit of hindsight, and often in hindsight we see God's actions more clearly than we did in the moment.

We must ask ourselves, "How do I expect God will answer my prayer?" I often find the answer requires the hands, the words, the prayers, and the actions of others in my life. Through family, friends, neighbors, coworkers and even sometimes the stranger at the bookstore or café, God can and does come to my aid. However, for God to take action, I must be vulnerable enough to let people in.

God of comfort and healing, give me hope in uncertain times. Help me to reach out for the support and encouragement I need and to trust you to be with me through the loving presence and actions of others. Amen.

We associate Elijah with whirlwinds, fire, and, of course, with Elisha—young, curious, steadfast Elisha. Elijah knows he will soon be taken up to heaven. Elisha is resolute in his loyalty to stay with him to the end: "As the LORD lives, and as you yourself live, I will not leave you."

When have you experienced the feeling that you were exactly where you needed to be and had close friends trying to dissuade you from being there? Elisha knows that Elijah, who is closer to him than a father, will be taken from him and there is nothing he can do about it. Elijah repeatedly tries to get Elisha to stay behind and not follow him. Why? We don't really know. What we do know is Elisha stands firm—over and over he says, "I will not leave you."

When Elijah asks what he can do for Elisha before he is taken from him, Elisha requests that he inherit a double portion of Elijah's spirit. While this may seem a bold and selfish request to us, in truth Elisha is asking to be treated as the oldest son, who would inherit twice what a younger son would be entitled to. But Elisha isn't after property or power; he wants to inherit the right to be Elijah's successor. Indeed, as Elijah is taken up in the whirlwind, his mantle is left behind. Elisha retrieves it and uses it to cross the Jordan the same way Elijah did—striking the water with the rolled-up mantle. The water parts, allowing him to cross over to the other side. Elisha is seen and accepted as Elijah's successor and carries on God's work for many years to come.

What would have happened if Elisha had stayed behind as Elijah asked him? What opportunities have you missed by not clinging tightly?

O God, strengthen me to stand firmly where you want me. Amen.

D IY: the acronym that leads the common person to thousands, if not millions, of avenues to creative freedom. Web sites, videos, and cable channels abound for how to "do it yourself" no matter what the "it" is. It expresses a thrilling freedom to make something yourself. We learn this at a young age, as my daughter—even before age two—would happily announce, "Do it myself, mommy!"

So, for what type of freedom does Christ set us free? Is it a do-it-myself or a do-as-I-please kind of freedom? It would seem that the freedom we receive in Christ comes with obligations. The first obligation is to Christ. The second obligation comes in how we relate to one another.

"The fruit of the Spirit is love, joy, peace, patience, kindness, generosity, faithfulness, gentleness, and self-control." This kind of fruit is not something we can DIY, not something we can even grow. This kind of fruit is not just for the individual. The fruit (singular) of the Spirit that Paul mentions is a communal gift, and only God can give the growth needed for this fruit—by way of the life-giving energy of the Spirit. Paul says that a church being led by the Spirit will be marked by the presence of these gifts.

Take a few minutes to reflect on your faith community. Try thinking back over a few decades (if you are fairly new to the community, ask a few longtime members to share their reflections). Look and listen for times of important or difficult decisions. Where do you see the evidence of decisions being Spirit-led? How did love of neighbor influence the Christ-given freedom in the decision making?

Holy Spirit, comforter and guide, bless me with a heart for the faith community you call me into. Help me to act on the freedom you give me to serve my community. May your work in the community bear much fruit. Amen.

Jesus' time is running short. His face is set toward Jerusalem, toward his suffering, death, and resurrection. Earlier in the chapter, Jesus tells the disciples directly, "The Son of Man must undergo great suffering, and be rejected by the elders, chief priests, and scribes, and be killed, and on the third day be raised" (9:22). But the disciples either don't hear or don't believe Jesus' words. When they face Samaritan rejection of Jesus, their first response involves the use of force. According to my NRSV Study Bible, some other ancient manuscripts read, Jesus "rebuked them and said, 'You do not know what spirit you are of, for the Son of Man has not come to destroy the lives of human beings but to save them.'" Jesus rebukes the violence; this land is a field of mission, not one of violence.

This unpleasant incident has far too many parallels today. Not many us will admit to thinking that violence offers the key to achieving anything—other than more violence. Yet violence pervades our world: road rage, drive-by shootings, bombings, cheating, stealing, and acts of arson, to name a few.

In the 1990s the phrase, "What Would Jesus Do" (WWJD), became popular. I would paraphrase the idea as remembering to stop and ask myself, "Are my actions reflective of how Jesus calls me to live?" I am even more interested in the question, "What *is* Jesus doing—in my life and the lives of those around me?" Are my actions reflective of what Jesus is doing in my life? Am I viewing my life as a mission field?

Does might make right? Does it matter if we consider our cause to be a holy one? What decisions do you face today that may tempt you to force matters to go your way?

Take a few minutes to ponder these questions. Close by writing a prayer asking God to help you when you face the temptation to use aggressive action, hostility, or violence.

Among the three or so books I read at once, one is usually a memoir. I especially appreciate spiritual memoirs. Reflecting on our spiritual journey and sharing our story is not only valuable to our own understanding of God at work in our life, it has immense value to others who are exploring their faith and learning to reflect on their own journey. It may be especially helpful to stop and take time to look back when we feel overwhelmed by the present. We remind ourselves of God's past activity in our lives and the lives of others so we can remember that today is but a single day. Looking back can bolster our sense of hope for today.

The psalmist writes, "I will call to mind the deeds of the LORD; I will remember your wonders of old. I will meditate on all your work and muse on your mighty deeds." His earlier crying out to be heard has opened his heart to remember God's presence, which is not always known or felt at the time. We often see that more easily after the fact.

For the last six months I have been the primary caregiver for my husband who is in hospice in our home. When I think back over this time or read in my journal, I can clearly see how God, through so many friends and family, has supported both of us in different and important ways.

Looking back and reflecting on all that God has done reassures the psalmist (and us) that God will continue to act, to love, to comfort, to provide, to encourage, to call us beyond what is hard or frustrating or fearful today, and to lead us into tomorrow and God's holy way.

God who works wonders, help me to be mindful today of all that you have done for me. Open my eyes and my heart to see how you are at work in my life; when I cannot, give me strength to live in faith and to trust your promise to love me with an everlasting love that will not let me go. Amen.

It takes just a few words to give someone the assurance they are not alone during a difficult journey. Recently my mailbox held just such a reminder. A small postcard with a pencil drawing of a solitary pilgrim walking down a barren and lonely looking road included the words, "My steps have held fast to your paths; my feet have not slipped" (Ps. 17:5). Below the scripture my friend wrote, "I thought of Paul (my husband) when I read this." These simple words lifted me.

In today's scripture the apostle Paul expresses the necessity of staying focused and faithful on the path. Fearing the church is being led off course by false teachings, Paul warns the Galatians that choosing a path of self-indulgence and a life marked by works demanded by strict adherence to the law is dangerous. Rather, Paul encourages them to remember that the Spirit has freed them from a life dominated by the law. He reminds them, "For the whole law is summed up in a single commandment, 'You shall love your neighbor as yourself.'"

Guided by the Spirit we are called to love and care for one another. We aren't forced to, but we are free to respond, as Jesus did, by serving God and one another for the well-being of the community. This kind of accountability keeps us focused on the path; indeed, without it we are more prone to isolating ourselves. In isolation we may easily make life all about "me." Then we are only steps away from turning our faith into a long list of dos and don'ts. At that point, we've given away the spirit of freedom we found in our life with Christ.

Looking again at the solitary figure pictured on my postcard, instead of seeing someone walking alone I see purpose in his steps. Perhaps he is on his way to visit a friend in need of a cup of coffee, a listening ear, and a word of encouragement.

May you respond with purpose to both the responsibility and the spirit of freedom to which the Spirit calls you today.

It seems safe to say that our lives are full of distractions. While we have wonderful time-saving devices, even more things clamor for our attention. Making decisions about how we spend our time isn't as simple as choosing between good and bad—far more often we are choosing between good, better, or best.

Three people indicate a desire to follow Jesus. The first person boldly promises to follow wherever he goes, but Jesus' warning about the living conditions of discipleship apparently discourage him. The responses of the other two people include the words, "Let me first. . . . "

I am a list maker. Making a to-do list is my attempt to accomplish as much of the *important* stuff as possible. But Jesus expresses no interest in our accomplishments. I realize that much of what I record under the title "important" has little or nothing to do with growing in my faith, sharing God's love, or proclaiming the kingdom. Mind you, some items on my list may fit in the "better" or even the "best" category. But Jesus challenges his disciples to sacrifice even the best of whatever might make us utter the disclaimer, "I will follow you, . . . but let me first. . . . " The priority to which Jesus calls us is beyond good, better, *and* best.

I affirm that most of us, myself included, would be as sorely lacking in commitment as these three would-be followers. We do have an edge over them because we are part of the body of Christ. We receive strength, encouragement, and opportunities to grow in service, in faith, and in community. As post-Resurrection people we walk with Jesus, knowing his face is no longer set toward Jerusalem.

God of the journey, help me turn aside from distractions and follow Jesus' call to proclaim your kingdom with all my heart. Amen.

A Time of Healing

JULY 1–7, 2013 • WILLIE JAMES JENNINGS

SCRIPTURE OVERVIEW: The story of 2 Kings 5:1-14 joins the beautiful portrait of Psalm 30 in presenting a God who comes to help us in our pain and suffering. These passages draw our attention not simply to the gift of healing but to the giver of the gift who calls us to relationship and life. The epistle lesson reminds us of the importance of caring for one another and striving to build community in the name of Jesus and by the power of the Holy Spirit. The Gospel lesson from Luke reminds us that the Lord will heal humanity through human hands. By sheer grace, we have been invited to join Jesus. His disciples announce the reign of God and the time that now is.

QUESTIONS AND THOUGHTS FOR REFLECTION

- Read 2 Kings 5:1-14. What is the relationship between how we see ourselves and the expectations that we have of God to help us?

- Read Psalm 30. In what ways have you experienced the presence of God in your difficult times?

- Read Galatians 6:1-16. In what specific ways might you make Christian community a more essential reality of your life and not just an option?

- Read Luke 10:1-11; 16-20. Jesus depends on his disciples to carry out the mission given him from his Father. Jesus also commits his authority and word to those same disciples. In what ways do you see that responsibility in your life?

Associate Professor of Theology and Black Church Studies, Duke University Divinity School; an ordained Baptist minister on staff at Mount Level Mission-ary Baptist Church, Durham, North Carolina

No one deserves sickness. No universal moral equation binds certain people to certain diseases, physical challenges, or traumatic bodily harm. As we gain more knowledge of the body, its genetic structures and predispositions, we face the danger of starting to imagine our lives like mathematical formulas. We are not formulas, and it would be much better for us if we move away from formulaic thinking about our lives.

This passage introduces us to Naaman, a person doing well in life but who also has a sickness. One aspect of his life does not balance out the other. Naaman, like so many others, wants to be healed. The desire to be healed joins us together in this world, rich and poor, influential and marginal, elites and lower classes, educated and uneducated, bypassing whatever hierarchies of existence we have formed to make sense of our social worlds. Sickness exposes the folly of both personal formulas for success and social formulas that establish status.

God also shuns formulas. God does not work in our lives by a formula. Naaman learns this lesson. He expects God to help him in ways that will be completely understandable to him, that match his social status in life, and that are convenient. But God often disrupts the way we imagine things coming together for our good in order to surprise us with divine grace. The danger Naaman faces in this story is to the willingness to give up hope in anger over the unorthodox way God is working in his life. We face this same challenge. We should never try to match our unorthodox God with a formula for how we should be helped, healed, or sustained in this life. If we do, we will miss out on God's blessing.

God, teach me to shun formulas for success or health and look to the surprises of healing that you will bring my way today. Amen.

Are not . . . the rivers of Damascus, better than all the waters of Israel?" Sometimes we struggle to see God in unfamiliar places. In this passage we encounter a furious Naaman who cannot understand why his healing requires him to step into a foreign river, the Jordan, and wash seven times. Naaman would have preferred to wash in waters familiar to him. It seemed to him senseless to do this not only in a strange place but also in waters that were to his mind less attractive than the rivers of home. But since he is away from home, the simple approach would be for Naaman to open himself to being healed and blessed right in the place where God has brought him.

Place is indeed important, especially the places we know as home and from where we gain our sense of belonging and identity. God comes to us in such places, making our home divine habitation. God does this as an inexhaustible sign of divine grace.

Yet those of us who have faith in the God of Israel are also asked to go where God leads. In new places and spaces God will give us blessing and healing. But being in new places often means not being in control of our surroundings and sometimes having to wait on the actions of others to get what we need or want. New places intensify our sense of vulnerability, but God invites us to walk in faith in precisely such places.

We must remember that our faith journey is never alone but always with the God who makes a place a home. The God we serve has a tremendous gift for turning strange places into home, not by first transforming the place but by changing us—if we are open to being changed.

Lord, I open myself today to being changed so that the place I am in right now might become a new home for me. Amen.

There is always a before and an after. The psalmist shows us life with God between this before and after. We go from despair to joy, from feeling utterly alone, cast down, and forgotten to feeling uplifted, supported, and healthy. We must be careful not to imagine this before and after of life as caused by God's toying with us. Nor would it be helpful to our souls to see life as endless cycles of absurdity moving continually back and forth between the sublime to the grotesque.

Both ways of seeing life constantly tempt us. The psalmist shows us a God who walks with us in time, seemingly content to be with us in life's every moment. Before you awoke this day God was there with you, waiting to enter it with you. Before you encounter the things that might disappoint or hurt or drive you toward despair, God is prepared to move you through the day. Even if this day brings you to mistakes that displease God and hurt your neighbor, God will not abandon you but will await your repentance and your turning again to the way of faith.

God is the God of the again and again, always wishing to bring us to an after: *after* we have fallen, *after* the disappointment, *after* the hurt. This is God's way, forever drawing us from the signs of death to the sight of life. Therefore we are bold both in our praise and our complaint to God, knowing that in either moment we live with a God with excellent hearing. The time between before and after can seem endless, but there will be an after, because God is faithful.

Lord, remind me in my difficult moments that there was a before and you were with me then, and there will be an after, because you are with me even now. Amen.

Bear one another's burdens." We often struggle to balance care for others with self-care. Few of us consistently achieve this balance. In truth, we can never achieve the balance as long as we seek it without help. It may seem counterintuitive to think of a matter as personal as self-care as requiring the help of others to achieve it, but in fact this is exactly what the Galatians passage helps us to understand. Being Christian not only calls us to life in community but also to live as though community is essential to living a healthy life. The call to form vital Christian community is always challenging because trusting in one's own abilities seems far more appealing than trusting in the shifting sands of relationships. Relationships carry the weight of disappointment, and sometimes our community can be destructive or life-draining.

We are, however, creatures created to enter community with God our Creator and with each other. The wise Christian understands that God has saved us and renews us in and through relationships. Anyone who shuns community also shuns health. We are a new creation recreated in Christ Jesus for good works and healthy life together.

So we should turn our energies toward building community. We look to help others and ask for help from our sisters and brothers. When we see others in need of help or being harmed by a community, we speak out and help them. When we need help we must allow ourselves to enter that vulnerable space of asking and receiving help offered to us. Authentic Christian community will only be found in the giving, asking, and receiving of mutual aid and support. This way leads to true balance. The first step toward self-care that this passage invites us to take is toward each other.

Lord, help me to build community by my actions this day. Amen.

We move from death to life. The Christian life exists in this movement. Yet many of us don't realize it. We tend to think of our lives through smaller transitions; for example, from college or graduate school to an anticipated career or from singleness to a lasting relationship or from life without permanent obligations to life as a parent. Some of us don't imagine any transitions except getting older.

Yet the most decisive transition happens all around us every day. As Christians, we are dying to worldly ways; that is, ways of living and thinking that are opposed to God and God's way of love. This is not a natural transition. It results from the cross of Jesus Christ through which the claims on us of every worldly order—social, political, interpersonal, and economic—have been put to death. Every demand that we live according to their logic has lost its power over us. Of course, there is tension in this transition; not only does the world not want to release us from its ways, but we also often continue to embrace the world's logic.

We are, however, a new creation in Christ Jesus. So we share one another's burdens rather than going it alone and expecting everyone else to do the same. We seek to strengthen one another rather than seeing each other as competitors for resources. We endeavor to follow the Spirit of God rather than live according to the habits of self-centeredness. We esteem *everyone*—not just those who show the trappings of influence and power. And we worship God in Spirit and truth and not simply to exhibit the signs of piety and correct religious form. So the Holy Spirit beckons us onward toward this new life and away from the chains of death that encircle the world.

Thank you, Jesus, for creating a path from death to life. Help me to walk joyfully in it today. Amen.

There is joy in being directed by God. Yet this joy lives in the midst of uncertainty, struggle, and challenge. Jesus directs the disciples into what will most assuredly be troublesome places. They will face temptations of anxiety over everything—from how they will survive to who will receive them and help them. Even as they are tempted to worry in the ways that we worry, they carry the authority and power of God with them. Fear and anxiety on the one hand, divine authority and power on the other hand—which will shape their expectations on their journey? We face the same question daily. God wishes to direct our journey just like the original disciples, filling us with a tangible joy that witnesses the reign of God through Jesus in our lives. And, like those early disciples, we must walk in the faith of Jesus, following his steps. Our journey is now his journey, and his journey is our journey.

The disciples of Jesus live in Jesus; from that place, they face complicated days knowing that Emmanuel is more than just a name. It is a way of life and living: God is with us. This is why Jesus speaks with such confidence in what his disciples can do as they journey. This is not pride in their abilities but trust in the God who will go with them. We may face each day with extraordinary confidence not in our own abilities but in the commitment of God in Christ Jesus to our life. Today's portion of your life journey then becomes quite special, because today brings another chance to bear witness in the simple gestures of life—eating, talking, helping—to a God who has come close, joining flesh to flesh in the Son, and who says to us, "I am with you."

Lord, thank you for another day of the extraordinary journey that is my life with you. Amen.

We who follow Jesus have power in his name—that power differs from worldly power. Worldly power draws us into its endless calculations—who has it or who does not. So many people live focused on getting power to obtain what they want or to influence others. Jesus invites us to focus on our heavenly citizenship. That focus frees us from the seductive pull of power because Jesus reigns for the sake of the world. We are citizens of heaven even now, and from that place of destiny we are called to live each day with a sense of hope rooted in the life of Jesus. We hope not for power but for our lives and the lives of others to be shaped by the reign of God. This hope sustains us especially in moments when we feel powerless.

When we face struggle with people or systems, we easily lose sight of our heavenly citizenship and go after worldly power. Yet worldly power is fleeting and life-draining because obtaining and securing it demands our constant focus. God has marked us for a life path freed from the hunt for power and which bears witness to divine authority in the name of Jesus. In his name we can resist evil and overcome it and stand with others against that which seeks to destroy God's creation.

Through the Son of God we have authority over evil. Yet such authority is not the cause of our joy. Our joy comes with knowing and being known by God. We are bound to the life of the triune God and bound for heaven. So when we are tempted to forsake what is already ours and pursue what the whole world vainly seeks after, we remember that real power already resides in Jesus' hands.

Gracious Savior, when I am tempted to seek worldly power, remind me that all power is in your hands today. Amen.

The Plumb Line

JULY 8–14, 2013 • DENISE SHAFFER

SCRIPTURE OVERVIEW: Amos appears to have lost all hope that the people would realize the serious nature of their sin and renounce it. Because Amos has now come to terms with this melancholy reality, he also understands that God's judgment must inevitably come. Psalm 82 proclaims the supreme rule of the God of Israel: those who forfeit loyalty to the true God will only have their lives dominated by false and destructive gods of their own creation. Colossians emphasizes the crucial place within the Christian life of the qualities of faith, love, and hope. In an ironic twist, the parable of the good Samaritan makes an outsider the one who is "good." We then can place ourselves in the ditch as the victim at the mercy of the very outsider who has been rejected.

QUESTIONS AND THOUGHTS FOR REFLECTION

- Read Amos 7:7-17. In what ways are you using God's "plumb line" to remain close to God and straight and true with others?

- Read Psalm 82. What gods distract you from God?

- Read Colossians 1:1-14. What fruit-bearing growth is your relationship with God yielding?

- Read Luke 10:25-37. Who are your neighbors, and how are you tending to their needs?

Christian education minister in the Church of the Nazarene; born and raised in a Nazarene parsonage, raised two daughters in a Nazarene parsonage, and now has the privilege of watching her five grandchildren being raised in the same heritage; school improvement specialist living in Rock Hill, New York

Amos's preaching emphasizes the righteousness and justice of God, a central theme of the Hebrew Scriptures. It helps us understand the concept of integrity in our relationships, especially to those in need.

Today's reading is the second vision of five witnessed by Amos. It begins with a word of destruction. Amos's vision shows God dropping a plumb line in the midst of the children of Israel. A plumb line, a builder's device, tests whether a wall is uniformly straight. A wall out of plumb would require correction. God holds the plumb line for Israel and for us to determine our sense of justice and our faithfulness.

The prophet Amos believes the people of Israel have turned from God in inauthentic worship and a willingness to take financial advantage of others. It would appear that Amos has lost patience with the people. God drops the plumb line of accountability. How do we measure up to the kind of relationships God desires of us with those in our families, our workplace, and our community—especially in our places of worship?

We easily get caught up in events around us. We may find ourselves bent out of shape by our own desires, twisted beyond an ability to help the needy. We may not stand "true" in God's alignment. Only by focusing on the "straight" alignment can we see where we are out of alignment with God's will.

God tells Amos that places of worship "shall be made desolate," the sanctuaries "laid waste." God disciplines. God corrects Israel for her constant straying from God's commands. That correction comes also to the twenty-first-century church when we stray. The plumb line drops in our midst. How "straight" are we? Are we ready to lead lives of integrity before God?

God, search our hearts for any area that needs to be straightened up. Amen.

This passage serves as a commercial break between visions. Amos goes on to relate the vision of the plumb line to Israel's current experience, and the news is not good. The priests of the high places and sanctuaries receive the protection of the king. They too have misaligned interests. Amaziah, the priest of Bethel, relays Amos's vision to the king. Words of death and exile make no friends among those who have deceived themselves about their accountability to God.

Amos tells the king and the people that God will measure against the plumb line. All will be held accountable, just as each of us is responsible for his or her own behavior and repentance. Our communion with God is one way to know where and how we stand. When we are out of plumb with God, God may seem distant; perhaps our lives even feel desolate.

Amos stands alone and undaunted in delivering his message to Israel. Neither the priest Amaziah nor the king wants to hear Amos's words. Amaziah tells Amos to leave the country; go prophesy somewhere else! When we are out of plumb with God, we may find it hard to hear the message. We may turn against the messenger.

Amos faced a difficult task: giving bad news to those in power and to the people he loved. Sent to be a prophet to Israel, he followed God's call, even though human orders countered God's will.

What messages are you hearing that you would rather not hear? When have you condemned the messenger? To whom are you listening today? Be resolute like Amos. Be a voice in your world to point others to God.

God, it is your voice and yours alone that I want to hear today. May I keep in mind that I am always in your presence. Amen.

The psalmist gives expression to God's concern in the "divine council." Seemingly lesser "gods" (perhaps those of the surrounding peoples) are not demonstrating justice. They show "partiality to the wicked" rather than "rescue the weak and the needy." As with those in power, so too God holds a plumb line for those responsible for justice to others. God stands over the gods whose power derives from God and to whom they must account. When we are out of plumb, we too have neither "knowledge nor understanding." The importance of justice related to accountability comes to the fore as God levels indicting accusations: God's people have failed to "give justice" and "maintain the right."

The psalmist offers a poetic profession of belief in the one God, the Most High. Allegiance to any other god thwarts justice and righteousness. When justice for the least falters, the foundations of the earth shake. Chaos draws closer.

We also find ourselves in the midst of many "gods." To whom do we give allegiance? How do we manifest justice? God has called us to be the hands and feet of Christ. For some of our acquaintances, we may be the only "picture" of God they will see and experience. So what message do we convey?

How do we as God's children handle those who are poor and needy? Do we view them through the eyes and heart of God, or do we "show partiality"? Where is God's plumb line in our midst, and how are we measuring up? When we provide care for the weak and the orphan, speak up for the lowly and destitute, then we will be glad when the psalmist cries, "Rise up, O God, judge the earth!"

God, move our hearts with what moves yours. Help us see all those we meet through your eyes, so that we may look on them with compassion and respond with justice. Amen.

THURSDAY, JULY 11 ~ *Read Colossians 1:1-8*

The epistles help me realize that the early church struggled with issues that were not much different from those that churches face today. Sometimes, early church members allowed life to get in the way of their ability to see Jesus and his way—and that's true for us. We find ourselves reading this letter, desiring to see how the way of Christ applies to us.

I find here in Colossians an interesting connection to Amos. Paul wants these relatively new Christians to understand that he and others in the faith community are praying for them. He acknowledges their faith and love, particularly the fruit bearing they have done in their community. Sounds like a plumb line is being held up to the church of Colossae—and they are measuring up! Paul affirms these fruit-bearing Christians who know that their relationship with God through faith leads to a growing relationship with others and a "love . . . for all the saints." The Colossian community has truly comprehended God's grace.

Paul grounds the Colossians' purpose in Christ and ties it to their hope in heaven, which helps them continue in faith and love. Jesus Christ, "the word of truth," keeps them and us straight and true—in line with God's plumb.

How is your faith community using Paul's positive words to the Colossian church to evaluate its ministry? How does your faith community measure up to the description of a fruit-bearing church that Paul speaks of?

Lord, may we remember the excitement of our first commitment to the faith. Help us to live in a way that pleases you. Amen.

Paul desires that these Colossian Christians "lead lives worthy of the Lord" and goes on to explain what that means: "fully pleasing to him, as you bear fruit in every good work and as you grow in the knowledge of God." These new Christians will stand next to the plumb line to see how they measure up.

Paul also prays that these believers will "be filled with the knowledge of God's will." This knowledge is not an end in itself but makes it possible for us to lead lives worthy of the Lord, lives of holiness. Holy living, in turn, leads to an increasing knowledge of God. What a wonderfully reciprocal relationship this forms!

I never tire of reading this passage. It reminds me that as I walk in Christ's way, I will "be made strong with all the strength that comes from his glorious power." We cannot walk this road without Christ's power. Have you ever tried to turn on a flashlight with dead batteries? You can try to turn it on; but without the a power source, it will never light up. Christ's power energizes us to bear trials patiently and even with joy.

Paul closes the letter with a threefold commendation of God's action on behalf of humanity: We share in the inheritance of the saints of light; we are rescued from the power of darkness; we receive forgiveness of our sins.

Jesus set the plumb line and prepared the way for this type of walk through his life and through his death on the cross. We have already been delivered! It is like reading the last chapter of a book first; we already know the ending: forgiveness and inheritance. That is good news!

God, thank you for your Son; may we grow in knowledge of you and lead lives of holiness. Amen.

Jesus begins a discussion with a lawyer. Or should I say a time of questions and answers—with answers the lawyer doesn't want to hear. The lawyer asks of Jesus, "What must I do to inherit eternal life?" Jesus responds with a question.

The lawyer replies, citing two passages from the Old Testament: Deuteronomy 6:5 and Leviticus 19:18, which bind together the love of God and neighbor. Jesus tells him he has answered correctly and that if he does this he will live. Perhaps the lawyer is looking for the plumb line when he asks, "Who is my neighbor?" And it is a legitimate question, because ancient authorities state that "neighbor" noted to in Leviticus refers to "your kin" or "any of your people." In response, Jesus tells the familiar parable of the good Samaritan.

How do we respond to loving God and neighbor? Do we want to live? Isn't the lawyer's question the one the church is asking today? With so many people and so many needs, who is my neighbor? And just how thin am I supposed to spread myself and my resources? Perhaps we, like the lawyer, don't want to hear Jesus' answer.

Caring for neighbor goes hand in hand with loving God. We don't have to choose between feeding on scripture and feeding the hungry, between reaching out to God and reaching out to those in need. The Christian walk requires both works of mercy and works of piety. We learn to expand our hearts to care for neighbors down the street and around the world.

Listen to yourself asking Jesus, "Who is my neighbor?" In preparation for tomorrow's meditation, listen for Jesus' specific answer to you. Be ready to list the neighbors Jesus says are yours.

God, may I see and respond to the needs of others. Amen.

W ho is my neighbor?" So Jesus tells a parable of four characters. The priest and the Levite are highly respected Jewish religious leaders, perhaps on their way to the temple in Jerusalem. The Samaritans descended from Israelites who intermarried with Gentile settlers beginning in 722 B.C. The Jews despised the Samaritans. The lawyer would be familiar with this history. Jews would walk miles out of their way to avoid Samaritan territory. Yet the Samaritan has compassion on the wounded Jew (character #4).

"Who is my neighbor?" Jesus stretches the boundaries of family and kin to include anyone in need. God's interest moves beyond family and racial prejudice. The choice of the Samaritan as the helper would leave Jesus' audience stunned.

We want to measure up to God's plumb line, so we will take the Samaritan's approach, which requires that we move out of our comfort zone to line up with God's will for us. I can almost hear a cry of protest, "But I can't help everyone!" We need to help those God places in our path by being ready and obedient servants.

"Who is my neighbor?" We usually know what is right, what God wills for us. The issue becomes this: will we follow through as the hands and feet of Jesus? Will we view people as Jesus sees them? Will we pray daily for God to show us God's heart? We know the standard.

Jesus, at the close of the parable asks, "Which of these three . . . was a neighbor?" The lawyer knows the answer: "The one who showed him mercy." Jesus' response then and now is, "Go and do likewise."

Lord, I want to know you so completely that I will be ready to do whatever you ask of me. I want to be your hands and feet for my neighbors. Amen.

Ripe for Compassion

JULY 15–21, 2013 • TOM CAMP

SCRIPTURE OVERVIEW: In the Amos lection, the vision of judgment is followed by a statement of God's impending justice. In Psalm 82 (the alternate psalm text) the God of Israel rules all. Those who do not remain loyal to this God will allow gods of their own making to dominate their lives. But God will not allow such tyranny to go unchecked and will ultimately vindicate those who have lived faithful lives. The Colossians hymn heightens the connection between the cosmic Christ and the church, his earthly body. The familiar complaint of Martha directed against her sister, Mary, constitutes the Gospel lection. The story of Martha and Mary maintains that doing without listening is futile.

QUESTIONS AND THOUGHTS FOR REFLECTION

- Read Amos 8:1-12. How will you open yourself to hear the word of God in the midst of profit motives, widening gaps between rich and needy, political and international hostilities, and environmental pollution?

- Read Psalm 82. The psalmist calls our attention to the many "gods" we honor, those centers of value and attraction that call our attention away from the one true God. How do you distinguish between false values and the deeper values in your life?

- Read Colossians 1:15-28. The writer proclaims Christ as the image of the invisible God and us as Christ's body. What practices enable you to be aware that you are participating daily as an active part of Christ's body?

- Read Luke 10:38-42. How do you balance daily tasks of living with an awareness of being in Christ's presence?

Pastoral counselor and spiritual director; Samaritan Counseling Center of Northeast Georgia; living in Athens, Georgia

The river was so bare, the water level so low, that the trash often concealed by the water was left exposed on the dry riverbed. I sat on the bank looking at what I once knew as a beautiful flowing river but which was now punctuated with dry clay islands. What happened? The combination of erosion, pollution, and drought altered the character of this river. I sat staring at the evidence of what we try so hard to ignore.

Our land trembles due to overuse, erosion, and pollution. I join people who mourn for beauty where there is ugliness, for fertile farmland to grow healthy food, for fresh oxygen-rich air where there is urban smog. People mourn for justice and fair sharing of the world's resources. How do we take seriously the problems we face and not feel overwhelmed and hopeless?

The prophet is merciless with us, as is reality. My father told me maturity involves moving beyond fantasy and denial to face the naked truth of reality. I never liked that teaching!

How do we find peace in this world filled with so many problems so publicly displayed? We may find it tempting to ignore the problems and deny the fears—or to pray for miracles. We certainly face the temptation of focusing on religious rituals and beliefs rather than following those rituals and beliefs to their moral implications.

Amos appears to deny any hope. He portrays stark reality and real consequences. Acknowledging reality is confession, the beginning of hope. As we face the stark reality of the consequences of our attitudes and behaviors, we receive the opportunity to change. Only as we embody God's divine love for ourselves, one another, and the world do we have motivation to make these needed changes.

Awesome God of the prophets who confronts us with truth, awaken in us courage and love for you and all you have created. Amen.

When the fruit and the people are ripe, the Lord will spare them no longer (NIV). With ripeness and maturity come responsibility and purpose. To be spared no longer means facing the absolute truth of our circumstances. In this time we are ripe to come to terms with the truth in at least two ways.

First, we are ripe in our minds. God has so guided our development over thousands of years that our minds have powerfully expanded capacities. We, like most animals, can monitor our feelings, environment, and bodies to defend ourselves from all sorts of threats. This capacity protects us; but by itself, it is self-centered. Our minds are ripe because we have developed *beyond* self-centeredness. Our human brain has specific structures that enable us to be compassionately aware of all other beings, which allows us to live together in community. We can monitor self-centered urges and make moral choices. We can recognize self-centered impulses and postpone reaction, consider long-term consequences and alternate actions, and be thoughtful of other people and things. We now have the ability and, therefore the responsibility, for compassion.

Second, we are ripe in our awareness of the interconnectedness of actions and consequences for ourselves, other people, and the whole environment. Science has opened to us the cycle of behavior and consequences in areas such as the food we eat and our health, our standard of living and its effect on the earth, and the relationship of injustice and oppression to crime and violence. We cannot act and assume our actions have no consequences. We are not spared the outcomes of our behaviors.

The capacity and opportunity for moral action and compassion are tremendous gifts. We are conscious human beings who can choose to incarnate the compassion of divine love.

Wonderful God of compassion, open our hearts to your compassion with us. Awaken our compassion to all beings. Amen.

How many "gods" are there? Our religion teaches there is only one God, yet the psalmist speaks of many "gods."

Sometimes I am painfully aware of the many gods in my life. I catch myself thinking I must have a new car, the best office, an expensive piece of clothing. I worry that my house needs better furnishings. I seek financial security and sexual satiation. In a world of great change, I yearn for stability. I want my enemies destroyed. I seek spiritual righteousness.

Wow, I've listed nine of my gods. Some spiritual directors tell us that three universal energy centers become our gods: security, pleasure, and power. The psalmist reminds us that these gods understand nothing, for they walk around in darkness. They have no awareness of long-term consequences or of other people as God's children. They defend the unjust and show partiality to the wicked; that is, they seek their own ends without regard for the effect on others.

To sing out, as the psalmist does, "Rise up, O God, judge the earth," is to pray for awareness of our many gods and the effects these gods have on us and our world. When we become aware of our gods, we then have power to deal with them.

Yet our true selves are made in the image of the one true God who does judge, and we yearn for oneness with this God. God's judging is not condemning but discerning. It makes clear what is real. God's judgment opens our eyes so that we no longer walk in darkness. We gain a heightened awareness of deeper, truer reality. We seek not security, pleasure, or power but love. We seek to be loved and to love as our true nature. The verb *love* is the incarnation of the one true God.

O God, judge us with love, so that we awaken to our true nature. Amen.

After morning worship with Holy Communion, my wife and I gathered with family and friends to eat lunch. As we sat around the table, partaking of the bounty of food and life experiences, I felt a deep sense of shared community. We each seemed to feel safe in this shared togetherness, and all shared both joy and challenge with relative ease. Somehow there was far more present in and around that table than people and food.

The writer of Colossians says that God has chosen "to make known the glorious riches of this mystery, which is Christ in you" (NIV). Christ is universal, the beginning and the end, the essence of all reality. Everything that exists has its being in Christ. Jesus somehow embodied the spirit of this primordial, life-giving essence that we know as God. We each experience Christ within so that when we gather together in openness and compassion, Christ is present in our midst.

When I gather with others who are seeking but fail to experience this openness and compassion, I feel alienated. When I feel defensive or aggressive, I see others as threats rather than fellow human beings. When I am open to myself, caring and respectful to others, I feel a connectedness that goes far beyond human community to the sense of Christ's presence in and among us.

Paul invites us to transcend self-protection and self-promotion so that we join him in "fill[ing] up in [our] flesh what is still lacking in regard to Christ's afflictions" (NIV). In opening ourselves to one another in the church—the body of Christ—we continue the presence and work of Christ in the world.

We only truly know Jesus' teachings when we *become* the teaching, when the spirit of Christ is incarnate in us.

O God, who came to us in Christ, awaken us to your eternal mysterious presence. Amen.

FRIDAY, JULY 19 ~ *Read Amos 8:11-12*

It started out to be a lovely evening with good food and conversation, but the evening news created anxiety. Forest fires, economic turbulence, political tensions, famines, and war brought awareness of so much danger in our world.

We live in a world filled with many dangers, and we expend a lot of energy trying to disregard them. I grew up in the time of threat of nuclear war, a threat we've learned to ignore today. Now we face threats of too many people for the earth to support, depletion of resources such as clean water, pollution of our environment, and hostilities and violence among people. These threats come as the consequences of human choices and behaviors that run contrary to the word of God. Our individual choices as well as our collective choices have real consequences.

The prophet does not avoid attention to the real dangers; indeed, his confrontation of the people with the naked reality forms the essence of prophecy. The prophet tells of an approaching famine of the word of God. God has given direction for obedient and faithful living.

Perhaps we travel so far from God's will that we no longer hear God's word. Maybe, in our fear, we hear only superficial comfort; and we mistake that for God's word. Or we are taken in by the social and cultural "gods" such as wealth, military power, possessions, and political ideologies. The prophet warns that those who follow false gods will fall and never rise again.

"The time is surely coming . . . when I will send a famine on the land." Once the consequences come, it is too late. God does not excuse us from responsibility. In our life today, some consequences have already occurred; but we still have the opportunity to face reality and make significant changes—ones that reflect the true will and purposes of God.

Powerful God, thank you for your direction in our lives. Give us courage to correct our ways before it is too late. Amen.

As I played with my infant granddaughter, I watched her crawl after every new thing within her sight, investigating this wonderful world. Her family's dogs, the patterns on the carpet, her toys, my knee, the dog's toys—all fascinate her. Her world is awesome, filled with mystery and adventure. She has not yet learned danger and fear, and her limits are set only by the protective hands of her caregivers. Her refreshing innocence and curiosity reconnected me with my own innocence and curiosity. I began to see the world with more color, deeper feeling, less matter-of-fact acceptance.

The next day I spoke with an elderly man whose wife had just died. His pain was tremendous, yet his accumulated wisdom from years of dealing with loss guided him. I sought to minister to his pain but found myself being ministered to by his pain. I noticed his mentoring of me in my own losses.

The fullness of God dwelled in Jesus as an example of how the fullness of God may dwell in all of us. We meet God in the infant filled with curiosity and the old man whose wisdom guides him through another wilderness. We meet God in the homeless who suffer from the inequalities of our world and the wealthy who realize riches do not provide that deep satisfaction we all seek. And we meet God in our own spiritual meditation, as our deep compassion for ourselves and the world emerges beyond our protective layers of awareness.

We all become servants according to God's commission. Through us the word of God will be fully known. The mysteries are now revealed to the saints. When we remember that each person is the image of God, a dwelling place of God's spirit, our relationship with God will deepen and widen, and our compassion for all of life will intensify.

O God, who dwells in Christ, remind us that you dwell in each of us at all times. There may we find you. Amen.

Sitting with my spiritual mentor in a beautiful garden, I acknowledged being in the presence of a truly compassionate person. I do not remember what my mentor said during that time, but I remember his face, the calm of his body, his bright cheerful eyes, and my deep peace in his presence. Whatever was happening in his own life, he made space for me in himself.

I see Mary seeking more than Jesus' words. She does not seek to learn or to receive a great teaching; she seeks to be in his presence. She hungers for his very being, a being imbued with unconditional love, permeated with compassion. Jesus invites her and makes space for her in himself. To be in the presence of one who loves so completely confirms our own being.

God invites each one of us to the feast of divine presence. At this feast we find ourselves saturated with divine love that creates space within us for others. Too often the cares of the world distract us from awareness of God's presence, and our agendas distract us from God's presence in each other. God is present with us in mystery and in community, through nature and through compassionate service. We find God's presence anywhere and everywhere we look.

My mentor stated clearly that spiritual mentoring was not about achieving some spiritual high but about developing love that bears fruit in relationships. Jesus' life and teachings served as my mentor's model. Jesus always calls us beyond simply basking in his love to unself-centered loving of others. Such loving comes not as a demand but as a natural outgrowth of being in divine presence, of being loved deeply and completely.

It is not simply being loved that confirms us as much as the experience of love flowing through us. This flowing love, this divine energy, enlivens us with abundant life.

O God, who is always and totally present even in our ignorance, awaken us to your permeating love. Amen.

Relationship with the Living God

JULY 22–28, 2013 • PATRICIA WILSON

SCRIPTURE OVERVIEW: The Hosea passage implies that the relationship between God and Israel is similar to a marriage that has been ruined by an unfaithful spouse. Yahweh has been scorned, and judgment is at hand. However, the prophet implants a reminder that Yahweh's final word is not destruction but redemption. Psalm 85 reveals a community of God's people who are suspended between the "already" and the "not yet." Colossians reminds the readers that no other force or personality may compete with Christ, for Christ and only Christ embodies "the whole fullness of deity." Faith and action are one. Luke's Gospel directs the disciples' attention to their real needs, as well as reminding them of the only one who can fulfill those needs.

QUESTIONS AND THOUGHTS FOR REFLECTION

- Read Hosea 1:2-10. How do you distance yourself from God? How have you experienced God's love and forgiveness?
- Read Psalm 85. In what ways do you dwell on your past history with God? What kinds of tribulation do you experience in your life? How can you learn to listen to God?
- Read Colossians 2:6-19. Do you feel deeply rooted in Christ? Have you been tempted by other spiritual practices? What did you do?
- Read Luke 11:1-13. How would you describe your prayer life? What has been your experience of the Holy Spirit when you pray?

Author of *Quiet Spaces, When You Come Unglued . . . Stick Close to God*, and *The Mindful Manager* (Upper Room Books); living in Nova Scotia, Canada

Did you feel a sense of unreality, perhaps even revulsion, as you read this text? How can God tell Hosea to marry a prostitute? Then God intervenes and names the three children of Hosea and Gomer. Did you recoil from those terrible, damning names that indicate the depth of God's anger toward Israel: "my punishment," "not loved," "not my people"?

If you read farther in the passage, you'll discover that Gomer leaves Hosea. She returns to her old way of life. Yet, Hosea publicly takes her back, an amazing act of forgiveness in a culture that could have stoned her.

This passage portrays a callous, vindictive God. Yet, when we read the last verse, the picture changes. Suddenly, we see a God who not only forgives those same people but promises a familial relationship.

Rather than reading this text as a literary story, try seeing it as a metaphor for the relationship between God and Israel. God represents Hosea, an upright man, who marries a prostitute. Gomer represents Israel, a nation in the midst of warfare and even anarchy, a nation worshiping false idols and forgetting its covenant with God. When Israel tries to separate itself from God, God brings Israel back.

In a present-day context, we worship the false idols of money and power. The fabric of our lives becomes acquisition and consumerism. Time and time again, we turn away from God because our minds and hearts are elsewhere. We forsake the relationship of love that God has promised us. Yet, like Hosea who forgave Gomer, God does not let us slip away. We are continually drawn back into God's presence, forgiven, and redeemed.

If I have strayed away from you, bring me back, Lord. If I have forgotten your great love for me, bring the remembrance of that love back to my heart as I come into your presence now. Amen.

An older fellow in the prayer group related all the things that God had done for him: taken away his desire to drink, restored his marriage, and found him a job. *What a great and glorious Lord we serve,* I thought.

In the first three verses of this passage, the psalmist does the same thing: he recounts God's treatment of the people of Israel. God has restored the fortunes of Jacob, forgiven the sins of the people, and set aside wrath and anger toward Israel.

In both cases, the storytellers are recounting a history with God. Their words convey a sense that God is an active, involved, caring God who is lovingly concerned with our lives. When God comes into the picture, things happen; fortunes are restored; relationships are healed; peoples and persons are changed forever.

Back to the prayer group. After the fellow finished his recounting of how God had changed his life so completely, the leader of the group spoke. "Bill," he said. "That happened thirty years ago. What has God done for you today?"

The same thing might have been said to the psalmist. "Writer, those things happened decades ago. What has God done for Israel today?"

It's easy to get stuck into a rut of what happened yesterday. Most of us can tell stories of God's hand in our lives: miracles, big and small; moments of God-with-us that we will never forget. Some of us get lost back there in the past glories of our walk with God. We forget that we have already traveled that road. We want to look back to where we have been instead of looking forward to where God leads us now. We forget that the God of our past is the God of our present and our future.

Lord, help me remember your goodness toward me, but only as I continue to walk with you daily. Help me also remember that you are a God of the present moment. Amen.

In talking with an older, retired minister, I shared my fairly recent conversion experience, my hopeful plans for the church, and my excitement over future possibilities. He sighed, shook his head, and said, "Oh, yes. The early enthusiasm. You'll get over it."

In this section of the psalm, the Israelites have gotten over it. They have forgotten all those wonderful stories of God's favor toward them as they turn from their God and turn toward the idols and false gods of their neighbors. In these few verses, we acknowledge a shift. God is now angry with them, and they are in need of God's restoration and love.

I've met a lot of Christians in the same boat. It all started out so well—joy, excitement, enthusiasm. Then, somewhere along the way, it all slowly faded, leaving them with a sense of abandonment and loss. Usually, they blame God for forsaking them, seldom acknowledging that they are the ones who moved out of the circle of God's love.

Any relationship involves that period of wonder and discovery as two people begin to form a bond together. They do not expect that the "honeymoon period" will last forever. Yet, relationships do endure beyond the early enthusiasms and become stronger and deeper as the years pass. The relationship journey can survive bumps in the road.

However, when we allow the rocky places to define the relationship, we run into trouble. God doesn't promise no valleys or bumps in our walk; God did promise us that we wouldn't have to travel alone. Knowing this, we can step out in faith today with the same feelings of enthusiasm, joy, and excitement that we first experienced at the beginning of our journey.

Lord God, restore in me the enthusiasm for the journey. Fill me with joy as I contemplate the days ahead, knowing that whatever they hold for me, you are with me. Amen.

The psalmist writes this portion of the psalm after telling us that Israel needs God's favor. We don't know whether he is talking about a drought, famine, exile, or war. We just know that Israel is in trouble.

We've all been in places of drought, famine, exile, and war —probably not in the literal sense, but certainly metaphorically speaking. Whether we're experiencing a period of spiritual dryness or a hunger for more of God, a feeling of being cut off from God or a breakdown in a relationship, at these times, like the Israelites, we turn to God.

One drawback of being human is that we often convince ourselves that we know exactly what God needs to do in order to set things right in our lives. In times of trouble and need, our prayers often become "to-do" lists for God.

"Let me hear what God the LORD will speak." So the psalmist begins his prayer for God's help. These words give us the starting point for an intimate dialogue with God. Before we say or do anything in our petitions before the throne of grace, God wants us to listen. That means being silent: silent in our thoughts, in our words, in our hearts, and in our minds. From that silence comes the still small voice of God speaking to us. In the midst of our tribulations, despite what has gone before, God is there, has always been there, will always be there. We just need to listen.

The psalmist also tells us the results of listening to God: peace, salvation, glory, love, faithfulness, and righteousness. For many people, this comes as a moment of clarity as the pathway opens before them. For some, it may be a deep sense of God's hand in the situation; others may experience a new closeness with God.

God of my life, teach me how to listen to you. May I listen now as I open myself to you. Amen.

It's all about the roots. Deep roots mean a healthy plant. Shallow roots make a plant susceptible to drought and storm. We can say the same thing about the roots of our Christian faith. If they go deep, nothing will move us. If not, we may fall prey to every new whim and idea that comes along.

Paul knew this. The Colossians find themselves surrounded by all kinds of religions and beliefs that he calls hollow and deceptive philosophies. He warns them against the elemental forces of this world that are not of God.

In our modern world, a plethora of information bombards us every moment of every day. Inevitably some of this information will be of a "spiritual" nature: promises of new hope, new lives, new power, new abundance, and even new bodies—if we just believe. We can easily discern that some of these new ideas are false, and we can set them aside. But many are insidious in that they lay claim to Christian elements. Somehow, God gets all tangled up in spiritual practices outside of our biblical frame of reference. Whether New Age or shamanism, Scientology or angel worship, pantheism or Spirit guides or any of the many alternatives available to us, none of these so-called religions can give us what today's reading promises: forgiveness of sins and a new life through the power of the Cross.

Christians not rooted deeply in Jesus can be lured into the belief that it's okay to explore other avenues of faith. Although they desire a deeper relationship with God through different spiritual practices, they fail to see how slippery the slope is and how easily they can be drawn away from God.

Paul makes it quite clear: Jesus Christ is the reality. All else is shadow.

Lord Jesus, I want to be deeply rooted in you. Nourish my faith with your love and presence in my life. Today, bring me into a closer walk with you. Amen.

The Lord's Prayer. Most everyone knows it. For most of us reading this, it's part of our weekly worship. But today's reading isn't the prayer we're familiar with. It's Luke's version—kind of a streamlined edition of Matthew's version.

Think of this shorter Lord's Prayer as our relationship with God in a nutshell. In these few verses, Luke gives us a daily prayer that describes how we are to view God and how God views us.

The first word, *Father*, tells us that we are part of a family. It's a highly personal way to address the Lord of lords, King of kings, the Alpha and the Omega, the Almighty God. It seems that we Christians have a lot of temerity, being on such familiar footing with God. Yet it sets the stage for us to acknowledge that we are God's children.

Before we get into the meat of the prayer, we also acknowledge that God is more than just a loved head of the family. God is holy ("hallowed"). And then, we remind ourselves that we are a waiting people. "Come, Lord Jesus, come," we are saying as we pray for God's kingdom here on earth.

Finally, the prayer presents three petitions to God. Boldly, we ask for bread to sustain our bodies each day. We ask to be forgiven of any wrongdoings, understanding that our task as God's people is to forgive others around us. And finally, we ask not to be tempted beyond our strength. In essence we ask God to be with us in all that comes to us each day.

To distill this prayer even further, we could pray, "Father, holy, come. Give, forgive, protect." Six words to describe an intimate relationship and a daily walk with God.

Father, hallowed be your name. Your kingdom come. Give us each day our daily bread. And forgive us our sins, for we ourselves forgive everyone indebted to us. And do not bring us to the time of trial. Amen.

We often read this passage as proof that God will give us anything we want if we just ask for it. The two parables could lead us to believe that all we need is a long shopping list and lots of determination when we approach God's throne.

But on closer reading, the parables don't say that at all. You'll notice that in the last verse Jesus tells the disciples what they will receive when they ask, seek, or knock. Surprised? I was. How do we miss the Holy Spirit in this passage? It's as if the Holy Spirit has slipped in when no one was looking.

At last, we have the final piece to our God-relationship puzzle. Our relationship with God includes the Holy Spirit. We know the Holy Spirit led Jesus into the desert and helped him overcome Satan's temptations. We know that Jesus promises the Holy Spirit after he has gone. We know that at some point the Holy Spirit comes to Jesus' followers at Pentecost. But now we know something more: when we petition God, we receive the Holy Spirit in response.

It's as if Jesus tells us not to fixate on the "things" we want; but instead, to align our hearts with God's heart. Then, when we begin to seek an answer to our prayers, that answer will come from the wisdom of the Holy Spirit within us. The undefined "it" of the previous verses is not the shopping cart full of the things we want but the gift of the Holy Spirit.

Our asking and seeking and knocking should be for the Holy Spirit before all else. Only then can we pray to God with a full expectation of receiving an answer.

Lord God, send the Holy Spirit to me so that when I pray for myself and others, I can follow the Holy Spirit's guidance. Help me bow to the Holy Spirit's wisdom and put aside my human wants and needs. Amen.

Gifts of Discipleship

JULY 29–AUGUST 4, 2013 • VANCE P. ROSS

SCRIPTURE OVERVIEW: The Hosea lection portrays the agony of God, who is torn between the demands of judgment and of grace. When justice and grace are weighed in God's balances, grace always prevails. Psalm 107's language applies to many experiences of alienation. Lostness, hunger, thirst, and weariness characterize the condition of those cut off from God; yet if they seem abandoned, they are not. For God has guided them out of the desert and back to their homes once again. The freedom to live in goodness is the subject of Colossians. The passage points readers beyond "things that are on earth" to "things that are above." Freedom from greed is the focus of Luke 12:13-21, a text that addresses the difficult issue of how the Christian is to deny the temptations of materialism while living in a very material world. The farmer is not condemned because he worked to produce a bumper crop, but his demise is viewed as tragic because he wrongly believed that his bulging barns would be his salvation.

QUESTIONS AND THOUGHTS FOR REFLECTION

- Read Hosea 11:1-11. How does the thought of God's pain at your misbehavior strike you? When have you experienced wrath as a gift?

- Read Psalm 107:1-9, 43. When has God led you through a "desert waste" to an "inhabited town"?

- Read Colossians 3:1-11. What behaviors and practices of your "old self" would you like to strip off?

- Read Luke 12:13-21. When have you allowed greed to affect your relationships?

Father to Bryant, Kristina, and Alyssa; Pop-Pop to Jaylie and Christopher; husband to Bridgette; Senior Pastor to Gordon Memorial United Methodist Church, Nashville, Tennessee

Saying that God hurts, Hosea places an amazing concept before us. The Invincible God experiences pain. The Designer God, Author of the Universe, feels the agony of human refusal to return love, the love that helps and heals the child. God hurts, ultimately, because God's child hurts and attracts more hurt.

The child attracts hurt by chasing puny gods that entice but own only the capacity to harm. Greed, as seen in the corporate malfeasance that led to the 2008 economic collapse, is one of those gods. Another is biased justice, as viewed in the contemporary practice meting out capital punishment almost exclusively to the financially disadvantaged. Individual unwillingness to forgive serves as another puny god that calls forth God's judgment. Any act of lust, serving gods that abuse others while serving selfish needs, makes a demand of God.

What demand? These idol-worshiping behaviors demand the God-gift of wrath. Yes, the God-gift of wrath. God's rage serves as much more than an envious response of a spurred parent. Anger expressed at mistreatment elevates the dignity of the oppressed one and serves notice that victimization cannot and will not be silently tolerated. God's fury demands a defending response to pain, a response that stops the unkindness. Only when unkindness ends can there be reconciliation.

God longs for our love, for us to be reconciled to God by loving treatment of one another. Hosea reminds us that God's heart breaks when we fail to love and that God will gift our failure with an angry response. It is not a threat. It is a promise! Amazingly, even with the promised anger, God dares to bring us home. Astonishing love it is—a love to be grateful for but not to be taken for granted.

God of love, help us to love as you ask and as you have shown, especially in the person of Jesus. We pray in his name. Amen.

Even at age fifty-four, I wrestle constantly with the notion of vulnerability as it applies to me. I despise the idea of personal weakness, perceived and actual. Growing up I often felt anxious about self-defense, physically and emotionally. I never wanted to be found in a position where anyone could hurt me or even know they hurt me.

This anxiety has not left me. Even with the God-gift of a wise and skillful Christian psychotherapist, I remain suspicious of the *V* word. Expressing vulnerability and pain does not come easily for me. My comfort level for weakness remains miniscule. Testifying to hurt is not a witness I choose to share.

Hosea contradicts me—and many others of us—as he relates God's capacity beyond anger, to explicitly share in the emotions of hurt. God knows that hurt. God does more than become enraged at faithless disobedience; God feels hurt with us.

When those we have nurtured—those whom we have taught to walk and ride bicycles or those we gave time and money to or those we shared intimacies with of every kind—turn from us to items that serve only to crush them, we seldom get angry first. Our culture conditions us to consider that, but it is not what happens. Before our anger shows, we suffer. We feel pain and hurt.

I am not alone in fearing the *V* word. The willingness to confess our hurt does not come easily in society or church. Admitting injury often is perceived as helpless, even cowardly, for those who will dare to express it.

Thanks be to God for this gift from the prophet. We do no wrong when we communicate offense. We do not sin to say that we have been wronged. God does it. Because God does, we are liberated to do the same.

Great God, help us dare to be reconciled in Jesus' name. Amen.

We can count on God. The psalmist recalls for us that God specializes in deliverance. Redemption is God's forte. God knows how to emancipate, liberate, and rescue. If God's people know anything about their history and religion, they know of God's ability to redeem.

This ability lays the foundation of faith and tops faith's impact on living. A religion that functions only in worship gatherings of the faithful is no religion at all. The book of Psalms, insisting on a full embrace of life, declares a faith that believes in the God who alone can be counted on. Followers of Jesus often forget this good news. The standards of our environments can betray us. They can keep us from enjoying life, from living the overcoming message we claim as foundational.

One snowy Sunday my son, Bryant, invited me to drive down an especially icy road in our neighborhood. He favored it for summer bike rides as well as winter sled rides. He thrilled at the dips and turns and wanted me to share the thrills in our Chevy Cavalier.

Not immune from such betrayal, I procrastinated and stalled our commuter conversation until the turn passed out of sight. It did not leave his mind, however. "Dad," he said, "we didn't go down Lincoln Avenue." I replied, "Son, we couldn't. If we got stuck, we might not get out for days." Bryant quickly intoned, "Dad, we won't get stuck. And if we do, God will bring us out. Don't you believe it? You preach it every Sunday!"

Our Lord's Day preachments and testimonies should bear up to the examination that Bryant made. Redeemed people should say and show what we have experienced and know. Our challenge today is to trust the God who can bring us out of any situation.

Almighty One, may we trust you to redeem the situations we encounter. In Jesus' name. Amen.

The psalmist invites those who claim insight and understanding to examine Israel's salvation history as a tribute to the love of God. Scripture texts such as this psalm speak powerfully to the unstinting love God showers on humankind. They emphasize the overall witness of the Holy Bible: God extravagantly loves humanity. Belief in scriptural primacy makes biblical reflection essential to Christian faith.

But what does my life experience speak? God's love blesses me. I know faith struggles. I have had desert days when God was silent and seemed absent. In unsure days of little peace, God spoke through family and friends. Colleagues, even foes, gave words of hope and help. Looking back, even in rough days God showed me love continually.

The psalmist defines the sovereignty of God as steadfast love, with the defining characteristics of compassion and forgiveness. All of us have known what the psalmist means when writing, "Some wandered in desert wastes, finding no way to an inhabited town; hungry and thirsty, their soul fainted within them. Then they cried to the LORD in their trouble, and he delivered them from their distress." Through it all, God's love sustained.

God hears our cries and delivers. God's steadfast love comes in concrete form in providing for those in need: through friends that we did not know were friends at all; through a phone call at just the right time; through parents and siblings who showed up just in time. God gave brothers and sisters who have been friends even when expressing anger toward one another. God gave disciples of Jesus, clergy and lay, who prayed with and for me, who encouraged me and challenged me. Is God's love steadfast? Along with the psalmist, and with a multitude in faith, my testimony is yes!

God, embolden us to testify to your goodness. Amen.

Christian faith declares the gift common to all as the ultimate. Jesus the Christ, our liberator and emancipator, lives as that common gift, God's excellent gift to the world. The gift of God in Jesus is fullness of life; that is to say, life in all of its glorious possibility.

We often misunderstand the "full" life in the faith. Many relegate holiness to denial of the senses, making flesh a problem for living rather than a wondrous part of life. Sex is a wondrous gift from God. Profound fervor is a superb gift from God. Sharing resources is a splendid gift, connecting our needs with the needs of others. Rich impatience for justice, enthusiasm that speaks and acts for right, serves as God's good gift.

Colossians discusses fornication, impurity, passion, evil desire, lying, greed, malice, slander, and abusive language as alternatives to God's good gifts. It defines *cravings* in life that have become *goals* of life. Sin has distorted and disordered life. Gifts have *become* life rather than instruments that *enhance* life. As such, when these become ends rather than means, they necessarily involve the abuse of God's people.

Only when gifts become disconnected from God do they create problems. Colossians 3 invites us not to be controlled by appetites. We are to live beyond the hungers that keep us turning on each other rather than to each other.

Rearranged priorities are fundamental to following Jesus. Divisions that make it convenient to abuse—nationality or religion, gender and credentialing, political status and economic class—all disappear when we have connected ourselves to Jesus. God's ultimate gift shifts our priorities, causing us to review and thus reorder. Then we gain fullness of life, now and in the world to come. With Jesus, appetites become aligned for abundant life. Glory to God!

God, lead me to control my appetites, in Jesus' name. Amen.

God loves you. Do you know that God loves you? Yes. God loves you, and God is blessing you. Do you know you are blessed? Yes, we are blessed; but when God blessed you and when God blessed me, God did not have just us in mind."

Above is one of my favorite benedictions. It speaks to God's gift of connecting us with others. It invites us to remember Wesley's "Blessed Connection" and to live it in our local contexts. I use it often as a blessing to remind me and those with whom I am privileged to serve, that God's blessings are communal in nature.

God blesses us to bless others. The Almighty touches us to create witnesses, persons who can introduce the God of Life to any who have seen and even sought only death. Life can indeed be better for any and all people, especially when we recall that it is never about anything more than the gift of our connections, our relating to God because of our relating to one another.

This connection is lost in the text. A man asks Jesus to arbitrate an inheritance dispute. It seems that he desires to get something, thereby abandoning relationship. Operating out of individual self-interest, he assumes that inheritance benefits life more than relationship. Rather than work it out with family, he seeks the potentially destructive stance of finding a judge.

Even today many spurn the God-gift of relationships for things. Items of wealth entice us. Sisters and brothers, husbands and wives, friends and partners lose the wealth of love daily because of material seductions.

God blessed you and me with relationships. How are we caring for those God has given us to love?

God, grant me, this day, to nurture those you gave me to love, in the name of the Christ. Amen.

Jesus asks, "Who set me to be a judge or arbitrator over you?" He then tells a story. Responding to one seeking judgment to gain inheritance and risking family relationship to do so, Jesus says, in effect, that time spent on material possessions is wasted time. It could be one's very undoing.

Society disagrees with Jesus. We live in "me-my-I" territory. Today's tyranny by possessions, ownership, and wealth controls us. Dominated as we are by wants, desires, and riches, often we have no limits as to what we will do to get them.

This tyranny consists of more than finances. Reputations are tarnished when people seek to own position, fame, celebrity and prominence for themselves alone. Character assassinations abound where this kind of oppression lays claim. Agonizingly, we witness such behavior among some who claim to follow Jesus, even in the church.

Investigating Jesus, however, shatters such claims. Jesus offers alternatives to economic and social tyranny. He reminds us in this cautionary parable that we pay a price for ignoring relationship with one another and God. By telling this story of the one who loses his life after spending it on foolishness, Jesus provides a way to reconcile beyond what is socially accepted.

Here is the gift: reconciliation comes by and through resistance. When we resist the popularity of cultural norms—the sins of abuse, the indulgence of greed—and replace these with the joy of relationship, we enter the presence of Jesus. We connect with the reign of God when we live—on earth—as citizens of that reign. As disciples of Jesus, we find this gift of resistance to be more than covenantal option. Glory to God, it is joyful obligation!

O God, help us to resist the world's enticements so that we can relate in love. Through Jesus we pray. Amen.

The Essentials

AUGUST 5–11, 2013 • BETH TAULMAN MILLER

SCRIPTURE OVERVIEW: The lesson from Isaiah and the psalm call the people of God to "Hear!" The message has to do with sacrifices and burnt offerings: God does not want them! The sacrificial system had come to be understood as a means of attempting to manipulate God for self-centered purposes, and the texts therefore call for worship that is God-centered. The Gospel lesson also calls the people of God to decision. Our use of financial resources is inextricably linked to our conviction that the future and our destiny lie ultimately with God. What we believe about the future affects how we live in the present. This affirmation is precisely the message of Hebrews. The entrusting of one's life and future to God is "the reality of things hoped for, the proof of things not seen." For those who trust in God's reign, "God is not ashamed to be called their God."

QUESTIONS AND THOUGHTS FOR REFLECTION

- Read Isaiah 1:1, 10-20. How do these verses demonstrate a connection between spiritual health and relational health?
- Read Psalm 50:1-8, 22-23. What is your basis for giving?
- Read Hebrews 11:1-3, 8-16. Who are your ancestors of the faith?
- Read Luke 12:32-40. What spiritual practices help you focus on a "perfect love" that casts out all fear?

Pastoral counselor with Thrive Resources, a company she and her husband have founded to serve those in recovery; member of First Congregational Church, West Dundee, Illinois

My sons grew up in a neighborhood full of boys and often played street hockey, a pick-up game of baseball, or ice hockey when the pond froze over. The neighborhood boys introduced them to sports they might not have discovered on their own. Part of the appeal of the new games was obtaining all the gear: the marker for paintball or the long board for skateboarding. At times the "stuff" of the sport became more important than the game itself. While they are older now and have each honed in on a single sport, the gear of the many sports dabbled in but not embraced decorates our garage. While the equipment serves as a sentimental reminder of days gone by, it is not accompanied by regular use and engagement in those games.

In this vision from Isaiah, God reprimands a rebellious nation for getting caught up in the ritual of sacrifice—as if that defined their relationship with God. Somehow people began substituting being around the "things of God" for a right relationship with God. God clearly articulates displeasure at sacrifice rather than obedience. And yet, what God asks for, God makes possible. "Wash yourselves; make yourselves clean," God declares and then goes on to clarify what is essential: an expression of faith defined by socially responsible involvement.

When our spiritual practices become the goal, we mistake ritual for relationship. If we are not careful, we can fall into believing that being around the things of God is the point. The words of these verses are clear: God desires our full engagement. When we seek to be spiritually healthy, it will have an impact on our relational health—to those we love and to those in need.

God, we are grateful for your grace that allows us to be cleansed where we are wrong. May our relationship with you penetrate our being, impacting the way we relate to and serve one another. Amen.

TUESDAY, AUGUST 6 ~ *Read Isaiah 1:18-20*

These words from Isaiah are familiar to many of us, particularly the King James Version: "Come now, and let us reason together." I've experienced that translation of these verses as comforting—yet further exploration of this passage indicates these words are probably more accurately understood in the context of a court case in which a decision will be rendered. The NRSV puts it this way: "Come now, let us argue it out." That translation seems to better capture the angry tenor of God's message. God desires right relationship more than going through religious motions.

I tend to embrace God's love more than I want to embrace God's justice. And, as is true in so much of life, these words represent the reality that God is both/and rather than either/or. It isn't that God is loving *or* vengeful. Rather, God is loving *and* calls us to own our sin. Our sins can be "like snow" and "become like wool," if we are "willing and obedient." These verses beautifully and metaphorically describe God's forgiveness, but we must choose that by our repentance and right living.

I am reminded of Jesus' conversation with the paralytic at the pool of Bethesda in which Jesus asks him if he wants to be well (John 5:6). Truly, it isn't enough to know that wellness is possible. Nor is healing and forgiveness an unconditional promise. We must willingly choose to step away from our sickness. Divine love and justice offers us the choice of health and wellness and the "good of the land" when we make that decision. Divine love and justice also supports our freedom to walk away, enforcing the consequences of our choices.

O God, who is both loving and just, grant us the courage to be willing and obedient. Amen.

Recently I heard someone describe her dad. He dressed well, carried himself with confidence, and exuded a sense of strength and kindness. She explained that she never tired of watching people's reactions when they met him; somehow it rearranged in their minds how they viewed her and, consequently, how she regarded herself.

Verses 1-6 of Psalm 50 give an imposing account of God, describing God's strength, righteousness, might, and rule over all of heaven and earth. The passage also refers to the Israelites as God's "people" and the "faithful ones" that made a covenant with God. While many psalms fall in the categories of songs or prayers, scholars often refer to Psalm 50 as "prophetic exhortation." Like the Isaiah passage, a courtroom scene comes to mind as God calls the people to account. God "does not keep silence." The Holy One calls the earth and heavens to witness the promise that the "faithful ones" have broken.

The Israelites have broken their covenant with God—and God calls them on it. They had fallen into the false belief that God desired their offerings more than God desired ethical living. When we lose sight of what matters to God, we wisely return our focus to God. From that vantage point, we gain a healthy perspective of how to view ourselves and how to live our lives. God's goodness and greatness influence and even "rearrange" how we see everything else. We begin with God, and all else flows from there.

What would change in your life, your relationships, your speech, your beliefs about yourself or others if you were to stop and truly focus on God?

Meditate on these words: "I am God. Your God." As you do, ask God how a fresh look at the covenant between you and God as Parent and child might reorder your life.

Mark this, then." God emphasizes the tragedy of remembering religion yet forgetting God. God communicates the destruction that occurs in our lives when God is overlooked. And, true to divine character, God issues a directive about what is wrong and sets forth a way to do it differently. The bottom line, God declares: you can forget me—or you can "bring thanksgiving" as your sacrifice.

You may have heard the phrase "an attitude of gratitude." Until recently, I believed persons simply decided to be grateful—to have that kind of attitude—and then, they became grateful people. I now feel it more likely that gratitude is a spiritual practice, and as such, must be practiced. It isn't a self-help campaign in which we will ourselves to change; rather, we choose to engage in the practices, observances, exercises, and even speech patterns that draw us into grateful living.

Choosing to live without gratitude embraces scarcity by focusing on what we don't have enough of, what someone else has more of, or how we can get by with giving little. Consider those places in your life where you cling to a scarcity mentality such as "I don't have enough" (money, time, energy, sleep), or "I'm not enough." The difference a shift toward gratitude makes in one's life is palpable. It opens the door to abundant living. We develop more of an awareness of what we have than what we don't, an awareness of what isn't, and gratitude for what is. The spiritual practice of gratitude opens us to a spirit of humility and a mind-set of abundance. When we express our gratitude regularly to God and others, gratefully acknowledge God's presence in our day, and seek to embrace an abundant mind-set—we are practicing gratitude. Out of that place of humility and softheartedness we are shown "the salvation of God."

Gracious One, may our practice of gratitude be a sweet, fragrant offering of thanksgiving to you. Amen.

It is no small matter to have a working definition of faith: the "assurance of things hoped for, the conviction of things not seen." It is beneficial to have defined what is so pivotal to us—and yet we use the word *faith* in different contexts. We try to "have faith" by believing in something or someone or expressing confidence in spiritual truths yet unseen. We can refer to "our faith" when speaking of our spiritual life holistically—as in "she is a woman of deep faith," or "my faith is important to me." And we speak in terms of "practicing our faith" as we live our lives.

Much like we practice other spiritual disciplines, we can also practice our faith. At times I have read this definition in Hebrews 11:1 and quickly assumed my faith was not up to par because of where I found myself on that given day on the continuum of assurance and conviction.

What if the definition of faith given above is the goal, but we understand there to be a range that allows room for wrestling and growth without its implying our unfaithfulness? In her book *Amazing Grace: A Vocabulary of Faith* Kathleen Norris suggests that part of how we practice faith is by recognizing that the continuum of faith includes "belief, doubt, and sacred ambiguity." It seems we often define the opposite of faith as uncertainty. And yet, wouldn't the more accurate antithesis of faith be disengagement and apathy rather than questions? Verse 2 of our Hebrews passage states that "by faith our ancestors received approval." Certainly our ancestors such as Noah, Abraham, Sarah, and Jacob practiced their faith as they wrestled with their beliefs, doubts, and sacred ambiguity.

O God, grant me the courage to name wherever I am on the continuum of faith as I grow toward assurance of things hoped for and conviction of things not seen. Amen.

Several years ago, my oldest son and I watched the first movie in the Lord of the Rings trilogy, *The Fellowship of the Ring*. He loved the story and had read the book prior to seeing the movie. Even though I knew the movie was the first install-ment of the project, I came to the viewing with my traditional movie filter, expecting an ending that brought closure. The movie ended, abruptly in my opinion, leaving me with more questions than answers. When I turned to him and asked, "It's over?" he reminded me that while it was the end of the movie, it wasn't the completion of the story.

We often refer to Hebrews 11 as the "roll call of faith." While not perfect, followers of God such as Abraham, Sarah, Jacob, and Isaac made many courageous, faithful choices in which they demonstrated an "assurance of things hoped for and a conviction of things not seen" (Heb. 11:1). They did receive the fulfillment of some promises—yet they lived with the faith that they had not yet seen the end of the Story. They "confessed that they were strangers and foreigners on the earth, . . . seeking a homeland." Desiring a "better country, that is, a heavenly one," resulted from their expressing faith in God and what was yet to come.

We can easily become shortsighted and see only the story currently going on around us or in our own lives—and get bogged down in the unanswered questions with which we wrestle. While faithfully living out what we sense God calling us to in the present is a way of expressing our faith, trusting that we have not yet seen the end of the Story is another.

God who is Alpha and Omega, may you quiet our hearts with the truth that you are the beginning and the end. In light of your Story, we can trust you with ours. Amen.

Fear comes in all shapes and sizes: worry, anxiety, dread, concern, dismay, uneasiness, or downright terror. It can manifest itself like a fog that hovers but cannot be grasped or one that doesn't allow us to see the hand in front of our face. It has been a part of the human condition through the ages as demonstrated in the number of times the scriptures speak to the topic. These verses open with a command that addresses the fear: "Do not be afraid, little flock." We can imagine Jesus speaking these words with a tone of tender strength.

Beginning with the command not to fear, Jesus points to a few truths that direct us toward peaceful, grounded living. First, claim the blessed assurance that it is "[God's] good pleasure to give you the kingdom." This rings true with how Jesus taught us to pray: "Thy kingdom come. Thy will be done" (Matt. 6:10, KJV). An antidote to fear resides in the kingdom power to change our lives, bringing peace rather than distress to relationships, questions of self-worth, finances, burdens, and the spiritual journey.

Second, while Jesus does not speak a moral imperative against possessions, he presumes a proper perspective on their importance to us. Our embracing a scarcity mentality toward money and belongings provides fertile soil for fear and anxiety. When we rightly order money in our lives, we position ourselves for wholehearted, meaningful living.

Finally, Jesus longs to bless those who focus on him. He sounds a call to watchfulness and readiness: be attentive, do not lose sight of what matters most. The old hymn says it best: "Turn your eyes upon Jesus, look full in his wonderful face, and the things of earth will grow strangely dim in the light of his glory and grace." (*The United Methodist Hymnal*, #349)

In the form of a breath prayer, pray this throughout your day: (Breathing in) O Perfect Love, (Breathing out) cast out my fear.

Choice and Focus

AUGUST 12–18, 2013 • ARTHUR F. GAFKE

SCRIPTURE OVERVIEW: Isaiah 5:1-7 and Psalm 80:8-19 employ similar images to represent the people of God—a vine or a vineyard. The image clearly communicates the divine commitment to God's people. Unfortunately, the people do not respond in kind, so God must destroy the vineyard. The people plead for restoration, and their future life will depend not on their repentance but on God's repentance! Jesus issues a radical call for human repentance in Luke. God will bear the burden of human disobedience, and God's gracious turning to humankind makes life possible. Hebrews demonstrates that the story of God's people does contain outstanding episodes and exemplars of faith and suggests that God never gives up on calling us to follow, to run the difficult race that leads to life.

QUESTIONS AND THOUGHTS FOR REFLECTION

- Read Isaiah 5:1-7. How do you monitor subtle shifts in yourself that turn faith to fear and grace to grief?

- Read Psalm 80:1-2, 8-19. In your laments, how have you blamed God for adverse events?

- Read Hebrews 11:29–12:2. What marathons have you chosen to run in your life even in the midst of life-threatening forces?

- Read Luke 12:49-56. How does Jesus' gospel counter the dominating claims on your life?

Consultant and trainer in leadership and organizational development, living in Las Vegas, Nevada

Each year in July the Badwater Ultramarathon populates the Mojave Desert of Death Valley, California, with approximately ninety of the world's toughest athletes and their supporters. Covering 135 miles from Death Valley to Mt. Whitney, California, in temperatures up to 130°F, this race is the most demanding and extreme running race anywhere on the planet.

The race requires that the runners be disciplined and focused. They practice their art of running all year long in preparation. Each runner requires a legion of helpers along the way. The conditions are life-threatening. Each runner must learn how to run in severe conditions.

In the same way, we must learn how to run our own race in the face of threatening forces. We are reminded daily of threats to our well-being. We can succumb to the forces that challenge us, or we can focus and live our lives as graced by God. The difference comes in *how* we run. Disciplined focus, a community of support, and prayerful reminders of God's grace form the core of the *how*.

Once the Badwater Ultramarathon has begun, runners probably consider giving up. Running day and night leaves ample opportunity to stop or quit. Some do leave the race. In our lives we too can choose to leave one race and begin another one. Regardless, we pick up our lives and continue to live out our days a step at a time.

Staying focused on what is most important calls for discipline and practice. God's grace surrounds us throughout our race, not simply at the end of it. This constant grace makes our running possible.

God of desert and forest, of heat and cold, we are thankful for the race that we get to run. Sustain us with your grace. Amen.

As I walk my neighborhood in Las Vegas, some front yard trees have roots muscling their way across the top of the soil, making yard maintenance difficult. These trees desperately seek the little surface water available. The exposed roots signal trees vulnerable to winds and droughts.

Observers say that our society has shallow roots that seek daily sustenance from surface entertainments. Our low pain threshold, our continual need for assurance, and our intolerance for risk signal the high anxiety of our age. We live connected to one or two generations of our history. Beyond that many of us are vague about our roots.

Today's passage sends us into deep places, away from the shallow roots of our society in which every trouble seems to be the worst that has ever been. The writer of Hebrews pours out a litany of challenges, troubles, and heartaches that our ancestors experienced. With shallow roots we might quickly read the listings in these verses and move on. With shallow roots we probably do not connect with these ancestors' experiences.

When the foundations of our society are shaken, when "normal" is broken, when our vulnerabilities are exposed—then come the times that test and measure our faith. Do we believe in God's abiding presence, even in the hard times?

As I read the listing in Hebrews, I wonder if those who risked themselves, those who faced torture and death, cried out "why me?" I invite you to make a list from today's verses. How many risk and loss experiences are on the list? Choose one among the list and imagine a story of someone for whom that experience was real. Imagine what faith in God meant for that person. Then turn the story around and let it be your story, praising God for life.

Lord, draw us deeply to what was. Draw us deeply to what is now and ever shall be. Amen.

The woman treasured the coin her aunt had given her when she was a child. Now in her eighties, the woman pulled the coin from its special place and gave it to her grandniece. This coin was not to be lost but saved, its value far exceeding its "street value."

As with the loving aunt, God gives us not a coin but a life with far greater value than its "street value." As we live our days sometimes we feel as though our lives are lost, wasted, used up, worn out. In those times we pray for God to save us. Especially in hard times of bad economy, illness, death, and loss, we pray.

The psalmist cries out with such prayer as his people face hard times. The desperation drives him to project upon God the purposeful destruction of the people. Laments are made of desperation. In such times we fashion God with human image and motive. We do this when we feel lost or besieged. We cry out, appealing to a greater power than ourselves to deliver us, to save us.

The God of all creation does not at one time save us and at another destroy us. The good news of Jesus is that we are saved—worthy, valuable, and sacred both in good times and hard times. In our lament we may forget this truth because the pains seem more real than God's grace. Yet we have the witness of others who came through hard times. The apostle Paul wrote to the Romans: "For I am convinced that neither death, nor life, nor angels, nor rulers, nor things present, nor things to come, nor powers, nor height, nor depth, nor anything else in all creation, will be able to separate us from the love of God in Christ Jesus our Lord" (Rom. 8:38-39). We are valued by God.

God who saves us and counts us worthy, may we receive your love and claim ourselves and others as valued in grace this day. Amen.

Isaiah chapter 5 begins with the hopefulness of love and the planting of a vineyard on a fertile hill. Pictures come to mind of rows of grapes planted on a hill, carefully tended and beautiful in the morning sun.

We do well to pause with this first verse and breathe in the beauty of the scene. In our fast-paced, Twitter world we hurry to conclusions with little pause for sweet beginnings. If we rush on to the next verses of Isaiah 5, we discover by verse 4 the harvest of wild, bad grapes. The lovely opening scene dissolves into negativity. So slow down and linger with the opening scene of beauty and good expectations. We do not have to read these verses jammed together. We can separate them, lingering for a time on each. Slowing down to cherish beginnings is a spiritual discipline.

Identify the beautiful, loving, high hopes in your own life. You do not have to rush on toward harsh conclusions. Pessimists and fearful voices of our world push us past the beginnings to negativity. Resist this push. The new day, the new expectations, the loves confirmed in these beginnings have a place of their own in our lives.

Slow down and linger with the beginnings. Let conclusions stand aside for hopeful beginnings.

As we slow down to cherish God's beginnings with us, we can find that the conclusions are transformed because we are transformed by beautiful beginnings.

God who inspires in us beginnings filled with hope, we thank you for the possibilities of new life that visit us this day. Amen.

Throughout human history people have raised anguished cries about the destruction of human community. This happened in Israel in the eighth century before Christ. The economic policies of the nation had pushed people from their land and shattered communities. God's covenant demands were disregarded. Piety prevailed but justice was absent. The prophet Isaiah speaks in protest. The leaders still consider themselves faithful; they believe they act out of good intentions.

The partial verse of Isaiah 5:7b shows just how subtle the change from God's good fruit to wild grapes can be. Read only in English, the shift between good and bad seems large. Justice is replaced by bloodshed and righteousness by a cry. But in the Hebrew language the change is slight and subtle. "He hoped for justice (*mishpat*), but there was bloodshed (*mispach*), for righteousness (*tsedakah*) but there was a cry of distress (*tse'akah*)." Examine the similarity of *mishpat* and *mispach*, of *tsedakah* and *tse'akah*.

In our practice of faithful living we do well to keep an eye on the subtle shifts in ourselves that turn faith to fear and grace to grief. Through prayer we can seek those places in our own heart and life that begin with God's good planting and yet have a slight variation that yields the opposite. Is there good intention to be loving to others, yet a hesitation to risk the action of love? Is there a desire for open communication, yet insecurity about being rejected that silences your voice?

Our intentions may not yield the good fruit we profess. Reclaim in your own life God's good planting. Act on the power and truth of it for yourself and others.

God who plants beauty and love in the human heart, may we discover and transform those places where we need to reclaim the beauty and love you plant in us. Amen.

The Gospel of Luke presents Jesus as a defining presence in an age when the world was crowded with authorities defining what was real. The world was awash with claims on human life in which people were the property of the ruling authority. Jesus defined the world based on love and grace. This redefinition radically differed from the world where authorities' claim on human life was enforced with power over others through taxation and military might.

Many in Jesus' world suffered greatly because of the claims on their lives by ruling authorities. These people hungered to receive the good message of Jesus. Those who believed Jesus' message gave up the old habits of living as the possession of a worldly power. Yet, the oppressive authorities did not dissolve or disappear. These kingdoms asserted their divinity and challenged anyone who did not submit. Those who profited from the benefits of the ruling authorities and those who feared to turn away from them found Jesus' message dangerous. They rejected that message as untimely and threatening. In this rejection lies the "division" that Jesus brought.

In our day authorities battle to define what is real in human life. Dominating corporations, demanding ideologies, shrill religious voices, and others clamor to define and claim human beings. Repeated slogans, image packaging, demonizing of opponents are common fare with which we live. Into this fray Jesus offers the message of a reign of grace.

Each of us must answer the questions: "To whom do I belong? What authority defines me?" In answering we divide ourselves not in defense or fear but in faith and in the choice to belong to God's kingdom.

God who was, who is, who will be, claim us this day. Define us as your beloved. Help us see the other claims on us for what they are. Amen.

This challenging passage from the Gospel of Luke has sadly been used as a justification for Christian aggression from near the beginning of the church. As with other worldly authorities, the leaders of the church sought to suppress, through bribery or torture, those who disagreed. Divine authority was claimed to enforce the exercise of defining might against all opposition. The early and systematic exclusion of women from leadership in church, and later, the brutality of the Inquisition are but two examples.

Such brutal authority mimics perfectly the authorities of Jesus' day, those he challenges with a new message of love and grace. The tactics of those who enforce "church" echo the scenes of Jesus' torture and execution. History repeats itself.

The division Jesus speaks of is not a continuation of oppressive policies but a new policy of grace, love, and justice. Jesus does not enforce his kingdom. He invites people to turn their lives around and live the way of his kingdom. He issues this invitation: "I am standing at the door, knocking; if you hear my voice and open the door, I will come in to you and eat with you, and you with me" (Rev. 3:20).

Worldly and religious powers established on fear must enforce their presence on people. God's kingdom thrives in human life as an invitation: hear, open, eat together. This kingdom is established through faith, not fear.

Faith in God's presence brings humility not arrogance. Faith in God's presence forms relationships across lines of difference and not self-righteousness. In faith we gain strength of love and grace. Exercise rigorous love and grace, and the world's divisions will be made plain to you.

God who comes with voice, speak to us of wisdom and sanity in a world of foolish offers and insane threats. Aid us in sorting out what is real and what is fearful pretense. Amen.

Divine Assignments

AUGUST 19–25, 2013 • ERIN M. HAWKINS

SCRIPTURE OVERVIEW: The Luke text portrays the healing that Jesus has just performed as a call to decision, a call to "repentance and changed lives." Hebrews proclaims to the readers that they "have come . . . to the city of the living God, the heavenly Jerusalem, . . . and to Jesus, the mediator of a new covenant." For Luke, Jesus and his wonderful works signal the accessibility of God's transforming power and thus signal also the time for repentance. The accessibility of God's transforming power is evident in the lessons from Jeremiah and the psalm, although Jeremiah has no choice! And amid opposition from the wicked, the psalmist affirms what Jeremiah had been told by God—that his life from its very beginning has belonged to God.

QUESTIONS AND THOUGHTS FOR REFLECTION

- Read Jeremiah 1:4-10. What does it mean to you to be formed, known, set apart, and appointed by God?

- Read Psalm 71:1-6. The psalmist exemplifies trust in God despite the circumstances of life. What life circumstances challenge you to place your complete trust in God?

- Read Hebrews 12:18-29. The author declares that God will shake heaven and earth to eliminate all that is nonessential to the coming realm of God. What nonessentials is God shaking up in your life to prepare you for the promise of a new heaven and a new earth?

- Read Luke 13:10-17. In what ways (physically, spiritually, mentally) are people in your society bent and broken, unable to stand tall?

General Secretary, General Commission on Religion and Race, The United Methodist Church, Washington, DC

I have a friend who enjoys jigsaw puzzles. She continually searches for intricate, unique, and beautiful puzzles. One day I asked her, "Why do these puzzles fascinate you?" She thought for a moment and replied, "I love to be a part of the plan. I know that within the box lies a wonderful creation. To have the pleasure of forming the jumbled heap of pieces into the beautiful picture on the cover is a sheer delight."

As I read this passage in which God calls Jeremiah to be a "prophet to the nations," God's purposefulness captures me. Verse 5 emphasizes a clear message: "I formed you; . . . I knew you; . . . I set you apart; . . . I appointed you." Other biblical passages explore God's activity in shaping us. Psalm 139:13, 15 states, "It was you who formed my inward parts; you knit me together in my mother's womb. . . . My frame was not hidden from you, when I was being made in secret, intricately woven in the depths of the earth."

To be formed, known, set apart, and appointed by God is a testament to God's love for and faith in us. Jeremiah's encounter reminds us that the Creator is not simply aware of our existence but is actively involved in our development and, most importantly, has a plan for each of us. God will not call all of us to be the "prophet to the nations," but God calls us for equally important and life-changing work—acting as a companion to the sick and dying, being a drum major for justice in the face of oppression, demonstrating God's preferential option for the poor, or raising up a new generation of world changers. As we respond to God's call we become a part of a grand plan where our jumbled pieces are transformed into the beautiful picture God intends.

God, make us available to be instruments of your peace, justice, love, and compassion in a hurting and broken world. Amen.

Imagine with me with this scene. I sense a tense atmosphere in the room. I can see Jeremiah—jaw clenched, shoulders hunched, brow furrowed. "I can't do it," says Jeremiah "I'm too young!"(AP) "Ah, but I can do anything," God responds (AP). I figure God finds it amusing and possibly irritating when we struggle against our calling. We believe we hold a more accurate view of ourselves than God. We falter under the illusion that our sense of identity trumps God's all-knowing, all-powerful presence.

When confronted by a challenge or a high calling, we may feel tempted to dredge up our weaknesses, shortcomings, and self-limiting beliefs as reasons for not stepping up to the moment with obedience and humility. The discipline of prayer and meditation can help us overcome this temptation. As we speak to and listen for God, our negative self-understanding is challenged and revised. God chastises Jeremiah for his self-perception as immature, inadequate, incapable. Hear the grace of God in the phrase, "Do not say, 'I am only . . . '" As children of God created in the image of God, we are hardwired for greatness—ordained by God and empowered by the Holy Spirit. Furthermore, God promises to be with us and to protect us.

So take heart! Human ability, wisdom, strength, or power are not the means by which God fulfills divine purposes in the world; rather, it is through the power of God at work in people with many perceived inadequacies. As Paul would later say in Second Corinthians, "We have this treasure in clay jars, so that it may be made clear that this extraordinary power belongs to God and does not come from us" (4:7).

O God, I believe that I am fearfully and wonderfully made. It is with your divine power and protection that I can be your hands and feet in the world. Amen.

Jared came home one day with a paper cup filled with soil and one tiny radish sprout. He beamed with pride. After some discussion Jared and his mom decided that they would start a garden in the backyard. One bright Saturday morning they started their project, first preparing a plot of ground for the garden. Jared yanked weeds out of the ground with his hands; he sifted the earth between his fingers, tossing away the rocks; he patted, dug, kneaded, and smoothed the dirt until he had transformed the rocky, dry, weed-infested soil into a soft, moist, welcoming habitat for his radish sprout.

The transformative nature of Jared's touch on the earth—rough and eager, gentle and soothing—reminds me of the transforming power of God's touch. Sometimes God shakes us up to get our attention. At other times God's gentle and soothing touch provides healing and restoration. God touches Jeremiah's mouth, and that action changes him forever. God's touch often comes with an assignment. Jeremiah's was to "uproot and tear down, to destroy and overthrow, to build and to plant."

In the face of extreme global poverty, economic upheaval, war, racism, environmental degradation, violence, and corruption, God shakes us up to be modern-day prophets. By the power of God we are called to uproot systems of injustice; to destroy the stratifying lines between the haves and the have-nots; to build community; and to plant seeds of peace, love, and justice.

God placed powerful, dangerous, and nurturing words in Jeremiah's mouth, words that destroyed the death-dealing forces in the world while planting seeds that built up the structures of life. May it be so with us.

Christ, through your suffering for us, we have eyes to see the suffering of the world. Give us strength, courage, and wisdom to be modern-day prophets. Amen.

An internet search of the phrase "lack of trust" will result in millions of articles about marriage and relationships, business and leadership, government and politicians, other beleaguered positions, institutions, and events. A lack of trust seems to be a pervasive occurrence in the world today. To trust in the midst of trying circumstances can be hard to do, but it is exactly what the psalmist demonstrates for us in this passage.

Here the psalmist appears to have reached the end of his resources. He makes several urgent appeals to God for deliverance from his enemies. Yet, throughout his prayer, he prefaces his appeals by confessing his trust in God as his only refuge and hope. In the midst of his struggle he looks back at his lifetime of experience with God, acknowledging that God had faithfully protected him in the past and declaring his trust that God will do it again. The psalmist knows God as the one who saves and maintains confidence that God will save.

We will all experience times in our lives where our circumstances seem too much to bear. In the midst of the stress, we may wonder if or how God is at work on our behalf. In those moments, we, like the psalmist, can look back over our lives and recall the countless times that God has saved, provided, comforted, blessed, and delivered us. We have every reason to trust God and to keep trusting God even in the midst of difficulty. We can pray like the psalmist, making our petitions known to God while offering praise for the saving power, grace, mercy, and love of the Holy One. Then we will experience the God of miracles who will provide what we need most in our time of despair.

O God, for all those around the world who are in the midst of struggle, we pray your deliverance and declare our unfailing trust in you. Amen.

Theology can be messy business. Many theologians, preachers, evangelists, and all manner of religious figures have attempted throughout history to provide definitive answers on the nature, mind, and ways of God. However, there are always (at least) two "sides" to the best Christian answer to any theological question. These sides often seem far apart and difficult to reconcile. Yet the sides are seldom really opposites, despite strong tensions between them.

The writer of this passage compares two mountains. The writer reminds us first of the experience of the Israelites at Mount Sinai: the flames of fire, the darkness and gloom, the trumpet blast, a Voice too terrible to endure, and the fear felt by the people—including Moses. Then the writer states that we have come to worship at Mount Zion, the home of God inhabited by Jesus and all the heavenly hosts.

The stark contrast between the two mountains can seem like polar opposite representations of God's relationship with the world. Sinai represents the fear, pain, and spectacle of the physical world, while Zion represents the peace, inclusion, and joy of the spiritual world to come. Rather than overemphasizing one image and neglecting the other, we accept the challenge to hold the two mountains together, to maintain a proper balance between seemingly opposite sides of the truth. God is both at work amidst the pain and flashy consumerism of this world and inhabiting a world that transcends all our earthly concerns. God calls us to live this both/and theology by faithfully working to care for all of God's creation, while at the same time anticipating and drawing strength from the fact that the troubles of this world are only temporary—the best is yet to come.

Dear God, continue to care for all the people of this world as you prepare us for the world that is to come. Amen.

Iremember the day vividly. I was sitting in my office when the building began to rattle. At first I simply thought a large truck was passing by; but after a few moments, I realized I was experiencing an earthquake. Since earthquakes are relatively rare in Washington, DC, this was quite an event for the region. The news stations reported damage to a few homes, construction sites, and even some historic monuments. The earthquake brought no serious damage and awakened many to the impermanence of life and its comforts.

This text lays before us the fact that the created order, the original heavens and earth, is temporary, capable of being shaken and intended from the beginning to give way to something better: the unshakable, transcendent order of the everlasting realm. Sometimes the shaking up of our world allows God to establish the unshakable in our midst. Our relationships get shaken in order to establish the unshakable values of trust, honesty, and loyalty; our material possessions are shaken loose from our grasp to establish an unshakable dependence on God; our political systems are shaken by change to make possible the establishment of shared power, ethical leadership, and community interests. And while the "shake-ups" in our lives may disorient and frustrate, we can be thankful for that which is unshakable now and in the world to come.

We express our thanksgiving for the hope of the future through worship, where we encounter God, hear God's voice, and are transformed. True worship does not leave us as we are, at ease with illusions of our own power and significance. Rather, it makes us aware of the fleeting nature of human life and institutions as we bow in awe before the permanence, might, and splendor of our God.

Christ our Savior, establish within us your unshakable kingdom by shaking loose all that distances us from you. Amen.

No one asked him to do it. No eager group of people ushering the broken woman to the front of the crowd; no one crying at his feet begging for mercy and healing; no expectations that a miracle will even occur that day. Just a faithful woman coming to hear Jesus teach in the synagogue who finds herself set free by his compassion.

Jesus demonstrates the power that courage and compassion have to set people free. He looks upon the woman with mercy, seeking nothing but to heal her affliction and make her whole. He does not wait to be asked; he sees a need and fills it. Jesus matches compassion with courage as he dares to break the rules in order to care for the woman. We need this kind of courage in the world today: courage to do what's right, to care for all members of the human family, to stand up for the rights and dignity of those weighed down by life's physical and social afflictions.

Too often we underestimate our power to set free those around us who are bound. The world is full of broken people, stigmatized by homelessness, joblessness, abuse, and other oppressive forces. We know them as friends and family, coworkers and church members. Perhaps they are strangers to us, their hearts, minds, spirits, and bodies bent by the weight of their suffering. We watch them unaffected and numb, never considering that a kind word or compassionate act might release the bonds that hold them. We need not wait to be asked to follow in Christ's footsteps. Armed with courage and compassion, we have all that we need to—as the prophet Isaiah commands—"loose the chains of injustice and untie the cords of the yoke, to set the oppressed free and break every yoke" (58:6, NIV).

Dear God, give us the courage and compassion to lighten the burden of your hurting and broken children. Amen.

True Worship

AUGUST 26–SEPTEMBER 1, 2013 • B. JOHN FRANKLIN

SCRIPTURE OVERVIEW: The admonition in Hebrews 13 "to show hospitality to strangers" is vividly illustrated by Jesus' advice to guests and hosts in Luke 14. In the topsy-turvy world of divine hospitality, everybody is family. Radical hospitality makes sense only in light of the conviction that God rules the world and therefore adequate repayment for our efforts is simply our relatedness to God and our conformity to what God intends. The texts from Jeremiah and the psalm call the people of God back to commitment to God alone, rather than to the gods of the nations and their values. God is no doubt still lamenting our failure to listen but is also, no doubt, still inviting us to take our humble place at a table that promises exaltation on a scale the world cannot even imagine.

QUESTIONS AND THOUGHTS FOR REFLECTION

- Read Jeremiah 2:4-13. When have you experienced the "greater love"?
- Read Psalm 81:1, 10-16. How open is your mouth to God's provision?
- Read Hebrews 13:1-8, 15-16. Who are the "prisoners" you know, and what might God be asking you to bring them?
- Read Luke 14:1, 7-14. Beyond your familiar circle, to whom might you extend God's hospitality?

Chaplain to the Anglican Bishop of Dunedin, New Zealand; Anglican priest, spiritual director, retreat leader; living in Dunedin, New Zealand

Xavier Beauvois based his 2010 film, *Of Gods and Men*, on the true story of a group of French Cistercian monks caught up (and ultimately killed) in the violence of 1990s Algeria. A tender moment comes near the beginning in a conversation between eighty-two-year-old Brother Luc (the doctor) and a young woman from the local village near the monastery. Sitting beside him on a bench outside the monastery wall, the young woman asks Brother Luc if he has ever been in love. The old monk leans over and replies that he has, several times; but then he encountered an even greater love, and he answered that love over sixty years ago.

Today, in Jeremiah, we see the greater love. God grieves that no one answers this love. God is asking, "What have I done wrong that you have screened me out?" No one has remembered the delivery of their ancestors in love from slavery; led through deserts, drought, and darkness; and brought safely to a new land—a land abundant with food, water, and space. Everything came as God's loving gift and provision.

The generation that Jeremiah addresses suffers from amnesia. He gives us a snapshot of a people who have lost their roots, lost their identity, and lost connection with the greater love that called them, formed them, and showered them with goodness.

Over two and half millennia later, Jeremiah's words serve as a wake-up call. Are we, children of love, in danger also of being subsumed by our prevailing culture and forgetting our first love? Our malls, entertainment centers, and sports fields exert their influence; but the soul, when called to awareness, knows that God alone can satisfy. Jeremiah calls us to awareness of the love that will not let us go.

We bless you, loving God, that our sin and indifference never deters you. To you we turn, for in your love alone is our life. Amen.

I accuse you," says the Lord. Surely God doesn't accuse! But love is at work, telling the truth. We see the grieving Lover naming the wrongdoing of the beloved, a wrongdoing that is destroying them. God levels accusation against the people's choices, naming these choices evil. But like a small child exercising independence, the house of Jacob and the families of Israel say, "I can do it myself!"

God's presence and grace is like living water. Living water flows clean and clear with no mud, chemicals, or giardia in it. More than tea, coffee, coke or alcohol, living water is what the body was designed to operate on. And God's children are choosing not to drink it. Instead, in the energy of human enterprise, they have dug cisterns, water catchment containers where water can sit and grow stagnant. But now their cisterns are cracked and can hold no water. With no water, the people perish.

God's passionate love speaks through the metaphor of water. "Look at your choices," God seems to be saying. "You forsake me and want to generate your own life water supply. And what do you get instead? Life?" Human nature has always been good at self-deception.

Priests and teachers have not helped to name truth, and the prophets speak for Baal. So God points to their neighbors to highlight examples. Examine with care, God says; have they changed their gods? The implicit answer is no. "Then why do you exchange your glory for nothing?" (AP)

Love calls us to look at our independence, our life choices, turning again and again to the One who supplies living water.

Drench us with your very self, loving One, that choosing you we may live and bathe in your goodness. Amen.

S ing aloud to God our strength; shout for joy to the God of Jacob." Why? The psalm answers with God's voice saying, "I am the LORD your God, who brought you up out of the land of Egypt. Open your mouth wide and I will fill it." God delivers and provides. That's why.

We too sing and shout with joy because God, pursuing us in love, makes God's self available for relationship. "I am your God." We relate with family, with land we stand on, and even the car; but relationship with God is something utterly other! Relationship with the Holy One, with the God and Father of our Lord Jesus Christ, with the Mysterium Tremendum, is not of our doing. God loves first and, in love, becomes accessible and available that we might respond. And with the singing and shouting, mortal flesh needs also to be silent, and in fear and trembling, stand before the wonder of it. God our Deliverer seeks relationship with us and awaits us laden with gifts! "Open your mouth wide and I will fill it." How do we respond to this invitation?

Israel, our archetypal self, doesn't listen. And the pride of human independence has no room for vulnerability to love. Love serves as a threat when we are busily making our kingdom come and getting our will done. Love threatens because imperial Me has to stand aside. Israel has no mind to do that. But negative responses do not put God off. Crying aloud, but not with joy, God shouts, "O that my people would listen to my voice." Besides dealing with our foes, God promises an abundance of good things for us. O that we too would listen.

Loving One, as we open to your love and choose to listen, our hearts shout for joy at your goodness. Amen.

Love became flesh and lived among us, full of grace and truth. And Love invites us to love, for we are Love's agents in the world.

How easily we warm up to what we don't have. We tell ourselves, "I would like to, but I don't have time." And while we say to others that we always have time for what is important, how important is it to us that mutual love continue? What does continuing mutual love look like? To help us get the picture, the writer to the Hebrews provides specifics.

Among other things, love offers hospitality to strangers. Cleopas and his companion welcomed a stranger they met on the Emmaus road, and what a surprise that led to! We experience our own delightful surprises as guest and as host. Hospitality can be the provision of a meal, a bed, or a ride. It can also include the offer of presence, companioning, and prayer. Whatever hospitality covers, there we find the One who is endlessly hospitable to us, making divine presence known, making "mutual" more than two.

We show love by remembering those in prison and empathizing with them in such a way that we understand to some extent their situation. We may visit a penal institution, but the "prisoner" may be shut up in a rest home, a hospital room, or may be locked into destructive behaviors, guilt, and unforgiveness. Wherever the prisoners are, the love of Christ that we bring can set them free.

Mutual love. We receive and give. We maintain balance through our openness to receive, that from receiving, we may give. And God the Source is in the flow, for our mutual love expresses the love that is God, a Holy Trinity of self-giving love.

Loving God, you are hospitality itself. Open our hearts to be bearers of your love. Amen.

Jesus is out for dinner again. And dinners with Jesus are seldom without incident. He tends to upend cultural values, question accepted practices, and defy conventions that block loving compassion. Imagine the banter as people enter with the expectations of a good meal and intelligent, even witty, conversation. Jesus is the honored guest. All eyes rest upon him, since on the way in, he healed a man—on the sabbath! But Jesus himself watches, noting how social order and customary dining etiquette play out. A dinner is an important social event where how one washes, where one sits, and with whom one sits become noteworthy.

Feel the respectful silence fall as Jesus begins to speak. He does not dine out with the crowds nor in the synagogue. At this private affair a select few get to hear him firsthand. "Imagine you are at a wedding breakfast,"(AP) he says. Everyone will remember their experiences of wedding feasts; the quality of the catering, where they sat, and with whom they talked. But he goes on. Those gathered expect to hear words of spiritual wisdom. So what does Jesus mean when he talks about not taking your rightful place of honor and receiving the recognition appropriate to your station in life? Is this a lesson on how to avoid social embarrassment?

The kingdom is clicking in. The first shall be last and the last first, says the one who emptied himself of place, glory, and honor. Jesus notes that discriminatory social norms and customs do not have the final word. He speaks the love of the Father in whom is equal space for all, honor for all, and unconditional love for all. Our status, titles, and honors count for nothing in the kingdom. Those who truly know their place are those who affirm that they stand in the sight of God, loved and honored as children of the Most High.

Father, we are yours, and our worth is in you alone. Amen.

Having addressed the guests, Jesus turns to the host. As he senses the attention turning to him, what does the host feel? Is he honored by the attention of the rabbi or embarrassed that all eyes focus on him? And when he hears what Jesus has to say, does he dare to take any food in his hands—does anyone else? What Jesus says would have applied to all present. What Jesus says is quite shocking, for when you are invited out, you return the favor, as is appropriate in our culture also. We feel comfortable with family, friends, and (equally) rich neighbors.

Here comes the kingdom again. "Who is your neighbor?" Jesus once asked in another telling story. Surely he doesn't literally mean the poor, the crippled, the lame, and the blind. The church soup kitchen and the welfare agencies that we support look after them. Literal or not, these kinds of people are outcasts in Jesus' world. Leviticus explicitly forbids many of these persons to be priests (Lev. 21). The Qumran community of Jesus' time completely barred them. But are they not also children of God? Exclusion. The early church wrestled with the same issue: who should one *not* eat with?

In contrast to an exclusive dinner party at a Pharisee's house, Jesus provided bread for five thousand out in the country; he gathered with disciples at Mary, Martha, and Lazarus's house. These gatherings—welcoming and inclusive—signaled God's hospitality.

Beyond meals, how hospitable are we? Jesus pushes us out of our comfort zones. As he says to his host and to the other guests, he says to us: show hospitality (in whatever form) to those who cannot repay you. As we are loved, so are we to love, for our love is the vehicle of God's love. "And," he adds, "you will be blessed."

Jesus, as you give us today our daily bread, may we be bearers of your bread to others. Amen.

We are blessed. Nothing we do will make God love us more, and nothing we do can make God love us less. No matter how independent, indifferent, and unavailable we may be, we see through this week's scriptures that God will not let us go. For God is love.

In Jeremiah, we find the Lord God Almighty, the Origin, Source, and Creator of all laments. God grieves because the people have removed themselves from divine embrace. In Psalm 81, the divine lament continues for much the same reason. God says, "I gave them over to their stubborn hearts, to follow their own counsels" (v. 12). This is the voice of the grieving parent, the sorrowful lover who watches on with longing love, desiring only the best for the loved one and fearing the worst. But the promise stands regardless. God subdues enemies and provides the finest wheat and honey from the rock.

Hebrews 13 presumes the triumph of love, showing us that God resides in our hospitality. Through us, God shows love to strangers, including those who are strangers to divine love. And we are blessed because, as the epistle writer notes, "If we love one another, God lives in us" (1 John 4:12).

Our Gospel reading displays Love incarnate. "In this is love, not that we loved God but that he loved us and sent his Son" (1 John 4:10). The Father's lament becomes saving action. So Jesus unapologetically comes to our table, stands in our culture's customs, and challenges our table manners. He is the host. He himself is living water, the very bread of life. In him the Love that will not let us go meets us where we are.

Come love of God, and we shall be changed! Amen.

Useful by Design

SEPTEMBER 2–8, 2013 • ADRIENNE MICHELLE DENSON

SCRIPTURE OVERVIEW: The Gospel lesson stresses the cost of discipleship. One of the costs involves family, but the implication is that there are compensations as well as costs. Belonging to God affects the way in which one belongs to others. Traditional patterns, kinship and otherwise, are transformed. This insight lies at the heart of Paul's letter to Philemon concerning Philemon's slave, Onesimus. Without directly requesting that Philemon set Onesimus free, Paul clearly suggests that the ties that bind persons as brothers and sisters in Christ transform traditional social patterns, including slavery. Both Jeremiah 18 and Psalm 139 affirm our belongingness to God, individually and corporately.

QUESTIONS AND THOUGHTS FOR REFLECTION

- Read Jeremiah 18:1-11. Jeremiah watches the potter at the wheel, forming clay in his hands. How do you discern the Potter's hand in your life when you find yourself or your situation marred?

- Read Psalm 139:1-6, 13-18. How can you better incorporate intentional lament and explicit praise into your time of prayer?

- Read Philemon 1-21. Paul affirms Onesimus's usefulness. How do you affirm your own worth, and how can you better employ your usefulness to the benefit of your church and community?

- Read Luke 14:25-33. Jesus encourages us to consider the cost of discipleship. How can you create and carve out time for intentional reflection and meditation?

Baptist minister, leader of the Young Adult Ministry, West Side Missionary Baptist Church, St. Louis, Missouri

Enslaved Africans in America penned the spiritual, "He's Got the Whole World in His Hands." Despite their marred situation, they imply and testify in the song to God's control. God is worthy of worship and holds them in God's good and capable hands.

Jeremiah goes to the potter's house and watches him work. The pottery wheel spins, the hands of the potter surround the clay; yet the pot in his hand is spoiled. We consider it good news to feel God's hands upon us. Though we may not always feel God's presence, hear God's voice, or see God at work in our lives, we rest assured that God's hand stays upon us. The Master Potter remains at the wheel, transforming our situations, shaping us for service, and envisioning good plans, a renewed hope, and a bright future. God reworks us into another vessel, as it "seems good."

Though strongholds may bind and sin mar, God will never wipe God's hands of us. Mercifully, the Master Potter desires our repentance and longs to rework us into vessels of honor, useful to God and prepared for good work. (See 2 Timothy 2:21.)

The clay, though "spoiled," remains clay. So it is that God's people, despite their sin, remain God's people. Always ready to forgive, God longs to remold and transform us. As Christians we affirm God's gift of Jesus to mend marred situations and to restore relationship with God. Through Jesus' salvific work, we now have access to the same Spirit that raised him from the dead. The Holy Spirit can resurrect our lives, transform our hearts, and sanctify us for God's good service. That same Spirit empowers us to create with God an honorable and just world.

Master Potter, rework us into worthy and useful vessels that are equipped for your good work. Amen.

It would take me nine long years to discern God's call for me to enter the ministry. During the fateful and ninth year, God got my attention one morning in jail. That day, I spoke with a client who did not know the Lord, yet he affirmed and confirmed God's call on my life. This client had eyes to see God's hand upon me. Once I finally comprehended God's intention for my life, I ran. I wanted to do my own thing, to be my own person, to follow my own heart, to pave my own path.

Like the people of Judah and the inhabitants of Jerusalem, I wanted to walk according to my own plans and to obey the dictates of my "evil will" (Jer. 18:12). I too shut my ears to the truth of God's word and shut my heart to the call for repentance. I continued to pursue my dreams and to execute my own plans.

The prophet brings to the people words of judgment *and* redemption. Judgment certainly weighs them in the balance; yet even now, redemption comes as God advises that we "amend [our] ways and [our] doings." The Potter has created us for so much more than we can ever plan or imagine. God fashions us with a purpose, designs us for usefulness, and intends good for our lives. The Holy One longs for us to discern God's hand upon us, to obey God's voice, and to repent readily when we chase after selfish goals rather than God's will and way.

Once I yielded to God's intention for my life and strove to make my ways and my doings good, I became more useful to God and to my community. When we allow the Great Potter to shape us into the likeness of Christ and into the people that God has called us to be, then we can more authentically proclaim the good news through our thoughts, our words, and our deeds.

Merciful God, grant us discernment to recognize your voice, grace to trust your plan, and courage to obey your will. Amen.

While I dislike being searched, I'm well known by the airport authorities and by uniformed officers at many a prison. I will never forget being searched at an Independence Day celebration in Namibia, a southern African country. The line for men at the entrance to the stadium was long and winding, yet the one for women was surprisingly empty. Perhaps the women knew what to expect. I, however, was caught unaware. Never in my life have I been handled with such vigor and intention. At its end, it became obvious that I carried no concealed weapon or any notion of privacy.

Likewise, the women at the prison where I work do not have the privilege of privacy. In prison, they are always subject to search and always under someone's watchful eye. Staff know their every move and note their daily patterns. Someone always knows when they are sitting and when they arise. It can be maddening and nerve-wracking to be watched so closely and to be known so intimately.

Just so, the psalmist notes God's knowing of his thoughts and words. He finds himself hemmed in "behind and before." This situation may seem threatening to some; the situation may feel more like a siege. Such confinement and intimate knowledge can feel like a battlefield or a prison camp.

Yet while God aims for surrender, this surrender produces freedom, not entrapment. When we surrender to the all-knowing God, we relinquish control over the things that hold us back from accomplishing God's will. When we surrender to the all-seeing God, we allow our lives and our gifts to be used for the glory of God and the benefit of our communities. Though God knows us intimately and searches us closely, God still loves us dearly and longs for our freedom.

O Lord, hem us in behind and before; bring us to our knees in prayer. Amen.

Ihave kept vigil at the hospital bed of dying veterans and have witnessed the sacred moment of death. As a hospital chaplain, I was often called to the room of dying patients to provide pastoral presence, a listening ear, and an encouraging word. In moments of sadness and impending death, I would lean upon the ancient hymn and prayer book known as the Psalms, particularly Psalm 139. As the nurses removed all forms of medical intervention, I would begin to read this psalm. By the time I finished, the patient usually had passed away. While the grief-stricken family may not remember the words from this chapter, I'm sure they recall that in the valley of the shadow of death, they were not alone.

The psalmist praises the God who remains steadfast, who knows us intimately, who loves us unconditionally, and who declares us fearfully and wonderfully made. We can never escape God's Spirit—from the time of conception to the moment of death and beyond.

Psalm 139 expresses praise for God's marvelous works, precious thoughts, and skillful hands, yet the psalmist falls under God's watchful eye. There is nowhere to flee from this surveillance, and God's hand in the womb has formed and knit his life together. This close relationship brings a special intimacy.

At death's door, we may praise God for a life well spent and for the promise of God's eternal presence; yet we too may lament, petitioning God for more time and for the miraculous healing of a body that God knows all too well. This psalm offers a powerful model of prayer; one where we both praise God and lament. May we be bold and honest enough with God and ourselves to pray likewise.

Spirit of the living God, may we make our petitions known and our praise explicit. Amen.

My mentor encourages me to take time to think. It seems commonplace and simple enough. Yet at work, we easily allow day-to day emergencies, modern technology, and general busyness to distract us. At home, I become preoccupied with my family, my hobbies, the world, and its glamor. Even spiritually, I can become distracted by well-doing and, like Martha, by much serving. When, however, I take time to think, I am more inclined to make wise decisions and to engage in strategic and mission-minded projects. When I take time to think, I am less likely to move aimlessly through my day and my life, doing much and accomplishing little.

Like my mentor, Jesus encourages us to think, to engage our heads as well as our hearts. He calls us to consider the cost of discipleship and the sacrifice necessary to follow him. In today's scripture lesson, he delivers surprising and seemingly bad news to the crowd. He tells them they must "hate" their loved ones and their own lives to be his disciple. Prone to hyperbolic speech, Jesus' use of the word *hate* falls within the comparative sense. Essentially, he suggests that we must love our families and ourselves much less than we love our Savior. "Signing on" for the long haul requires a reprioritization of our commitments. We join a "new" family that demands our time and resources.

Jesus surprises the masses by proclaiming this upside-down kingdom, where little becomes much, where you must lose your life to gain it, where you must hate to show your love. Though the crowd may have followed him for free health care or a hot meal, Jesus encourages them instead to count the cost of discipleship and to sacrifice all for their faith. I imagine it didn't take too long or too much thought for the crowd to realize that it's far easier to follow after Jesus than it is to be his disciple.

Lord Jesus, teach us to count the cost and the blessings of being your disciple. Amen.

When I was a young child, my parents often told me that my actions reflected my upbringing. My words and deeds could bring honor to my family or shame to our name. Like my parents, Jesus delivers this cautionary tale to the great multitude. He invites—moreover, insists—that they consider the cost of discipleship.

Jesus offers examples of leaders who first count the cost: the builder who must decide whether he can complete his tower and the king who must determine whether his army will reign victorious. If the builder cannot finish the job and the king cannot defeat his foe, Jesus suggests that each pursue an alternative project or another approach.

In essence, I believe Jesus is saying, "Do not put me to shame; do not mock my name or reputation." He wants his followers to take discipleship seriously, to calculate the cost of releasing that which is most dear—whether that be family or possessions. Jesus does not issue a call to wariness about discipleship but a sober call to consider what discipleship entails. Without consideration one may be lured into defeat or retreat.

Which of us will not "first sit down and estimate the cost" or consider the number of troops before going to war? The answer: None of us! Otherwise we face ridicule and defeat. Discipleship requires a strategy. Jesus will soon carry his own cross, and he identifies cross bearing (in the present tense) as an expectation of those who follow him. By weighing the costs and choosing to be a disciple of Jesus, we determine to follow him by any means necessary. We don't, however, do this in our own strength but in the power of One who began a good work in us and who is able to bring it to completion. (See Philippians 1:6.)

Merciful Jesus, when we commit to being your disciples, grant us strength to carry our own cross and to complete honorably the good work that you began. Amen.

When I was in my early twenties, members of my church would not free me from the shadow of my mother or my sister; they saw me solely in relation to them. They would ask questions like, Are you the one (read: daughter) who is married? Are you one who has a baby? Are you the one who is a pastor? "No," I would reply. "That would be my sister."

Few people could believe that I was happy with the life I had fashioned. At the time, I was a capital defense investigator, working with men and women facing the death penalty. I risked life and limb to help my clients receive the best possible sentence; yet the members at my church encouraged me to return to school. They could not see the worth in my work.

In contrast, the Christian community highly values Philemon's work. Known for his love, his faith, and the refreshment he brought to the saints, Philemon further benefited the body of Christ by allowing his home to become a community church. Paul underscores not only Philemon's usefulness but the usefulness of Onesimus. Paul publicly encourages Philemon to release his runaway slave from bondage and from any impending punishment. Paul even promises to settle Onesimus's account and requests that the former servant return to Philemon as a brother in ministry and in Christ. One cannot be a brother in Christ and a slave in the flesh.

Paul writes with his own hand, appealing to Philemon's willingness to go above and beyond in the Christian community. He could make demands but prefers to appeal to Philemon's Christian sensibilities. He appeals in love. By accepting Onesimus as a beloved brother, Philemon refreshes Paul's heart. He becomes useful to the kingdom and a blessing to all.

Gracious God, teach us to love as you love and to affirm the worth in ourselves and in all whom we encounter. Amen.

God's Lost and Found

SEPTEMBER 9–15, 2013 • J. STEPHEN LANG

SCRIPTURE OVERVIEW: The apparent message of Jeremiah 4:11-12, 22-28 is total despair, but verse 27 offers a soft note of grace. God's redemptive purposes for the people will not ultimately be thwarted. Psalm 14 suggests that foolishness and perversity characterize all humanity, but God can gather from among sinful humankind a community of people who will find their refuge in God. In First Timothy, the writer points to his own life as an example of God's ability to reclaim and redeem persons. Luke 15 suggests just how far God is willing to go to reclaim the lost. In the parables of the lost sheep and the lost coin, God is portrayed as remarkably and even recklessly active in pursuit of wayward persons. God goes after them.

QUESTIONS AND THOUGHTS FOR REFLECTION

- Read Jeremiah 4:11-12, 22-28. In what ways do you behave like "senseless children" who have "no understanding"?

- Read Psalm 14, which reminds us that "all" people at times "turn aside" from God. How does it affect you, knowing that everyone, even very religious people, are "lost" and in need of salvation?

- Read 1 Timothy 1:12-17. Take a moment to do what Paul does in this passage: contrast your present walk with God with your previous life apart from God.

- Read Luke 15:1-10. Consider the Pharisees' criticism of Jesus' reaching out to lost people. Does your attitude resemble that of the Pharisees or the shepherd in Jesus' parable?

Author of thirty-six books, including *Know the Bible in Thirty Days*; *1,001 Things You Always Wanted to Know about the Bible*; and *The 100 Most Important Events in Christian History*; living in Seminole, Florida

Reading the Bible helps us make more friends for the soul. We become acquainted with the individuals who have been inspired by God—and that includes Jeremiah, known as the "weeping prophet" because of his laments over the people's sins. Reading almost any passage from Jeremiah wrings a groan from the heart. Here we read about a deeply sensitive man with a whole-souled commitment to his God—a man who cannot help but grieve over his nation, Judah, knowing the people are spiritually lost.

"My people are fools; they do not know me. They are sense-less children; they have no understanding. They are skilled in doing evil; they know not how to do good" (NIV). Notice the contrast: the people are "senseless children" with "no under-standing"—and yet they are "skilled in doing evil." Skill comes from practice. Through continued abuse and exploitation of their neighbors, the people gain proficiency in evil and move farther from God. They do not "know" God, as they prove by ignoring divine authority. In Jeremiah's lifetime, the saintly King Josiah had instituted a much-needed religious reform, but the changes were short-lived. With Josiah gone, the people have snapped their minds shut, paying no heed to the dire warnings of Jeremiah and other prophets.

Jeremiah foretells punishment by a "scorching wind" from the desert. His prophecy comes to pass a few years later when the Babylonians conquer Judah, destroy the Temple, and carry leading citizens into exile. The image of the scorching wind stands as a warning for all ages and peoples, signaling the time for people "skilled in doing evil" to grow up, morally and spiritually, and stop being "senseless children."

God, thank you for the words of your prophets that still speak to us across the centuries. Amen.

The theme of Psalm 14 revolves around practical atheism. Theoretical atheism refers to the intellectual belief that no God exists, period. Practical atheism means behaving as if God does not exist. In the history of the world, we have witnessed few theoretical atheists, since most people believe in some divine force. But countless practical atheists have come on the scene, people like the "fool" in Psalm 14, the person whose belief that "there is no God" really means "there is no God watching me and expecting me to behave a certain way." The fool cannot see beyond the narrow compass of the present life.

And what results from practical atheism? "Corrupt" people, "vile" deeds. They "devour" their neighbors and "frustrate the plans of the poor." Anyone behaving this way is a "fool"—not one lacking intellectual knowledge but one whose heart is not right, who ignores God's claim on his or her life. The Hebrew word translated "corrupt" implies a sense of spoiling or being ruined. God designed human beings for a good purpose (to love each other and love God), but lack of regard for God and neighbor makes them worthless and spoiled.

Like many of the Psalms, this one begins with lamentation but ends in hope and triumph. Although fools and evildoers distress and oppress their neighbors, "God is present in the company of the righteous" and "the LORD is their refuge." God stands with the righteous.

The last verse of the psalm proclaims a hopeful prayer: "Oh, that salvation for Israel would come." The psalmist looks forward to a time when the fools, who have "turned aside" from God, will recognize their lostness and seek God.

God, keep us ever aware of your presence, and let it guide our words and deeds. Amen.

We could title this passage "Genesis 1, Reversed." Jeremiah "looked at the earth, and it was formless and empty." Genesis 1:2 uses the same words when referring to the primeval state of things before God creates all things and declares them "good." In Jeremiah's vision, the light has gone; the mountains, seemingly so solid and steadfast, are "quaking." Humanity's stubborn and selfish refusal to love God and neighbor affects all creation. Creation's chaos conveys God's "fierce anger."

God's wrath is not a popular subject these days. Writers and preachers prefer to emphasize God's love, not God's wrath. I once passed a church with a sign that posted the topic of the upcoming sermon: "A wrathful God of mercy." That is a good summary of what the Bible tells us about God. Those who juxtapose an Old Testament God of wrath with a New Testament God of mercy fail to recall that both Testaments bear witness to the same God and to the same attitude toward human failings. The way human beings treat one another kindles God's anger. We seem "skilled at doing evil" while ignorant and inept about doing good.

This passage from Jeremiah shows, in unforgettable images, how seriously God takes human sin. Sin throws the whole creation out of kilter. God created all things and called them "good," just as the Creator made human beings to live in love and fellowship. When humans choose their own paths, chaos results. Despite the seriousness of sin, God tempers wrath with mercy: God will not completely destroy the land. In wrath and mercy, God remains relentless.

God, keep us mindful of your anger toward sin and mindful of your great mercy. Amen.

The passages from Psalms and Jeremiah speak of the lostness of the human race. Today's reading from Luke looks at the divine solution to the problem. God hates sin—but loves sinners. In fact, God loves sinners more than the religious people of Jesus' day, the Pharisees, can comprehend. Cozily smug in their righteousness and possessing an elitist view of religion, the Pharisees and teachers of the law "muttered" because Jesus sat down at the table with sinners. We can sense their contemptuous sneers when they refer to "this man" who rubs elbows with sinners.

Jesus responds to their scorn with two parables. The first deals with a shepherd who has a flock of one hundred sheep. One wanders away into the wilderness where it could be killed by predators or be injured or simply starve to death. The shepherd still has ninety-nine sheep in the flock—strictly speaking, he does not need the straying sheep. Nonetheless, he searches until he finds it. The shepherd does not grumble about carrying the wayward sheep on his shoulders; he feels joy and calls on others to share the joy.

God isn't just the Righteous One sitting sternly in heaven awaiting people's repentance—God actively seeks people out. The surest sign of this is Jesus himself, Son of God—not distancing himself from the lost but dining with them. To the Pharisees' criticism that "this man welcomes sinners and eats with them," an appropriate response might be, "Thank God!" The earliest Christian art does not show Jesus on the cross—but rather, Jesus as a shepherd bearing a sheep on his shoulders.

Lord, we thank you for reaching out to us in our lostness. Make us eager to do the same for others. Amen.

FRIDAY, SEPTEMBER 13 ~ *Read Luke 15:8-10*

In Luke 14, Jesus teaches the people about being "salt" in the world and committing themselves wholly to God. In chapter 15 we see that the tax collectors and sinners gather around to hear him. The "lost" people give him their ears, while the smug Pharisees criticize his association with sinners. To these critics, lost sinners do not merit anyone's attention; Jesus debases himself by associating with such people.

Pause a moment to consider Jesus' occupation: a carpenter, a person who supplied timber for houses and built farm implements and furniture. He plied his trade in the world, doing business with a wide variety of people. Unlike the Pharisees and rabbis who gather together to debate scripture and theology, keeping their distance from the rabble, Jesus is in the world, a world full of lost people in need of salvation. The Son of God came to earth not to keep his distance from people but to seek out the lost.

The parable of the poor woman who searches frantically for the lost coin in her home speaks to both the depth of divine love and the searching nature of God. The parable gives rise to some gentle humor: the flustered woman turns her house upside down to find the coin; when she finds it, she shares her elation with her neighbors. Surely, if a human can "search diligently" for a lost coin, God even more diligently seeks out sinners. And when the lost sinner is found, there is great rejoicing in heaven. At the heart of the gospel is this amazing truth: Almighty God, Maker of heaven and earth, reaches out to the lost soul and rejoices at repentance.

Merciful God, make us more like Jesus, reaching out in love to a lost and hurting world. Amen.

Saul, a devout Pharisee and zealous for the Jewish law, studied under the noted rabbi Gamaliel who in Acts 5 advises his fellow Jews not to persecute the Christians, for if the Christian movement has its origin in God, humans cannot stop it. Saul does not imitate his teacher's tolerant wait-and-see attitude. Saul approves the stoning of the first Christian martyr, Stephen, and tries to stamp out the movement, regarding all Christians as heretics and blasphemers. His dramatic conversion on the road to Damascus (Acts 9) changes the persecutor into one of the greatest figures in Christian history.

Even before his conversion, Saul was a man of stern energy and fizzing vitality. Such a person could be of great value in the growing—and persecuted—church. So Saul, the Pharisee, found inner peace as a Christian, with his zeal still intact and put to good use.

Writing to his young protégé, Timothy, Paul recalls the time he spent as "a blasphemer and persecutor and violent man." He was the enemy of God's people, yet God shows mercy to him. He has been one of the self-righteous Pharisees—the people who, in Luke 15, criticize Jesus for spending time with sinners. Paul comes to understand that devoutly religious people like himself can be spiritually lost, in need of rescue by the good shepherd of Jesus' parable.

Paul says that among sinners, he has been the *protos*—a Greek word usually translated "first" but which in this context means "chief" or "foremost" or even "worst." His dramatic, life-changing, history-changing transformation proves that no lost soul lies beyond God's reach.

God of miraculous transformations, teach us that no person is beyond hope, that your love and mercy know no limits. Amen.

As a child, I complained about being stuck indoors on a rainy day. My grandmother would say, "Rainy days make you appreciate sunny days"—a wise response. Would we value good times if there were no bad times? Would we appreciate our health—physical, emotional, or spiritual—if we had never been sick? Would we appreciate being secure and content if we were never lost?

Paul thanks and praises God for his amazing conversion. He contrasts his days as a self-righteous but lost man, the "worst" of sinners, with his present life as an apostle. Paul has behaved abominably, working to destroy God's community of faith—but "the grace of our Lord was poured out on me abundantly" and "I was shown mercy" and "unlimited patience." Paul can't help bursting out with joy and gratitude: "To the King eternal, immortal, invisible, the only God, be honor and glory forever and ever. Amen." Paul's doxology quivers with exhilaration because his former state is engraved in his memory. The people who fully appreciate divine mercy are those who know how much there was to forgive; people who can say, in the words of the classic hymn, "I once was lost but now am found."

Did Paul really see himself as the "worst" of sinners? Paul might reply, "Yes—the worst I really know." Back in Genesis, Adam and Eve had been evasive when caught in sin: Adam blamed it on the woman God had given him, and Eve blamed the serpent. Paul understood spiritual maturity: you take an objective look at yourself and make no excuses. You regret your failings and thank God for providing a Savior. Frustration and regret over our flaws, then contentment and gratitude to God: This is the heart of Paul's gospel message.

Loving God, we thank you and praise you for your infinite mercy and patience. Amen.

Out of Bounds

SEPTEMBER 16–22, 2013 • CLAIRE KEENE

SCRIPTURE OVERVIEW: Three of the texts for this Sunday deal with intercession; and although they certainly will not make praying any easier, they may make it more hopeful. The readings from both Jeremiah and the psalm depict the anguish of one who identifies with the pain of God's faithless people. Prophet and psalmist grieve with and for the people and join in the persistent and impatient plea for health and renewal. But God turns out to be not an impassive or distant deity but one bound up with the anguish of the prophet and the anguish of the people. Likewise, the psalmist discovers that the God who refuses to tolerate Israel's faithlessness nevertheless cannot finally abandon the chosen community. First Timothy also challenges readers to offer prayers of intercession and specifies that they be made for those in positions of political leadership.

QUESTIONS AND THOUGHTS FOR REFLECTION

- Read Jeremiah 8:18–9:1. What signs of salvation do you expect as you move from one season of life to another? What happens if they do not appear?

- Read Psalm 79:1-9. The psalmist asks God to send his suffering people quick compassion, but prays for vengeance on invading nations. Can we trust God's compassion without seeing our violators suffer?

- Read 1 Timothy 2:1-7. For whom do you choose not to pray? What effect does their stance have on your resistance?

- Read Luke 16:1-13. What crisis would move you to reclaim God's gifts to you as "true riches"?

Poet, potter, priest, and preacher; "Grammy" to Socorro and Emily; alto to her husband's baritone; rector, Episcopal Church of the Resurrection, Loudon, Tennessee

Starting over. It almost always means change, rethinking, turning in a different direction.

It usually comes from a rousing jolt of failure—a firing, like that of the unfaithful manager; a relationship that's turned cold and hard at the core; a clear-eyed, shocking glimpse that we've become the very demon we've been running from. Often, our cognizance wounds us at the source of pride: a dancer with rheumatoid arthritis, a teacher whose knowledge is being ravaged by Alzheimer's, a devoted parent whose child retreats into self-destruction, an athlete with a spinal cord injury. Our life will not be what we thought. What now, if the achievements in which we have invested our lives, day after day, year after year, bring no satisfaction or security?

Perhaps we, like the manager, can start over—this time investing our well-being in the lives of others. We cut people some slack and welcome the tumbling and tossing of life with others, which smooths, rounds, reveals, and reinforces us. We can begin to follow the path of yielding ourselves generously—the way small springs trickle into tributaries, yield to rivers, and push rivers toward the sea.

Our lives have never been simply our own to facet and polish into gemstones. This time we can start over less anxiously. This time we offer our ashes, our dust, our water for the common feast. And the Spirit, hovering, turns them into prodigal variety, turns them into lives that are fruitful and multiply.

O Lord, we forget that our treasure is really yours. Honing our gifts and hiding our limitations, we fear failure constantly; we are famished for hope and possibility. We forget that we thrive only in the give-and-take of your household. Widen our horizons, Lord. Turn us toward each other, that we may not despair of your grace. We ask for Jesus' sake. Amen.

Expectations grow from experience. So our souls layer them like tree rings: they thicken, season, solidify. They ossify into entitlement, into a solidly sculpted, artful life. We have learned to expect the sun to rise, the rain to fall, creeks and rivers to fill and flow. We can predict tides, lunar cycles. We expect what we plant to sprout, to flower, and to yield food enough. We engineer our houses to sustain serenity. We expect clear warnings about change. We're entitled to basic predictability, right?

And then an oil spill smothers the Gulf Coast. An earthquake tumbles Haitian cities. A tsunami in Japan breaks up edifices, fills traffic arteries with sludge, rinses away thousands who depended on one another, and imperils generations with radiation. Tornadoes eat big holes in cities, spitting out the rubble hundreds of miles away. Whole families and communities disappear. Halfway around the world, governments struggle to stay afloat on the swells of one uprising after another.

The ancient Israelites in Babylon aren't the only ones who ask, Is this God's doing or not? Has God, like an unfaithful lover, abandoned us for a more attractive people? Or is our God impotent? Neither yes nor no satisfies.

God is as essential to our famines as to our feasts. We also are somehow essential. We and God measure out meanings; we bake them into tomorrow's bread. "Hear, O Israel: The LORD our God, the LORD is one" (Deut. 6:4, NIV). We castaways on this God-embraced world are one too. We belong to one another. And thus the people of Israel and the prophet Jeremiah cry. For this reason we cry, we fear, we hope, and we awake to thrive. This grace of belonging is not an entitlement, but with shocked-wide eyes we might just reach for it, this balm in which God wraps every wound.

Eternal God, still us, entwine us, and grow the future's roots among us. Amen.

When the economy that ballooned our retirement accounts and our real estate values suddenly deflates them, shouldn't someone other than us pay for it? When our government makes no one happy, isn't it the other party's fault? When our schools slide down a slippery slope, mustn't it be the teachers' fault or the parents' fault or perhaps the fault of those spoiled, privileged children or all those poor immigrant kids? If our country is at war on multiple fronts, isn't it because those other nations don't know how the world ought to run? If the environment is prostituted for short-term pleasures, isn't it our ancestors' fault for creating the automobile, suburban sprawl, and air-conditioning in the first place?

And by the way, why hasn't God submitted for our review a proposal for getting us out of this mess?

Our preferred response to calamity remains, "We don't deserve this; it's not our fault." We seldom, it seems, get past trying to make our hearts and hands look less dirty by pointing out others' fingerprints on the wall. We aim ferocious energies at reasserting our honor or at least getting an explanation that soothes our dignity. We expect an answer for our pain. We call even God on the carpet.

Our strategy for justice and peace is usually smoke and mirrors. Smoke, in that we're trying quietly to burn the record of our own dirty hands and hearts. Mirrors, because what really horrifies us is the truth: we are part of the murky mix; all of us— both sparkles and muck. If we say "yes" to our imperfections, we must say "yes" to those of others.

A world at enmity with itself cannot find its way. Blame and shame cannot set the world right. Only our repentance and our forgiveness set us plumb and level with God's future.

Dear Lord, because we cannot set the world straight, we hope in your mercy and trust in your faithful love. Amen.

Every day we work and eat and do business with people who are as different from us as the Gentiles were from former Pharisee, Paul. Our archetypal stories don't match. Characters from scripture dear to us may be just names to them: Isaac, Elijah, Mary, Peter. The rituals through which we embrace our identity and hope—baptism and Holy Communion—may seem just plain weird. Unlocking Christianity for folks who did not grow up under its roof is a puzzle. How do we open windows to the gospel light within us?

First, Paul says to pray for all people. For *all* people. Offer supplications, prayers, intercessions, and thanksgiving for them. Do this even for people in power, the strangers most likely to oppose and oppress us. This is no small challenge, to pray as if we are all alike before God.

The goal of our praying for everyone does not primarily hinge on their conversion: "O God, make them see things our way, which we are sure is your way." No, the one-size-holds-all prayer Paul recommends is evangelical. It commits *our* hearts to lives we thought we had God's permission to ignore, to keep our distance from, perhaps even to despise. Inclusive prayer places us under the spotlight of reconciliation, where the family resemblance to those we fear or ignore becomes obvious. *Their* story is *our* story with chapters of blessedness, sin, judgment, and redemption much like ours. It is God's love story, told in flesh and blood through Christ's sharing it, Christ's blessing it, Christ's healing it, and finally through Christ's yielding it to us through the Spirit.

Praying for all people, no matter what, clears our vision to see everyone as Jesus sees us: as we are and as we may become, radiant with our one Father's light.

Gracious and generous God, stretch our prayer to fit your heart. Amen.

Summer has ended; winter has come, and there are no refreshing rains. The people of Israel "are not saved." The people fear God's absence, and Jeremiah cries out to God in grief for the people. The drought becomes a metaphor for Judah's alienation from God. So the prophet weeps, desiring to cry a fountain of tears, a spring of water that would "quench" the suffering of the drought-stricken people.

When tears break through, we can begin to heal. But it's not always easy to get there. It takes waiting past the defensive rush. It takes digging down to where reality's splinter sticks in our soul, festering. Tears can flush out the wound.

Deep wounds don't bleed clean. They bore in until they grate against our souls like broken rib against lung. Then we cry, "No! Stop it; something's wrong!" Finally, we pull back the crust of doing just fine, thank you. We allow tenderness. We bend and bond and brave reality once again, naked before God and each other, as in Eden. New life starts now.

Salvation does not start with a laundry list of faults to rectify. Our witness to God's power doesn't begin with our conquering temptations. Salvation begins with tears, with a baptism into the goodness of our genesis in God. We yield again to belovedness. How could we ever share wine so lavishly at the wedding feast, rejoice with the prodigal's return, caress lepers, send the lame home with their pallets if first we had to be strong, brave, and true? God's justice begins with welcome, in the font of tears and tenderness. This balm of Gilead makes all us wounded ones whole.

Dear Lord, make us willing to start where we really are, letting you flush out the buried grime and grit that's making us miserable. Then send us on your way. Amen.

Comparisons start the day we're born. How much does he weigh; how long is she? After that, we compare our children's development, whether they eat vegetables or sleep well, when they begin to talk or walk. Right from the start we emphasize whatever distinguishes one person from another. We rank ourselves by demographics. It's a hard habit to break.

Admit it—you would dress more carefully for Prince William and Kate Middleton's wedding than for your niece's. You would tidy your house more for the bishop's visit than for your best friend's. You might tell your child, "I don't know" but would worry about admitting ignorance in a job interview. You might reveal your golf score publicly but not your bank account balance—who wants to be ranked by last month's overdraft?

The writer of First Timothy urges prayer for all—including those authorities who wield power over our lives. Why? Because there is *one* God and *one* mediator over *one* people. However, we cannot measure two dimensions of human life: our rootedness in God and our interdependence with one another. These soul-dimensions are givens, like time and space. We cannot rank ourselves by them because we all get the same score—*one*. *One* life before *one* God in *one* common humanity.

Our relationships with God and one another establish the planes within which the single dot of our existence becomes three-dimensional life. We cannot escape the graces or the tensions of this triangular life: we exist for mutual delight. And therein lies the need for us to pray beyond every boundary. Therein lies the need for us to claim Christ's only intent: to bring us all home to the Holy One, who sees beyond distinctions and loves us beyond all measure.

Enlarge our vision, Lord, to see you in every life, so that we may trust your life within us. Amen.

My family members thought we knew how to vacation in this place. But Thursday at dusk, a tornado blew across the river, climbed the steep bank toward our cabin, and ripped at the pines and birches of the North Country. No electricity, no water, no air-conditioning, no landline, no cell reception, no television, no radio. Once-towering trees lay down in protest across the roads. The sign identifying our road had disappeared. Meat for the holiday barbecue warmed in the dead refrigerator. No friends or relatives here. What now?

We were safe and, at first, content with the sudden simplicity. But days passed, toilets filled, milk warmed, skin exuded oil and sweat, sleep fled. We experienced a brief desolation, but a desolation nevertheless. Privileges disappeared. Like the deer, eagles, raccoons, and bears around us, we scrounged and made do. Only the river remained as ever, rolling below us, murmuring.

"Know that the LORD has set apart the faithful for himself." Yet, what is faithfulness when way becomes wilderness, when familiar signposts no longer direct our approach to God? We have relied on these maps, milestones, and well-marked exits: AAA-guided expressway living. But our route suddenly leads to nowhere. How do we keep covenant when rules of the road no longer apply? Are our lives lost to us?

Perhaps real life is more awakened than plotted. We make our passage now by the river's lead, descending without compass, leaving known vistas behind. We follow like fish, with no cargo but trust. We must lean with the river, must learn to notice that God is moving—swiftly or slowly—gathering us, pushing us beyond ourselves. The Lord puts "gladness" in our hearts and makes us "lie down in safety."

Receive us, Lord, into the deep currents, where we know your love by following it. Amen.

Values and Security

SEPTEMBER 23–29, 2013 • ÜLLAS TANKLER

SCRIPTURE OVERVIEW: The Bible warns about the delusions that wealth brings, repeatedly directing readers' attention to the poor and the destitute. Luke's Gospel text culminates in Jesus' story of the rich man and Lazarus. Only in the next life, when the rich man is rid of his riches, can he see Lazarus, now secure at Abraham's side. First Timothy contains a series of warnings to prosperous readers that having the basic necessities of life should be enough. Greed diverts attention away from the God "who richly provides us with everything for our enjoyment." And against the best wisdom of all the financial planners of Judah, Jeremiah purchases the field at Anathoth. The prophet invests his money in the divine promise, in the outlandish conviction that God is faithful.

QUESTIONS AND THOUGHTS FOR REFLECTION

- Read Jeremiah 32:1-3a, 6-15. When have you taken a bold stand in a situation that seemed hopeless to others? How did your words or actions redeem the situation?
- Read Psalm 91:1-6, 14-16. What do you need to make yourself feel secure?
- Read 1 Timothy 6:6-19. When have you allowed yourself to trust in "the uncertainty of riches"?
- Read Luke 16:19-31. What in your value system needs adjustment from the perspective of eternity?

United Methodist pastor from Estonia; executive secretary for Europe, Middle East, and North Africa with the Board of Global Ministries

Zedekiah, the king of Judah, thinks he can stop the future by imprisoning Jeremiah. With Jeremiah in solitary confinement, he believes the prophet's warning will not be heard.

I grew up in Estonia when the Soviet Union occupied it. The Communist leaders thought that by throwing people into prisons or sending them to Siberian labor camps, they would alter the future. They wanted to maintain the power they so greatly misused. The Communist leaders felt threatened by those who dared to imply or imagine that this order of things would not last. They believed that by silencing the prophets who proclaimed doom to our society, the doom would not come. But they were not naive; they suffered from self-imposed blindness.

Jeremiah's proclamation in his day runs contrary to the patriotic propaganda of the nation's leadership. "This is what the LORD says: I am about to hand this city over to the king of Babylon and he will capture it" (NIV). This kind of message not only undermines patriotic feelings but undermines the status of those in power. Zedekiah is unready to "go there." His concern revolves around his own power and authority—not whether the word comes from the Lord.

We are not kings. Most of us probably do not exercise authority over many people. But chances are, most of us would rather keep to our wishful thinking about better days ahead than face the truth about our circumstances, our decisions, our character. The idea of false security encourages us to believe that what we do and who we are is right.

The future did not depend on whether Jeremiah was free or locked up. The future depended—then and now—on the Lord of world and history.

Lord, may we not rely on the feelings of false security we have created ourselves. Help us embrace the truth and trust that you will never forsake us. Amen.

According to common understanding, good news means that something we like will happen now or very soon. When God called Jeremiah, the Lord appointed him to be "over nations and kingdoms to uproot and tear down, to destroy and overthrow, to build and to plant" (Jer. 1:10, NIV). Does Jeremiah serve as a bearer of good news or bad news? The Christian emphasis on God's love might create a limited understanding, as if good news means that God only relays pleasant information.

Jeremiah seems to proclaim bad news and good news at the same time. I wonder if some of the leaders pushed him to make up his mind! Are you telling us that a foreign king will capture us (Jer. 32:3) or that we will prosper in our economy (32:15)? According to your message, should we feel safe and secure—or prepare for a disaster?

Jeremiah as a true prophet of the Lord sees the big picture and realizes that God's actions and words represent good news. Indeed, the people of Judah, who have not attended to God's commands, will face the punishment that comes through the king of Babylon. Yet, in the midst of proclaiming that judgment and while imprisoned, Jeremiah chooses to act out redemption.

Jeremiah buys a piece of worthless property for seventeen shekels from his cousin. He goes to great lengths to make this sale visible: money exchanging hands, witnesses to the deal, and the deed of purchase itself. Jeremiah's secretary, Baruch, will then store the deed in a jar, where it will last a long time.

Jeremiah "voices" the good news that God assures us of a future. We may rest in God's love. "Houses and fields and vineyards shall again be bought in this land."

Lord, your word is always good news to us. Give us grace to accept it fully. Amen.

Security has been a core value of humanity throughout its existence. We may discuss at length how our contemporary culture differs so drastically from the people whose lives were determined by the culture of biblical times. However, most people place security as a top priority. Relationships flourish in a secure environment. Envy and mistrust, born out of insecurity, undermine relationships.

The concept of security has many facets and factors. Much depends on interpretation, as well as context. Some people think first of world markets and investments. For others the weather and its impact on rice fields comes first. And for many the first connection to security revolves around aging family and those for whom threatening violence is as real as the air they breathe. Everyone defines security in a different way, depending on personal or communal context.

King Zedekiah attacks Jeremiah for his message about the upcoming destruction by the Babylonians, yet the king and the prophet in some ways agree with each other. The king does not want Judah's destruction, while the prophet looks into the future when God's blessing will provide prosperity.

The king's view relies on security created by the self. The prophet knows the fragility of the security built by power and might; he relies on God. It is Jeremiah who sings the lyrics of this song with integrity: "You who live in the shelter of the Most High, who abide in the shadow of the Almighty, will say to the LORD, 'My refuge and my fortress; my God, in whom I trust.'"

Lord, in the midst of many expected and unexpected fears in this world, let my heart dwell in your shelter. Amen.

When people feel concerned or insecure, they sometimes pray. Some consider this option as the "last straw" to which they resort. For others prayer constitutes a regular part of their lives. When a problem arises, they pray. Many who do not call themselves Christians or believers reach out to somebody or something "out there" when a serious crisis occurs. They form words that call for help in their minds and hearts. We might say that in these times people believe God might hear them—but too often they do not believe in listening to God.

The Bible, however, emphasizes the truth that a relationship with God provides not only an opportunity to cry when we face trouble but gives God an opportunity to speak to us. God desires our listening. Silence of the heart is a heavenly attribute. In that kind of silence we really begin to hear.

A troubled heart that wants to cry out all its needs and concerns to the all-powerful God may then perhaps become aware that this God—not necessarily "out there" but "right here"—has something to say. And maybe one can then hear the words that the psalmist hears: "Those who love me, I will deliver. I will protect those who know my name. When they call to me, I will answer them; I will be with them in trouble, I will rescue them and honor them" (NIV).

God offers comprehensive coverage and protection. What a great gift of grace that we may speak with our heavenly Father and trust that God listens and responds to us. When we call, God will answer. When we find ourselves in trouble, God will not only rescue us but will honor us.

Lord, may my prayers include listening as well as speaking. Amen.

I remember the years that led to the Soviet collapse in the early 1990s. Hyperinflation meant that we knew what the few things in our empty stores cost yesterday. We had no idea what they would cost tomorrow. The value of the Soviet ruble deteriorated within hours. The goal was to buy anything—whatever was available and as much as possible—scissors, sugar, panty hose, pillows—just to get something for this money that would be worthless tomorrow. In those days, when we saw people lining up in a long queue, we would first quickly take a place in the line and only then ask what the store sold.

In the intervening time, market economy has flourished in my country. The economy has been up again. Priorities that most people pursue today differ greatly in terms of technology and price, but we seem as materialistic and self-centered as two decades ago. After the innumerable examples and experiences from history, humanity might have learned the lesson that we do not live by bread alone.

Consider the strength of the words in this passage. Godliness with contentment is "great gain." We brought "nothing" into the world; we take "nothing" out of it. One should "flee" from the evil that comes from the love of money and "pursue" righteousness. Setting our heart and mind on values that last is not a pursuit that is being settled once and for all. Rather, we make an endless number of choices every day, based on directions given to us in the word of God.

Lord, in some areas of my life I should be content and, in others, contentment is carelessness. Guide me as I learn the difference. Amen.

Are you rich? No, no, no! Most of us would deny that label, perhaps mentioning in passing a few famous names that we associate with wealth—or those on the *Forbes* magazine list. So does this release us from the admonition given to Timothy to "command the [rich] not to be haughty" in the present age? Perhaps these three verses of the Bible actually do not belong to the main text but might appear in the appendixes, under the title "Readings for those who consider themselves rich."

Are you rich? And this time, let those who belong to the overwhelming majority of the world's population give an answer. The concept is relative. Therefore, rather than calculating our assets and bank accounts, which may add up to categorizing us as "rich," let us examine the message: those who happen to be wealthier than others are not necessarily evil or dishonest. The passage says nothing about the "wrongness" of being rich—or even of desiring wealth. The verses' concern pinpoints haughtiness or arrogance and setting hopes "on the uncertainty of riches."

An attitude of arrogance can pervade our living. Arrogance implies a worldview that revolves around self. *I* have achieved because of who *I* am, because of what *I* can do, because of what *I* own. The *I* here is vastly disproportionate, becoming so big that it casts a shadow on all life's values; hence, the warning in these verses. After addressing the temptations of wealth and the gain of contentment in faith, we return once more to the specific attributes of wealthy Christians in the community of faith. Attitude is all-important, and persons with wealth can do good through their generosity and sharing.

We all long to contribute in a meaningful way. Long before we began to wonder what is really valuable, God created us to enjoy and hold to "the life that really is life."

Lord, free our hearts so that we share what we have. Amen.

The Bible does not quite satisfy our curiosity about what heaven might be like. Rather, many passages actually seem to indicate that we would be better off not trying to guess: "What no one ever saw or heard, what no one ever thought could happen, is the very thing God prepared for those who love him" (1 Cor. 2:9, GNT). Clearly, everlasting life "up there" is not meant to be the primary motivation to get there.

We seldom glimpse insights into the life to come from the perspective of this age. However, today's passage offers an insight into our life *here* from the perspective of eternity through the story of the rich man and Lazarus. To understand what is truly valuable, we need to do more than simply consider yesterday, today, and our immediate environment. To identify true and lasting values and to gain the ability to set priorities in this life, we need guidance from the life to come. Our living appropriately today requires that we allow God to enlighten us in matters where we are naturally shortsighted.

Indeed, our shortsightedness may keep us from noticing someone at our own gate. Lazarus is poor by choice—not by his own but by someone else's choice. This someone feels so secure with his possessions that they consume him and become his top priority. The rich man does not treat Lazarus poorly or abuse him; he simply does not *see* him at all.

Only after death does the situation reverse itself. The rich man suddenly "sees" Lazarus. It appears that the seeing has come too late for him, but perhaps it is not too late for us. We and the five brothers still have a chance. The Lord wants us to view this life through the perspective of eternal values.

Lord, open my eyes to see the values in this life from the perspective of eternity. Amen.

From Exile to Freedom to Service

SEPTEMBER 30–OCTOBER 6, 2013 • JOHN R. TERRILL

SCRIPTURE OVERVIEW: Moving from the sadness of Lamentations 1 to the thanksgiving prayer of 2 Timothy 1 is to move from total darkness to "the appearing of our Savior Christ Jesus, who abolished death and brought life and immortality to light through the gospel." Lamentations 1 and Psalm 137 are both painful laments from the vantage point of the exile. Both laments dramatize the expression of honest pain, which offers to God anger as well as grief. In contrast, the New Testament texts speak of faith. The writer of the epistle delights in Timothy's heritage of faith, nurtured by mother and grandmother and empowered by divine gifts of love and self-discipline. But it is a heritage that must put itself at risk for the sake of the gospel and not flinch in the face of inevitable suffering. The disciples ask Jesus for "more" faith, only to be told that faith cannot be quantified.

QUESTIONS AND THOUGHTS FOR REFLECTION

- Read Lamentations 1:1-6. Seasons of desolation are a part of life. In what ways are you in exile today?

- Read Psalm 137. The Israelites offer an authentic prayer that recounts God's faithfulness and invites divine justice. Is your prayer life characterized by such authenticity?

- Read 2 Timothy 1:1-14. How does your identity in Christ make a difference in your everyday living?

- Read Luke 17:5-10. What does service in the kingdom of God look like to you? What character traits are you developing as a result?

Director of the Center for Integrity in Business, Seattle Pacific University; regular contributor to print and Web-based journals on matters related to business, ethics, and Christian theology; Seattle, Washington

Lamentations is the first in a series of books that chronicle the experiences and emotions associated with living in exile. Written sometime after the fall of Jerusalem to Babylonia, the book of Lamentations captures the grief of a people displaced by war and removed from the familiarity and comfort of home. Jerusalem is sacked, and the Temple, the visible reminder of God's presence and care, is destroyed.

Recently, I had the opportunity to tour the Newseum in Washington DC—a museum that chronicles the history of American news. One striking exhibit covers the devastation of Katrina, a strong category 3 hurricane that wreaked havoc on the U.S. central Gulf Coast in 2005. The storm first hit New Orleans on a Monday, like today. Its surge produced devastating flooding that exiled huge populations. Homeland Security estimates that 800,000 men, women, and children were displaced. Forced to flee for their lives, many have never returned. A rolling wall of water destroyed memories, dreams, and physical property. In a matter of hours, this vibrant city was transformed from a proud, festive, and buoyant community to a people gasping and struggling for life.

Jerusalem, long rejecting the ways of the Lord and culpable for its own demise, suffered a similar fate. But rather than succumbing to natural forces, it was besieged by a human army that sought to stamp out its identity.

"How lonely sits the city that once was full of people!" The experience of exile comes in many forms. We find ourselves in desolation through losses and conflicts of all kinds. While God promises never to desert God's people, this passage closes with a picture of total forsakenness: "From daughter Zion has departed all her majesty." God, have mercy.

Help me to trust you, Lord, in times of trouble. Amen.

The experience of exile continues in Psalm 137. The tears and weeping linger in the far-off land of Babylon as a banished community remembers the good life once enjoyed in Jerusalem. Everything feels wrong about the new address, so much so that lyres, once instruments of joy and celebration, hang abandoned in the nearby trees.

Worse yet, tormentors mock them, demanding blissful melodies that will force the Israelites to remember the good days long gone. Can anything be worse than pretending to be happy when pain and loss consume your heart? The Israelites will have nothing of it. How can they rejoice in such a wasteland under the command of such vile oppressors?

As we considered yesterday, the music also stopped in New Orleans when Katrina rolled into town. Sirens replaced trumpets, and collapsing structures dispelled the tap-tap-tap of dance and jollity. But as the waters slowly receded, a melody began to emerge. The people of New Orleans found strength to begin the long process of rebuilding through their shared history of song and dance.

Israel quietly sang a different song, one that recalled God's faithfulness and goodness, yet demanded divine justice for the tyranny they had endured.

"O daughter Babylon, you devastator! Happy shall they be who pay you back what you have done to us! Happy shall they be who take your little ones and dash them against the rock!"

We may find Israel's refrain discordant and dangerous, but it exudes honesty. God invites authentic relationship. Are you willing to cry out in trust as the Israelites did?

God, help us sing a song to you this day. Remind us that our melody doesn't always need to be joyful but, rather, can be filled with chords of pain, anger, disillusionment, and the longing for you to make things right. Amen.

In a world of e-mail, instant messaging, and texting, we often value convenience over content. But the construction and tone of our words matter. The apostle Paul, a master communicator with thirteen epistles attributed to his name, carefully crafted letters that addressed thorny theological and practical matters.

Paul writes this second letter to Timothy to encourage his younger colleague to persevere in gospel work in spite of suffering and challenge. The opening verses note the theme and focus of the pastoral epistles as Paul stresses his apostleship "for the sake of the promise of life that is in Christ Jesus." Paul then becomes more personal in his address to Timothy. He writes a love letter of sorts from an older friend and mentor to a younger, cherished leader of the next generation. "To Timothy, my beloved child: . . . I remember you constantly in my prayers night and day. Recalling your tears, I long to see you so that I may be filled with joy. "

We all need to find persons like Timothy in whom we can invest; but we also need the mentors like Paul who can encourage us toward faith and service. For me, one of the privileges of the Christian life involves playing both roles. I keep a desk file with notes of reassurance that I've received over the years, "love letters" from friends and mentors who have invested in me. When I need a heartening word, I pull out the file and read. "I delight in your partnership. . . . I thank God for you. . . . You are a good and loyal friend to many." We are both the investor and the invested. May you draw on the strength and kindness of those who have invested in you! And may you encourage others, becoming a living epistle of love.

Lord Jesus, thank you for friends and mentors who remind me of my true identity in you. As you remind me that I am beloved, prompt me to reach out to others with words that encourage and inspire. Amen.

THURSDAY, OCTOBER 3 ~ *Read 2 Timothy 1:5-7*

In encouraging Timothy to persevere and "to fan into flame the gift of God" (ESV) that has been entrusted to him, Paul pursues two parallel paths. First, he reminds Timothy of his God-given identity and "holy calling" made possible through the salvific acts of Christ Jesus, "who abolished death and brought life and immortality to light through the gospel" (ESV). This is good theology, and Paul never misses an opportunity to expound on such topics.

But Paul includes a second "path" when he reminds Timothy of the nurturing role that his human family and spiritual community played in his development. Specifically, Paul recounts for his protégé the "sincere faith" of his grandmother and mother, as well as the equipping function of the community of faith through the "laying on" of hands.

Some of us come from a strong faith lineage like Timothy's, while others do not. But most of us know people in our lives who invested in us, believed in us, and prepared us for service and witness in the world. When we think back to such interactions, we hear aptly spoken words that affirm, embolden, and call us to greater possibilities. Timothy would have heard such words, even through the casual speaking of his name, which means "God's honor."

Our names and descriptions—for better or for worse—influence the way we live. Christians are blessed to receive the label, "children of God." Just as Timothy was nourished through a lofty given name and the "laying on" of hands, we as Christians possess an extraordinary identity and are equipped for service in the reign of God. Paul writes not only to encourage a colleague but to challenge Timothy to make a choice: will he continue to live a life of honor or settle for something less? How about you?

Loving God, help me to embrace my full identity in you and to live up to my holy name! Amen.

Paul launches into a theological treatise in verses 8-14, reminding Timothy of his Christ-focused calling and God-given identity made possible by the saving work of Jesus Christ. This calling, "which [God] gave us in Christ Jesus before the ages began" (ESV), provides the foundation for Paul and Timothy's ministry.

An embedded nature in Christ allows Timothy to be as Paul: unashamed to preach the gospel, able and willing to endure suffering, and wholeheartedly convinced of God's ability to guard his mission in the world until the time of final accounting. Paul ends with a more direct exhortation, "Guard the good deposit entrusted to you" (ESV). In other words, embrace fully your gift of vocation and calling in the world.

Guarding "the good deposit" looks different for each one of us. Paul and Timothy reflected the good deposit through more traditional church work and missionary service. Others will express it through faithful service in the home and marketplace. All of life is sacred and abounds with kingdom possibilities. While Paul urges Timothy to remain rooted in his specific role, his words, more broadly, speak to our unique opportunities and contributions in the world.

How do you invest your experiences, interests, and gifts in ways that contribute to human flourishing in all realms of life? "Created in Christ Jesus for good works" (Eph. 2:10, ESV), you remain true to God's calling through these investments. When you fail to invest, you mar your identity and that of the greater body of Christ, reflecting less than who you were created to be as an image-bearer, a co-creator with God, and a life-giving restorer.

Gracious God, help me to be a faithful steward in all contexts of life and to embrace the world as laden with kingdom possibilities. Amen.

We have been on a journey this week, from the raw emotions and frayed nerves of a people in exile, to the struggles and challenges of the budding community in the New Testament church. At each juncture, we see that fear and faith reside simultaneously in the people of God. Jesus understood this tension, as did his disciples. In today's text, the disciples respond to Jesus' preaching on the necessity to forgive others by crying out in need to him, "Increase our faith!"

The customary interpretation of this passage goes something like this: If only we had more faith, all would go well. But what does Jesus intend to convey in his reply to the disciples? His response does not center on having *mere* faith or *more* faith. Even though the twelve waver at times, they have given up much to follow the Lord.

Might Jesus be redirecting them in the object of their belief? This doesn't seem likely either. Jesus stands directly before them. Jesus is seemingly teaching on the nature of faith. Faith, like a mustard seed, depends on the acts of outside forces. As a seed needs soil, water, and sun, faith needs provisions that come from God alone. Often people interpret this parable as speaking of the greatness that can come from little things.

But for Jesus, spiritual growth relies on receptivity. "If you had faith the size of a mustard seed" seems to imply that at this point, the disciples lack even that much faith and trust. Maturing faith, a gift from God, will always produce a response. Just as a mustard seed grows, genuine faith blossoms into something beautiful and beneficial.

Without a growing faith and trust, the disciples will be unable to forgive someone who sins repeatedly against them.

Lord, thank you for the gift of faith. May my belief bud, grow, and expand like that of a mustard seed. Amen.

In Jesus' day, servants carried out the field and household work of the master for wages. No questions asked—just do your job and do it well. "When you have done all that you were commanded, say, 'We are unworthy servants; we have only done what was our duty'" (ESV).

At first glance, the text feels jarring and contradictory, especially when we consider Jesus' interactions with his followers in other settings. Is our membership in God's kingdom characterized by obligatory duty and a less-than-full citizenship with loss of accompanying rights and privileges?

Earlier in the book of Luke, Jesus teaches about the blessedness of servants who stand ready for their master's return, and he paints a different picture of servitude. In recognition of the alertness of his subjects, the master upon arriving home responds with gratitude. He clothes himself for service, invites the servants to recline at his table, and then prepares to attend to their needs. (See Luke 12:37.) In an even more dramatic example in John 13:1-16, shortly before his crucifixion, Jesus humbles himself through an extreme form of servitude by washing his disciples' feet.

As children of God, we have all the rights and privileges of full-fledged members of the royal household. Out of this relationship we take delight in serving God and humbling ourselves for the benefit of others. The Christian life is often not one of prestige and glamour but of service, duty, and devotion. When you help others, do you expect praise? Or has your freedom and identity in Christ allowed you to serve others more freely?

Lord, teach me to seek your kingdom first. Remind me that I am both part of the royal family and here to serve you. Amen.

Home Away from Home

OCTOBER 7–13, 2013 • NAOMI ANNANDALE

SCRIPTURE OVERVIEW: One might have expected Jeremiah to advise the exiles to maintain their independence and be ready to return to Judah. Instead, he tells them to settle in, to build and plant, to seek the welfare of Babylon, even to pray for its prosperity. The judging purposes of God call for extended exile and not impatient rebellion. In the story of the ten lepers in Luke, one returns to praise and thank Jesus for giving him health. Only then do we learn that he is a Samaritan. The ultimate outsider becomes the model of faith. Second Timothy bears witness to the awesome character of God that always honors divine commitments, thereby appearing to humans full of surprises. For the psalmist God merits the worship of all the earth.

QUESTIONS AND THOUGHTS FOR REFLECTION

- Read Jeremiah 29:1, 4-7. When have you lived in a place where making a life seemed impossible?
- Read Psalm 66:1-12. How have you been tried and tested?
- Read 2 Timothy 2:8-15. What does Paul's suffering and his willingness to suffer for the sake of the gospel mean to you?
- Read Luke 17:11-19. When you first read this passage, do your thoughts go first to the one leper who returned or to the nine who go on to the priest? Why?

Doctoral student studying religion, psychology, and culture at Vanderbilt University, Nashville, Tennessee

Ｗe tend to think of wilderness as a place undisturbed by human hands—a place of trees or desert, of streams or rocky mountains. Not a city with marketplaces, hanging gardens, homes, and great wealth—such as Babylon. And yet, for the Judeans—conquered, humiliated, and driven from home to exile in this city of their conquerors—Babylon is a sort of wilderness. They find it strange, confusing. They do not speak the language; they have no map to guide daily life; they have no way of knowing if they face a few weeks of misery or a couple generations of upheaval. Homesick, anxious, and painfully aware that they are no longer in control, their lives have been "heaved up."

Many of us have also felt our lives "heaved up." We have faced all sorts of wildernesses: the loss of a loved one; job loss or disappointment; economic challenges; changes in ability. A wilderness, I have come to think, is simply that place where the old answers don't work anymore. Often, it's a place we want to escape. Most likely, that's what the Judeans wanted, and this prophecy addresses that issue. They need to hear the word of the Lord not only in the midst of suffering, worry, and change—but in spite of it.

I once got lost on a small mountain at dusk. When I realized my lostness, I panicked, and ran. The Judeans want to flee too or at least hunker down, put their lives on pause until they can go home. But God won't let them. Even in that urban wilderness, with an open and uncertain future, God calls them to live, to move forward, to be fruitful, to experience the simple pleasures of family and community—to sense a simple grace even in this place that might never really feel like home.

Today, think about a wilderness you have faced, and consider what has helped you to survive it.

Today *normal* is a word fraught with political implications. As our worlds have widened, and we have been made aware that practices and understandings commonplace to us are not necessarily those of other times, places, and people, we acknowledge that *normal* is a contested word. As our worlds have widened, we have become more aware that practices and understandings commonplace to us are not necessarily those of other times, places and people. In my own studies I have learned that the shapes, beliefs, and practices of families and communities vary dramatically through time and space.

What we are likely to share, however, is a tendency to care most for those who are closest to us. This is normal, at least in the sense of being common. We find it harder to care for those who have hurt us, who have made "normal" life impossible. And yet, God calls the Judeans to attend to these people and their home.

I used to think this text asks us to take care of our communities. I appreciated the idea of working for the welfare of the city, with its homes and gardens and families. I envisioned homeless people offered shelter, streets cleaned of drug paraphernalia, eager children learning in vibrant schools. In a way, God does call for these possibilities. The challenge that pushes this call beyond the "normal" is that the city for which you care shelters the enemy. Working for the welfare of Babylon, the place of our exile? There is nothing "normal" about this.

Not many of us have experienced the world-shattering effects of invasion and exile. But I imagine all of us have experienced hurt. God calls us beyond our "normal" response, which is to care first and foremost for ourselves and those closest to us. Instead, God calls us to work for the welfare of all, no matter how strange it may seem.

God, help me to work for the welfare of the place where you lead me today. Amen.

I'm tempted to focus on the one leper who becomes the star, but then I realize I'm interested in all ten. Their complete subjugation to a climate of fear fascinates me. Read carefully: They are out on the road (lepers had to live outside of town). They keep their distance (lepers had to stay a distance away from others). They call out when Jesus approaches (lepers had to cry out "unclean" when others came near). They do as they are told (they begin walking to the priests when Jesus tells them to, even though they are not yet healed). Perhaps most importantly, nine of them avoid the risk of further vulnerability through meaningful engagement with this strange man who has had something to do with the disappearance of the sores that made them social outcasts in their world.

Vulnerability requires engagement. We often perceive vulnerability as a defect, something to fix, fill, compensate for, or at least hide—surely not add to. Few of us advertise our imperfections or take actions that will further stress our weakest places.

I wonder if maybe we might take the risk. I wonder what we lose by focusing more on shoring up the vulnerabilities than on connecting with God's human community. I am in the midst of considering possibilities for my doctoral research. I feel poorly prepared for anything involving numbers. And in my field, I can easily avoid them. But I have given serious thought to statistical work, in part because of what it will necessitate: that I build a human community of mentorship, support, and care. And that I be honest and vulnerable in those relationships.

The nine lepers scurry off to the priests. Vulnerable relationship was too costly. How do we hide from vulnerability with God and one another? What might we gain by opening ourselves more fully to God's transforming love?

Pray that you might allow yourself to experience the gift of vulnerability.

Sometimes it's difficult to see the difference between *clean* and *well*. Sometimes the world doesn't want us to see. The lepers lived a limited, harsh existence. People viewed them as contaminated and contaminating. They made people uncomfortable. We tend to look back from a stance of enlightenment, assuming we have come so far. But we forget that our world still shuts out those who are sick, disabled, or simply different. Recently, I learned of a boy and his mother who were removed from an Easter worship service because the boy, who is intellectually disabled, made too much noise. He was celebrating the resurrection of Jesus in his own way, but apparently, his way was distracting. He made people uncomfortable.

Jesus makes ten lepers *clean*; one becomes *well*. What is the difference? Maybe it comes down to what we can see. The ten made clean can see they are cured. The disfiguring sores that marked them as lepers are gone. That satisfies them; they go to the priests who will verify the cure and render them acceptable by the standards of their world. This is a good thing for these people, though it does not question the norms that have shut them out in the first place.

A preferred condition would be to be made well, as the Samaritan is. What does it mean, to be made well? To be well implies not only—maybe even not necessarily—cure. To be well brings the ability to see the inbreaking of God's grace even in the midst of suffering and to acknowledge the utter vastness and freeing power of that grace. When our faith has made us well, we can see the mercy and love showered upon us by no merit of our own. It changes how we see the rest of the world.

Today, think about how your faith community has stepped beyond the norm to offer grace to others often viewed as outsiders, or how it might do so.

To whom does the writer speak? Sometimes this psalm addresses people, calling them to give praise or to remember their history. Sometimes the psalm speaks to God, offering praise and remembrance. At the same time, the psalm writer seems to be working out the question of his or her own identity as an individual and as part of the whole people of God.

Look, for example, at verse 6: "They passed through the river on foot. There we rejoiced in him." Who passed through the river? Who rejoiced? Was it they? Was it us? Was it both? Maybe this psalmist isn't confused; maybe this psalmist knows exactly what he or she is doing and is working hard to help us ascertain an important bit of information.

As a pastor, I often heard that people didn't like the Old Testament. It is long. There are all those strange names. It is violent. People just couldn't relate. And I get it. I certainly have not seen a sea separate before my eyes, walked between two walls of water, and then had the guilty pleasure of watching the water rush back upon those who wanted to hurt me.

I have, however, borne burdens that felt as if they might destroy me. I have walked right into disappointment by failing to listen to God speaking through my heart. I have faced challenges and come through them a little stronger. I have, most definitely, felt myself carried through the most painful moments in my life. I do, indeed, know what it is to land in a spacious place, a place of safety, security, abundance.

The Exodus happens again and again, always in a new setting, and that is why we read, learn, and relearn it. I think it is also why the psalmist doesn't state whether the psalm is about them—or us. It is about both. They are us. We are them.

O God, hear my praise, my song of thanks for the ways in which you have carried me through this life. Amen.

R**emember** Jesus Christ." For the writer, that powerful memory sustains him through persecution and suffering. How can we find that sustenance? What does it mean to remember Jesus? The Pauline letters usually call the people of God to remember something: the poor (Gal. 2:10), Paul's chains (Col. 4:18), our work (1 Thess. 1:3)—not Jesus himself. And the call can easily be translated as "keep on remembering."

I like that. Rather than an isolated mental note ("remember to buy milk on the way home"), "keep on remembering" sounds like an imperative we do and continue doing every moment of every day of our lives. It sounds as a demand for constancy in our lives as Christ followers. I need this.

Many of us want to remember Jesus Christ, and so we employ many items as memory aids: crosses on necklaces, fish on cars, scripture-tattooed bodies. How else might we try to keep on remembering; what might deepen our relationship with God and nurture our relationship with God's world?

The breath prayer, an ancient practice meant to keep us in constant connection with the Holy, uses a short phrase, half spoken upon inhale, half upon exhale, that a person repeats silently or aloud, throughout the day. ("Lord Jesus Christ/Have mercy on me, a sinner" is a classic; I like "Holy wisdom/Guide me.")

I wonder if practicing the breath prayer might help us remember that we embody this relationship and its grace in all of life. Only then can we keep on remembering Jesus as we work, play, love, and live. Then all we are and all we do might be a remembering of Jesus' merciful, gracious, all-encompassing love. Keep on remembering.

Today, think about a phrase that might be a meaningful breath prayer for you. Take several moments to repeat it silently. Then continue to repeat it in your head as you go throughout your day.

In my basement, I feel myself accused of disorganization, of procrastination, of overconsumption. Why? Because it is full. I want to clean it out, but I have little time. And with four people in the house, most items I consider discarding have meaning for someone. I thought about one item—a pile of heavy, clanking chains that I have tried to get rid of several times—as I thought about these words to Timothy.

The chains are a prop left over from a Holy Week worship experience called The Reproaches, an ancient practice meant to challenge the church to see the ways it often fails to respond to God's great gift of salvation and grace. The Reproaches can be a moving, passion-filled experience that connects Jesus' passion with the continuing life of Christians in the world today.

In the early church, and for the writer of Second Timothy, the matter of "leaving the church" literally bespoke an abandonment of the faith. The writer alludes to Paul's physical imprisonment, "chained like a criminal." God's word being "unchained" allows Paul to endure his chains.

Every time I see those chains and consider tossing them, I recall the many ways in which the word of God can be and has been denied, suppressed, or has suffered at the hands of human fallibility. The word relies on us, on our willingness to be honest and good workers, as verse 15 of this chapter states, so that it might spread and be known.

The word of God remains unchained. We may be faithless, but God remains faithful. Each of us makes the word known in our small piece of God's creation. The word of God is not chained. It lives freely in our hearts.

Today, consider how you know the freedom of the word of God in your heart. How might you share that with others?

Will There Be Faith on Earth?

OCTOBER 14–20, 2013 • LORETTA F. ROSS

SCRIPTURE OVERVIEW: Christians want help in understanding the significance of the Bible. Psalm 19 delights in the instruction of Yahweh. The text of the Torah is valued, not as a legal document but as an occasion for meditation and for the shaping of values, intuitions, and sensitivities. Scripture in Second Timothy is the gift of God and a guide for the practical life of God's people. Its instructive role equips believers for every good work. Jeremiah 31 anticipates the time when God will write the law on the hearts of the people and reminds readers that at the core of "the law" is the covenant relation God establishes: "I will be their God, and they shall be my people." The parable of the persistent widow directs us to the companion of Bible study: prayer.

QUESTIONS AND THOUGHTS FOR REFLECTION

- Read Luke 18:1-8. What spiritual practices or life events have deepened your belief in God's goodness and love for you?

- Read Psalm 19. Reflect on a time when some encounter with God's word has filled your heart with remorse or the awareness of your own sin.

- Read 2 Timothy 3:14–4: 5. Timothy faced a culture hostile to the gospel. What threats to the word of God do you see in today's world?

- Read Jeremiah 31:27-34. Jeremiah prophesies of a coming time of personal responsibility to God and personal knowledge of God. How might the age of digital communication, the deconstruction of many institutions and hierarchies, and the emerging church be heralds of such a change?

Director of the Sanctuary Foundation for Prayer, Presbyterian minister, spiritual director; living in Topeka, Kansas

She has been doing this for years—getting up each day and banging her head against a brick wall. We wonder how she does it. Some of us try to convince her to give up and get on with her life. She only shakes her head and says, "But don't you see? I must do this." Sometimes at night, when she can't sleep, she worries that the end to her suffering and oppression will never come. Then she gets up, kneels down, and beseeches God for mercy.

Never displaying bitterness or resentment, she remains calm in the face of her persecutors. And here is what astonishes us: she is peaceful—peaceful in the lack of her success, peaceful in the face of her enemies, peaceful in not knowing how or when the situation would be resolved.

And, oh yes, she got her vindication. Things turned out better than we could have imagined. When we asked her how she felt, she said, "God is good. All I did was have faith in that goodness."

Jesus' parable of the persistent widow facing the unjust judge presents a dramatic example of unflinching faith against impossible odds. If an evil, uncaring judge is worn down by this woman, how much more will God, who loves us, respond to our need? Jesus is not advising his followers to make a nuisance of themselves but rather to trust in the abiding goodness and mercy of God active in their lives.

Where in your life do you feel you are banging your head against a wall? Ask God what is required for you to find the hope and peace you need in order to persevere.

This week we will consider how faith is formed in us and how we may nurture it. Where does faith come from? We begin by recognizing faith as a gift, given through God's self-revelation. How does that revelation occur?

We live in a time of great anxiety, historic tumult, and change. The world cries out for creative, innovative thinkers, strong leaders, and wisdom. Christians are empowered to bring to the world our unique and vital faith. Our global society does not need our anxiety, anger, blame, or resentment. The world needs the faith of the prayerful, persistent bearers of hope.

Psalm 19 combines two poems, which note two ways of knowing God. Today's reading, verses 1-6, recounts the first: God's revelation through the created order of the universe. God speaks creation into existence. God speaks, and worlds come into being and resonate with God's word. So the heavens tell of God's glory; day speaks to night. Using no words, creation instructs humanity about God's reign. In beholding creation, we overhear this conversation.

For many of us, nature and relationships with other people provide powerful places for encounter with God. Yet we may also sadly neglect this form of revelation and faith nurture when nature becomes something we have to drive through to get to work. Other people get in our way and become frustrating objects that we must placate, manipulate, or somehow endure.

Only when we take the time to "hear" the glory of God and pay attention to the all-encompassing breadth of creation will that piece of faith revelation take shape. Otherwise, we miss the dynamic quality of life that sings constantly of God's wonders.

How does the creation deepen your faith in God? Take five minutes today to listen for God speaking to you through the creation. What do you hear?

The word of God speaks to us not only from the world around us but also through the stories of our experiences of God passed down through oral tradition, printing press, and the algorithms of the digital age.

The glory of the heavens witnesses to God's power in nature. The law reveals God's power in history. The word *law* in modern usage usually refers to complicated legalese of dry ordinances and fine print. The law in society, as we know it today, is hardly perfect and rarely experienced as soul-refreshing. However, for the psalmist the law contains the life-giving energy of God.

The law of God sets the boundaries that promote a way of living, a way that gives energy, meaning, and deep security to the obedient. The law as God's word points the way to joy, ful-fillment, and peace.

In the second letter to Timothy, we find the church under threats from a world hostile to its message. Various groups relay competing gospels. In response to these influences the writer urges Timothy to "stand by the truths you have learned and are assured of. . . . Remember . . . the sacred writings which have power to make you wise and lead you to salvation" (REB). The letter charges Timothy to bear witness with dogged determina-tion to the message of Jesus Christ. Timothy is to "keep calm and sane at all times" (AP).

No indulgent self-pity allowed. No drama. No hissy fits. No throwing up the hands and walking out. No plotting against enemies or sending nasty e-mails. We must keep calm and sane at all times. Like that widow. Like the word tells us to do.

Today, practice staying calm and sane in the midst of chaos.

For the prophet Jeremiah, God is not a doctrine, a religious idea, or a profession. God is up close and *very* personal. Jeremiah's faith does not come to the fore through religious rituals and practices of the Temple; but rather through his personal communion with God, as harrowing as that would prove to be for him at times.

"I will put my law within them, and I will write it on their hearts; and I will be their God, and they shall be my people," sums up the message to Jeremiah.

Such claims to intimacy with God often upset establishment religion. All sorts of things may go wrong when one individual claims to speak for the Holy One. Yet scripture, tradition, creeds, confessions, and church polity offer checks and balances in the community of faith to hold us to the truth of God's word.

As unsettling and as often abused as it may be, this internal "law" written on the heart remains at the core of personal faith. This knowledge of God comes with personal responsibility: "all shall die for their own sins." Yet we cannot persist in faith by itself. We need the community, the wisdom tradition of those who have gone before us, and the word of God in creation and scripture.

Who gets us up in the morning to calmly and sanely face once again a hostile world? Is it not the accessible, intimate God who dwells in our hearts? Is it not the wordless communion, the animating exchange with the Living Word that deepens, frees, and empowers us to bring faith into the world?

This capacity is available to all. God says, "They shall all know me, from the least of them to the greatest." We suffer and cause others harm when we fail to tend to the love our hearts share with God.

Holy God, in whom I live and move and find my being, open my heart to deeper awareness of your presence within me. Amen.

FRIDAY, OCTOBER 18 ~ *Read Luke 18:1-8*

At the beginning of Jesus' parable, we read that the purpose of this story is encouragement to persevere in prayer. Receiving faith and the revelation of God requires that we get our heads out of the books, push away from the TV and computer monitor, and lift our minds toward the mind of God. We shift our attention from ourselves to the One beyond human manipulation and control.

We reach beyond ourselves—our facts, figures, and pundits. We turn from tunnel vision to a larger vision. Like the poor widow, who sees something beyond the apparent foolishness of her enterprise with the unjust judge, in prayer we reach into the yet-to-be-conceived possibilities of God.

In anxious times our first response may be to take action, make an inquiry, or blame someone. In contrast Jesus asks, regarding the future and his return, not will the disciples be smart, capable, and in control of things; but rather, will they have faith? Will they be able to see beyond their own sin, greed, egos, and foolishness to possibilities not yet manifest?

Through this parable, Jesus prepares his followers for anxious times ahead. He encourages them to pray always and not lose heart. Prayer inspires us to take a longer view than the narrow, strained focus on the immediate. Prayer liberates us from our fearful selves and establishes us in the peace of Christ.

Take time to pray as you share your concerns and worries with God. Then step back from a narrow focus on what is wrong and how helpless you may feel, in order to dwell for several minutes in the steadfast, eternal power of God. Allow yourself to enter into the strength of your God and trust in what you cannot yet imagine.

This week the Gospel writer encouraged us to trust that a good and loving God hears and responds to our prayers. The psalmist lifted our hearts with the beauty and grandeur of God's word speaking through creation. We found security in God's law, the word that gives life and joy to the obedient. Second Timothy reminded us of the continuing threats to the truth and the importance of perseverance in proclaiming the gospel. With Jeremiah we discovered an intimate, personal God within us. And Jesus exhorted us to pray always and not lose heart.

One thing remains. We will not be able to do *all* these things *all* the time. We will forget the word of God. We will miss the mark. We will—let us name it clearly—*sin*.

The psalmist exclaims, in a sobering bit of insight, "But who can detect their errors?" We may believe we are keeping the law, but our faults may be hidden from our own awareness! Have you ever had a moment like that, when the awareness of your own capacity for sin, your own presumption and arrogance, is laid bare before you?

Through this week's reading in Jeremiah, God announces a new era of personal responsibility and accountability. In the coming days younger generations will not have to pay the price for their elders' sins. Instead, each person will be held responsible for his or her own sins. And further, God will forgive those sins and remember them no more.

Finally in Jesus Christ, we affirm the culmination of God's word, now made flesh. Here we discover the extent and reach of God's love for us and the depth and cost of divine forgiveness.

"Let the words of my mouth and the meditation of my heart be acceptable to you, O LORD, my rock and my redeemer." Amen.

W ill [there be] faith on earth?" asks Jesus. Why does our faith matter to Jesus? Throughout the Bible we see a relationship between our faith and God's expression of power in the world. This connection baffles me—that an omnipotent God would choose to love and rely on such unstable flakes and losers as human beings. You might think that porpoises or whales would have been a better choice.

God's need for our faith appears to baffle Jesus as well. When he goes to his hometown, he discovers that "he could do no deeds of power there, except that he laid his hands on a few sick people and cured them. And he was amazed at their unbelief" (Mark 6:5-6). How would you feel if the ability to relay your message and heal the sick depended on a bunch of sinners and their faith in God?

Where do we find the faith to persevere as Jeremiah, as the widow in Jesus' parable, as Timothy, or as countless others who hang in there as a calm, sane presence in this crazy world?

The texts this week offer some answers. Faith is formed through transforming contact with the word of God. We encounter that word as it speaks in the creation, as we read it in scripture study and reflection, as it is written on our hearts.

God has all the bases covered and speaks to us unceasingly. We cannot escape. Why not give up your anxiety and let Jesus use your faith to perform miracles in your hometown?

Does God await your faith in order to perform a miracle in your life—something you could not do in your own strength and knowledge? What are you waiting for? Start deepening that faith.

Lord, Have Mercy!

OCTOBER 21–27, 2013 • RICK LANDON

SCRIPTURE OVERVIEW: The Hebrew scripture readings declare the salvation of humankind and insist that the initiative for that salvation comes from God alone. The prophet Joel looks forward to the day when all Israel's sons and daughters will become as prophets in the land. Psalm 65 is a psalm of thanksgiving for the "God of our salvation." The writer of Second Timothy elevates his own achievements by means of athletic imagery, but the reading concludes with an acknowledgment that strength and deliverance have come and will come from God. The story of the prayers of the Pharisee and the tax collector in Luke suggests the perils of ignoring the fundamental truth of Joel 2 and Psalm 65. The Pharisee presumes that his achievements are his alone; the tax collector knows that prayer begins and ends with a cry to God for mercy.

QUESTIONS AND THOUGHTS FOR REFLECTION

- Read Joel 2:23-32. What has been your plague of locusts, and where was God? How do you recognize God's Spirit in your daily activities?

- Read Psalm 65. How often do you pray without making requests of God?

- Read 2 Timothy 4:6-8, 16-18. How do you feel you are being poured out as a libation in your Christian journey?

- Read Luke 18:9-14. How can we take pleasure in our Christian work and not become Pharisees?

Director of the Interfaith Counseling Center, Lexington, Kentucky; adjunct professor with the Baptist Seminary of Kentucky and the Lexington Theological Seminary

Psalm 65 gives us an order for prayer: praise, confession, and then recognition of blessing. The psalmist begins with praise due the God to whom we make our vows and who answers our prayers. What a wonderful description of God as "Thou who dost hear prayer" (ASV). I've sometimes felt that my prayers weren't even getting out of the room. The psalmist reminds me that the efficacy of prayer doesn't depend upon how I feel.

After praising the God who answers prayers, we bring our confessions. We can confess even when our sins seem to overwhelm us. The psalmist prays, "As for our transgressions, thou wilt forgive them" (ASV). God not only forgives our sins but brings us into a living relationship in which the goodness of God's presence satisfies. The psalmist acknowledges God's blessings in that we are the "one[s] whom Thou dost choose, and bring near to Thee, to dwell in Thy courts" (ASV). God wants us to live nearby. Thanks to God's forgiveness, we are not only invited into the divine presence but we also acknowledge God's "awesome deeds." We recognize and admit the blessings God has bestowed on us. In the psalmist's agrarian culture, God's blessings come as a good harvest and meadows full of flocks.

An interesting aspect of this psalm as a prayer guide is that the psalmist asks for nothing but forgiveness. Too frequently our prayers are a litany of requests made to God. I have friends from whom I never hear unless they want something. I love those friends, although I weary of their constant requests. I suspect that God sometimes just wants to hear from us with a simple prayer of praise and thanks.

Thank you, God, for loving me into a merciful relationship with you. Amen.

I'm old enough to remember with fondness the *Hee-Haw* television show which had a group that sang almost every week, "If it weren't for bad luck, I'd have no luck at all." That vocal group must have known Joel, the prophet. In his time, the crops have been ravaged by a plague of locusts and grasshoppers. Joel says it represented God's retribution, which requires repentance. Having grown up in Oklahoma, I've seen crops that have been ravaged by locusts and grasshoppers. They resemble a mighty army that destroys every plant in their path. Nevertheless, Joel speaks of God's faithfulness, assuring the people that the plague isn't permanent. There is hope. Whatever else hope may involve, it certainly means that we have a future story. We have hope because God is with us and God is the future.

> You shall know that I am
>   in the midst of Israel;
> and that I, the LORD, am your God
>   and there is no other.
> And my people shall never again
>   be put to shame.

My friend lies in a nursing home, dying slowly of lung cancer and congestive heart failure. In conversation, he said that he was thankful to God because he was going to be healed. Knowing he was not the type who necessarily believed in miracles, I asked what he meant. He replied that God was going to heal him in the eternal dimensions of life because this world doesn't have a cure for his condition. He smiled and said, "God is always faithful and good. We really can trust God."

We can pray verse 27 full of hope by inserting our name and situation in the place of Israel.

"You shall know that I am in the midst of _____; I am the Lord, your God, and there is no other." Amen.

The prophet Joel tells us that God's Spirit shows up in some of the most unlikely people and places. The Spirit may show up in men, women, youth, as well as children. The Spirit sometimes surprises us by showing up not with our leaders but with the servants. At one point in the Bible, God's Spirit even showed up in a donkey. The Spirit acts freely, beyond our control. Our task comes in being aware and sensitive to God's Spirit anywhere and anytime.

Often our desire to control is a major obstacle in our spiritual life. We pray that God will help us meet *our* goals and desires. Both God and we would be better served if we prayed that God would help us meet *God's* goals and desires. It requires constant spiritual discipline to be sensitive to God's Spirit, whenever and with whomever the Spirit shows up.

I was recently involved in a small-group Bible study. Our preparation for that study had focused on a particular scripture passage and getting ready for an interesting discussion. Before we began our meeting, a woman spoke about having been on a silent retreat. She mentioned the many voices in her head and how she tried to learn to quiet them so she could be more of a prayerful listener than a talker.

I can't recall what in-depth discussion we had on that Bible passage, but those few minutes of conversation about the silent retreat seemed like a holy nudge to me from God's Spirit. It certainly wasn't what I was expecting from God on that day. Since then I've gone on several silent retreats and learned that God really does speak when I'm quiet enough to listen. By the way, the woman who spoke about the silent retreat wasn't one of our participants; she was a hotel employee who was setting out the coffee.

Lord, help me to be attentive to your presence throughout the day. Amen.

My father often said, "If you don't have time to finish the job correctly, how will you ever find the time to do it all over again?" I'm sure that my father and Paul would like each other because Paul seems to be saying that he not only finished the job but did it correctly. He now faces imminent death. He has stayed the course and will receive the crown of righteousness.

On many occasions in Paul's life, he could have quit. He had many opportunities to stop, and none of us would have blamed him. I probably would have quit if I had been imprisoned, shipwrecked, abandoned by colleagues, and suffered from some physical condition for which I repeatedly begged God unsuccessfully for healing. In spite of his conditions and situations, Paul stayed the course. Maybe he was just stubborn and hardheaded.

However, Paul's motivation was rooted in something more than mere stubbornness. He was in love with Jesus. That love not only motivated him but energized him during very difficult times. It also gave him hope—hope in the sense that he knew his present situation wasn't permanent. Hope, whatever else it may mean, certainly implies a future with meaning and purpose, even if those outcomes can't be seen at present. Hope enables us to persevere.

I have missionary friends who work among some of the most despised people of Europe. They've been steadfast over many years, hosting a Bible study in their home when most often the participants were just themselves and their children. They continue to invite others with their gift of hospitality. They, like Paul, are being poured out as a libation. When we hear the call to self-emptying, do we stay the course?

Lord, remind me again during this day that you are faithful. Help me to be faithful to you. Amen.

Paul's ministry is coming to a close. Some of his colleagues have not only deserted him but turned against him. He knows, however, that he is not alone—the Lord is with him. The Lord will rescue and save. Even with the assurance of the Lord's presence, Paul probably misses his friends and companions. Often we just need people.

Perhaps you have heard of the grandchild who stays at the farm with his grandparents. The night brings him keen awareness of strange sounds and images. Grandmother asks the child to go out on the back porch and bring in the broom. The darkness and strange sounds frighten the child. Grandmother reassures the child that all is well because Jesus is with him. So, the child slowly opens the back door and says, "Jesus, if you are out there, hand me Granny's broom." Even knowing that Jesus is with us, we often need people.

Loneliness encompasses more than just having people around us. Loneliness comes from the thought or feeling that we don't really matter to others. Some people may want us around because we are useful to them. We need relationships in which other people know us and care about us. *Who we are*, not just *what we do*, matters to them.

Paul, in company with others, and now by himself, continues to "fully proclaim" God's message, which is our calling as well. For this reason we need church. We need others who embody Christ with their presence, singing, touch, concern, fellowship, worship, and prayers. But when the touch and care of others eludes us, we can remember God's presence, rescue, and salvation.

Lord, make me keenly aware of your presence through the presence of others. May I be in such close relationship with you that I may be your presence for others. Amen.

For a long time I had the idea that if I didn't tell God what I was thinking or feeling, God wouldn't know. Frequently, I felt ashamed of my thoughts and feelings, and I certainly wasn't going to be telling anyone, especially God. I wanted God to think well of me.

Luke's Gospel offers many lessons on prayer, and today is no exception. Two men come to pray: a Pharisee and a tax collector. The surprise of the story would be apparent to those who heard it: the professional religious man walks away *unjustified*!

The tax collector prays his thoughts and feelings, conscious of his sinfulness. The Pharisee, however, seems more concerned about how others might view him. Clearly, he wants others to consider him to be generous, honest, faithful, one who fasts and gives to the church even more than is expected. Perhaps he is being truthful, and all his descriptions are accurate. However, he allows his ego to get in the way as he awaits God's affirmation and confirmation of his piety.

Several years ago, I was considering a vocational change. I spoke with my spiritual director of my concerns about how others might interpret my vocational change. After carefully listening to my story, he said, "You seem to be full of vainglory." His words shocked me. Not me; I was a pastor! Vainglory sounded terrible. My director suggested that I pray, do some research, and return in a couple of weeks. I researched *vainglory* and discovered that indeed I was full of it. My concern about what others might think of my decision precluded my asking for God's direction. My sin humbled me, and I could only pray, "Lord, have mercy on me, a sinner." Vainglory can easily slip in and inhabit our spiritual life. Maybe that is what happened to the Pharisee. At least, it happened to me.

"Lord, be merciful to me, a sinner." Amen.

T̲he Way of a Pilgrim describes a simple prayer called the Jesus Prayer. A man asks how to obey the scriptures that teach us to pray without ceasing. He receives the following words to pray, "Lord Jesus, Son of God, have mercy on me a sinner." He is further instructed to pray this simple prayer in rhythm with his breathing.

This prayer is based on the tax collector's prayer. In contrast to the Pharisee whose prayer described all the good things he has done in the name of God, the tax collector stands away from the others, with downcast eyes and breast-beating to pray, "God be merciful to me, a sinner!" (NASV). This simple and humble prayer seeks mercy. In the parable, Jesus says that the tax collector went home justified. The result of being justified or made right in the presence of God has much to do with being humble.

The goal of the Jesus Prayer comes in praying it so frequently and genuinely that it prays itself into you. You can pray this prayer as you stand in line at the grocery store or as you wait for the red light to change at the intersection. Pray it as you rock your infant to sleep or as you lie in the hospital bed waiting for the medicine's healing work. You can pray it anywhere and anytime.

This prayer has fundamental elements of a healthy theology. It recognizes God. It asks for God's mercy. It recognizes me as a sinner and is prayed in humility. What more can there be to a healthy prayer? The Pharisee's prayer may have accomplished what he desired, which was the admiration of others. The tax collector, however, went home justified.

Lord Jesus, Son of God, have mercy on me. Amen.

Write the Vision Plainly

OCTOBER 28–NOVEMBER 3, 2013 • ELISE ESLINGER

SCRIPTURE OVERVIEW: Habakkuk stands aghast at the "destruction and violence" all around and wonders why justice never seems to conquer. At the end of the reading, God contrasts the proud, whose spirit "is not right in them," with the righteous who live by faith. The psalmist delights in God's righteousness and in the commandments of God; however, he admits that "I am small and despised." The psalmist's "trouble and anguish" appear in Second Thessalonians also, but here the "persecutions and the afflictions" endured by the faithful serve a particular end: they stand as signs of the imminent return of Jesus Christ. In the Gospel reading Jesus tells Zacchaeus, "Today salvation has come to this house," which reminds us that the righteous who live by faith are not necessarily the socially or religiously acceptable.

QUESTIONS AND THOUGHTS FOR REFLECTION

- Read Habakkuk 1:1-4; 2:1-4. How would you articulate "the vision" to be freshly expressed in today's world, by today's churches, through the ministries of all Christians?

- Read 2 Thessalonians 1:1-4, 11-12. What does it mean to live past-present-future in Christ, both personally and within your faith community?

- Read Luke 19:1-10. Reflect on persons who have made a transformative difference in your life; give thanks for these by name.

- Read Ephesians 1:11-23. What does it mean to "live in praise of [God's] glory"? What would it mean to have your life (and its every breath) "become a song" to God?

Consultant in worship, music, and spiritual formation; compiler and editor, *The Upper Room Worshipbook*; adjunct faculty, Academy for Spiritual Formation; living in Dayton, Ohio

W rite the vision plainly, so that a runner may read it" (AP). What challenging words to launch our reflections this week! I wonder how a response plays out in our digital culture—perhaps with a blinking display on one of those huge signs? What is the vision posted on this sign—or in our texting and tweeting?

"Why do you make me see wrongdoing and look at trouble? Destruction and violence are before me; strife and contention arise." I know how *that* plays out in our digital culture: we cannot escape instant images of war, famine, natural disasters, murder on the streets, much less the strife and contention ever visible in families, government bodies, and churches. It's overwhelming—what can one person do? "The righteous live by their faith." Oh dear, oh yes. How does that play out personally and communally, on behalf of God's shalom intentions, in any kind of culture, in any time or place?

The prophet Habakkuk experiences times of great besiegement; yet after voicing his complaint, he chooses to keep watch and to await God's response. What a contrast to many of our contemporary behavior patterns; yet, our hearts are called even now to such attentiveness and trust. We need certainly to lament authentically; to pray honest complaint; and then to listen, look, watch, and pray for guidance. Perhaps our opened eyes will come to see how God is at work in our beleaguered world, and our ears will hear the call to participate in that grace. We may be urged not only to "write the vision; make it plain," but, indeed, to live it plainly, just as the saints have through the ages.

God of the ages, we thank you for the vision written plainly in the life of Jesus and pray that we who follow him will bear faithful witness. Amen.

Psalm 119 is the lengthiest of the Psalms, an epic poem of acrostic meditation on Torah, the word, the law of God. Today's lines reflect devotion to the judgments, decrees, precepts, as well as trust in the righteousness and faithfulness of God. Three of the eight poetic lines, however, express poignant longing for deliverance (in other words, trouble and anguish are the poet's lot: he is "small and despised"). These feelings are woven, we note, within the affirming fabric of steadfast faithfulness and love. The psalmist identifies himself as God's servant. The servant of God loves and desires what God desires. Because God is one of righteousness, the psalmist feels comfortable voicing his personal need for justice, even as he delights in God's commandments. At the end of these verses, the poet prays for understanding, "that I may live."

Prayers for strength in tribulation and thankfulness for the way God's grace sustains persons in the midst of life's trials—such has been expressed in the psalms, hymns, and spiritual songs of the church over many generations. In the fullness of worship, we sing lament and praise, thanksgiving and petition. We express honestly our fears and hopes, our sorrows and our joy. When we do this as servants of God, we rehearse and celebrate the trustworthy word:

> How firm a foundation, ye saints of the Lord,
> is laid for your faith in [God's] excellent word!
> . . . .
> When through the deep waters I call thee to go,
> the rivers of woe shall not thee overflow.

Here begins understanding, "that I may live."

What are some of your songs of lament? For what and whom would you pray this day? For what are you thankful? How might you express your love of God's word in a poem, psalm-prayer, song, dance, painting, or embodied service?

"Christ has died, Christ is risen, Christ will come again," many traditions proclaim confidently at the Lord's Table. We do affirm with thanksgiving the gift of Jesus' death and resurrection, personally and communally, the *kerygma* of the church through centuries. The "coming again" part, though, concerns the future, which remains an unknown quantity. How do we declare and live our faith confidently as we venture into the unknown? This is as much an issue in our contemporary cultural context as in the decades of the early church, at the time of Paul's writing to the Thessalonians.

It is timely for us to consider these verses, especially noting the gracious thanksgiving expressed for the Thessalonian community. Their faith is "growing abundantly," as is their love for one another. Even more, Paul celebrates the community's steadfastness and faith during persecution and affliction. That can offer an inspiring word to our congregations today and to all those who try to be worthy of the call to ministry in Christ's name.

As Christians, we are a people who live the past-present-future simultaneously—what some have called "the eternal Now." We log *kronos* realities day by day (clock and calendar) but are graced as *kairos* communities toward eternal timekeeping and expectant love-sharing. May we declare with the Swedish diplomat Dag Hammarskjöld, "For all that has been, thanks; for all that will be, yes!"

God of all our days, in all times and places, may we trust your eternal Now. Strengthen us to be grateful participants in your work in our world, while living into the promise of your eternal and everlasting reign on earth as in heaven. Amen.

Zacchaeus: a short man who climbs high in the sycamore tree for a good view of Jesus who journeys through crowded Jericho that day. Jesus approaches the tree, spies the man and commands, "Zacchaeus, hurry and come down; for I must stay at your house today!" Zacchaeus has elevated himself, hoping to see Jesus; Jesus stands on the ground, yet seeks Zacchaeus aloft.

This chief tax collector for the Romans makes his living at the expense of his neighbors; his fellow Jews openly despise him. Grumbling in the crowd begins when Jesus, yet again, seeks the hospitality of a sinner. In Jerusalem, Jesus will pay the price for such repeated offense. We know that soon he will "face the music," a death dirge.

In the birth narrative that introduces this Gospel, divine music of the heavenly angels brings cosmic good news to poor shepherds in the field: "Glory to God in the highest heaven, and on earth peace among those whom he favors" (2:14). Now, on the ground in Jericho, Jesus offers heavenly good news to a wealthy one. When Zacchaeus comes down to earth again, he has become a new creation in Christ. He subsequently declares publicly his intention to share half his wealth with the poor, along with reparations (fourfold) to the ones he may have defrauded. Then he lives up to his birth name, "righteous one."

The kingdom of heaven is enlarged with the inclusion of a "new" Zacchaeus along with any and all of us who choose, with the saints of God, to echo the angels' song by living our "yes" to Christ, whose suffering, death, and resurrection embrace all heaven and all earth, including sycamore trees.

Gracious God, on this All Saints eve, we give thanks for all the communion of saints (including Zacchaeus). May we too say "yes" to your welcome and bidding, and follow in their footsteps of faithful witness. Amen.

ALL SAINTS DAY

B lessed are you!" Not the usual greeting offered to suffering and oppressed people. What does this mean? In Luke's Gospel, Jesus addresses his "sermon on the plain" specifically to his disciples rather than the crowd. It includes half the number of "beatitudes" found within Matthew's "sermon on the mount." Furthermore, Luke includes beatitude opposites: woes to those who bask now in wealth, power, and self-sufficiency to the exclusion of those in need.

All of Luke's potent version of the Beatitudes relates to life and ministry on behalf of the poor ones (not just the "poor in spirit," as in Matthew) whom Jesus came to seek and to save. Here, speaking plainly on the plain, Jesus bids the disciples (and others who would follow him) to take up his ministry of shalom with the poor and downtrodden in this world. It is ministry in the Magnificat spirit! It is ministry to be undertaken by disciples who themselves may face rejection, persecution, and be downtrodden on this earth, but who may gain eternal significance in the reign of God.

All those who follow Jesus participate in this reign of God on earth, here and now. Concern for all God's children means that love motivates the life and work of the disciple. Behaviors are to be selfless, nonviolent, nonretaliatory, and merciful. This sounds like the lives of the saints, and, yes, the martyrs. Can such a way of living and dying characterize us "ordinary saints"? Can we too take root in the earth (and minister joyfully and faithfully here) while being awed to heaven?

Loving God, may our souls and our bodies be consecrated in joy to Christ even as we weep for others and ourselves, as we experience hunger and thirst while seeking to feed others, and as we find ourselves rejected when reaching out to embrace the stranger. Blessed are you, in Christ's name. Amen.

That familiar story of a young, courageous, and trusting Jewish boy named Daniel, imprisoned in Babylonia yet delivered miraculously from the lion's den, is a classic biblical tale of mythic proportion. Today's reading from this apocalyptic book, while not of the lion's den, also contains threat. Here, we learn of Daniel's vision in a dream during the first year of King Balshazzar's reign. Daniel, part of the king's court, writes of his dream of four winds stirring up a great sea from which emerge four fierce and distinctively terrifying beasts.

Quite disturbed by the vision, Daniel approaches an attendant for assistance in interpretation. The attendant states that the beasts represent four oppressive earthly rulers (usually now assumed to be Babylonian, Median, Persian, and Greek). However, the "holy ones of the most High" will receive the eternal kingdom. In other words, evil, tyrannical earthly kingdoms will not ultimately prevail within God's eternal reign over heaven and earth.

Apocalyptic fears and dire predictions, not to mention perennial experiences of disaster and violence, often dominate the news and sometimes our personal lives. There are lots of Beasts out there, and Beauty does not usually seem to transform them with a kiss. We do well to hear with Daniel that "the holy ones" are the true recipients and guardians of the eternal kingdom. As we celebrate the saints, may we look once again toward the countless holy ones who keep the kingdom and serve as guardians and proclaimers of the eternal truth of God's sovereignty forever. May we be numbered with them in faithfulness.

Loving God of all heaven and earth, thank you for the "holy ones" in heaven and on earth who love and serve you with confidence and trust. Give us grace to withstand times of terror and threat and to stand firm in our own faith in your eternal reign of shalom. Amen.

During a memorable autumn retreat, the All Saints worship celebration featured a lengthy, golden paper chain. On each prayer-full link was inscribed the name of a canonized saint or an extraordinary-ordinary person of beloved memory. A quote from Saint Symeon the New Theologian evoked the creation of the golden chain: "The saints in each generation, joined to those who have gone before, and filled like them with light, become a golden chain, in which each saint is a separate link, united to the next by faith, works, and love. So in the One God they form a single chain that cannot quickly be broken."

Celebration of faithfulness among Ephesian saints reminds me that each person in Christ's church has indeed been created to be a golden (light-reflecting) link in "praise of [God's] glory." Within present contexts of life and ministry, throughout the generations, and with the saints and angels whose song we join at the Eucharist, we are enlivened by Christ himself, who is "the fullness of [the One] who fills all in all."

As Christians we best exemplify living "in praise of [God's] glory" when we remain connected in community, marked by the Spirit. Here we may find, with the Ephesians, that "the eyes of [our] heart" are enlightened. Here we are called and equipped for service in the name and spirit of Christ. Here we may come to know the hope and the glorious inheritance of the saints, as we also seek to be part of that single golden chain of "faith, works, and love." May it be so, as we sing with the psalmist our praise—with every instrument, with all our breath, in all times and places. Alleluia!

"Gracious God, grant that what we sing with our lips we may believe in our hearts, and what we believe in our hearts we may practice in our lives . . . with all the saints, in praise of your glory." Amen.

Places of Intimacy with God

NOVEMBER 4–10, 2013 • BENONI R. SILVA-NETTO

SCRIPTURE OVERVIEW: The rebuilding of the Jerusalem temple became a test of God's promise. The prophetic word of Haggai insists on courage and labor, reminding the people that God's Spirit is already present among them and points toward the future. In Second Thessalonians, some Christians have grown extremely agitated by claims that the "day of the Lord" has already come. The passage recalls what Jesus and God have already accomplished and insists that God's future may also be trusted. Jesus' response to the Sadducees confutes them, not merely by its cleverness (their question also is clever), but by its truth. The eschatological future cannot be understood simply as an extension of the present, except in one profound sense: God is Lord both of the present and the future. This profound truth demands the praise to which Psalm 145 summons all creatures.

QUESTIONS AND THOUGHTS FOR REFLECTION

- Read Haggai 1:15b–2:9. What are the temples of God that have been or are in the process of being destroyed? being rebuilt?

- Read Psalm 145:1-5, 17-21. What in your current experiences points you to God's greatness?

- Read 2 Thessalonians 2:1-5, 13-17. In one sense, Christ is already with us, but we live with the promise of Christ's return. How will you prepare for Christ's coming?

- Read Luke 20:27-38. In what arenas do you find yourself operating by the letter of the law? How might you become more compassionate?

Professor, Union Theological Seminary, the Philippines; Associate General Secretary of the General Council on Ministry of The United Methodist Church

The prophet Haggai encourages the people of God to rebuild the Temple that was destroyed many years earlier. For two decades after the exile and the homecoming, the Jews have planted crops and built homes, but the house of the Lord remains in ruins. People recalled the splendor and glory of Solomon's temple; how were they to create such an edifice now? Ezra 3 relates the weeping of those who envisioned the previous Temple when compared to the one being rebuilt. Yet the Temple had been a sacred place where people communed with the Holy.

For Haggai, restoring the building seems to be as important an act of worship and faithful obedience as praying or singing praise to God. Worship is essentially intimacy with God. I have experienced such intimacy often in times of solitude, within the cloistered spaces of my consciousness, within the hallowed hall of my soul, within the sacred spaces of my spirit, within the holy corridors of my personal life, within the inner chambers of my solitary existence. But there remains an invitation to meet God also within the temples of worship where we join God's people in fellowship and worship. This community can light the spark of passion and faith within me.

People from across different cultures worship in different kinds of places: within magnificent cathedrals in Europe or the U.S., or within thatched huts and mud-bricked buildings in Africa, or within the bamboo and coconut buildings in rural Philippines. Many places represent the feeble attempts of God's people to respond to the call to build or rebuild God's Temple.

O God, grant that your invitation to meet you in the sacred places and intimate spaces of our lives continues to be compelling and immensely irresistible. Amen.

Another place of intimacy with God comes in our dreams and visions. Haggai reports that God gave him the task of stirring up the people to dream of rebuilding the Temple. The earth and the human body have been referred to as the temples of God. It will not be too far-fetched to think that God desires that we "rebuild" these temples as well.

The English language defines the word *vision* in two ways: to see present reality clearly (as in having 20/20 vision) and to see future possibility through imagination (as in dreaming a world transformed).

I imagine the prophet telling the people with fire in his words and passion in his voice, "[God] called for a drought on the land and the hills, on the grain, the new wine, the oil, on what the soil produces, on human beings and animals, and on all their labors" (Hag. 1:10). In some ways this describes our present reality. Haggai stirs up the people to dream dreams and see the vision of the Temple rebuilt, of a world regenerated, of God's reign coming upon this earth—stretching their awareness beyond present reality to future possibility.

On many occasions my family and I spent summer vacations camping under the magnificent sequoia trees in northern California. In those sacred times we bonded as a family and gained deeper appreciation for God's world. The trees stood like holy cathedrals with their steeples pointing to the sky. Our conversations often revolved around the threat of irresponsible logging that would bring down the ancient trees and irreparably destroy the environment along with God's creatures that have found their dwelling in these sacred forests. We have participated in destroying God's Temple, and now God wants us to rebuild it.

Grant, O Lord of creation, that the joyful blending of vision and passion may bring us to the future that welcomes us with an unfolding world where your love and grace reign. Amen.

The psalmist begins with his personal experiences and reasons to praise God. And then as the psalm progresses he mentions "one generation shall laud your works to another." And as in the rippling waves upon the pond, he closes the psalm by stating, "All flesh will bless his holy name forever and ever." Praise of God is not just for individuals; it is the work of creation itself. And in these first five short verses, the psalmist moves beyond praise to extol, bless, laud, declare, and meditate. Praise is both contemplative and active.

I supervised a number of pastors and churches in California. Often as I would visit the churches, I would find myself drawn to the side of the road by the sight of a beautiful sunset bursting with spectacular colors as the sun bid farewell to a glorious day. Or I would watch the waves in the northern coastal region sometimes gently kissing the silent sand on the beach while at other times violently smashing against the protruding rocks, creating a sensational burst of white foam. Or I would see the vast canvas of the sky upon which fascinating cloud formations painted a moving picture and the Master Painter used the sun as a paintbrush to add glorious colors to a magnificent work of art. I often met God in the midst of those profound mysteries and found myself rejoicing over and praising that which I fall short in naming and understanding.

I believe that my experience of God's greatness and majesty that moves me to awe and wonder and worship is shared by people across generations. And the time will come when the hope of the psalmist shall be a reality: "All flesh will bless his holy name."

O magnificent Parent, may we catch a bit of your grace and a glimpse of your greatness as we touch and are touched by the beauty of your creation. Amen.

This passage points to the intimate places of remembrance and anticipation. Early Christians lived in joyful expectancy of the second coming of Christ. Future generations as well have anchored their faith on this exciting anticipation. But the writer also invites believers to remember the former teachings, which will help ground them in this anxious world.

Some of my lasting memories from my seminary years at Union Theological Seminary in the Philippines came when Bishop Benjamin Guanzing, who was then the president of the seminary, pulled me aside for engaging conversation. His telling me that I had been chosen stirred me to dream dreams and to look toward the future with great expectation.

The president stressed the importance of remembering my cultural and religious heritage as I pursued my dreams. In essence, I heard him say that I must open the dusty and forgotten pages of the past as I try to chase the future of my emerging world. Heritage is of utmost importance in our pilgrimage. The gift of roots is as important as the gift of wings. His voice still rings clear in my ears as he reminded me of the ancient Filipino adage: "The one who is not willing to look back to the past with much appreciation and gratitude will not reach the intended future destination with success."

So the Thessalonians remember. By remaining faithful, they and we discover the division between truth and falsehood. Thanksgiving then leads to steadfastness; we are not deceived. We can engage in holy remembrance when we read the stories of faith in scriptures, when we participate in communal rituals, when we sing the hymns of the faith. Might those sacred memories be places of intimacy with God?

O Living Christ, capture our spirits as we immerse ourselves in meaningful memories that intersect with the joyous anticipation of our hopes and promises. Amen.

The Sadducees pose a question to Jesus; Jesus does not back away nor does he stand with the religious leaders. As we read, we may even conclude that Jesus blasts the Sadducees in their ignorant arrogance. Jesus had several options in dealing with problem people whose aim was to entrap him or to make a mockery of his theological position: avoid, appease, or alter. He could have just ignored them and brushed them off as impertinent. He could have accepted their position and embraced their ignorance. Or he could change their understanding of realities and possibilities.

Usually Jesus chose to listen to the questions, look through their eyes into their hearts, and see the disquieting images of their aching souls. In this question-and-answer period, he makes several points: The Sadducees belong to "this age"; they find themselves so tied to levirate law that they cannot perceive God's future in which all matters will change. Jesus separates the here and now from the future, "that age" in which the Sadducees have no stake. So the conversation ends with the scribes saying, "'Teacher, you have spoken well.' For they no longer dared to ask him another question" (Luke 20:39).

Meaningful conversations can offer occasions for significant conversions. Today's passage seems to reflect a stand-off. However, when we enter conversation with an openness to the Spirit's guidance, we may experience transformation and genuine change happening in us and in the other. God can be intimately present with us in our conversations, even in controversial ones.

All-knowing God, may I see your face and feel your presence, even in the midst of chaotic relationships and unsettling conflict. Amen.

"'Get to work, all you people!'—God is speaking. 'Yes, get to work! For I am with you!'" (THE MESSAGE).

This week's readings have focused on identifying the places where we experience intimate relationship with God: within the sacred places of worship (the Temple), in our dreams and visions, in our experiences of awe and wonder, within the holy corridors of our memories and expectations, and at the heart of our questions and doubts. Today, we return to the prophet Haggai whose book seems to point to an understanding that such intimate relationship happens in the following:

- When we listen to God's compelling invitation, in this case, to rebuild the Temple;
- When we respond in obedient discipleship; that is, we take courage and get to work; and
- When we experience divine empowerment through the promise of God's presence and abundant resources.

Although God is present with us every moment of our life, awareness of God's intimate presence usually comes during those moments when we hear and respond to the call that gives meaning and direction to our life journey.

"Get to work! For I am with you!" becomes a poignant invitation to find meaning in the work we have been called to do and to rest assured that God accompanies us in every step and down every road. God's "spirit abides among [us]; do not fear."

Every day may we gaze upon the unfolding of your grace, O God, and respond with joyful and passionate obedience to where you direct our paths. Amen.

The psalmist ends our week of meditations with an exciting punctuation mark: "The LORD watches over all who love him. . . . My mouth will speak the praise of the LORD, and all flesh will bless his holy name forever and ever."

These verses sum up the meaning of intimacy with the Divine. It is living our life in the keen awareness and genuine confidence that God watches over us. We relate to God in passionate love, and we live our life praising God in whatever we do, with whoever we are, and wherever we go.

These verses emphasize God's justice and kindness. This God is near, one who hears cries and saves. Those who acknowledge divine sovereignty and "call on," "fear," "cry to God" will experience God's presence, provision, and protection. These do not come as reward but as a result of intimacy with God.

I believe that if I can stretch my love for God to reach out to those whom God loves—the lost, the last, the least, and the leftover folks of society—I shall find more places of divine intimacy. In the final analysis, relationships matter—relationships with God, with neighbor, with the earth. Our lives will ultimately be measured by what we have done for the least of our brothers and sisters. (See Matthew 25:31-40.)

God upholds a high purpose for humanity. Nothing will remain untouched by God's redemptive love. All flesh will bless God's holy name forever.

We pray that we will trust you, O God, in spite of the unknown. And finding life as an exciting adventure in faith, we would be led toward a deeper understanding of your will, a closer and intimate relationship with you. Amen.

Dreads and Dreams

NOVEMBER 11–17, 2013 • NANCY MAIRS

SCRIPTURE OVERVIEW: Isaiah 65:17-25 looks forward to God's creation of "new heavens and a new earth." Jerusalem itself is not to be restored but created anew, a place in which life will be revered and protected and in which God will permit no harm to any of creation. The New Testament lessons remind us of the reality—the sometimes painful reality—of the present. Second Thessalonians 3:6-13 warns against the disorderly conduct of those who believe that the newness of the eschatological future permits them license in the present. Luke 21:5-19 adds an element of sobriety to the singing of new songs and the expectation of a new future. The faithful are called to bear witness to God's future in the present, precisely when the new future cannot be seen and even when it seems most improbable.

QUESTIONS AND THOUGHTS FOR REFLECTION

- Read Isaiah 65:17-25. 1. In Isaiah's vision, "natural" enemies are reconciled and live together in peace. What steps would bring about this kind of reconciliation among human beings?

- Read Psalm 118. In what ways is God your salvation? What leads you to your belief? How do you express it?

- Read 2 Thessalonians 3:6-13. Do you agree with Paul that only those who work may eat? What exceptions would you make?

- Read Luke 21:5-19. Do you see any of the signs Jesus mentions in his vision of the future? If so, what are they? What is your response?

Poet and essayist, member of the interfaith peace-and-justice Community of Christ of the Desert, Tucson, Arizona; her books include *Ordinary Time* and *A Dynamic God*

Critical scholars agree that the writer of the Gospel of Luke, commonly identified as a Greek physician, did not know Jesus. Therefore, the book offers a cultural view but not an eyewitness account of Jesus' life and teaching. The writer may well have experienced, or at least talked to those who experienced, the horrific events culminating in the destruction of the Temple in 70 CE, however. Indeed, one stone was not left upon another, the Romans having dismantled the structure stone by stone in order to salvage the gold that had melted between them. These details are matters of historical fact.

The Gospel of Luke appears to have been written following this destruction. Using the literary device of foreshadowing, the writer places the description of the Roman slaughter of the Jews (including the early followers of Jesus) and the ravaging of Jerusalem in Jesus' mouth to illustrate his prophetic power.

The writer is well aware of the suffering the followers have endured, before and during this holocaust, at the hands of both Romans and other Jews. As they have practiced their emerging faith, they have been persecuted by those in power, reviled by family and friends, and even tortured and murdered. Luke reassures them that they have the strength to employ these trials to spread the word about Jesus' teachings, strength bolstered by their belief. The final words of the passage are triumphant enough to give anyone heart.

Luke may or may not have been a physician, but he certainly is a healer, addressing an audience who must have been deeply traumatized by chaos and cruelty. In recounting the narrative and words of Jesus—himself presented as a healer in the Gospel of Luke—this Gospel gives us a prescription for mending and transcending pain through faith in the comforting power of the Holy.

God, increase our confidence in Jesus' power to heal. Amen.

Part of the Gospel of Luke presents an apocalyptic vision of what will follow the period of personal suffering that Jesus' followers will endure. This prophecy seems to involve all humankind in catastrophe, signifying the end of the world.

For followers of Jesus, the Jesus who speaks of apocalypse seems remote, the message unbelievable and frightening. He speaks out of a long tradition of doomsday prophets.

However, we need not read this passage out of context. The verses that follow this passage make clear that Jesus' predictions pertain to Jerusalem and the Jewish people. In the light of the suffering endured during and after the destruction of the Second Temple in 70 CE, Luke's audience would well understand the vision's horror. The world as they knew it had shattered, and they must have viewed the events as signifying the end times.

Metaphorically speaking, the world is always ending for someone. Just ask the inmate on death row in the hours before execution or the survivors in a Middle Eastern village just after a drone has dropped its cargo. Ask the tornado victims in Joplin, the hurricane victims in New Orleans, the flood victims in Waterbury, Vermont.

Even those of us not immediately affected by wars and natural disasters confront The End in various ways: the end of fresh water, of rain in the desert, of air safe to breathe and food safe to eat, the end of creatures great and small, from aphid to polar bear to . . . us. However, we are cocreators with God of a livable space. If we want to prevent, or at least postpone, the end of the world as we know it, we must alter our way of being in it altogether. We must conceive our lives in terms of deed and not of doom.

God of justice, keep us mindful of all those who suffer. Strengthen us to work with diligence in creating a safe and sustainable world for all. Amen.

At the beginning of 2 Thessalonians 3, Paul exhorts the community to pray "that we may be rescued from wicked and evil people; for not all have faith." In the passage that follows, he cautions them not merely against people outside the faith but also against "believers who are living in idleness and not according to the tradition that they received from us."

Faced with the task of forming a cohesive community, Paul has begun to lay down rules, which will be elaborated and codified over the coming centuries as an institution called "the church." Some regulation is necessary, because much of Christian behavior goes against natural inclination. That's part of its strength: it demands deliberation and discipline to act on behalf of an entire group, not merely the self.

Paul, Silas, and Timothy visited the Thessalonian community to demonstrate the behavior fundamental to group cohesion: working hard in order to avoid draining the community of its resources. In this situation, laggards and meddlers weaken the social fabric others have labored hard to weave. Nevertheless, scolding may arouse shame, resentment, defiance, even antagonism, but probably not a willing spirit or a contrite heart.

I feel sure that Paul might have addressed the Thessalonians in a more productive fashion by encouraging ways they might assist in the process of community building. Give them work to do rather than criticize them for the work they are not doing. Ignore negative behavior and encourage them whenever they are silent and diligent. In the end, they may come to "doing what is right" purely for goodness' sake.

Jesus, Teacher and Friend, accompany us as we learn to embrace and assist our companions on the journey toward perfect love of one another and all God's creation. Amen.

Isympathize with Paul's vision of a beloved community. One of the deepest-seated characteristics of the Jewish tradition is an emphasis on community: the family, the tribe, and eventually, overarching all, the people of God. Jesus rooted his teachings in Hebrew scripture, and as they spread to both Jews and Gentiles, the emphasis on group identity remained.

By the time Thessalonians was written, followers of Christ may even have called themselves *Christians*, but they still may not have grasped its full meaning. A writer on the Web site Got-Questions.org says that some Thessalonians thought the Day of the Lord had already come, so they stopped working.

Paul lays down some (but by no means all) behaviors necessary for functioning as a community, addressing all the members but clearly pointing to some and not others. In the verses preceding this passage, he has praised the group effort: "We have confidence in the Lord concerning you, that you are doing and will go on doing the things that we command."

Paul's decree is strict: "Anyone unwilling to work should not eat." He tries to teach this group that forming a community demands cooperation and exertion from *all* for the betterment of all. Continuing to function as a group, especially as a beloved community, can be lot of hard work. The task of maintaining cohesion never ends since the individual members are bound to come and go. As the *Pirke Avot* (a work of rabbinic Judaism) states of our daunting task to heal the world (*tikkun olam*), "It is not up to you to complete the work, but neither may you desist from it." Created carefully, however, community supports all of us so that no one wearies in "doing what is right." The message is simple: take care of one another.

God of all, give us guidance and companionship as we live in communities that carry out your word and work in the world. Amen.

FRIDAY, NOVEMBER 15 ~ *Read Isaiah 65:17-23*

Isaiah presents a vivid eschatalogical vision that seems to be innate in the human psyche. The details may vary from culture to culture, but the dream of a perfected world has persisted temporally and geographically. The common elements of the dream include abundance and the end of suffering. The people will have, in Isaiah's prophecy, long life, home and land ownership, fruitful labor, social justice, and freedom from disaster.

To what extent has this dream been realized? To our shame, not much. People who live in parts of the world that have good sanitation and medical care, live to ages most of Isaiah's contemporaries could only dream of. Some own their own shelter and have the means to support themselves, but many others live on the streets and subsist on a couple of dollars a day. They have no hope of meaningful employment and fair compensation for their labor. Increasingly, as the climate changes, people endure drought and famine, violent weather and floods, widespread disease, and degraded land, air, and oceans. Earthquakes destroy property and kill thousands of people and animals.

All in all, our world seems far from perfect. God may be creating a new world, but God does not create alone. We are the bearers of God in the world; the responsibility for the well-being of that world rests with us. We cannot throw our hands up in despair. We must not turn our well-being over to soulless corporations, greedy financiers, self-serving politicians, or anyone who shirks the task of helping God to create a new earth in which all can thrive. God demands full creative involvement of every one of us in the new order God intends.

Creator God, we love the world you gave us, but we also know it falls short of its full potential. We regret our failure to work with you toward its perfection, and we ask you to strengthen our resolve to create with you a new earth brimming with blessings for us all. Amen.

God promises to anticipate the needs of the people and fulfill their requests even before they have finished asking. God will rebuild Jerusalem, which now lies in ruins, and restore it to the people.

The transcendent element in Isaiah's vision of God's new earth revolves around the peaceable kingdom symbolized by accord between natural enemies, wolf and lamb, lion and ox. These vivid images, filled with contradictions in the "real" world, have inspired writers and artists for generations.

The details are not purely figurative, however. They tell us exactly how we must behave in order to bring about the perfect peace God intends for us. At the root of our discord lies fear, which condemns us to narrow, bitter, and hateful lives. Too often we blame others for the dread we feel, believing that their actions and attitudes make us afraid and thus lead us to relinquish power over our responses.

In reality, we choose our anxieties and suspicions; and if we react to the perceived danger with hostility, we invite conflict. The animal world works differently. If I, the lamb, face you, the lion, calmly, odds are you will eat me up. But if I, an Israeli, greet you, a Palestinian, with friendship, although you might still kill me, the chances are less likely than if I approached you with a gun. If we both set aside fear, we might find ourselves exchanging not insults but pictures of our grandchildren.

Unlike animals, human beings, with God's initiative, have the power to create a peaceable kingdom by responding to one another as members of God's beloved community.

O God, your Son bequeathed us peace, and we have done painfully little with the salvific gift. Teach us to trust in you and one another so that we no longer hurt or destroy anything and conflict becomes cooperation on your holy mountain. Amen.

Although Isaiah casts his psalm of joy in the future, it seems to me we would do well to start singing it now. It never hurts to start praising what is to come. If we do, we bring what we dream of into our waking life and begin to live it now. In too many ways humankind flounders in dark and dire straits. We may be tempted to howl helplessly in anguish. Better to raise our voices in anthems of delight.

We usually project anything beyond our control (from a broken toe to a tornado) onto a wrathful deity. We can spend a long time growing beyond dread until we finally take comfort in the beneficence of the Holy. At this point we can experience our salvation: our liberation from want and other ills, moving into freedom and security in God's good world.

Here we find cause for thanksgiving and celebration. Feeling delight in our own blessings, we proclaim and praise God's goodness throughout the world. Isaiah calls for shouting and singing, although most of us will probably opt for quieter forms of exultation. The noise level doesn't matter. We simply share our joy and encourage others to find their own ways into the delightful realm of the Holy.

Practically speaking, we can't exist perpetually in the state of giddiness my words imply. I don't mean to suggest that we can or ought to do so. However, we can choose responses and attitudes toward life in all its diversity as it unfolds around us. To the extent that we choose to laugh rather than to weep, to sing rather than to moan, we can spend most of our lives at ease in the coming reign of God.

O God, creator and keeper of all, we praise you for the blessings you pour out on us day after day. May we be aware of the joys of our lives and alert to the needs of others for support and encouragement as they search for their own joys. Amen.

Attentiveness to Christ's Reign

NOVEMBER 18–24, 2013 • DANIEL T. BENEDICT

SCRIPTURE OVERVIEW: Each of the passages for this week addresses the ends served by divine power. Jeremiah characterizes kingship by wisdom, justice, and safety. The exercise of kingly power is on behalf of God's people rather than against them. The reading from Colossians praises the cosmic dimensions of Christ whose exaltation is not an end in itself, for the task of Christ is one of reconciliation. The goal of Christ's kingship moves to center stage in the Lukan lection. The bystanders and one of the criminals executed with Jesus know what it means to be a king, so they taunt Jesus with the demand that he use his power to save himself. For Jesus, a king is not one who saves himself but one who saves others.

QUESTIONS AND THOUGHTS FOR REFLECTION

- Read Jeremiah 23:1-6. What strikes you about God in this reading? What do you hear God asking you to do or change in your life as you attend to this passage?

- Read Luke 1:68-79. Zechariah's song is one of four canticles (scripture songs) in Luke, chapters 1 and 2, that we use in worship (Song of Mary, Song of Zechariah, The Angel's Song, and Song of Simeon). What do these songs have in common?

- Read Colossians 1:11-20. Paul equates "forgiveness of sins" with redemption. How do you respond to that?

- Read Luke 23:33-43. The estimation of Christ Jesus in Colossians 1:15-20 and Luke's narration of Jesus as King of the Jews stand in stark contrast. How do you interpret and integrate the two pictures, and why?

Abbot of the Order of Saint Luke, writer, teacher, practitioner of the contemplative life; living in Waialua, Hawaii

It is ironic that in many churches a lay reader will read this text while the ordained pastor (shepherd of the flock) will hear these words of accusation and the promise of a worthy successor. Hearers beware! Jeremiah speaks plainly in pressing home God's charges against the pastors (the religious and civil rulers of his day): "Woe to the shepherds who destroy and scatter the sheep of my pasture!"

Attending is the word in play. The shepherds have not attended to the flock, so God will now attend to the abusive shepherds. A quick consult with the dictionary opens up the rich meanings of *attend*: "to look after, to take care of, to take charge of, to listen to, to be present with, to accompany, to be mindful, to be ready to serve." Israel's rulers have not attended to the sheep, so God will intervene. God will gather, bring back, and raise up rulers who will shepherd them beyond fear and dismay. The phrase *no one will be missing* brings comfort to a world of missing persons, errant drones, roadside bombs, and devastating tsunamis.

Pastoral duties and mutual oversight can be systematized and efficient. Still, the ways in which we exercise attentiveness gets to the heart of ongoing spiritual formation for all of the baptized. In total ministry, all are accountable for shepherding. Bernard of Clairvaux said that true piety is leaving room for consideration—with God as the chief object of that consideration. If God is attentive to the sheep, then our consistent thoughtful regard will lead us to attend to God in the midst of the flock.

Learning to accompany one another requires paying attention to God in our primary practices of worship, prayer, reflection on scripture and life and seeing people, not as numbers but as unique and beloved companions.

How is God calling you to attend to others in the congregation? in the other spheres of your daily life?

God's promised attentiveness to Israel by raising up a "righteous Branch" is in continuity with God's covenant with David, the icon of a human ruler and a man after God's own heart. This stirs the Christian imagination to find the promise fulfilled in Jesus, the Messiah, as witnessed by much of our Advent poetry and hymnody. That is one way to play the text.

However, might Jeremiah's words have a more proximate and practical fulfillment in view? Whether God will bring a transformed and repentant Zedekiah (see Jer. 21:1ff) back from exile or raise up another, the salvation effected by this "righteous" branch will be practical. This ruler will deal wisely, attend to justice, and order right relationships. Whether divinely established or popularly elected, in outline this is the work of good shepherds and righteous rulers.

In a seemingly post-moral culture, we yearn with Jeremiah for leaders and citizens in church and state who possess a centered wisdom and who seek alignments and relationships that reconcile rather than alienate and impoverish. Where does such practical leadership and rule come from?

Drawing upon yesterday's consideration, practicing presence to God, to others, to self, and to the natural order around us remains central and endlessly renewing. We do not achieve righteousness; we receive it, using the means of grace. At minimum, these include the sacraments, the rich array of prayer practices, ongoing reflection on our living in dialogue with the Bible, and living daily the baptismal covenant in the full range of relationships. In these, "The LORD is our righteousness," raising up many shepherds to ensure that all the baptized graze in good pastures for the life of the world.

O God, grant that when we hear the Good Shepherd's voice we may know who calls and may follow where he leads. Amen.

Y ou go, Zechariah! You once-muted priest in the delivery room: now the promises are fulfilled (v. 20), and you can sing! Zechariah gets his voice back, and he hymns words that the church has used daily in Morning Prayer for centuries. Monks, nuns, office workers, and farmers recite or chant the song at sunrise. What God promised through Jeremiah, Zechariah waits on tiptoe to see. The birth of John as the forerunner is for him the guarantee of God raising up "a mighty savior . . . in the house of his servant David." Hope is about to be fulfilled, and promises made long ago are about to be kept.

This poetry connects with and addresses the shadows of our inner and outer worlds. The song gathers up the yearnings of God's people remembering David, recalls ancient promises, embraces the vocation of living in righteousness, and piles up images of salvation: "[God] has looked favorably on his people and redeemed them . . . has raised up a mighty savior . . . has shown the mercy promised to our ancestors . . . has remembered his holy covenant." God's action continues!

God's actions serve a holy purpose: "that we, being rescued from the hands of our enemies, might serve [God] without fear, in holiness and righteousness before him all our days."

This is the church's song, not only its specific words but its thrust that acknowledges the sovereign Savior as the fulfillment of God's promises and the call to be the vanguard of the New Creation. There hatred, enmity, darkness of spirit, fear, sin, and death are consumed in light, mercy, holy service, knowledge of salvation, forgiveness, and peace. Of such our hymns and songs are made, and in such singing our spirits are reborn and refreshed.

What darkness in your life or in the life of your congregation needs consuming in light? What hymn or song gives voice to your attentiveness to God's redemption?

Paying attention to our location has its gifts and demands. I live a few steps from the ocean. Paying attention to where I live means both enjoying the beaches and picking up assorted pieces of plastic that might otherwise add to the "Great Pacific Garbage Patch" that endangers marine life. It also means preparing for tsunamis and hurricanes. Our location, both geographic and spiritual, lays claims on our attention.

In baptism God claims us and relocates us, transferring us from darkness into the reign of God's beloved Son. Redemption comes through relocation! We are now "in Christ."

We may want to question the writer's equating redemption with the forgiveness of sins. "Isn't redemption so much *more* than forgiveness?" Not so fast! Maria Boulding in *Gateway to Resurrection* demonstrates that forgiveness, both God's and ours, is central to life as we live in community, whether the divine-human community, the family, the church, or the larger world.

Life in community requires not forensic but embodied and enacted forgiveness. Why? In order to wipe up (not wipe out!) the messiness and disenchantment that accompanies human failure and sin. Our location, both in our persons and in the social fabric around us, remains broken and messy.

So, the mystery of redemption is enacted through forgiveness—God's and ours—and baptism's washing becomes real. In forgiveness God restores community and manifests "the kingdom of God's beloved Son."

Holy Thursday's enactment of foot washing exemplifies paying attention to those who have disappointed us. Here, dirt is washed away and Christ makes us "part" of him when we have fallen into "no part" of him. (See John 13:8.) Likewise, every Eucharist is a new beginning. Both are paradigmatic kingdom scenes. Pay attention.

Thank you, God, for relocating me to your Son's reign. Amen.

Paul fully exploits the cosmic identity and significance of Christ Jesus. Much preaching and teaching reduces Jesus to a good teacher, a timebound exemplar, even a willing victim and sacrifice. Popular culture knows him as a "superstar" and a religious icon. Paul demolishes these lesser conventions with as high a Christology as exists in all of scripture, encompassing the visible and invisible, and declaring, "All things have been created through him and for him."

How do we humans appreciate and stand before this portrait of Christ? We are left to shrink before it! We decry our arrogance and self-inflation in creation. Here again, we find ourselves relocated, displaced from our usurpation of the center. This location calls for doxology!

Where words fail, art, physics, and music may succeed. Maybe we have to stand before Graham Sutherland's tapestry of *Christ in Glory* at Coventry Cathedral or look at pictures of the Hubble Eagle Nebula or listen to Handel's "Worthy Is the Lamb" to enter imaginatively into this cosmic and deeply healing declaration.

One consequence of a more imaginative reading of the text could be awakening to human eccentricity! We are not the center of the universe or the sole object of redemption and reconciliation. (See verses 16 and 20.) If we are to travel well in a spiritual world, then the sovereign Christ who is before all things and in whom all things hold together is our interpreter and guide.

In the end the text raises spiritual concerns: the why and how of our origins, the meaning of our social and ecological relations, the nature of our ecclesial life and mission, and the destiny of creation.

Spend time with some art, music, or scientific masterpiece, and be aware of what it evokes in you with regard to the day's text.

"This is the King of the Jews." The subject of authority and rule is tossed around in various ways here—in jest and mockery, as well as in hope and faith. The bystanders, soldiers and one of the thieves scoff at his title, daring him to prove otherwise. The repentant thief pleads for a sovereign's kindness and remembrance when his reign begins. The inscription serves as a humiliating down payment on the assertion of kingship, and nothing seems remotely regal here but Jesus' prayer asking forgiveness for his tormentors and his reassurance to the frightened thief. The "elegant robe" (v. 11) is long gone.

In the Gospels, even in John, Jesus' identity is unclear, debated, and struggled with. All of the Gospels focus and refocus to make a proper assessment of who he is and what he means to them. Just when it seems that Jesus has come into focus, the cross blurs it all again.

"If you are the King of the Jews, save yourself." That Jesus could or would pull this out of the bag in a last-minute demonstration of power was out of the question. Of course, we know what is coming. We know of the Resurrection and that "in him all the fullness of God was pleased to dwell" (Col. 1:19). We know that whatever the theory of atonement, Jesus was crucified under an inscription that was true—but not in the way it was meant.

That is the twist in the story: here is a king who doesn't look in any way like a sovereign because he is sovereign in the face of hell and death. His way of taking up his rule was to succumb, be captive, and then be delivered to be "made . . . both Lord and Messiah, this Jesus whom you crucified" (Acts 2:36).

Spend some time in front of a crucifix or a favorite rendering of the crucifixion and simply rest in contemplation. Afterward, journal your reflections.

THE REIGN OF CHRIST SUNDAY

Christ the King or the Reign of Christ Sunday appears on the calendar as a day to cap the liturgical year and to echo Easter's victory at history's ultimate horizon. However, we do well to pay attention to its point-counterpoint.

The sovereignty of a crucified man is a strange power to the world. Paul was up front about it: "We proclaim Christ crucified, a stumbling block to Jews and foolishness to Gentiles" (1 Cor. 1:23). The Messiah's "downward" pattern so prominent in the synoptic Gospels remains equally suspect today, even among those who profess to follow the crucified sovereign. Jesus had stated it plainly: "'Let these words sink into your ears: The Son of Man is going to be betrayed into human hands'" (Luke 9:44). This manner of ascent to kingship was always over his head, and ours too! We would rather be located next to the Christ of Colossians than next to Luke's Christ of The Skull.

This reading both surprises us and opposes our tendency to triumphalism. Triumphalism is the excessive belief that our brand of religion or politics is superior to any other, an altogether familiar trend in our day. We all have the capacity under the right conditions to lapse into such bad manners.

Luke shows us a side of the Messiah that shelves such excess and calls us to baptismal living in which we take our place upon the cross with him, proclaiming and enacting the kind of rule and authority he exercises. His rule and authority is bestowed in suffering, not seized; awakened to, not possessed. Colossians offers the Big Picture; Luke gives an "on-the-ground" narration. Reconciling the two pictures becomes the work of spiritual formation—learning and embodying the way of discipleship for the reconciliation of the world.

Where in your life does triumphalism crop up? How does this reading of Christ's way of ruling lead you to repentance?

A Vision for Peace

NOVEMBER 25–DECEMBER 1, 2013 • JOE PENNEL

SCRIPTURE OVERVIEW: Advent is a new year, a new time, a new life: a genuine newness wrought by God in the world. As both the prophetic oracle and the psalm attest, Israel hopes for justice, peace, and well-being. The biblical community knows God's intention for these matters and trusts God's faithful promise. Thus Advent begins in a vision of a healed alternative for the world. The New Testament readings intensify the long-standing hopes and make the promises of God immediate prospects. The intensity and present tense of New Testament faith revolve around the presence of Jesus, whose very person initiates a new beginning in the world. The church at Advent watches in order to notice where God is bringing justice, peace, and well-being.

QUESTIONS AND THOUGHTS FOR REFLECTION

- Read Isaiah 2:1-5. How do you move from hopeful intention to action, and in what arenas?

- Read Psalm 122. The writer defines Jerusalem as "sacred places that put our souls in touch with holy gladness." Where is your Jerusalem?

- Read Romans 13:11-14. How has "putting on Christ" been both disturbing and comforting to you?

- Read Matthew 24:36-44. How will you prepare to meet Christ this Advent season?

Retired bishop, The United Methodist Church; Professor of Pastoral Leadership, Vanderbilt Divinity School; living in Franklin, Tennessee

Visions pull us forward, opening us to new ways of seeing and living. They help us to see new possibilities. Isaiah had a vision for the possibility of peace, a time when people would cease to learn about war. He dreamed of a time of leveling of national distinctions. He longed for a time when God's ways would become the ways for all nations. That vision still beats in the hearts of those who believe that peace is a real possibility.

Many people believe that the nations can "walk in God's paths." We have a hard time conceiving of Isaiah's vision for peace because members of the human family have not learned how to live together. For example, thousands of Americans and Vietnamese died in the Vietnam War. Those who perished were not numbers on a page. They were someone's child, someone's roommate, someone's tennis partner, and someone who came to the table for Holy Communion. Isaiah's vision entailed a day when nations would no longer "learn war anymore."

God's promise to Isaiah makes clear the difference between what is and what will be. Persons are to move beyond hopeful intention to action: beating swords into plowshares and spears into pruning hooks.

Like Isaiah, Jesus calls his followers to live by a higher righteousness. In Jesus' day the law stated clearly that people should not murder one another. But Jesus called people to a higher standard by teaching that it is not only wrong to murder, it is also morally wrong to hate. For Jesus, the inward disposition becomes more important than the overt act. The motive becomes more important than the deed. Who we are becomes more important than what we do. This is the better way. This is the vision of Jesus, and it was rooted in the vision of Isaiah.

God of peace, help me to live as if love already reigns. May the day come when "nation shall not lift up sword against nation." Amen.

Jerusalem is a sacred city to both Jews and Christians, and Muslims claim it as their third most important city. Jerusalem is mentioned in almost two-thirds of the books of the Hebrew Bible and the New Testament. Jerusalem means "city of peace" or "cornerstone of peace."

I have been to many of the celebrated and distinguished cities of the world, but not one of them has the power to touch the mystical feelings of my heart as does Jerusalem. I can emotionally relate to the psalmist when he said, "I was glad when they said to me, 'Let us go to the house of the LORD.'"

I experience gladness within the walls of the old city— a holy gladness that I cannot explain or interpret with finite words. I have visited Jerusalem six times, and each time the feeling of holy gladness has been more and more pronounced.

As people of faith we need our "Jerusalems." We need those sacred places that put our souls in touch with holy gladness. When we have found our Jerusalem, we will return to it time and time again as did the Hebrew tribes who went to their Jerusalem "to give thanks to the name of the LORD."

When I arise in the morning, I go to my upstairs office for a time of prayer, spiritual reading, and meditation. I fight with myself over not turning on the computer. It takes great discipline on my part to practice quietness, to write in my journal, to go over my prayer list, and to search the scriptures. With the keeping of these disciplines and the passing of time, my office has become my Jerusalem. If I consistently go to my upstairs office, I can better experience holy gladness in the many moments of daily life. I do not feel as deeply or see as clearly when I fail to "stand within the gates" of my Jerusalem.

Lord, grant me the discipline to go to "Jerusalem" so that holy gladness might fill my soul. Amen.

The psalmist longs for the day when peace will come to Jerusalem. He echoes the feelings of the writer of Lamentations who said, "She has no one to comfort her" (1:2). As pilgrims come to Jerusalem the psalmist wants them to pray for peace within the walls of Jerusalem, for the absence of social conflict, for peace with the enemies and for "peace within you."

Since 1996 I have preached in over four hundred congregations. In each of these I have listened to prayers of the people and pastoral prayers. In all of these places I have heard few prayers for peace. I have heard prayers for the military and for the families of those in harm's way, but I have not heard earnest heartfelt peace prayers for the "Jerusalems" of our day and time.

At the same time I must honestly say that as a pastor I have not followed the call of Psalm 122 to pray for peace, nor have I faithfully entreated my congregations to do the same. How can peace come if we, as Christians, do not pray for it?

The psalmist invites all pilgrims to "pray for the peace of Jerusalem." For him, this peace comes with justice, with the promotion of well-being for the people. Those who love Jerusalem commit themselves to her welfare. Consider what might happen if members of the great world religions prayed for one another's welfare and well-being, always seeking the other's good.

As strange as it seems, the more we pray for peace in the world the more we will experience peace within ourselves as we struggle with misdirected impulses and conflicting emotions. When peace dwells within us, we will make acquaintance with more goodness, steadfastness, wisdom, justice, and love.

God whose name is love, help me to be faithful in my prayers for peace so that I might find peace within myself. Amen.

THANKSGIVING DAY, USA

If we are not careful we will develop amnesia about the meaning of Thanksgiving. Psalm 100 calls to mind the deeper meaning of the day. It reminds us that we are not God. We are not independent and self-made as Henry Ford was fond of saying. The psalmist reminds us that "the LORD is God" and not those of us who think we are the center of the universe.

Psalm 100 will not let us forget that God provides the essentials of life. In one church I pastored, the altar guild would place a lovely cornucopia on the altar for Thanksgiving. It served as an elegant and exquisite reminder of a God whose love ever provides.

The high meaning of Thanksgiving does not come through people dressed up like pilgrims or the Macy's parade or the afternoon football game or tables piled high with food or doing those things that cause us to turn in upon ourselves.

I am thankful for Thanksgiving because it helps me to remember that there is someone to thank. This day and every day reminds us that we can transcend our prosperity and that we can be superior to our wealth. When we come to this rich understanding we can "make a joyful noise to the LORD."

As Americans celebrate our national Thanksgiving, may we express gratitude for all the benedictions that make life good and beautiful. Let us not forget that God has flooded the outer world with sunshine and that beams of grace bring hope to discouragement.

O God, we pray for those who will find it hard to be thankful. For those hard pressed with difficulty, oppressed by anxiety, brokenhearted with bereavement, disillusioned with disappointment, whose words of gratitude will be stayed upon their lips as Thanksgiving comes. Help us and all your children to be thankful for thanksgiving. Amen.

Consider how clothing serves many functions in more affluent cultures. What we wear enhances our looks, helps us to fit in, and makes us more comfortable within our skin and with others. Clothing can give us a way to define ourselves for others. For example, when we wear our school colors on game day, we make a loyalty statement. Or when I pin on my Episcopal lapel pin I am making a statement about my responsibilities in the church. Likewise, our scripture reading for today beckons us to define ourselves by putting on Christ.

Like putting on our physical clothing, putting on Christ is something we need to do on a daily basis. Just as we intentionally choose our daily dress, our putting on Christ also requires a daily decision. We will grow spiritually if we give as much thought to putting on Christ as we do in making every effort to select just the proper garment to fit the activities of a certain day.

One of the august aspects of putting on Christ is that we do not have to decide about color combination, style, dressing down or up, matching the belt with the shoes, or the fit of the threads. The attire remains the same every day. The question for the Christian is this: "Will I choose to wear it or not?"

We do not purchase this covering in the marketplace; it comes as sheer gift. Our challenge is to live as if we have opened our hearts to welcome this benefaction.

When we put on Christ we can expect to be both disturbed and comforted. We will be disturbed because Christ kicks up the evil spirits in us, and we will be comforted because Christ mends our broken places.

Gracious God, grant me the constant and steadfast discipline to put on Christ each and every day. Amen.

Matthew knew that Christ had come and believed that Christ would come to us in the course of our daily life. He also affirmed that Christ would someday come in a final consummation. However, there is an unpredictability to Christ's coming. No one will know the time, the day, or the hour. Not even the angels will know. It will be like in the days of Noah when no one knew when the flood would come. Christ's coming will be so unpredictable and unexpected that of two people in the field, one will be taken and one will be left. Of two women grinding meal, one will be transported and one will continue her task.

According to Matthew, since we do not know when Christ will be unveiled, we watch with great anticipation and with great expectation. You can say this for Matthew—he gives us nothing predictable to hang on to. Instead, he tells us about the unexpected appearance of Christ.

This is a rather unsettling passage for me because I like to soak myself in the familiar during the season of Advent. So we are wise if we accept the fact that there is something about Advent that we cannot manage, plan, or program. Christ will come not when I want Christ to come but when Christ is ready to come. We best prepare for Advent by understanding that Christ will come incognito, in disguise. During Advent Christ does not strong-arm us into believing. Rather he comes to us in ways and through people that we least expect.

Our first step in preparing for Advent is to make an inward commitment to be observant, watchful, and attentive to those people and places where we will meet Christ.

Lord, give us eyes to see, ears to hear, and a heart to know when you come to us so that we will not miss an experience of the Holy. Amen.

SUNDAY, DECEMBER 1 ~ *Read Matthew 24:43-44*

First Sunday of Advent

In 1966 I served on the staff of a United Methodist congregation in Memphis, Tennessee. On a lovely Thursday afternoon, the White House called to tell us that the vice president of the United States would be worshiping with us the following Sunday at the 8:30 A.M. service. From the time that call came until the choral call to worship, the coming of Vice President Humphrey gave shape to how the church staff members spent much of our time and thought. His coming determined how we filled those few days. Our desire for readiness was shaped by the future.

Matthew earnestly believed that the second coming of Christ should shape a life. He held the strong conviction that the church should be prepared for Christ's advent, just as St. Luke's Church needed to be ready for the coming of the vice president. This readiness was one of the towering marks of the early church. If we believe that Christ will come among us this Advent, that belief will determine how we live in the present.

I believe that Christ will come to us this Advent. Christ will come to us in the pain of the world. At a local prison, I encountered a couple who visited every Sunday afternoon. I asked them, "Why do you come here?" Without hesitating they replied, "Because we meet Christ here."

Christ will also come to us in the joy of everyday life. He will advent with a family gathered around a table, in the return of a friend, and as we kneel for Holy Communion. Let us not dismiss Matthew when he writes, "Therefore you also must be ready, for the Son of Man is coming at an unexpected hour."

Advent God, shape me by the sure belief that you have come and that you will come again. Amen.

God's Dream

DECEMBER 2–8, 2013 • CHARLES W. ALLEN

SCRIPTURE OVERVIEW: The Old Testament roots of Advent hope are cast in royal imagery. The psalm marks the king as one whose work is to bring justice to the weak. The new king makes a new world possible. The Gospel reading is both invitation and warning that we must make concrete decisions to reorder our life in ways appropriate to God's new intention. Characteristically Paul makes the grand, sweeping claim: The new behavior appropriate to God's new governance is that the strong and the weak, the haves and have-nots, relate to each other in new faithfulness. Advent is spent pondering specific decisions about bringing our daily life into sync with God's rule.

QUESTIONS AND THOUGHTS FOR REFLECTION

- Read Isaiah 11:1-10. How do you view the relationship between verses 1-5 and verses 6-10? What do justice and peace have to do with predators and prey?

- Read Psalm 72:1-7, 18-19. What qualities do you desire in a leader?

- Read Romans 15:4-13. In the faith community at Rome, what stumbling block prevented people from welcoming one another? How can we avoid that stumbling block?

- Read Matthew 3:1-12. How did Jesus' ministry fulfill or challenge John's prophecy?

Chaplain for Grace Unlimited (Lutheran-Episcopal Campus Ministry) and Affiliate Professor of Theology at Christian Theological Seminary, Indianapolis, Indiana

Why do you read the Bible? Do you read it to win arguments? Maybe. I know I have. But Paul stresses a deeper reason. The scriptures were written to encourage our hope. That's how Paul has come to read and understand the scriptures, and it behooves us to read scripture in the same fashion and for the same reason: to encourage our hope.

We recall that Paul started out as an overenthusiastic religious bigot. He thought he correctly interpreted the scripture. Then the God of Hebrew Scriptures spoke to him in the voice of a man he had despised. He realized that he had been persecuting God and God's people—in the name of God and God's people!

Even more amazing, God recruits Paul instead of punishing him. He has been welcomed, unconditionally welcomed, and then recruited to share the news of God-in-Christ's welcome, not just with people like him but with people he has regarded as unworthy outsiders. Paul affirms that Jesus Christ was a Jew. Jesus assumed a particular identity with the people of Israel and yet threw open wide the radical welcome to those outside the Jewish faith. After his experience, Paul cannot look at scripture in the same way. He now sees every passage, every word, as reflective of this new community inhabited by God's spirit in Jesus Christ.

The community isn't new any more, but it's still inhabited by God's spirit in Jesus Christ; you and I are being welcomed into it daily. We read and listen to scripture, trusting that we'll find our hope encouraged by the same God who already welcomes us. We hope that some day we will learn to live in a harmony that extends to everyone. "Let all the peoples praise him."

Greet us, O God, with outstretched arms, that as we read words written in former times we may find our hope renewed. Amen.

R epent, for the kingdom of heaven has come near." The call to repentance formed the basis of John the Baptist's sermon and Jesus' too. Were they crazy or what? If the kingdom of heaven, God's reign, had come near, where is it now? It's been two thousand years. Is the world any less conflicted? Are lives any less broken? Were they just wrong?

I guess that depends on what John and Jesus meant by "has come near." John seems to imply that everybody will get their comeuppance. Somebody more powerful than John will show up any day to gather in the deserving, the "wheat," and burn the undeserving, the "chaff," with unquenchable fire: a crowd-pleasing conclusion for just about any blockbuster action movie.

When Jesus comes along, John believes the more powerful somebody is on the scene. But Jesus turns everything around. He starts gathering in the undeserving. He has sharp words and warnings for those expecting privileged treatment, but he wields no "unquenchable fire."

What Jesus made of John's message is so unexpected that John begins to wonder if he's made a mistake. Jesus answers that the nearness of God's reign brings wholeness to broken lives, and that's that. (See Matthew 11:2-6.) Maybe that answer mollified John; we're never told.

So what about today? Has God's reign come near? If we've been waiting for a crowd-pleasing conclusion, the answer is no. But God is still here, nearer than we can imagine, bringing wholeness to broken lives, gathering in the undeserving, warning us not to expect privileged treatment. More importantly, God calls us to repent; that is, to turn—to turn away from waiting for God's reign so that together we might start to *be* God's reign. The kingdom of heaven has come near. Turn now.

Open our eyes, O God, to the nearness of your reign, that we may walk with you to bring wholeness to broken lives. Amen.

Ihave a cat. I like birds, fish, rodents, and reptiles too. But right now it's probably not a good idea to keep any as pets while I have a cat. Some cats do seem to get along with smaller animals, but if you leave them unsupervised you may be sorry. That's the price of living with a semidomesticated predator.

God, says Isaiah, dreams of a day when none of us will be predators. Even lions would learn how to graze. There will be no pets, apparently, because on God's holy mountain we'd all belong to one another and to God. And we'd know it. Even snakes would know God, and it wouldn't stop at snakes. Every tiny thing would be drenched with the knowledge of God. "They will not hurt or destroy on all my holy mountain; for the earth will be full of the knowledge of the LORD as the waters cover the sea."

I can't help thinking of the sixth day of creation (Gen. 1:24-31): no predators, no crafty snakes (not yet, anyway), a world where children will not be harmed by nature or by conflicted grown-ups. However, in Genesis we are to "fill the earth and subdue it."

In Isaiah none of us subdues the earth. A wise, Spirit-filled ruler from David's line, who seems to serve more as an adviser for the world as a whole, a signal to the peoples, will judge with righteousness. But the earth is filled, not by us but by the knowledge of God. God rules by filling us with knowledge and wisdom. When we live in the fullness of Isaiah's vision, there is no need to subdue anybody or anything because we all will have learned how to play well with others.

I look at my cat and wonder if that vision is a foolish dream. But what's foolish about dreaming it? Why not encourage it?

Dream with us, O God, that our belonging to one another may grow to embrace your whole creation. Amen.

God's Dream

There was an election recently. There's always a recent election. Wouldn't it be wonderful if the candidate you supported actually accomplished everything promised? When was the last time that happened?

Psalm 72 contains words composed for the enthronement of a new king. It reflects a present hope for a newly established leader. You may interpret verses 2-7 as predictions (NIV) or as wishes (NRSV). Either way it's wishful thinking. With a new leader we always hope that our world will be set right and made whole. That can happen in a few instances: a war ended, an unfair practice halted, a rise in employment. But it's seldom close to all that was promised or to all that we dared hope this time around.

Why do we keep doing that? We know that our leaders are only human. We know that nobody gets elected without some compromises, especially in a complicated culture with clashing views of the common good. We wouldn't even think of reviving a monarchy, but we still catch ourselves hoping that a new leader might come along and put *everything* right.

Some would say that we need to grow up and stop dreaming. But are people who stop dreaming grown up? I shudder to think what our world would be like if people before us hadn't dreamed. We're told to hope for the best and prepare for the worst. That sounds like balanced advice, but there's always a danger that when we start preparing for the worst, we'll stop hoping for the best.

Advent is a time to renew outrageous hopes. "May righteousness flourish and peace abound."

Trouble leaders and people, O God, with your uncompromising vision of goodness, justice, and shalom. Amen.

Paul works tirelessly to eliminate divisions among the people of God. He hopes that the new community in Christ will always have plenty of room for observant Jews along with the flood of new people who will never keep kosher. He wants this Jewish-Gentile community to be the way forward for everyone.

It doesn't happen. Most Jews want a stronger sense of identity, so they choose to keep renewing their everlasting covenant with God on more familiar terms. Paul's new community in Christ sees itself as the new Israel, but before long Jews become the minority and begin to feel unwelcome. That leads to a division of opinion between Jewish and Gentile Christians. Christians have grown quite adept at splitting themselves even further. Healing those divisions has become a complicated process; we can't seem to agree on what's important and what isn't.

And yet Paul's words won't let us go: "Welcome one another, therefore, just as Christ has welcomed you, for the glory of God." That doesn't mean we wait until our faith communities work through all their differences.

Welcoming starts when I realize that Christ is not noticeably more impressed with my favorite doctrines and rules than with anybody else's. What we believe and how we behave certainly matters, but our ultimate Word is an embodied personal presence, not a list of doctrines and rules—not even a really good list.

Welcoming starts when I realize that in Christ's presence our being together and belonging to one another matters more than holding the same opinions. We can do that right now.

Speak through our differences, O God, that we may belong to one another in your shared life. Amen.

Kill the wicked; crush the oppressor; burn the chaff. Three of our four readings this week speak of violence against the wicked, the oppressor, the "chaff." All three Abrahamic faiths have used texts like these to support killing entire populations in God's name.

It helps, maybe, to remember that we read scripture from the standpoint of a community where oppressors like Paul were not killed, crushed, or burned but halted (temporarily blinded), welcomed, and recruited by God. While barely polite with Paul, God presented him with a new future, as opposed to no future at all. Many of us pray prayers of confession. In doing that we acknowledge that we do not fall in a different category from the wicked, the oppressor, or the "chaff." Yet we, like Paul, find ourselves welcomed and recruited (after halting for confession). Harmful acts have consequences, but the consequences in a community like this open a new future.

When we read Isaiah 11:1-10 from that standpoint, we notice some helpful clues. A stump gives birth to a shoot. What seems lifeless produces a branch upon which the spirit of the Lord will rest. Yet the shoot or branch from Jesse's stump is not literally a plant but a person, a person who clothes himself with righteousness and faithfulness. When the spirit of the Lord blows, it fosters relationship and creates a new ordering. Lions eating straw? That's surely an exaggeration, though an appealing one. We cannot take any image here at face value—and that goes for killing the wicked. Isaiah presents a vision of a world where wickedness and oppression give way to goodness, justice, and wholeness.

Halt us from our harmful bent, O God, that we may join you in offering goodness, justice, and wholeness to all without exception. Amen.

SECOND SUNDAY OF ADVENT

Good news doesn't always sound good. You see a bumper sticker that reads *Smile, God loves you*, and maybe that sounds nice. But that's only because we fail to realize what an unsettling thing it is to be loved by God.

This God moves in and starts redecorating—without any consultation—and then has the nerve to throw a party at your place for guests you never would have invited. God's love, God's very life with us and in us, is that unsettling.

If that's what is in store for me, I wouldn't mind getting a fair warning. That's what John the Baptist provides. Get ready to be baptized with the Holy Spirit and with fire. Get ready to have everything rearranged. And above all, don't presume to think that you don't need a makeover, you brood of vipers.

The crowds who show up to hear John's words are full of churchgoing scripture readers who can't imagine they need to change. They're the people of God. They're already insiders, and they've shown up to watch the outsiders get washed.

But John the Baptist's message reminds us that by the time God gets through, we'll have no way of measuring who's changed the most. And we won't even care. As far as God's welcome is concerned, it doesn't matter where we started. It only matters where we're going. It only matters if we're on the way to becoming as welcoming as God already is. You brood of vipers, you churchgoers, you Bible readers, get ready for God to move in. Get ready to be made new. That's today's good news.

Move into our lives, O God, and though we are not ready to be changed, make us new anyway. Amen.

Restoration and Healing

DECEMBER 9–15, 2013 • GEORGE HOVANESS DONIGIAN

SCRIPTURE OVERVIEW: These readings convey that the coming of God, or the coming of the Messiah, will be profoundly transformative. The promises of messianic possibility work against our exhaustion, our despair, and our sense of being subject to fate. The psalm provides a comprehensive summary of the miracles wrought by God in the past to make new life possible. Jesus' life and ministry embodied these large expectations of Israel. The prophetic oracle, psalm, and Gospel reading all move toward the practicality of the epistle reading, which demands that we allow this claim of new human possibility to permeate all of life. Our life is directed to the reality of God, the very God whom we discern in our present and to whom we entrust our future.

QUESTIONS AND THOUGHTS FOR REFLECTION

- Read Isaiah 35:1-10. How does Isaiah's vision shape your daily life?
- Read Luke 1:47-55 and Psalm 146:5-10. What song of praise do you offer God in response to life?
- Read James 5:7-10. James speaks of patience. For what do you wait impatiently?
- Read Matthew 11:2-11. What specific examples of healing and restoration can you cite from contemporary life?

United Methodist pastor serving in South Carolina, activist concerning Armenian matters

We think of Advent as a time of preparation for Christmas. For many people, that preparation embraces the world of consumer goods and the realm of the spirit. Some of us feel a sense of joy when we see symbols of Christmas on the streets and in houses and churches. Some of us grow grouchy when we see television commercials that feature adapted religious symbols to sell shavers and cars and jewelry. Some of us shun television and commercial media as an Advent practice, similar to the sacrificial tradition of Lent, and use the time to prepare to celebrate the birth of the Christ.

John the Baptist remains imprisoned when he sends some disciples to confirm that Jesus is indeed the Messiah. They ask Jesus a simple question, which Jesus does not answer in a simple way. "Tell John what you hear and see. . . ." We know that miracles happen throughout Jesus' ministry. The miracles that we witness point us to the healing and restorative aspects of God's reign. New life comes as a result of these miracles. Our text assumes that John's disciples witnessed such miracles and returned to John with their evidence. The immediate text does not make visible those who received gifts from Jesus, but they are powerfully present here and throughout the Gospels.

I invite you to consider questions that come from the experience of these "invisible" ones: What do you see in the way of healing and restoration? How is healing happening in your community? How are you experiencing restoration?

Move beyond the individual level to that of community and mission: How will your congregation communicate the good news of Jesus to others? What stories of healing and restoration will the community tell? What healing and restoration will others experience?

God of healing, restore to us the hope that comes with the good news of Jesus Christ. Amen.

Western Christianity identifies the third Sunday of Advent as *Gaudete* (Latin for "rejoice") Sunday. Advent wreaths may include a pink candle on this Sunday to remind us of joy. Isaiah 35 offers us images of joy that go beyond a particular color. The text opens us to see with fresh eyes the extraordinary miracles in everyday life.

I once lived in an unreal wilderness—not a physical wilderness but a time in which I experienced a sense of desolation and great discomfort. Nothing felt particularly holy, and nothing seemed to promise holiness. The experience lasted much longer than forty days, and many temptations came. My gravest temptation came in my willingness to believe that misery was the only choice, that life was purposeless and hence something my stoic self should simply accept.

In the midst of that long temptation, something bloomed. Perhaps, as Isaiah suggests, a crocus blossomed, perhaps a friendship. Maybe I experienced the transformation that comes after going through the dark night of the soul. Perhaps it was simply the end of a long process in which God's love for the world became more real and evoked a deeper sense of wonder. Restoration occurred, but it was restoration to a new state of being and a different kind of wholeness.

Since that chapter of my life, I have read and heard the words, "Be strong, do not fear! Here is your God." I have grown in awareness of healing that takes place—healing for fresh wounds, healing for old wounds, healing for generational wounds. We do well to point our friends and acquaintances to the healing God offers—at Christmas and throughout our days—and not allow the consumer culture to set this time as a season of desire and greed.

Strengthen the weak hands and make firm the feeble knees, loving God, and especially strengthen our fearful hearts. Amen.

The prophet offers a vision of God's reign and includes signs of wholeness. Many of these feature common physical conditions of Isaiah's time, but the prophet's word is not limited to physical conditions. These verses present a vision for the health of the whole community and a vision that embraces all the earth. As I read Isaiah 35, I see a highway built in the wilderness. The highway leads all people to Zion, the place of transformation, wholeness, and worship.

I've known people who have attended annual family reunions. Sometimes they complained about the preparations, and sometimes they would be delighted to meet new relatives. My family of origin was much too small for such events: the Armenian genocide claimed the lives of my father's brothers as well as some members of my mother's family. As a pastor, I served churches that hosted annual homecoming celebrations. In these settings I observed the joy people expressed and experienced when they renewed acquaintances, reminisced, recalled those now part of the cloud of witnesses, and remembered that they are part of God's movement on earth and in heaven. Think about homecomings and gatherings that you may have experienced while you read Isaiah 35. How do those gatherings reflect Isaiah's vision?

Focus now on the highway in the wilderness. Isaiah does not state explicitly that the highway leads us into change and the future, but it can take us nowhere else. It carries us continually into the fullness of God's loving reign. (I hope that you will enjoy the note of grace in verse 8: "No traveler, not even fools, shall go astray on the highway.") Take time to remember and reflect on the highway you have traveled through life and to know that others travel on other highways to the same place.

Grant us such a vision, God, to see all those you have ransomed return to Zion. Amen.

The text is Mary's song of praise, but I find that context helps our understanding. Remember that Mary traveled to the hill country to the house of Elizabeth and Zechariah. Elizabeth offered words of blessing and hope. In response to Elizabeth's gracious words, Mary offers her own song of praise. Would that all our family gatherings yielded such responses! Family joy and the history of Israel meld in this moment in Mary's life. Mary's history conjoins the nation's future in the Magnificat.

Focus on verses 46-49. How does your spirit rejoice in God our Savior? For some of us, the sacred music of Christmas uplifts our spirits in praise. Some of us find the abundance of Advent and Christmas symbols uplifting. Clerks in stores offer greetings of the season. We see long-absent acquaintances at church services. Some of us, however, find ourselves trapped in cynical responses to this season. Perhaps the most dangerous temptation is this: We want to abandon ourselves to the joy expressed by Mary, but we cannot let go of the cynical edge that became attached to us. What will it take for us to release or abandon that old clinging self?

Mary's words offer guidance to allow for such release. Her words reflect our own human condition and our relationship with God. God "has looked with favor on the lowliness" of this servant. As we continue reading the passage, we see that Mary claims God's holy elevation of her. Does not God also look with favor on us and elevate us? While we may not be Mary, the Christ bearer, we are each the beloved of God—and we can magnify the Lord and rejoice! In the midst of Advent busyness, remember that you are God's beloved.

Loving God, you have done great things for me, and I give thanks for your gifts. Amen.

The Magnificat moves beyond praise and offers us a vision of restoration and healing. Mary praises God and then sings of God's justice on earth. Focus today on verses 50-55. Consider the actions in the text:

- God scattered the proud.
- God brought down the powerful.
- God lifted up the lowly.
- God filled the hungry.
- God sent the rich empty away.

Before Mary sings about these actions, she reminds us that God's mercy is for all who fear God. Think of fear as "having reverential awe." Reverential awe guides the remaining text. Those who fear God recognize their dependence on God's grace. As we open to grace, we realize our need for healing and restoration.

Mary's song extends the vision of Isaiah 35. The redeemed, according to Isaiah, return to Zion. The redeemed, according to Mary, are all those who love God. In the grand equalizing of God's homecoming celebration, those who have been mighty in status and power will be brought low, and those who have been oppressed and poor will be lifted up. In the reign of God, all will enjoy equal status with one another and with God. In the healing that comes with such a homecoming, we will be freed from our deeply established prejudices.

In your mind's eye, how do you envision this grand homecoming? Who would you embrace after you embrace family members? With whom would you most enjoy God's reconciliation? Consider creating a list of those persons with whom you would enjoy this type of bonding and harmony.

In your mercy, O God, give us a vision of your radical healing. Amen.

The passage in James offers serious counsel to be patient. I understand on the surface, but I object: I've never been very patient—at least not with myself. James responds and reminds me that the farmer waits for the crop from the earth. Again I object: I did not grow up on a farm. I grew up in the corner grocery store. Again James counsels patience and offers the example of the prophets. I try to object again: Which prophet? The epistle chooses not to respond to my objection. I understand that the epistle appeals to a knowledge of the history of Israel.

But why be patient and strengthen the heart if "the coming of the Lord is near"? Those who await the Lord's coming gain a measure of insight from the farmer who plants and waits; the needed rain comes from God. The farmer waits, relying on God's promise.

The Major Prophets and Minor Prophets lived during times of corruption, oppression, and exile. Their messages differ because of conditions faced by the Hebrew people; however, their messages testify to a unifying vision. Whether Isaiah or Zechariah or Micah, the prophets call the people to turn to God and to live as covenant people. The prophets place before the people a vision of God's justice and mercy. They speak of the full restoration of God's kingdom. The vision continues to show us a vision of hope and healing, of justice and mercy, of restoration and the setting right of all things. To proclaim such a counter-cultural vision in the midst of oppressive rule does demonstrate patience on the part of the prophets. They are the .001% who speak to the 99.999%.

Like those prophets, we are to wait with patience, exhibiting active confidence in God.

God, your prophets and saints have invited us to a vision of your reign. Let that vision become part of our daily desire and hope. Amen.

THIRD SUNDAY OF ADVENT

In the wilderness John proclaimed a message that called people to repent of their evil ways and to prepare for the coming of God's kingdom. Such preaching made John popular for a time, but then those in authority felt the pinch of what he said. They imprisoned him. Such is the way of culture with prophets.

Imagine John the Baptist in prison. What does John want? Perhaps he, like all of us, wants to know that he has not ministered in vain, that he has come to the correct conclusions. So he sends his followers to ask Jesus to confirm his identity as the Messiah. After John's followers leave, Jesus turns to those around him, those who had trailed after John in the wilderness and who now follow after him. He affirms John's ministry and asks them, "What then did you go out to see?" What do *we* expect to see—not of John the Baptist but of the reign of God? The prophets answer: restoration, healing, justice, and mercy.

Many people demand justice, but they identify only retributive justice, seeking revenge for crimes. The justice I read in the prophets demands restorative justice, actions that bring healing and hope rather than vengeance. Prophetic justice tells us to love our enemies.

Restoration scares people. We are used to certain lifestyles, which are based on the visible and invisible oppression of others. We may not, for example, participate directly in the forced labor of children or the unjust conditions of migrant workers, but we may support such evil indirectly through our purchases. What would happen if restoration happened in such a way that these conditions were no more? Today and in all days, let healing and restoration shape your center.

God, we move toward the celebration of the Incarnation. Help us to live the values of your reign. Amen.

It's Not about the Baby

DECEMBER 16–22, 2013 • BETSY SCHWARZENTRAUB

SCRIPTURE OVERVIEW: We are close to the reality of Jesus, in whom we have invested so much of our life and faith. Jesus is larger than life, shattering all the categories of conventional religious recognition. On the one hand, it is asserted that this is the "Son of David," in continuity with the old dynasty and the old promises. On the other hand, this is one "from the Holy Spirit," not at all derived from the human dynasty. This twofold way of speaking about Jesus does not reflect vacillation or confusion in the community. Rather, it is an awareness that many things must be said about Jesus, because no single claim says enough.

QUESTIONS AND THOUGHTS FOR REFLECTION

- Read Isaiah 7:10-16. As you prepare to celebrate the coming of Christ into your life in deeper ways, what aspects of Jesus could most unsettle and challenge your current ways of living?

- Read Psalm 80:1-7, 17-19. What penitence or spiritual preparation have you yet to make at this time? Where are you called into community to share your hope in God?

- Read Romans 1:1-7. In what ways have you been set apart for the gospel? How are you doing as you seek to live "in Christ"?

- Read Matthew 1:18-25. What would make you trust the Holy Spirit as deeply as Joseph did? Where have you experienced God's surprising grace?

Consultant in stewardship and generosity; author of *Afire with God: Becoming Spirited Stewards*; living in Garden Valley, California

This time of year, many of us find our mailboxes besieged with manger-scene Christmas cards depicting Mary, Joseph, and the baby Jesus. Now don't get me wrong: I am not against the baby Jesus. It is the sentimentalized image of a sweet babe removed from reality, surrounded by cooing doves and little lambs that can lead us astray.

What God has promised—and delivered—is Jesus, a real human baby who grew up into a strong, passionate, vulnerable human being. Jesus reveals the personhood of God. He is God incarnate, in human flesh, the One who ultimately fulfills Isaiah's prophecy and whose life, ministry, death, and resurrection have reoriented human history.

Isaiah 7 does not focus on a sweet, little baby. King Ahaz teeters on the brink of a disastrous military alliance for his people's security. But the prophet tells him and his top counselors that such an alliance will fail. Their security rests elsewhere: in complete confidence in God's trustworthiness.

Isaiah challenges the king to ask God for a sign, but Ahaz is afraid to ask. So Isaiah declares God's sign anyway. A certain young woman whom they both know is pregnant. By the time her son is old enough to know basic right from wrong, the two nations whom Ahaz now dreads will be deserted. And that little boy will experience a day when once-proud city dwellers will be in such crisis that they will be thankful for the basic food of their wilderness ancestors.

Our only true security is in our relationship with God. Isaiah's message is about what the soon-to-be-born baby will point to: the importance of trusting only, ultimately, in God alone.

Faithful God, help us to trust you with all that we are, finding our only security in you. This we pray in the name of Jesus. Amen.

It is no coincidence that both Advent and Lent are seasons of spiritual preparation and watchful waiting. Traditionally both bear the mark of the color purple in our worship places: the color associated with not only royalty but also with suffering and penitence.

Penitence is hardly a popular aspect of living. Most of us struggle with being willing to realize our wrongdoing, to regret our misdeeds, and to resolve to change. But sometimes life throws up a mirror before us as individuals or as nations, and we must face the great chasm between God's faithfulness, justice, and mercy, and our indifferent, ungodly ways of living.

The tribes of Israel face such a time—shortly before the fall of the Northern Kingdom. Enemy invaders destroy and plunder their cities, and neighboring people quarrel over who will take possession of them. The worshiping community knew their situation resulted from their turning their backs on God and exploiting the vulnerable people among them.

"Restore us, O God," the people cried. "Let your face shine, that we might be saved." The Hebrew word for *restore* refers both to changing desperate external circumstances and to turning the human soul back to God. The desperate external situation leads them to beseech God for help, throwing themselves wholeheartedly into God's arms and knowing that only God can save them. Sometimes individuals cry out for repentance; here, an entire faith community and nation acknowledges its need for God.

We may be experiencing such a time, as well: a time to face our cruelties as a people and turn our own lives around to face God. This can be a time of watchful waiting as we promise, "We will never turn back from you; give us life, and we will call on your name" (Ps. 80:18).

Restore us, holy and awesome God. Let your face turn toward us and shine, that we may be saved. Amen.

It is a fearful thing to feel far away from the one you love. Sometimes we measure the distance in kilometers or miles, but we can also mark it by hollow silences, heavy hearts, or stony indifference. When someone has betrayed or abandoned us, it feels terrible. When we have betrayed or abandoned others, it seems even worse.

So how must God feel when we turn our backs on God as a people or in our own personal lives? We are the church, part of God's covenant community down through history, and yet often we grievously offend God. God must weep.

Yet even this situation offers hope. In the midst of calamity, the worshipers who recite Psalm 80 gather from their various tribes to seek a direct encounter with God. God has afflicted them for injustice and yet can still deliver them, choosing to forgive and redeem their lives.

What courage it takes to approach such a God! Yet these persons know their God as the "God of hosts." That title can signify "God of all armies" or "God of the heavenly armies" (of angels). Or it can mean "God of the totality of all earthly and heavenly creatures." This third phrase makes the most sense, since God reigns sovereign over all creatures everywhere and in every time.

So here also resides our hope. God's face shining forth brings us light and life. The image of God's light evidences divine beauty and power, vengeance and vindication (the same word in Hebrew, as seen by both perpetrator and victim), radiance and glory.

God of hosts, we boldly ask to encounter you personally once more and to find our hope in you alone. We promise to turn back to you in grateful love. Amen.

This season focuses on Jesus, but God's promises began our preparation for him centuries before his birth. Prophets like Isaiah address situations in their time, but God speaks through them for generations to come. So for example, we can hear in the soaring music of Handel's *Messiah* not only Isaiah's words of comfort to fellow exiles long ago but also our Christian understanding of their ultimate fulfillment in Jesus Christ.

God's promises come to us through the prophets and scriptures, but they also come through the lives of people utterly committed to God's good news. Consider Paul of the early church. His faith in Jesus and gutsy, life-transcending discipleship continue to put a laser focus on God's message. Paul has been "set apart for the gospel of God," which he describes later in the first chapter of Romans as "the power of God for salvation" (v. 16) for everyone who has faith—that is, who entrusts his or her life to God.

God the Holy Spirit gives each one of us the power to respond to God with faith, as Jesus responded. God gives us this awesome power, which enables us to live a certain way: the way Jesus lived and continues to live through us. Life "in Christ" has been promised to us and is offered to us all, right now, through the Spirit.

It's all about Jesus and those of us "who are called to be saints" (v. 7). But it's also all about how we live his way today.

God of promises fulfilled, thank you for your gospel, your offer of salvation, and the Holy Spirit who encourages us and empowers us into new life in Christ. We pray this in Jesus' name. Amen.

Paul packs his letters to the first house churches with pragmatic advice, but the epistles start with the cosmic breadth and depth of God's good news for all through Jesus Christ. Take Paul's letter to the Roman Christians as an example. He starts with the gospel of God; reaches back to the promises of the prophets; summarizes the impact of Jesus' life, death and resurrection, and then surges forward through his own life to our apostleship and calling to belong to Jesus Christ. And that is all in the first sentence.

Paul may want to theologize step by step, but his intensity pushes him to press for the "So what?" question. The prophets, the scriptures, and Jesus himself urge us to make a heart decision: to belong entirely to Jesus Christ and so to join "the saints," meaning those who seek to follow Jesus in their everyday ways of living.

Paul states that the content of the good news is Jesus Christ himself, through whom you and I have received God's grace. We have received our apostleship through Jesus, as well. In other words, God has sent us (not just Paul) to proclaim the full-throttle gospel of Jesus' impact upon our world.

I don't know about you, but I did not expect all this. I thought I was just getting ready for another Christmas. You know: caroling, cards, manger scene, the sweet baby Jesus. But it's not about the baby (not in that way, anyway). It is about the fullness of Jesus who was born, lived, died, and is now risen.

God of grace, of promises and faith, and of Jesus, grab hold of us now and help us become all-out apostles of your good news. This we pray through the person of Jesus himself. Amen.

Joseph, a decent man, must have cared deeply about Mary since he resolves to break off their engagement quietly instead of publicly shaming her, which was his right by law. As soon as Joseph makes that decision, an angel shows up in a dream and tells him, "Do not be afraid to take Mary as your wife, for the child conceived in her is from the Holy Spirit."

Who in the world would believe that story? Is this angel truly a messenger from God? Will God's Spirit, which first blew over the surface of the waters at the beginning of creation, actually enter into a human life, a human body, in order to translate God's good news for all humanity into a mortal life?

Despite the Gospel writer's initial intent to relate how the birth of Jesus took place, many of the intervening verses deal with Jesus' conception and naming. Matthew wants to make it clear that this conception is God's doing. Jesus is the result of a new and startling divine initiative. And the name bears witness to the life Jesus will live out.

See, even the angel's announcement about the baby is less about the baby and more about trusting God. Will Joseph listen to his own reason and the opinions of relatives, friends, and neighbors? What kind of fool will overlook such a human transgression? Or will he believe the angel, set aside all his fears, and enfold Mary's future in his own?

Grace upon grace, Joseph chooses to believe the preposterous message and to trust God—and Mary—with his good name and his life.

Holy Spirit God, guide us to trust you beyond all reason, to set aside our fears, and to let you use us as you will. This we pray in Jesus' name. Amen.

FOURTH SUNDAY OF ADVENT

So Joseph takes the risk and accepts Mary. He names the baby *Jesus*, which means "The LORD [YHWH] saves."

God saves us: rescues us, heals us, and makes us whole. This God revealed the divine name in ancient times to Moses at the burning bush. This God is not only the Creator of all that exists but is the Sustainer of all living beings, which is the meaning of the verb used to make God's personal name.

This very nature of God was poured into one trembling human life, in Jesus. Yes, he came as a baby, shockingly vulnerable and powerless in our midst. But we celebrate his birth among us because of his entire life, his ministry on this earth, his willingness even to die for us, and his risen presence among us now, which has changed our lives for eternity.

Here Joseph learns one more thing. This God who creates, sustains, and saves us is actually *with us*. Our God is Emmanuel, God-With-Us.

What the prophet Isaiah learned and proclaimed so long ago not only encouraged the worshipers in Psalm 80 to seek God's forgiveness and help but also empowered Paul to declare hope in God's sovereignty and love. This same proclamation of God-With-Us came to Joseph and comes to you and me today.

So the Christmas message moves far beyond the sweet baby in the manger. The message entails all of who Jesus is—with us, for us, and through us and others to all generations. It's about Emmanuel, God-With-Us, who afflicts out of holiness, forgives and vindicates out of mercy, and always reaches out to travel with us in life, in death, and beyond.

Creator, Sustainer, and Redeemer God, thank you for your incredible gift of grace through Jesus! This we pray in his name. Amen.

The Word Made Flesh

DECEMBER 23–29, 2013 • ANDY LANGFORD

SCRIPTURE OVERVIEW: These texts conclude the season of Advent and lead us into the days of Christmas. They culminate with the classic scriptures of praise for God's mighty gift of the Word made flesh. The reading from Third Isaiah remembers the mighty works of God in the past and the present. The key word in that text is *hesed*, the dynamic unfolding of God's love for us. Psalm 148 is a poem of thanksgiving for all God's creation. The text for Christmas Day, the prologue of John, sets the coming of Jesus into the creation of the world and the promise of salvation for all God's people. Hebrews reminds us that the Incarnation is not just a feel-good story but a sign of God's humility and identification with the sufferings of this world. Finally, the shocking story of the exodus to Egypt, the slaughter of the innocents, and the return to Nazareth locate Jesus in the divine narrative of the children of Abraham and Sarah.

QUESTIONS AND THOUGHTS FOR REFLECTION

- Read Isaiah 63:7-9. How has God treated you with compassion? When have you taken time to remember God's acts of love amidst the busyness of these holy days?

- Read Psalm 148. Sing praises to God. List all the ways God has blessed you in these holidays.

- Read Hebrews 2:10-18. What is the relationship between the humanity of Jesus and his exaltation as the high priest of God?

- Read Matthew 2:13-23. What exodus journeys have you lived, and how have they influenced how you live today?

Pastor, Central United Methodist Church, Concord, North Carolina

A s we end our Advent journey, we stand at the threshold of the Incarnation. Isaiah is the prophet of Advent and Christmas. Over two-thirds of all Old Testament lessons in these two seasons come from Isaiah. Try to hear the brief and clear text for Sunday anew: "I will recount the LORD's faithful acts; I will sing the LORD's praises, because of all the LORD did for us, for God's great favor toward the house of Israel. God treated them compassionately and with deep affection. God said, 'Truly, they are my people, children who won't do what is wrong.' God became their savior. . . . In love [*hesed* or "steadfast love" or "loving kindness"] and mercy God redeemed them, lifting and carrying them throughout earlier times" (CEB).

Throughout this Advent, we have witnessed God's early faithfulness to the psalmist, John the Baptist, and Joseph of Nazareth. As we prepare for Christmas Eve tomorrow, the long nights of waiting are almost over. The Lord God has sent to us new messengers: heavenly angels, a young woman named Mary, and a host of other people gathering in a stable in Bethlehem. In love and mercy, the day of God's Savior is almost at hand.

The 1947 movie *Miracle on 34th Street* remains my favorite holiday movie. In that movie, Kris Kringle says, "Seems we're all so busy trying to beat the other fellow in making things go faster and look shinier and cost less that Christmas and I are sort of getting lost in the shuffle." Today, pray that you will not lose the coming Christ in the busy shuffle in these last days before Jesus' birth. May we catch our breath, slow down, watch for angels, give thanks for God's *hesed*, and be ready to receive the coming Savior.

God of darkness and light, help us overcome the shuffling of life to be ready to receive our Savior. Amen.

CHRISTMAS EVE

Throughout Advent, we have been decorating our sanctuaries and our homes. We have been buying presents and going to parties. We have listened to Christmas music and baked cookies. Yet, will we know when Jesus is with us? Will we see the Christ when he comes?

Pieter the Elder Brueghel, a Flemish artist in 1566, painted his vision of Mary and Joseph's arrival in Bethlehem in *The Numbering at Bethlehem*. The painting is dark and complex. The scene depicts a small, medieval Dutch village during the cold of winter. The artist uses only browns, grays, blacks, and an off-color white. Dirty snow covers a dozen stone buildings. Hundreds of people wrapped up in heavy coats and hats pursue their daily activities. Men butcher a pig. Two women bake bread over an outdoor fire. Children play together on frozen ponds. Bundled against the cold, everyone simply goes about his or her daily business, ignoring all else.

But, if you look closely, right in the bottom center of the painting, you can see a small, inconspicuous couple arriving in town for the census. A young woman with her head covered from the cold rides a donkey. A stooped-over man carries a saw. Mary and Joseph have arrived in Bethlehem.

In Brueghel's painting, none of the other villagers notices Mary and Joseph. The village people are preoccupied with their own everyday activities. No one watches for visitors from out of town. Mary and Joseph are simply lost among the multitude.

We too can just as easily overlook the Holy Family. Maybe, like the villagers, we become so caught up in our lives that we overlook God who is in our midst. On this night, above all nights, do not miss the arrival of the Christ child.

On this holy night, Incarnate One, prepare my heart to receive your coming. Amen.

CHRISTMAS DAY

Today, with all the stores closed and all the shopping over, take a deep breath and remember the finest Christmas gift. I am not referring to your favorite presents or the gifts of gold, frankincense, and myrrh. Instead, remember the very first Christmas gift, the gift of the child born in Bethlehem, the Word made flesh, who came to dwell among us.

For many people around us, God being born as a peasant child in a developing country two thousand years ago seems an absurd notion. Many folks imagine God as a being who is perfect and perfectly content to sit in heaven. Christians claim an alternate view. We have experienced a God who loved us from the creation of the world and calls each human being "very good." We know a God who feels anger and tenderness, despair and hope, and anguish and optimism.

Jesus Christ personifies God's love. Throughout this year, as we have met Jesus, listened to Jesus, watched Jesus heal the sick, observed Jesus' death on the cross and his resurrection, we know that Jesus was God's love made flesh. Jesus did not just point people toward God; Jesus *was* God. The first letter of John says it best: "Dear friends, let's love each other, because love is from God. . . . God is love. This is how the love of God is revealed to us: God has sent his only Son into the world so that we can live through him" (4:7-9, CEB).

The bottom line of our relationship with the Word made flesh is love. Love is what Christmas is all about: God coming to the world in love, in the person of a child. In the birth of a baby, the Word of God from the creation of the world becomes known to us. Welcome this new life into your life.

Incarnate God, in you love has come down among us. Amen.

Christmas Day has come and gone. The church has closed its doors. Dried candle wax from evening services stains carpets and pew cushions. Only a few pieces of straw remind us of the children's nativity. The after-Christmas sales have begun. We find ourselves exhausted from the holiday hassles. It is time for family to go home. We have to clean the dishes, throw out the trash, disassemble the decorations, and return to our routines.

Yet, before all this flurry of activity, let us praise the Lord. The Lord Jesus Christ, the child born in Bethlehem, is among us. Psalm 148 raises a cacophony of praise throughout all creation— from the highest heavens to the depths of the earth. The angels in heaven, the sun, moon, and stars praise the Lord. All sea monsters and violent forces of nature praise the Lord. Every living creature on the face of the earth praises the Lord. All people, from rulers to peasants, from young to old, praise the Lord. We have seen God's glory in Mary's child.

Before you return to life after Christmas, praise the Lord. Where have you seen God in Christ Jesus this week? When you sang carols in worship with your Christian community or while praying a prayer with family? When you lit a candle? When children fumbled through the old, old story, and you heard it afresh? When someone unexpectedly said "Merry Christmas"? When you opened an unexpected gift? When your gift to another brought a smile? When you gathered with loved ones around a festive meal? When you served a meal to people who have no reason to be festive?

Every day of this season, if we have eyes to see and hearts to feel, God has been, is now, and will be present among us. Join the psalmist and all creation, and praise the Lord.

Praise God in highest heaven, praise the child in a manger, praise the Spirit that stills your heart. Amen.

Hebrews is an anonymous letter to early Christians in the midst of hardship and distress. Throughout this epistle, Jesus Christ stands as the great high priest who offers the perfect sacrifice for us. We must, however, remember that before the Word became higher than the angels, the Word first became flesh and knew the pain that the children of Adam and Eve feel.

This text echoes the most ancient hymn of the church found in Paul's letter to the Philippians: "Though he was in the form of God, he did not consider being equal with God something to exploit. But he emptied himself by taking the form of a slave and by becoming like human beings. When he found himself in the form of a human, he humbled himself by becoming obedient to the point of death, even death on a cross. Therefore, God highly honored him and gave him a name above all names" (Phil. 2:6-9, CEB). Only by becoming human could Jesus Christ become complete and, as a priest, show us the way to God.

When the Word became flesh, God become like us so that we could become like God. Without the Incarnation, there would be no salvation. Without Jesus' becoming one with us, we could not become one with God. Through the Incarnation we are the sisters and brothers of Jesus Christ and thus children of God.

While this week of Christmas seems full of warmth, gift-giving, gift-receiving, family reunions, bright lights, and cheerful carols, we must not overlook the foundation of our joy. Our joy comes because God in Christ set aside glory, came as a child born in Bethlehem, walked as a servant among us, suffered death on a cross, and rose from the dead. Only through this journey did the infant from Bethlehem become the high priest of the heavens.

Jesus Christ, our Great High Priest, through your humility show us the path to the heavens. Amen.

Throughout the scriptures, a recurring story narrates faithful people leaving the Promised Land and traveling to Egypt. Abram and Sarai settle in Canaan, but in the midst of a famine they retreat to Egypt for food (Gen. 12). When the sons of Jacob face starvation, they travel to Egypt, the breadbasket of the Near East. The brothers find food and their brother Joseph whom they had sold into slavery (Gen. 42–50). Now Joseph, Mary, and the Holy One follow in the footsteps of Abram and Sarai and Jacob's family. It is an old, old story told anew.

One of the oldest churches in the world, the Hanging Church, stands in Cairo. Tradition declares that the church stands on top of the home in which Mary, Joseph, and Jesus lived during their Egyptian exile. How did they survive in Egypt as aliens in a foreign land? Tradition witnesses that the Holy Family used the gifts of gold, frankincense, and myrrh given to them by the Magi to pay their bills.

Yet, the Holy Family left behind great tragedy in Bethlehem. The massacre of innocent children provided a painful undertone to the refuge found by the Holy Family. Usually, we are too tired from all the Christmas activities to hear such stories. We like to hear about sweet baby Jesus, not the death of Rachel's children.

Today we still proclaim the faithfulness of God in a world devastated by painful realities. While some find refuge, many other children around the world die by the millions from hunger and illness. Some children in our own communities had no Christmas cheer. We can only fully understand the security of God by contrasting God's reign to the harsh world around us. During the holidays, remember the pain of the children.

God of the innocent ones, open our eyes to see the darkness that yet needs to be overcome by your light. Amen.

Abram and Sarai, facing famine, traveled to Egypt and then returned to the land flowing with milk and honey (Gen. 12). When the children of Jacob completed years of slavery, Moses led them to freedom through the sea and back to the Promised Land (Exodus). And now, an angel speaks to Joseph and leads the Holy Family back to the land promised to Abram and Sarai. They settle in the small village of Nazareth.

In the contemporary village of Narazeth stands the modern Church of the Annunciation. In the basement of that building is a small home, which tradition tells us was the childhood home of Jesus. The courtyard walls of the church display a collection of mosaics of Mary and the baby Jesus. Each mosaic portrays mother and child as indigenous to many different peoples: Chinese, African, Indian, and dozens of other ethnicities. While mother and child were Jews from the Promised Land, they were not just Nazarenes but citizens of the whole world.

The Word incarnate fulfilled the promise made to his ancestors Abram and Sarai: "all the families of earth will be blessed because of you" (Gen. 12:3, CEB). While a child of one people of one culture at one time, Jesus of Nazareth proclaimed the reign of God to all people. Whether we are North American or Australian, African or Chinese, European or Indian, or whatever we are, we are heirs of that divine promise.

On this last Sunday of the year, as we near the end of our journey with Jesus Christ, remember that the journey is not over. We have seen the glory of God in Jesus Christ. Our task in the year to come is to share his story with all the nations, with generations yet to come: the Word has become flesh and lives among us.

Jesus of Nazareth, as you have journeyed with us this year, continue to walk beside us for lifetimes yet to come. Amen.

Seeing and Believing

DECEMBER 30-31, 2013 • MELISSA TIDWELL

SCRIPTURE OVERVIEW: This week's readings invoke praise and thanksgiving to God for God's outrageous generosity in the gift of Jesus Christ. The readings all contrast that generosity with the situation of humanity apart from God's intervention. Jeremiah 31:7–14 portrays for us a people in exile, a people for whom despair and grief seem to be the only option. The apparent eternity of winter's grasp dominates Psalm 147:12–20, with its picture of God sending "snow like wool" and "frost like ashes." Common to both of these texts is not only the assertion of human helplessness and hopelessness apart from God, but also the proclamation that God has already invaded the world and caused a new world to come into being.

QUESTIONS AND THOUGHTS FOR REFLECTION

- Read Jeremiah 31:7-14. Jeremiah's role as a prophet is not to predict the future but to reveal God's presence and offer hope for the future. Where in our times of turmoil do you see evidence of God's presence? What spiritual practices or tools do you use for guidance?

- Read Psalm 147:12-20. Substitute, in verse 12, the name of your own community instead of Jerusalem. What can you name in your community that reflects God's active presence? What things point to the yet unfulfilled promise of the psalm?

Former editor, *Alive Now* magazine; freelance writer and editor, Atlanta, Georgia

While I get my news from several sources, I make it a point to tune in to one particular news program when possible. I really appreciate the way the commentator puts the day's news into context for me, giving perspective on not just the events of the day but the larger movements of history and culture.

In some ways the role of the news commentator resembles Jeremiah's calling as a prophet. Jeremiah is not just a talking head, pronouncing words of warning about the future. Jeremiah puts God's message into a context that the people can hear and respond to, use as an impetus for change and as a strategy for surviving exile.

This passage reminds the Israelites that the covenant they have with God will not be forgotten. God promises to draw them back to Zion, to restore them, and to be in close communion with them. Using some images that might have evoked another famous journey, that of the Exodus, Jeremiah promises that unlike that arduous trek where water was scarce and many perished, this journey will be along "brooks of water, in a straight path in which they shall not stumble."

Jeremiah's words hang between exile and restoration, between judgment and mercy. In these days between the passing of the old year and the beginning of the new, we might ask ourselves where our journey is taking us. Perhaps the next few days provide a good time to review our context, to trace our own story for passages that seemed hopeless but turned out for good or that seemed promising but proved to be occasions for sin. How does our story become an addition to the larger history of how God's people live with the courage to hope?

God, give us the vision to perceive your grace active in the world and in our lives. Amen.

As a child I would spend hours poring over the family photographs my grandmother kept. I found it fun to see evidence of the past, familiar family features in unfamiliar clothes. I especially loved it when my grandmother would tell me the story behind each picture. Sometimes she would laugh over a remembered prank; at other times she would wipe away a tear, connecting to a painful memory.

The Psalms are like this: a storehouse of family artifacts, some carrying great pride in our lineage, some revealing our limitations and excesses. Psalm 147 elevates us by the grandeur of the natural world, of God's intimate presence in the tiniest snowflake, God's immense power in the unbearable cold. But we notice the gap between the real and the ideal, as in verse 12, which praises God for giving peace to Jerusalem. Would only that it were so, that the holy city stood as a beacon of justice and righteousness.

As we end one year and begin another, it is a good time to think of the items on our prayer lists that represent a hope unfulfilled, a dream that eludes us. Does that hope stand as a reminder of God's hope for us, of which we must not weary but for which we must continue striving? What actions can we take to draw the reality closer, or what attitudes can we continue to grow into? Perhaps we could make a list of these and keep them as a guide to the coming year. We might write our own form of the psalm to reflect the blessings we believe God will deliver and is delivering through our life and the workings of the Spirit among us.

The Psalms, like our lives, contain both promise and loss, glory and pain. Seeing those things, not as separate but woven together in one truth, is the beginning of the wisdom that the Psalms teach.

Lord, make me an instrument of your peace. Amen.

The Revised Common Lectionary* for 2013
Year C – Advent / Christmas Year A
(Disciplines Edition)

January 1–6
NEW YEAR'S DAY
Ecclesiastes 3:1-13
Psalm 8
Revelation 21:1-6a
Matthew 25:31-46

January 6
EPIPHANY
Isaiah 60:1-6
Psalm 72:1-7, 10-14
Ephesians 3:1-12
Matthew 2:1-12

January 7–13
BAPTISM OF THE LORD
Isaiah 43:1-7
Psalm 29
Acts 8:14-17
Luke 3:15-17, 21-22

January 14–20
Isaiah 62:1-5
Psalm 36:5-10
1 Corinthians 12:1-11
John 2:1-11

January 21–27
Nehemiah 8:1-3, 5-6, 8-10
Psalm 19
1 Corinthians 12:12-31
Luke 4:14-21

January 28–February 3
Jeremiah 1:4-10
Psalm 71:1-6
1 Corinthians 13
Luke 4:21-30

February 4–10
TRANSFIGURATION
Exodus 34:29-35
Psalm 99
2 Corinthians 3:12–4:2
Luke 9:28-43

February 13
ASH WEDNESDAY
Joel 2:1-2, 12-17 or
  Isaiah 58:1-12
Psalm 51:1-17
2 Corinthians 5:20b–6:10
Matthew 6:1-6, 16-21

February 11–17
FIRST SUNDAY IN LENT
Deuteronomy 26:1-11
Psalm 91:1-2, 9-16
Romans 10:8b-13
Luke 4:1-13

February 18–24
SECOND SUNDAY IN LENT
Genesis 15:1-12, 17-18
Psalm 27
Philippians 3:17–4:1
Luke 13:31-35

February 25–March 3
THIRD SUNDAY IN LENT
Isaiah 55:1-9
Psalm 63:1-8
1 Corinthians 10:1-13
Luke 13:1-9

March 4–10
FOURTH SUNDAY IN LENT
Joshua 5:9-12
Psalm 32
2 Corinthians 5:16-21
Luke 15:1-3, 11b-32

March 11–17
FIFTH SUNDAY IN LENT
Isaiah 43:16-21
Psalm 126
Philippians 3:4*b*-14
John 12:1-8

March 18–24
PALM/PASSION SUNDAY

Liturgy of the Palms
Psalm 118:1-2, 19-29
Luke 19:28-40

Liturgy of the Passion
Isaiah 50:4-9*a*
Psalm 31:9-16
Philippians 2:5-11
Luke 22:14–23:56

March 25-31
HOLY WEEK

Monday
Isaiah 42:1-9
Psalm 36:5-11
Hebrews 9:11-15
John 12:1-11

Tuesday
Isaiah 49:1-7
Psalm 71:1-14
1 Corinthians 1:18-31
John 12:20-36

Wednesday
Isaiah 50:4-9a
Psalm 70
Hebrews 12:1-3
John 13:21-32

Maundy Thursday
Exodus 12:1-14
Psalm 116:1-2, 12-19
1 Corinthians 11:23-26
John 13:1-17, 31b-35

Good Friday
Isaiah 52:13–53:12
Psalm 22
Hebrews 10:16-25
John 18:1–19:42

Easter
Acts 10:34-43
Psalm 118:1-2, 14-24
1 Corinthians 15:19-26
John 20:1-18
Luke 24:1-12

April 1–7
Acts 5:27-32
Psalm 150
Revelation 1:4-8
John 20:19-31

April 8–14
Acts 9:1-6, 7-20
Psalm 30
Revelation 5:11-14
John 21:1-19

April 15–21
Acts 9:36-43
Psalm 23
Revelation 7:9-17
John 10:22-30

April 22–28
Acts 11:1-18
Psalm 148
Revelation 21:1-6
John 13:31-35

April 29–May 5
Acts 16:9-15
Psalm 67
Revelation 21:10, 22–22:5
John 14:23-29

May 6–12
Acts 16:16-34
Psalm 97
Revelation 22:12-14, 16-17, 20-21
John 17:20-26

May 9
ASCENSION DAY
Acts 1:1-11
Psalm 47
Ephesians 1:15-23
Luke 24:44-53

May 13–19
PENTECOST
Acts 2:1-21
Psalm 104:24-34, 35b
Romans 8:14-17
John 14:8-17, 25-27

May 20–26
TRINITY SUNDAY
Proverbs 8:1-4, 22-31
Psalm 8
Romans 5:1-5
John 16:12-15

May 27–June 2
1 Kings 18:20-39
Psalm 96
Galatians 1:1-12
Luke 7:1-10

June 3–9
1 Kings 17:8-24
Psalm 146
Galatians 1:11-24
Luke 7:11-17

June 10–16
1 Kings 21:1-21a
Psalm 5:1-8
Galatians 2:15-21
Luke 7:36–8:3

June 17–23
I Kings 19:1-15a
Psalm 42
Galatians 3:23-29
Luke 8:26-39

June 24–30
2 Kings 2:1-2, 6-14
Psalm 77:1-2, 11-20
Galatians 5:1, 13-25
Luke 9:51-62

July 1–7
2 Kings 5:1-14
Psalm 30
Galatians 6:1-16
Luke 10:1-11, 16-20

July 8–14
Amos 7:7-17
Psalm 82
Colossians 1:1-14
Luke 10:25-37

July 15–21
Amos 8:1-12
Psalm 52 *or* Psalm 82
Colossians 1:15-28
Luke 10:38-42

July 22–28
Hosea 1:2-10
Psalm 85
Colossians 2:6-19
Luke 11:1-13

July 29–August 4
Hosea 11:1-11
Psalm 107:1-9, 43
Colossians 3:1-11
Luke 12:13-21

August 5–11
Isaiah 1:1, 10-20
Psalm 50:1-8, 22-23
Hebrews 11:1-3, 8-16
Luke 12:32-40

August 12–18
Isaiah 5:1-7
Psalm 80:1-2, 8-19
Hebrews 11:29–12:2
Luke 12:49-56

August 19–25
Jeremiah 1:4-10
Psalm 71:1-6
Hebrews 12:18-29
Luke 13:10-17

August 26–September 1
Jeremiah 2:4-13
Psalm 81:1, 10-16
Hebrews 13:1-8, 15-16
Luke 14:1, 7-14

September 2-8
Jeremiah 18:1-11
Psalm 139:1-6, 13-18
Philemon 1-21
Luke 14:25-33

September 9–15
Jeremiah 4:11-12, 22-28
Psalm 14
1 Timothy 1:12-17
Luke 15:1-10

September 16–22
Jeremiah 8:18–9:1
Psalm 79:1-9 or Psalm 4
1 Timothy 2:1-7
Luke 16:1-13

September 23–29
Jeremiah 32:1-3a, 6-15
Psalm 91:1-6, 14-16
1 Timothy 6:6-19
Luke 16:19-31

September 30–October 6
Lamentations 1:1-6
Psalm 137
2 Timothy 1:1-14
Luke 17:5-10

October 7–13
Jeremiah 29:1, 4-7
Psalm 66:1-12
2 Timothy 2:8-15
Luke 17:11-19

October 7
THANKSGIVING DAY
CANADA
Deuteronomy 26:1-11
Psalm 100
Philippians 4:4-9
John 6:25-35

October 14–20
Jeremiah 31:27-34
Psalm 119:97-104 or Psalm 19
2 Timothy 3:14–4:5
Luke 18:1-8

October 21–27
Joel 2:23-32
Psalm 65
2 Timothy 4:6-8, 16-18
Luke 18:9-14

October 28–November 3
Habakkuk 1:1-4; 2:1-4
Psalm 119:137-144
2 Thessalonians 1:1-4, 11-12
Luke 19:1-10

November 1
ALL SAINTS DAY
Daniel 7:1-3, 15-18
Psalm 149 or Psalm 150
Ephesians 1:11-23
Luke 6:20-31

November 4–10
Haggai 1:15*b*–2:9
Psalm 145:1-5, 17-21
2 Thessalonians 2:1-5, 13-17
Luke 20:27-38

November 11–17
Isaiah 65:17-25
Isaiah 12 *or* Psalm 118
2 Thessalonians 3:6-13
Luke 21:5-19

November 18–24
THE REIGN OF CHRIST
Jeremiah 23:1-6
Luke 1:68-79
Colossians 1:11-20
Luke 23:33-43

November 25–December 1
FIRST SUNDAY OF ADVENT
Isaiah 2:1-5
Psalm 122
Romans 13:11-14
Matthew 24:36-44

November 28
THANKSGIVING DAY, USA
Deuteronomy 26:1-11
Psalm 100
Philippians 4:4-9
John 6:25-35

December 2–8
SECOND SUNDAY OF ADVENT
Isaiah 11:1-10
Psalm 72:1-7, 18-19
Romans 15:4-13
Matthew 3:1-12

December 9–15
THIRD SUNDAY OF ADVENT
Isaiah 35:1-10
Luke 1:47-55
Psalm 146:5-10
James 5:7-10
Matthew 11:2-11

December 16–22
FOURTH SUNDAY OF ADVENT
Isaiah 7:10-16
Psalm 80:1-7, 17-19
Romans 1:1-7
Matthew 1:18-25

December 23–29
FIRST SUNDAY AFTER
CHRISTMAS
Isaiah 63:7-9
Psalm 148
Hebrews 2:10-18
Matthew 2:13-23

December 24
CHRISTMAS EVE
Isaiah 9:2-7
Psalm 96
Titus 2:11-14
Luke 2:1-20

December 25
CHRISTMAS DAY
Isaiah 52:7-10
Psalm 98
Hebrews 1:1-12
John 1:1-14

December 30–31
Jeremiah 31:7-14
Psalm 147:12-20
Ephesians 1:3-14
John 1:1-18

A Guide to Daily Prayer

These prayers imply worship time with a group; feel free to adapt the plural pronouns for personal use.

MORNING PRAYER

"In the morning, O LORD, you hear my voice;
　　in the morning I lay my requests before you
　　and wait in expectation."

　　　　　　　　　　　　　　　　—Psalm 5:3

Gathering and Silence

Call to Praise and Prayer
　　God said: Let there be light; and there was light.
　　And God saw that the light was good.

Psalm 63:2-6

　　God, my God, you I crave;
　　my soul thirsts for you,
　　my body aches for you
　　like a dry and weary land.
　　　　Let me gaze on you in your temple:
　　　　a Vision of strength and glory
　　　　Your love is better than life,
　　　　my speech is full of praise.
　　　　I give you a lifetime of worship,
　　　　my hands raised in your name.
　　　　I feast at a rich table
　　　　my lips sing of your glory.

Prayer of Thanksgiving

We praise you with joy, loving God, for your grace is better than life itself. You have sustained us through the darkness: and you bless us with life in this new day. In the shadow of your wings we sing for joy and bless your holy name. Amen.

Scripture Reading

Silence

Prayers of the People

The Lord's Prayer (see Midday Prayer for text)

Blessing

May the light of your mercy shine brightly on all who walk in your presence today, O Lord.

"I will extol the LORD at all times;
     God's praise will always be on my lips."

                                —Psalm 34:1

Gathering and Silence

Call to Praise and Prayer

> O LORD, my Savior, teach me your ways.
>   My hope is in you all day long.

Prayer of Thanksgiving

> God of mercy, we acknowledge this midday pause of refreshment as one of your many generous gifts. Look kindly upon our work this day; may it be made perfect in your time. May our purpose and prayers be pleasing to you. This we ask through Christ our Lord. Amen.

Scripture Reading

Silence

Prayers of the People

The Lord's Prayer (ecumenical text)

> Our Father in heaven,
>   hallowed be your name,
>   your kingdom come,
>   your will be done,
>   on earth as in heaven.
> Give us today our daily bread.
> Forgive us our sins as we forgive
>   those who sin against us.

Save us from the time of trial,
and deliver us from evil.
For the kingdom, the power, and the glory
are yours, now and forever. Amen.

Blessing

Strong is the love embracing us, faithful the Lord from morning to night.

"My soul finds rest in God alone;
  my salvation comes from God."
                            —Psalm 62:1

Gathering and Silence

Call to Praise and Prayer

From the rising of the sun to its setting,
  let the name of the LORD be praised.

Psalm 134

Bless the Lord,
  all who serve in God's house,
  who stand watch
  throughout the night.

Lift up your hands
  in the holy place
  and bless the Lord.

And may God,
  the maker of earth and sky,
  bless you from Zion.

Prayer of Thanksgiving

Sovereign God, You have been our help during the day and you promise to be with us at night. Receive this prayer as a sign of our trust in you. Save us from all evil, keep us from all harm, and guide us in your way. We belong to you, Lord. Protect us by the power of your name, in Jesus Christ we pray. Amen.

Scripture Reading

Silence

Prayers of the People

The Lord's Prayer (see Midday Prayer for text)

Blessing

> May your unfailing love rest upon us, O LORD,
> even as we hope in you.

This Guide to Prayer was compiled from scripture and other resources by Rueben P. Job and then adapted by the Pathways Center for Spiritual Leadership while under the direction of Marjorie J. Thompson.

The Role of the Small-Group Leader

Leading a group for spiritual formation differs in many ways from teaching a class. The most obvious difference is in your basic goal as group leader. In a class, you generally want to convey particular facts or interpretations and encourage discussion of ideas. You can gauge your success at the end of a class by how well participants demonstrate some grasp of the information. In a group for spiritual formation, your goal is to enable spiritual growth in each group member. You work in partnership with the Holy Spirit, who alone brings about transformation of the heart. Here, gaining wisdom is more important than gaining knowledge, and growing in holiness is more important than either knowledge or wisdom. *Success*, if that word has any meaning in this context, will be evident over months and even years in the changed lives of group members.

Classes tend to be task-oriented in order to "cover ground." Groups for spiritual formation tend to be process-oriented. Even though group members will have done common preparation in reading and daily prayer, group reflections may move in directions you do not expect. You will need to be open to the movement of the Holy Spirit while at the same time discerning the difference between following the Spirit's lead and going off on a tangent. Such discernment requires careful, prayerful listening—a far more important skill for a small-group leader than talking.

Finally, classes tend to focus on external sources: the Bible, another book, a film, current events. In contrast, spiritual formation groups focus more on internal realities: personal faith experience in daily life and spiritual practice. Group members seek to understand and receive the graced revealing of God. When participants reflect on a scripture text, the basis for group interaction is not "What did the author intend to say to readers of that time?" but "How does this passage speak to my life or illuminate my experience?" Group reflections focus on the sharing of insights, not debate over ideas. As leader, you will model such sharing with your group. Your leadership differs substantially from that of a traditional adult class teacher. As a "participant-leader" you will read the daily meditations along with everyone else, bringing your thoughts and reflections to share with the group. You will lead by offering your honest reflections and by enabling group members to listen carefully to one another and to the Spirit in your midst.

Leading a spiritual formation group requires particular qualities. Foremost among these are patience and trust. You need patience to allow sessions to unfold as they will. Spiritual formation is a lifelong process. Identifying visible personal growth in group members over the course of the year may be difficult. It may take a while for participants to adjust to the purpose and style of formational group process. As leader, resolve to ask questions with no "right" answers in mind and to encourage group members to talk about their own experiences. Sharing your own experience rather than proclaiming abstract truths or talking about the experiences of other well-known Christians will accelerate this shift from an informational to a formational process. Trust that the Holy Spirit will indeed help group members see or hear what they really need. You may offer what you consider a great insight to which no one responds. If the group needs it, the Spirit will bring it around again at a more opportune time. Susan Muto, a modern writer on spiritual formation, often says that we need to "make space for the pace of grace." There are no shortcuts to spiritual growth. Be patient and trust the Spirit.

Listening is another critical quality for a formational group leader. This does not mean simply listening for people to say what you hope they will say so you can reinforce them. Listen for what is actually going on in participants' minds and hearts, which may differ from what you expect after reading the material yourself. While listening, jot down brief notes about themes that surface. Does sharing seem to revolve around a certain type of experience? Is a hint of direction or common understanding emerging—a clue to God's will or at least a shared sense of meaning for the group? What do you hear again and again? What action might group members take together or individually to respond to an emerging sense of call?

A group leader also needs to be accepting. Accept that group members may have spiritual perceptions quite unlike yours and that people often see common experiences in different ways. Some may be struck by an aspect that did not impress you at all, while others may be left cold by dimensions that really move you. As you model acceptance, you foster acceptance of differences within the group. Beyond this, you will need to accept lack of closure. Group meetings rarely tie up all loose ends in a neat package. Burning questions will be left hanging. You can trust the Spirit to bring resolution in time, if resolution is needed. Also be prepared to accept people's emotions along with their thoughts and experiences. Tears, fears, joy, and anger are legitimate responses during times together. One important expression of acceptance is permission-giving. Permit group members to grow and share at their own pace. Let them know in your first meeting that while you encourage full participation in every part of the process, they are free to opt out of anything that makes them feel uncomfortable. No one will be forced to share or pray without consent. "Where the Spirit of the Lord is, there is freedom" (2 Cor. 3:17).

It is important to avoid three common tendencies of small groups and their leaders:

1. Fixing. When someone presents a personal or theological problem, you may be tempted to find a solution or give your "priceless" advice. Problem solving generally makes

you feel better. Perhaps it makes you feel wise or helps to break the tension, but it rarely helps the other to grow. Moreover, you might prescribe the wrong "fix." If you have faced a similar problem, speak only from your own experience.

2. Proselytizing. You know what has brought you closer to God; naturally you would like everyone to try it. You can offer your own experience to the group, but trying to convince others to follow your path is spiritually dangerous. Here, your knowledge and wisdom come into play. Teresa of Ávila wrote that if she had to choose between a director who was spiritual and one who was learned, she would pick the learned one. The saint might be able to talk only about his or her own spiritual path. The learned one might at least recognize another person's experience from reading about it. Clarifying and celebrating someone else's experience is far more useful than urging others to follow your way.

3. Controlling. Many of us are accustomed to filling in silence with comment. You may be tempted to think you should have an appropriate response to whatever anyone says; that is, you may tend to dominate and control the conversation. Here again, patience and listening are essential. Do not be afraid of silence. Being comfortable with silence allows you to be a relaxed presence in the group. If you cannot bear a long silence, break it with an invitation for someone who has been quiet so far to share a thought, feeling, or question rather than with a comment of your own.